Forbidden Fruit

Forbidden Fruit

COUNTERFACTUALS AND INTERNATIONAL RELATIONS

Richard Ned Lebow

PRINCETON UNIVERSITY PRESS

PRINCETON AND OXFORD

Published by Princeton University Press, 41 William Street, Princeton, New Jersey 08540
In the United Kingdom: Princeton University Press, 6 Oxford Street, Woodstock,
Oxfordshire OX20 1TW

Library of Congress Cataloging-in-Publication Data

Lebow, Richard Ned.
   Forbidden fruit : counterfactuals and international relations / Richard Ned Lebow.
      p. cm.
   Includes bibliographical references and index.
   ISBN 978-0-691-13289-1 (cloth : alk. Paper) — ISBN 978-0-691-13290-7 (pbk. : alk.
Paper)   1. International relations—Research. 2. World politics—Research. 3. Cold War.
4. Imaginary histories. 5. Counterfactuals (Logic) I. Title.
   JZ1234.L43 2010
   327.1072—dc22   2009018726

British Library Cataloging-in-Publication Data is available.

This book has been composed in Sabon

Printed on acid-free paper. ∞

press.princeton.edu

Printed in the United States of America

10 9 8 7 6 5 4 3 2 1

To all those who transgress disciplinary boundaries and recognize the need to embed our understanding of international relations in a wider cultural and historical context.

Contents

Acknowledgments   ix

Part One

Chapter One
Making Sense of the World   3

Chapter Two
Counterfactual Thought Experiments   29

Part Two

Chapter Three
Franz Ferdinand Found Alive: World War I Unnecessary   69

Chapter Four
Leadership and the End of the Cold War: Did It Have to
End This Way?   103
   Coauthored with George W. Breslauer

Part Three

Chapter Five
Scholars and Causation 1   137
   Coauthored with Philip E. Tetlock

Chapter Six
Scholars and Causation 2   166
   Appendix
   Experiment 4, Instrument 1: Unmaking American Tragedies   196

Chapter Seven
If Mozart Had Died at Your Age: Psycho-logic versus
Statistical Inference   205

Chapter Eight
Heil to the Chief: Sinclair Lewis, Philip Roth, and Fascism   222

Conclusions   259

Notes   287

Index   329

Acknowledgments

FORBIDDEN FRUIT was the product of many years of reflection, research, and the writing of individual articles and book chapters that ultimately came together in a book. Five of the nine chapters have appeared elsewhere, and two of those have been extensively rewritten to incorporate new evidence and what I hope is progress in the evolution of my thinking about counterfactuals and their implications for causation and judgment. Two of the chapters are coauthored: chapter 4 with George Breslauer and chapter 5 with Philip E. Tetlock. I made only the most minor changes in these chapters and am very grateful to George and Phil for allowing me to reprint them here. I also thank Phil and Aaron Belkin for organizing a conference on counterfactuals and international relations in Berkeley in January 1995. It provided the stimulus for me to write my first paper on counterfactuals. Coauthor Janice Gross Stein and I showed how Kennedy and Khrushchev used counterfactuals to help formulate their respective policies and how evidence that had since become available indicated that most of them were based on erroneous assumptions.[1]

That paper and the conference encouraged me to pursue my investigations further. I wrote two more papers, published in *World Politics* and the *Political Science Quarterly*, in which I developed protocols for conducting historical counterfactual thought experiments and then applied them to the origins of the First World War.[2] By this time Phil had moved to Ohio State, where we collaborated on the correlational and experimental study reprinted here as chapter 5.[3] With Geoffrey Parker, an early modern historian, we went on to coedit a book that used counterfactuals to probe the reasons for and contingency of the phenomenal success of Western civilization in the modern era.[4] At roughly the same time, Rick Herrmann and I ran a multi-institution collaborative project on the end of the Cold War and coedited a book on the subject. George Breslauer and I produced a chapter that used counterfactuals to probe the role of leaders and asked if the Cold War would have ended when and how it did in the absence of Gorbachev and Reagan.[5] Subsequent research, the fruits of which appear in this volume, I conducted on my own. I became increasingly interested in using counterfactuals to probe how scholars address causation in an open-ended and nonlinear world and what counterfactuals can tell us about the perplexing binaries of fact and fiction.

Most of this book was written since I moved to Dartmouth College in 2002 and I am grateful to my international relations colleagues for their interest in my research and willingness to provide useful feedback in numerous conversations. Steve Brooks, Ben Valentino, and Bill Wohlforth were particularly responsive. I wrote the chapter on Sinclair Lewis and Philip Roth while a fellow of the Centre for International Studies and St. John's College at the University of Cambridge. I am indebted to Centre director Christopher Hill and then master of St. John's, Richard Perham. I finished the manuscript in London, where I hold a visiting appointment as Centennial Professor of International Relations at the London School of Economics and Political Science I am grateful to my LSE colleagues for their feedback, and especially to Mick Cox, Christopher Coker, and George Lawson, the latter of whom was kind enough to organize a faculty seminar on the book. Special thanks go to Rick Herrmann, Holger Herwig, Dorry Noyes, and Paul Schroeder, who were kind enough to read and comment on chapters, and to Carol Bohmer, David Lebow, and Nick Onuf for reading and giving me feedback on the entire manuscript. I am very grateful for the support and excellent editorial guidance I received from Chuck Myers and the fine copyediting of Marsha Kunin and proofreading of Reyad Allie and Josh Roselman.

PART ONE

CHAPTER ONE

Making Sense of the World

> Had Pyrrhus not fallen by a beldam's hand in Argos or Caesar
> not been knifed to death? They are not to be thought away.
> Time has branded them and fettered they are ledged in the
> room of the infinite possibilities seeing that they never were?
> Or was that only possible which came to pass? Weave, weaver
> of the wind.
>
> —*James Joyce*

FORBIDDEN FRUIT is an avowedly provocative but also inviting title. The two, as Eve knew, are often reinforcing. Her offer of the apple to Adam is an invitation to eat from the Tree of Knowledge and possibly transcend their human condition. It is a provocation because it involved violating the one proscription laid down by their creator.[1] Eating from the Tree of Knowledge, the couple soon discover, entails expulsion from the Garden of Eden, hard work to survive, pain in childbirth, and mortality.[2] Counterfactuals can be considered an analog to the apple, and the invitation to engage with them a provocation to those who believe that social science or history can only be corrupted by their use. I sense that the number of scholars who feel this way, while substantial, is on the decline. They believe we live in a metaphorical Garden of Eden, where the social and physical worlds are ordered, predictable, and related in a holistic way. For those of us who recognize that humankind left Eden long ago—if it ever existed—counterfactuals must be considered one more tool to help us make sense of our chaotic and unordered world, where knowledge sometimes has the effect of accelerating disorder.

I use counterfactuals to probe nonlinear causation and the understandings policymakers, historians, and international relations scholars have of historical causation. Toward this end and the broader goal of exploring the relationship between fact and fiction, and factual and counterfactual, I employ historical case studies, surveys, experiments, a short story, and an essay of literary criticism. An avowedly interdisciplinary book aspires to a multidisciplinary readership, and I believe my study has something of interest to say to social scientists, historians, and humanists. Casting my net this wide nevertheless invites problems of presentation and language that could limit my audience. Disciplines and fields or approaches within them often have distinct languages and concepts. To use any one of them is to identify with a particular discipline or methodological approach, but to use multiple languages and concepts is to risk incoherence. There is no way to finesse this problem, but I try to minimize its effects by keeping my language as consistent as possible, explaining concepts that may be unfamiliar to readers from other disciplines and, above all, by trying to speak to problems of common interest to these several disciplines and even to diverse approaches within them.

Different methods (e.g., case studies, experiments, literary criticism) employ different languages to conduct research and convey findings to the communities who routinely use these methods. I accordingly adopt, with some minor but important modifications, the language appropriate to each method I use and ask readers from other disciplines for their forbearance. At times, this practice may appear to involve me in contradictions. Social psychologists use the language of positivism, as they conceive of their discipline as a science. Historians and social scientists of the constructivist persuasion conduct case studies in the *verstehen* tradition, eschewing the language and goals of science. Constructivists and others who reject the quest for covering laws envisage social theory as a loose ensemble of concepts whose utility varies as a function of the kinds of questions one asks. Many of these researchers are nevertheless committed to formulating and evaluating propositions in accord with carefully established if ever evolving procedures.[3] I conduct my case studies from this perspective, using the concepts and language of history and constructivism.

My project achieves coherence not from any uniformity in language and concepts across chapters, but from my use of the same protocols to conduct and evaluate all counterfactuals, and more importantly, from the ways in which all the chapters in this book contribute to my overarching goals. Some readers might still find it inappropriate to approach social knowledge from the *erklären* tradition in one set of chapters and its *verstehen* counterpart in others. This too, I believe, is defensible in light of my objective for providing insights useful to these distinctive communities.

Let me expand on the above points and use this elaboration as a vehicle for introducing the book. So-called normal social science is based on Humean causation. It studies observable phenomena to discover regularities in human behavior. Researchers sometimes discover regularities they subsequently seek to explain, as in the case of the Democratic Peace.[4] More often, regularities are hypothesized in the form of propositions, and efforts are then made to validate them—more accurately, to falsify them—using appropriate data sets.[5] To qualify as meaningful, statistical regularities require explanations that identify the causal mechanisms responsible for them.[6] Regularities and associated causal mechanisms attract considerable attention when they appear capable of accounting for and, better yet, of predicting, outcomes of importance to us. My general orientation is constructivist, and in the course of this chapter I will critique the way positivist research in international relations is most frequently conducted. My purpose is not to author yet another critique of positivism, let alone drive a stake through the heart of mainstream social science. My criticisms of theory building in social science have a different and more positive goal. In the first instance, they aim to assist those committed to theory building by using counterfactuals to understand the conditions under which generalizations are likely to hold and some of the reasons and dynamics by which those conditions change.

From Max Weber on, good social scientists have recognized that any regularities in behavior must be understood in terms of their cultural setting, and endure only as long as this setting remains stable and the regularities themselves go unrecognized by relevant actors. At best, the social world can be described in terms of punctuated equilibria. Regularities exist within bounded social domains, but those domains are often subject to sharp discontinuities that can change the pattern of practices, how they are understood, or even the ends that they are seen to serve.[7] The search for regularities needs to be complemented by the investigation of ruptures, sometimes caused by changes in both ideational and material conditions, that undermine existing regularities and the understandings of the actors on which they are often based. Counterfactual analysis is particularly suited to this task because it allows us to explore the workings and consequences of nonlinear interactions in open-ended systems in ways many other methods do not.

My research speaks to mainstream social scientists in a second important way. I use counterfactuals to demonstrate the contingency of cases like the origins World War I that are critical for construction of theories (i.e., balance of power, power transition) or offered as evidence in support of them. By demonstrating the contingency of World War I, and of other critical twentieth-century events that followed from it, I not only raise questions about these theories but, more importantly, show the extent to which our most fundamental assumptions about how the political world works are highly contingent. Counterfactual thought experiments provide a vantage point for taking ourselves outside of our world and our assumptions about it where they can be subjected to active and open interrogation. Such an exercise not only makes us aware of assumptions that are so deeply ingrained that we take them for granted, but facilitates imaginative leaps in theory and hypothesis formation.

The preceding comments are directed primarily at political scientists and those among them who study international relations. My book also speaks to psychologists, and in a double sense. Chapters 5 and 6 build on existing work in cognitive psychology by using surveys and experiments to investigate questions this literature deems important. I believe these chapters make a modest contribution in this connection. For the most part, psychologists seek to discover the conditions under which people use counterfactual modes of thought and the character of the counterfactuals they invoke. I am more interested in using counterfactuals to probe the understandings people have of causation and what their receptivity to different counterfactuals reveals about their belief systems. These questions should appeal to many psychologists, and so should my efforts to relate my findings to international relations.

Historians are another targeted audience. The origin of World War I has long been a central question for historians of modern Europe, and the end of the Cold War has become an important question for them and international history more generally. My chapters on 1914 and 1989 address these events from a relatively novel methodological perspective and offer an original interpretation rooted in nonlinearity and confluence. They also represent, in my judgment, the most sophisticated effort to date to assess the contingency of these outcomes. These chapters speak to historians in their use of primary and secondary evidence but use the language of social science when discussing causation. Chaos and complexity are not novel in their application to European history, so many historians will already be familiar with these concepts.[8] Counterfactuals have always been controversial within this historical community. E. H. Carr dismissed them as flights of fancy, fun over a beer or two in the faculty club, but not the stuff of serious research.[9] In recent years, there has been a veritable explosion of counterfactual research in history, and I trust that many historians will welcome not only the application of counterfactuals to important historical events but the development of more rigorous protocols to guide and improve the quality of historical counterfactual research.[10] In this connection, I hasten to point out that I do not use counterfactuals to make the case for alternative worlds, but use the construction of those worlds to probe the causes and contingency of the world we know.

Students of literature will, I hope, find merit in my chapter on Sinclair Lewis and Philip Roth. In keeping with the practice of literary criticism, I offer close readings of these texts and analyze them with reference to literary genres and other well-established categories. As a political scientist, I bring an additional expertise to what are two very political texts. Drawing on my knowledge of political science and psychology, I analyze the counterfactuals that lie at the core of *The Plot Against America* and use this analysis as my key for opening up the meaning of the text. In turn, I use my readings of these texts to reflect back upon the understanding history and social science have of the past, the motives that move actors, and the respective claims to explain much of what is important about social relations. Some social scientists, I hope, will be intrigued by my efforts to use literature and to evaluate social science and its project, just as I hope humanists will find worthwhile my attempt to explore their domain with some of the tools of social science.

I begin my investigation with a brief discussion of World War I. I do so to illustrate the lengths to which policymakers and many of my colleagues will go to deny the contingency of key events that shape our world and how we think about it. The World War I case nicely illustrates the critical importance of non-observables and nonsystematic factors in understanding major international outcomes. I conclude with an overview of the remaining chapters and a discussion of how they contribute to the overall goals of the book.

World War I was the dominant international event of the twentieth century. It hastened the ascendancy of the United States as the world's leading economic power; led to the breakup of the German, Austro-Hungarian, Russian, and Ottoman empires; and set in motion a chain of events that ultimately led to the demise of the British, French, Spanish, and Portuguese empires as well. The war decimated a generation of young men and killed millions of civilians made vulnerable to influenza and other pathogens by the ravages of war, dislocation, ethnic cleansing, and the Allied blockade. It triggered a revolution in Russia, which had echoes in eastern and central Europe and more lasting resonance in China and Southeast Asia. Collectively, these developments made it almost impossible to restore political and economic stability to Europe, helping to pave the way for Hitler's rise to power, the Holocaust, and a second, far more deadly, bid for hegemony by Germany in alliance with Italy and Japan. World War II in turn gave rise to a Cold War between the Soviet bloc and the West that kept Europe divided for fifty years and the target of thousands of nuclear weapons that at the push of a button could have turned the continent into a desolate, uninhabitable no-man's land.

World War I and the events that followed had equally profound cultural and intellectual consequences. Europe's self-confidence was lost along with its leading role in the world, encouraging forms of artistic expression that communicated defiance, doubt, confusion, and alienation. Many artists and intellectuals sought refuge in a highly idealized image of Soviet-style socialism. Europe's internecine struggles and exhaustion after World War II dramatically accelerated the hegemony of the United States. After 1945, the latter became the leader of the self-proclaimed "Free World," helped finance the reconstruction of Western Europe and Japan, imposed its political and economic institutions and practices wherever it could, and gained wider influence through aid, trade and investment. Extraordinary levels of investment at home in education and research, charitable support for the arts and the immigration of thousands of Europe's leading scientists, artists and intellectuals made the United States the world's leader in medicine, science, space exploration, and the creative and performing arts. American popular culture became global in its appeal, leading some intellectuals to worry about Hollywood's hegemony and debasement of real culture, and others to celebrate it as a "soft power" resource.[11]

Many social scientists and international relations scholars consider these outcomes overdetermined. Until quite recently, the conventional wisdom among historians was that Europe in 1914 was like dry kindling just waiting to be set aflame by a match.[12] If the assassinations at Sarajevo had not triggered a continental war, some other provocation would have. International relations scholars have developed theories like power transition and offensive dominance to explain why a European war was all but inevitable. World War II appears at least as inevitable to many scholars given German dissatisfaction with the Treaty of Versailles and the aggressive goals and risk-taking propensity of Hitler, Mussolini, and Japanese leaders. So does the Cold War in the light of the power vacuum in the heart of Europe at the end of World War II and the antagonistic social systems of the two victorious superpowers. The end of the Cold War, the collapse of the Soviet Union, and the emergence of the United States as a "unipole" appear just as inevitable to some observers. Students of the former Soviet Union, liberal theorists, and proponents of globalization provide numerous reinforcing reasons why Soviet-style communism was doomed and American-style capitalist democracy was the wave of the future.[13]

The view that our world is the only possible world, or at least the most likely of all worlds, has multiple and reinforcing causes. There is the hindsight bias, by which we upgrade the probability of events once they have occurred and come to regard the past as overdetermined—but the future as highly contingent.[14] The hindsight bias is reinforced by the very nature of the scholarly enterprise. Historians and social scientists make reputations for themselves by proposing new explanations or theories to account for major events like the fall of the Roman Empire, the industrial and French revolutions, the world wars and the Cold War. Confronted by ever growing explanations for events of this kind, none of which can generally be dismissed out of hand, these events appear massively overdetermined. The need for psychological closure also plays a role. In chapter 5, I report on an experiment Phil Tetlock and I conducted to probe how people understand the consequences of their beliefs. Those who see the world as to a great extent ordered and predictable display a need for psychological closure and are hostile to suggestions of contingency—unless it helps to explain away an outcome inconsistent with their worldviews or preferred theories. Not surprisingly, many international relations scholars cluster toward the order and predictability end of the continuum. Whether they are socialized into understanding the world this way, or choose to become social scientists in part for this reason, the end result is the same: they are generally unwilling to recognize, or uncomfortable with the thought, if they do, that important social outcomes could be the result of agency, chance, or simply bad weather.

Discussions in the coffee lounge with thoughtful colleagues, and feedback from faculty and graduate students at institutions where I gave seminars on my book, indicate considerable interest in counterfactuals as a research tool but widespread confidence in the high probability, if not near inevitability, of major twentieth-century international outcomes, including those described in the paragraphs above. When I suggested that World War I might have been avoided if Franz Ferdinand and his wife had not been murdered by Serbian nationalists, I was frequently told that Europe was on the precipice of war and surely would have been tipped over the edge by some other concatenation of events. Behind this claim lay the belief that World War I was the product of systemic causes. When I raised the possibility of the Cuban missile crisis provoking a superpower war, I met similar objections but a different argument. Policymakers are not entirely irrational, I was frequently told, and, given the conventional advantage of the United States in the Caribbean and the overwhelming U.S. strategic nuclear advantage at the time, the Soviet Union had no choice but to capitulate. This argument was made during the crisis by Maxwell Taylor, who insisted that if Khrushchev had other ideas, more sober Soviet officials would soon assert their authority.[15] Not surprisingly, I found few colleagues convinced by my argument that, had a European or world war in the first two decades of the twentieth century been averted, or if the Germans had won it, we might be living in a world in which authoritarian corporatism might have competed successfully against democratic, laissez-faire capitalism. These counterfactuals elicited a third generic argument: that the social world resembles nature in its competitiveness and natural selection. Practices and institutions that work efficiently will win out over those that do not. Democratic capitalism would ultimately have triumphed.

Policymakers rarely act in response to explicit theories but commonly rely on more informal understandings of how the world works. They display the same belief in the retrospective near inevitability of important historical outcomes as their academic counterparts. In interviews with numerous American, Soviet, and European politicians, diplomats and military officers who played prominent roles in the end of the Cold War, Richard Herrmann and I found that almost all of them believed that the Cold War had to end when and how it did. At the same time, these policymakers insisted on the contingency of developments critical to this outcome in which they played a major role. They told us how easily such developments (e.g., arms control, the unification of Germany) could have been forestalled or worked out differently if it had not been for their skill, relationships with their opposite numbers, or ability to collaborate with them behind the backs of their respective governments. They seemed unaware of the contradiction between these two positions and struggled to reconcile them when pushed by us to do so.[16]

There is something wrong with this story. If major historical developments are so inevitable, the pattern of events leading to them should not be so contingent. If events are overdetermined, the underlying conditions responsible for these events should have been apparent at the time to scholars and policymakers alike, making them—although not their timing and specific expression—to some degree predictable. None of the events in question were self-evident at the time. In the decade prior to 1914 there was a general expectation among many military authorities and some, but by no means all, political leaders that a European war was likely. There was nevertheless remarkable optimism, within the diplomatic and business community, that mutual trade and investment had made war increasingly irrational and less likely. On the eve of the war, books advancing both arguments were runaway best sellers.[17] European opinion was also divided on World War II, with many of those in power in France and Britain and the Soviet Union convinced that Hitler had limited aims or could be bought off with territorial and other concessions. For quite different reasons, Churchill and Roosevelt expected to be able to do business with the Soviet Union after World War II. Writing in 1959, John Herz reminds us that the advent of bipolarity was as unexpected as the atomic age, in part responsible for it.[18] Hardly anybody predicted the onset of the Cold War or its demise, let alone the collapse of the Soviet Union. In the early decades of the Cold War, American foreign policy experts worried that the Soviet model would be more appealing to so-called Third World countries than liberal capitalism. In its latter decades, members of the U.S. national security community thought it possible, if not likely, that the Soviet Union would pull ahead militarily and act more aggressively. Both expectations were wide of the mark.

Single events are admittedly the most difficult kind to predict.[19] However, our record is arguably no better when it comes to trends, patterns, and macro-outcomes where prediction rests on the role of reason, social selection, or some other alleged feature of the environment. A socialist world, which Marx thought would require revolution, and later revisionists hoped to bring about through the ballot box, is perhaps the best-known example. Socialists and conservatives alike assumed that education and economic development would make the world increasingly secular and that the power of religion would recede into history. Premature triumphalism by neoconservatives about liberal democracy and laissez-faire capitalism, which found voice in such best sellers as Daniel Bell's *End of Ideology* and Francis Fukuyama's *The End of History and the Last Man* also proved far off the mark.[20] It is too early to pass judgment on predictions like those of Thomas Friedman that globalization will usher in an age of peaceful, liberal trading states—or, as its opponents insist, an era of vast disparities in wealth and crushing cultural uniformity.[21] I suspect that the future will once again defy prediction based on narrowly formulated logical arguments and linear projections.[22]

I learned this lesson early in my academic career; my first teaching post was at Brooklyn College in 1965, just as the social-political revolution of the 1960s moved into high gear. The civil rights movement had been under way for some time and the antiwar movement was about to begin. Woodstock was three years off, but flower power was in full bloom, bras were beginning to go the way of girdles, and the air was redolent with the pungent aroma of pot and joss sticks. To my senior colleagues, these developments were as unanticipated as they were unpalatable. There are good reasons why they were caught off guard. In retrospect, the transformation of the 1960s was a classic example of a nonlinear confluence. The postwar economic boom made rock and roll possible, and both developments, along with access to automobiles and burgeoning college enrollments, generated a distinctive youth culture. The birth control pill, the civil rights movement and the Vietnam War, all of which arrived hard on the heels of rock and roll, made that culture increasingly defiant. Systematic factors, including key international developments, were an important part of this story, but so were timing, chance, and accident.

All forms of complex causation, and especially nonlinear transformations, admittedly stack the deck against prediction. Linear describes an outcome produced by one or more variables where the effect is additive. Any other interaction is nonlinear. This would include outcomes that involve step functions or phase transitions. The hard sciences routinely describe nonlinear phenomena. Making predictions about them becomes increasingly problematic when multiple variables are involved that have complex interactions. Some simple nonlinear systems can quickly become unpredictable when small variations in their inputs are introduced.[23] As so much of the social world is nonlinear, fifty plus years of behavioral research and theory building have not led to any noticeable improvement in our ability to predict events. This is most evident in the case of transformative events like the social-political revolution of the 1960s, the end of the Cold War, and the rise and growing political influence of fundamentalist religious groups.

Radical skepticism about prediction of any but the most short-term outcomes is fully warranted. This does not mean that we can throw our hands up in the face of uncertainty, contingency, and unpredictability. In a complex society, individuals, organizations, and states require a high degree of confidence—even if it is misplaced—in the short-term future and a reasonable degree of confidence about the longer term. In its absence they could not commit themselves to decisions, investments, and policies. Like nudging the frame of a pinball machine to influence the path of the ball, we cope with the dilemma of uncertainty by doing what we can to make our expectations of the future self-fulfilling. We seek to control the social and physical worlds not only to make them more predictable but to reduce the likelihood of disruptive and damaging shocks (e.g., floods, epidemics, stock market crashes, foreign attacks). Our fallback strategy is denial. We convince ourselves that the future will more or less resemble the past, or deviate from it in predictable or manageable ways. We remain unreasonably confident in our beliefs despite the dramatic discontinuities of even the recent past—some of them caused by shocks we could not predict or control. The hindsight bias makes us exaggerate our estimates of the probability of events that actually occur, while belief-system defenses lead us to exaggerate the reasonableness of our prior expectations that other outcomes would occur.[24] Belief system defenses reinforce the hindsight bias and help to explain away predictive failures.

There may be something more fundamental than either the hindsight bias or the need to believe in rationality that makes people—not just international relations scholars—reluctant to accept the important role of contingency in the social world. Prominent thinkers suggest that human beings harbor deep-seated fears about uncertainty and accordingly do their best to convince themselves that they can predict, even control, the future. David Hume believed that "everything that is unexpected affrights us."[25] Martin Heidegger theorized at length about the anxiety generated by uncertainty and mortality.[26] Terror Management Theory builds on this insight as do Anthony Giddens and the ontological security research program.[27] In earlier times the universal human need to reduce anxiety about the future through some form of control found expression in efforts to propitiate the gods. Max Weber believed that modern people could no longer credibly invoke spirits and magic to control their environment, but prayer is alive and well in our society—and becoming more prevalent according to some surveys—despite the absence of any evidence of its efficacy.[28] The enduring belief in the power of prayer is undoubtedly another sign of people's need to believe that they can influence the future, and all the more so when they live in uncertain and dangerous times.

The behavioral revolution in social science might be understood as another expression of this primal need. Its bedrock assumption is that the social environment is sufficiently ordered to be described by universal, or at least widely applicable, laws. Regularities in behavior make the past comprehensible and the future to some degree predictable. The appeal of deterrence during the Cold War—to theorists and policymakers alike—offers a telling example. It was psychologically and politically reassuring to think that the bogey of nuclear war could be kept at bay by the rational practice of deterrence against the Soviet Union. Empirical support for deterrence was entirely counterfactual: the widespread belief that World War II and its horrors might have been prevented if only major European powers had stood firm against Hitler in 1936 or 1938. During the Cold War, deterrence repeatedly failed (i.e., did not prevent challenges it was intended to) but was repeatedly confirmed tautologically. Political scientists interpreted encounters like the two Berlin and Taiwan Straits crises as deterrence successes, assuming that the Soviet Union or China would have attacked Berlin or Taiwan in the absence of immediate American deterrence.[29] Deterrence failures like the Soviet missile deployment in Cuba were explained away with the counterfactual argument that these challenges could have been prevented if American presidents had practiced deterrence more forcibly. Evidence that came to light at the end of the Cold War would reveal that Soviet and Chinese leaders never doubted American resolve and that the forceful practice of deterrence by both sides—in the form of arms build-up, forward deployments, and bellicose rhetoric—repeatedly provoked behavior it was intended to prevent. The two Berlin crises and Cuba being cases in point.[30]

In the United States—as distinct from Europe—faith in the science of politics remains high despite the inability of several generations of behavioral scientists to discover the kinds of laws that exist in the hard sciences. There is a widespread belief that the social world is governed by the same kinds of regularities as the physical world and that discovery of them will allow us to explain past developments and make reasonable predictions of a probabilistic nature. I do not deny the existence of regularities in social behavior; there is ample evidence for them—and for the power of constraints and opportunities to shape the behavior of actors. As Max Weber observed, these regularities, and the "laws" to which they allegedly give rise, are short-lived because of the reflective nature of human beings and the open-ended nature of the social world.[31] Once regularities are known, actors take them into account, undermining their validity, as in the case of the famous "January effect" in the stock market.[32] Alternatively, they are undercut by changes in the environment that alter the underlying conditions on which the regularity depends, as in the case of party identification to predict voting patterns in American elections.[33]

The regularities that do exist in politics are generally incapable of explaining more than a small percentage of the variance. This point is unwittingly driven home in a widely cited article by James Fearon and David Laitin on ethnicity, insurgency, and war.[34] They claim to demonstrate that internal war can be explained by a combination of poverty, political instability, rough terrain, and large population. Only at the end of the article do they address the substantive as opposed to statistical value of the claims. The strongest effects they find increase the probability of civil war from roughly 5 to 15 percent for a country sometime in the next five years. This holds only for countries with extreme scores on their several variables (tenth percentile and below, or ninetieth percentile and above). As the overwhelming majority of countries fall inside these extremes, and include countries that are or have recently experienced internal wars, the regularities they allege to have discovered tell us nothing meaningful about the real world. In international relations, some scholars insist that their theories (e.g., neorealism, balance of power, deterrence, power transition, the democratic peace) account for key developments like peace and war. These claims are rightly rejected by critics who maintain that these theories have little to no predictive value, and that what explanatory power they claim all too frequently rests on ex post facto and historically questionable efforts to square the theories in question with failed predictions. Examples include deterrence theory and the Cuban missile crisis and the 1973 Middle East war, and realism and the end of the Cold War and survival of NATO.

Insight into the future is rooted in our understanding of the past, our socially constructed, psychologically motivated, and ideologically filtered reconstruction of past events and imputation of their "lessons." We use these understandings to affirm the validity of, and occasionally to reformulate, the analytical categories we use to make sense of the world, identify problems that require our attention, and select strategies to cope with them. Our presumed ability to make sense of the past—to discover patterns that allow us to explain social behavior in terms of its enduring regularities—makes us unreasonably confident of our ability to predict, or at least to cope with the future. Theories represent a formal means of turning understandings of the past into guides for the future and are enormously appealing to intellectuals who want or need to believe that we can think about the future in rigorous and more successful ways. Social scientists committed to theory building of this kind are correspondingly reluctant to admit the failings of their theories, let alone the overall difficulties encountered by the predictive enterprise. Like other professionals who make predictions, they invoke a range of defenses to explain away their failures, all of them intended to preserve their theories.[35] International relations scholars commonly deploy an additional defense; they fail to specify their theories in a manner that would make them falsifiable. This facilitates ex post facto efforts to square outcomes with theories.[36]

The general reluctance of political scientists to take nonsystematic factors seriously is adequate provocation to direct our attention to them. Are they really inconsequential for theory building or do they confound predictive theories in ways that are little understood or appreciated? Could key events like World War I have been untracked by credible minimal rewrites of history? What if Franz Ferdinand had not been assassinated and there had been no European war in 1914? What if Hitler had died on the western front during World War I instead of surviving, against all odds, almost four years of trench warfare? What if President Hindenburg had exercised his emergency powers more responsibly and Hitler had never come to power? What if Britain and France had prevented Hitler's remilitarization of the Rhineland in March 1936 or had stood firm with the Soviet Union at Munich in 1938? What if Kennedy had given in to hawkish demands for an air strike against the Soviet missiles in Cuba? What if Chernenko had not been succeeded by Gorbachev but by another aging party hack intent on postponing any meaningful reform, rightly fearing its domestic and foreign consequences?

Any of these outcomes were possible and some were arguably more likely than not. The list of cases can easily be extended. Counterfactual historians have identified numerous "bifurcation points" where they contend history could easily have taken a radically different course. They run the gamut from military and political events like the ones noted above to more complex developments like the rise of religions and the industrial revolution.[37] In chapter 3 I show how easily the assassinations of Franz Ferdinand and his wife, Sophie, could have been avoided and the many reasons to think that, if there had been no continental war in 1914, Europe had at least an even chance to evolve peacefully over the next decade. A peaceful Europe would have been dominated by Germany, the economic and intellectual powerhouse of the continent. German would have rivaled English as the language of business and science, and its corporate model of capitalism would have provided an alternative to the more laissez-faire practices of Britain and the United States. A German-dominated continent would have aborted the birth of the Soviet Union, and while Russia would have survived in some shrunken form, it is less likely that it would have become a superpower. Britain would probably have moved closer to the United States as a means of offsetting German influence. In a multipolar world, international relations theory would have concerned itself with a different set of problems.

Consider a darker scenario arising from an American invasion of Cuba in 1962. The Kennedy administration did not know that Soviet combat forces in Cuba were equipped with nuclear-tipped Luna ground-to-ground missiles and authorized to use them against an invasion force.[38] If they had destroyed the American invasion fleet, the United States might have responded with a nuclear attack against the Soviet Union. Even if escalation had stopped short of an all-out nuclear war, the Cold War would have been put on a very different and more confrontational course. Dé-tente would have been much less likely and so too the gradual evolu-tion of the Soviet Union away from its commitment to communism and the Cold War. Damaged and humiliated by American nuclear strikes, the post-Khrushchev leadership might have become more aggressive in its foreign policy. If the destruction of the American invasion fleet had led to a wider nuclear war there might not have been a Soviet Union in its aftermath. The United States and western Europe would almost certainly have been the targets of nuclear weapons in such an exchange, giving rise to a bleak and largely unpredictable future.

Social scientists in either of these worlds would have described them as largely determined. In a Europe that avoided a continental war in 1914, or any time afterward, liberalism would have been the dominant paradigm in the United Kingdom and the United States, and socialism would have retained it appeal to intellectuals on the continent. Liberal international relations scholars would have developed theories about the restraining consequences of industrial development, international trade, international law, and trade union movements. Sociologists would have stressed the beneficial consequences of education, widespread affluence, smaller families, and longer life expectancy. If Germany had democra-tized, it seems likely that some variant of the democratic peace thesis would have emerged. The imaginary critic in my story in chapter 7 makes many of these arguments, and uses them to demonstrate why our world could never have come to pass.

If the Cuban missile crisis had led to war, conventional or nuclear, historians would have constructed a causal chain leading ineluctably to this outcome. It might begin with the Russian Revolution and the ideo-logical cleavage it created between East and West, and go on to include the mistrust and hostility created by the different but equally self-serving ways the Western democracies and the Soviet Union responded to the threat of Nazi Germany, the subsequent division of Europe, efforts by both superpowers to destabilize and penetrate the other's sphere of influ-ence, the spread of their competition to other parts of the world, nuclear arms racing and threats, and finally, a crisis spiral (Berlin, Laos, Cuba) badly managed by insecure and risk-prone leaders (Kennedy and Khrush-chev). Instead of explaining the "long peace," historians would have com-pared the run-up to World War III to the pre-1914 division of Europe into competing alliance systems and the series of crises that led to the July crisis and World War I. Realism would be the dominant paradigm in international relations, although its proponents would see no distinc-tion between bi- and multipolar systems. Counterfactual speculation that a superpower war could have been avoided and the Cold War brought to a peaceful end by the transformation and de facto capitulation by the

Soviet Union would be greeted with the same degree of incredulity that suggestions of a peaceful twentieth-century Europe meet in ours.

This book does not engage in counterfactual speculation merely to make the case for the plausibility of alternative worlds. The contingency of our world should be self-evident to any serious reader of history. I use counterfactuals to probe the limits of Humean causation and to develop better means of understanding causation in a largely open-ended, non-linear, highly contingent world.[39] If regularities are short-lived, we have an equal interest in discovering them *and* their limitations and shelf lives. To date, social scientists have directed their efforts to the discovery of regularities, not to the conditions and dynamics that degrade them. Those who believe in systematic or structural approaches to social science—terms I use interchangeably to refer to theorizing based on the discovery of regularities—ought to be equally interested in this latter question. I contend that counterfactual probing of transformations is a first and necessary step toward this goal. My two case study chapters speak directly to these problems, as they probe contingency and the causes of international transformations. In the conclusion I elaborate a method for better determining the contingency of outcomes.

I also use counterfactuals to probe how social scientists and historians understand causation. To the extent that our understandings of the past are in thrall to cognitive and motivated biases, counterfactuals can help us recognize and overcome these impediments to greater openness and objectivity. Chapters 5 and 6 address this problem and demonstrate the power of beliefs to influence receptivity to counterfactuals but also the ability of counterfactuals to increase our estimates of contingency. These chapters also probe the relationship between belief systems and openness to counterfactuals that make and unmake history in ways that reinforce or undercut beliefs.

Finally, I show how counterfactuals can be used to provide otherwise unattainable perspectives on our world. We cannot easily step outside of this world and the beliefs we hold about it. Alternative worlds not only make this possible, they compel us to do so if we take them seriously. By providing distance from our world they are an indispensable means of evaluating it, empirically and normatively. They also provide insight into how we make sense of our world and why we are drawn to certain kinds of assumptions and theories. Such insight is helpful, if not essential, to theory building and evaluation. Toward this end I use a short story and an analysis of two political novels, one of them counterfactual. In contrast to good social science, good literature tells stories that draw readers in, emotionally as well as intellectually. They provide macrolevel insights by placing readers in microlevel encounters, relationships, and situations. Literature and its analysis accordingly have the potential to contribute to social science in important ways. This is a theme I began to explore in *The Tragic Vision of Politics* where I argued, pace Nietzsche, that music, art, and literature provide knowledge and experience that cannot be expressed in words and, by doing so, refresh our soul, heighten or provide new visions on that part of the world we seek to understand through language and concepts and the kind of knowledge they enable.[40] The arts, humanities, and the social sciences, while fundamentally different in their methods and often in the responses they invoke in us, should nevertheless be regarded as parallel projects leading to greater understanding of ourselves and our world. In this volume, I try to substantiate this claim by showing how counterfactual literature offers insights into history and international relations that social science cannot and how these insights can further the task of history and social science.

Let me now return to social science and its theory-building enterprise. Counterfactuals and the alternative worlds they create generally privilege the importance of specific events as opposed to underlying trends or features of the environment that might have helped to cause them. These are not only "data points," as some quantitative researchers regard them, but starting (or end) points for theories. We do not pull theories out of the air; they often grow out of our effort to explain important or anomalous events. Theorists work backward from cases to generalizations that might account for these and other events, which theory can now reorder as "cases." Whether we embed these understandings in theories from which we then deduce propositions, or simply develop propositions, individual events are generally the source material for insights into the social and political world. Scientific theories can sometimes be based on phenomena that have a very low probability—supernovas, for example—but they must start from this recognition and attempt to identity conditions under which otherwise rare events may become likely. In international relations theory, researchers just assume that important cases like World War I are representative of a broader and not uncommon class of events. This assumption may reflect a cognitive bias to attribute important causes to important events. Commenting on this bias, Deidre McCloskey notes that "disdain for assigning large events small causes is not rational in a world that is partly non-linear."[41] Counterfactual probing of cases can help us overcome this bias and determine the extent to which the events from which we derive our theories are representative or not of the phenomenon under study. Combined with assessments of their relative contingency, we can evaluate more rigorously their utility as starting points for theories.

Social scientists of the neopositivist persuasion believe in the possibility of universal social laws and theories. An increasing number of social scientists are willing to admit that causal relationships only function within a specific cultural sphere. Max Weber is generally understood to have argued that culturally and temporally specific generalizations are the most social science can hope to produce. Even this goal must be questioned if the world in which we live is to a significant degree shaped by agency, accident, and confluence. If so, theories—including those that make no claims beyond a specific cultural and temporal setting—can do no more than offer a first cut into a problem. They may be helpful in organizing our thinking, but are incapable of explaining outcomes in and of themselves and even less capable of making meaningful predictions.[42]

Weber had more fundamental objections to the kind of theory many American social scientists still seek. He recognized that the relationship between the knower and the known was historically situated and must be considered in tandem. Methods in the social sciences are not universal but culturally determined: epistemology is best understood as a historically situated philosophy that presupposes certain social phenomena and is therefore a social phenomenon in its own right. It must also be treated as an object of sociological study. Weber, like Nietzsche, understood that the project of value-free knowledge—about whose efficacy he had serious doubts—could only arise in a world in which the mythic had been rejected in favor of rationalization.[43] Demystification (*Entzauberung*) led ineluctably to the recognition by intellectuals that values were the product of will and choice, not of science. In a telling reference to the Garden of Eden, Weber warned that the "fate of an epoch which has eaten from the tree of knowledge" was to live in a world in which the limits of knowledge must be acknowledged. "We must know that we cannot learn the meaning of the world from the results of our analysis, be it ever so perfect; it must rather be in a position to create this meaning itself." Intellectual liberation encourages the belief that reason can unlock the secrets of the world but actually compels us to renounce the temptation to make holistic sense of the world.[44] Intellectuals, he recognized, are loath to accept this limitation; they constantly try to make the world appear more ordered and predictable than it is because they lack the moral grounding to face the truth on which honest and persuasive inquiry depends.[45]

As Weber expected, most social scientists remain committed to the world of theory building and downplay or ignore the cultural and historical localism of their approach and its limitations. Most theories in political science pretend that systematic factors are determining and that nonsystematic factors (agents, accidents, confluences) are transitory and without lasting significance. King, Keohane, and Verba, whose *Designing Social Inquiry* is widely used in graduate scope and methods courses, are typical in this regard. They assert that nonsystematic factors are worth examining only insofar as they enable us to determine what is systematic—to separate, so to speak, the wheat from the chaff.[46] This approach to theory would make sense only in a world in which systematic factors explain most of the variance. This is no reason to believe that we live in such a world, and certainly King, Keohane, and Verba offer no evidence in support of this their most fundamental and critical assumption.

In international relations there appear to be few, if any, discernible patterns beyond a few obvious ones (e.g., neighbors are likely to be historical adversaries, my enemy's enemy is my friend, hegemonic powers tend to overreach themselves). They were all common knowledge before the era of theory building. These patterns are to some degree robust but unreliable predictors of behavior and far from universal. Neighboring political units have frequently gone to war, or waged cold wars, but many have normalized their relationships over time.[47] States often, but not always, have close relations with adversaries of their adversaries, and their efforts to draw close can restrain or provoke their neighbors, making their consequences for war and peace uncertain. Hegemonic powers routinely overreach themselves in efforts to lock in their advantages (e.g., Athens, Spain under Philip II, France of Louis XIV and Napoleon), but do not always do so; contrast Bismarck's Germany to Wilhelm's, or Clinton's America to George W. Bush's. Nor do dominant powers necessarily provoke catastrophic wars when they act this way. Rising powers are assumed to challenge hegemons but the Soviet Union was careful to avoid war with the United States, and opinion is divided in the West as to whether China, undeniably a rising power, is preparing to challenge the United States or accept the status quo.[48] Each of these so-called patterns is indeterminate, as their consequences depend on nonsystematic and often idiosyncratic factors.

The relative importance of systemic and nonsystemic factors in bringing about an outcome is an empirical question, and one I address in the next two chapters. If the outcomes of individual cases are invariably indeterminate, aggregating cases will not change this reality. As I noted earlier, data sets and statistical manipulations often reveal significant correlations but the substantive power of the propositions or theories being tested is extremely limited. They may identify factors statistically associated with war and peace but do not explain or predict these outcomes. Their statistical findings are not infrequently artifacts of the data set or its coding. The democratic peace thesis and studies that allegedly demonstrate the efficacy of general and immediate deterrence have been severely criticized on these grounds.[49]

Statistical studies of international conflict, war, peace, and conflict resolution confront a number of difficult, if not insurmountable obstacles. The universe of cases, no matter how we define it, is limited. Most cases cannot be considered independent because relevant policymakers most often act on the basis of the lessons they drew from what they consider relevant previous cases. The conditions under which they act (e.g., nature of the regime, domestic constraints, alliance patterns, military balance, and technology) differ from case to case, and often do so dramatically over time. To construct a sample large enough to warrant statistical analysis, it is generally necessary to include cases that violate the conditions of independence and comparability. Even if we allow for the discovery of certain regularities, they would at best explain only a small part of the variance. To improve our understanding of outcomes—in individual cases and more generally—we need to take nonsystematic factors into account. Rather than dismissing them as "idiographic," and of only incidental interest to "nomothetic" (read serious) researchers, we must begin to think about nonsystematic factors in a systematic way. Knowledge of nonsystematic causes, when combined with the product of research into systematic causes can give us better explanations of events and better understandings of the limits of theory.

As noted earlier, the relationship between so-called underlying (systemic) and immediate causes and their implications for theory building is one of the core questions of this book and is addressed by all of its chapters in one form or another. This chapter has laid out the problem and the case for the utility of counterfactuals in exploring it. Chapter 2 focuses more specifically on counterfactuals, providing a definition of them, describing three kinds of counterfactuals, and exploring their respective utility for formulating policy, evaluating outcomes, and understanding their causes and contingency.[50]

Chapter 2 also advances a novel and provocative epistemological claim: that the difference between so-called factual and counterfactual arguments is more one of degree than of kind. Both rest on assumptions about the world and how it works and connect hypothesized causes to outcomes by means of a chain of logic consistent with available evidence. In factual arguments there is rarely, if ever, a "smoking gun" that allows researchers to maintain with any degree of certainty that a particular cause was responsible for an outcome. The plausibility of factual and counterfactual arguments alike rests on the appeal of their assumptions, the tightness of the logic connecting cause to effect and the richness of the evidence that supports them. The fundamental similarity between the structure of counterfactual and factual arguments means that many of the criteria for assessing the plausibility of one kind of argument are appropriate to the other. There are nevertheless additional criteria for good counterfactual arguments, and here we must be careful to distinguish good from valid counterfactuals. The criteria for good counterfactuals says a lot about their utility for purposes of analysis but nothing about their external validity. External validity can sometimes be tested on the basis of evidence. Like all propositions, counterfactuals can be falsified but never validated.

The protocols for conducting counterfactual thought experiments depend on the social domain in which they are used. The most important feature of this domain is the extent to which it is amenable to statistical laws and generalizations. For the reasons I provided, history and international relations generally lie outside this domain and accordingly require a set of protocols that are different from those used for counterfactual experimentation in the sciences. Chapter 2 develops a set of protocols more appropriate to history and international relations and in doing so also highlights some of the limitations and problems in using counterfactuals in these domains. The concluding section of the chapter uses earlier sections of the chapter as a foundation to construct a method for assessing the relative importance of systematic and nonsystematic factors—determination versus contingency—in specific historical outcomes. For my example, I use the phenomenal success of the West in the modern world.

Chapters 3 and 4 follow the protocols developed in chapter 2 to conduct counterfactual analysis of two important historical events: the origins of the First World War and the end of the Cold War, responsible for what international relations scholars generally consider two of the three transformations of the international system in the twentieth century—the other being the product of World War II. They are important cases substantively but also intellectually because they demonstrate the key role of nonsystematic factors and nonlinear causation. As noted earlier, these cases provide the basis for a procedure, elaborated in the conclusion, for unpacking cases to determine their contingency and the relative importance of structure, agency, and accident. This in turn can provide important insights into how nonlinear causation works in international relations.

Chapter 3, "Franz Ferdinand Found Alive: World War I Unnecessary," is a much reworked and expanded version of an article that first appeared in the *Political Science Quarterly*.[51] In the last decade new evidence and interpretations based on them have shifted our understandings of the origins of the war and I have updated my own arguments to incorporate and reflect the latest scholarship. This in turn led me to rewrite the conclusions, which address the broader implications of the case for international relations theory. The new evidence buttresses my contention that World War I was contingent in both its underlying and immediate causes. Historians have proposed a variety of underlying causes for World War I, from social Darwinism to nationalism, the alliance structure, offensive dominance, and shifts in the balance of power. What made Europe ripe for war, I maintain, was not this multitude of alleged causes, but the nature of the interactions among them. The First World War is best understood as a nonlinear confluence of three largely independent chains of causation that produced independent but more or less simultaneous gestalt shifts in Vienna and Berlin, and a slightly earlier one in Russia. Had the timing of the Austrian and German shifts been off by as little as two years, Austrian leaders would not have been so intent on destroying Serbia or German leaders might not have encouraged them to do so and the Russians would not have been willing to risk war in Serbia's defense.

Chapter 4, "Leadership and the End of the Cold War: Did It Have to End This Way?" is coauthored with George W. Breslauer and originally appeared in a volume I co-edited on the end of the Cold War.[52] The conventional wisdom about the resolution of this conflict emphasizes—correctly in my view—the important role of actors, notably Mikhail Gorbachev and Ronald Reagan. Gorbachev was different from previous Soviet leaders in his commitment to end the Cold War and his willingness to take political risks at home and abroad to do so. Reagan differed from other presidents and presidential candidates in the initial intensity of his hostility to the Soviet Union but also in his subsequent willingness to take the rhetoric of a Soviet leader seriously and work with him to reduce superpower nuclear arsenals and end the Cold War. Breslauer and I imagine East-West relations without Gorbachev, Reagan, or Bush and by doing so make the case for the determining role of leaders. We identify other leaders that might have come to power and consider the most plausible policies they would have pursued toward one another's country. This generates a wide range of possible scenarios in the late 1980s that range from intensification of the Cold War to its resolution on terms that might have allowed for the continued existence of the Soviet Union. We argue that the end of the Cold War, the terms on which it ended, and their consequences for the post–Cold War world, were contingent and highly dependent on leaders.

Part I of my book offers ontological arguments for why systemic theories of international relations are inadequate and attempts to devise methods for thinking more systematically about nonsystematic factors. Part II is concerned with psychological limitations on theory building and uses counterfactual surveys and experiments to probe how foreign policy experts, historians, and international relations scholars understand causation. It uses history as a resource rather than a focus of analysis. Its findings lend additional support to psychological critiques of systemic theories that contend that advances in theory building are seriously hindered by substantive and methodological commitments of researchers that are often impervious to evidence. In keeping with my objective to facilitate, not just critique theory building, I suggest several strategies to help overcome, or at least cope with these cognitive limitations.

Chapter 5, "Scholars and Causation 1," is coauthored with Philip E. Tetlock and originally appeared in the *American Political Science Review*.[53]

It conducts correlational studies to determine the degree to which professional observers of world politics rely on abstract principles and laws (e.g., the national interest, the balance of power, deterrence theory) to assess the plausibility of real and imagined past outcomes. It uses experiments to test the effects of "close-call" counterfactuals on their judgments. Close-call counterfactuals are minimal rewrites of history close to the event whose outcome we wish to mutate.

We theorize a sharp divide between "generalizers" who believe that behavior and outcomes display sufficient regularity to be described, even predicted, by principles or laws, and "particularizers" who foreground the role of agency and chance, doubt the efficacy of prediction, and emphasize the idiosyncrasy of individual cases. The conflict between these worldviews is made readily apparent by how participants respond to close-call counterfactual scenarios that use plausible rewrites of the past to move history on to an increasingly divergent path. Close-call counterfactuals make the case for the determining features of context, which make them anathema to generalizers but music to the ears of particularizers. The findings of both the correlational studies and experiments suggest strong links between belief systems and psychological orientations and the resistance of both to alternative worldviews or historical interpretations.

Chapter 6, "Scholars and Causation 2," builds on the findings of the previous chapter. Tetlock and I found that participants in our experiments considered the contingency of events to diminish the closer we approach them in time. Counterfactual priming made participants more open to contingency, and more so when the counterfactuals were packaged in narrative accounts that embedded them in local context. In this chapter, I attempt to see if the same pattern holds when historians and international relations scholars are asked to devise their own close-call counterfactuals. Participants with a high need for closure should respond positively to this task when the case is at odds with their view of the world or preferred theory, and be resistant, or at least cross-pressured, when it is a case they consider supportive. The cross-pressure, I surmise, arises from their need to demonstrate their imagination, historical knowledge, and competence in constructing arguments versus their need to defend their views of the world.

I also probe understandings of causation through the novel use of what I call long-shot counterfactuals. These are minimal rewrites of history at considerable temporal remove from the outcome I want to mutate. They entail a long chain of events between antecedent and consequent, and many enabling counterfactuals. Long-shot counterfactuals should be inherently less credible than their close-call counterparts because of these differences. The experiments in chapter 5 indicate that historians and international relations scholars estimate events to be more contingent the farther back in time from them they are asked to make an assessment. Experiments using long-shot counterfactuals nevertheless suggest that such counterfactuals are difficult to make plausible. When they are judged implausible, historians and international relations scholars lower their estimate of the overall contingency of the event in question. Counterfactual priming with close-call and long-shot counterfactuals appears to have divergent consequences. Following Tversky and Kahneman, I argue that both outcomes are due to the effect of vividness, which draws participants into a scenario, narrowing their conceptual horizon. If they judge the scenario plausible—a judgment much easier to bring about in a close-call counterfactual—they raise their estimates of the overall contingency of the event, and vice versa, if not.

Close-call and long-shot counterfactuals pose different kinds of challenges to participants. The latter encourage them to think about how remote and improbable our world would have appeared from the vantage point of the antecedent. They also highlight causal connections across social domains that are normally separate fields of study and by doing so emphasize the open-ended nature of the social world. I explore these features of long-shot counterfactuals and the cognitive tensions, even contradictions, that my experiments highlight in follow-up interviews with participants. Overall, these experiments and surveys indicate that neither historians nor international relations scholars display what might be considered rational thinking when they consider the contingency of alternative or actual outcomes that are perceived as having important implications for their beliefs about the world and how it works.

Part III turns to fiction on the grounds that it provides the most compelling and persuasive exploration of alternative worlds. The move from social science to literature and the humanities, I argued earlier, is fully justified given the goals of my inquiry. Nor is it as great a leap as it may appear to some readers. Fact and fiction have always been intertwined in the human mind and share a common etymology in most Western languages. History at the outset was inseparable from myth. It was only in mid-fifth-century Greece that the concept of myth was formulated, and with it, the possibility of distinguishing history from fiction. A century later, Aristotle argued that fiction—by which he meant all forms of poetry, including tragedy—was superior to history, which merely described events, because it had the power to order them in abstract ways and thereby convey deeper truths.[54]

The idea of the "fact" as a description of the world independent of theory is an invention of the seventeenth century.[55] This innovation is generally attributed to Francis Bacon or his followers.[56] In the eighteenth century, the understanding of "facts" as a form of "uninterested knowledge" had profound consequences for philosophy, history, and literature.

Traditional European history was shaped by the Christian belief that it encodes a pattern and purpose that can be discovered. The search for history's immanent plot, which used poetry for a model, tied it closely to literature. Literature in turn became implicated with history. Many novels of the middle to late eighteenth century, including those of Richardson, Fielding, and the plays of Steele, sought to mediate between figurative and empirical discourses, between discourses rooted in biblical narrative and those founded on observation. Novels of the period had yet to establish stable boundaries, and their authors often described them as a form of history. Only later would novelists come to understand their work as a form of poetry, but many still reserved the right to engage history.[57]

British empiricists of the latter half of the eighteenth century were drawn to history because they understood the present to be constructed on the understanding of the past. They sought rules for gathering and evaluating facts, became champions of quantitative data, and tried to develop more transparent modes of presentation. David Hume rejected interpretations that were not based on particulars that could be observed, and brought his understanding of induction to the study of history. He effectively debunked the idea that history told a story about a decline from a past golden age. His involvement with history nevertheless led him to conclude that it is functionally indistinguishable from novels and epic poetry because, like these forms, it is only made meaningful by fictional emplotment, a mere recital of past events being nothing more than a chronicle. For Hume, history, freed of its Christian and mythical roots, is the proper paradigm of human understanding because it connects our consciousness with what lies outside of it. It is a "moral science" because the conventions that govern human behavior are the unintended result of individuals' engagement with one another and the world. History helps to clarify these conventions and make them more meaningful by describing their emergence and evolution.[58] Many eighteenth-century historical works contain features that we associate with the novel because they seek to generate knowledge through the vehicle of conversation with the reader and elicit identification with the author who appears as the principal "character" of his or her work.[59]

Thanks to Hume and his continental counterparts, by the mid-nineteenth century history had replaced poetry as the principal source of knowledge and wisdom about humanity. Poetry was subsumed under the rubric of fiction, which by now had emerged as a generic category. This reversal of the relative standing of history and poetry, or more broadly speaking, of fact and fiction, was never fully accepted by creative artists and some philosophers. Modernist writers, among them Joyce, Pound, and Eliot, insisted that no era had a monopoly on experience, understanding, and wisdom and that recovery of the past was essential to human fulfillment. They embraced poetry as the appropriate vehicle toward this end.[60] Nietzsche went a step further and insisted that art and music spoke a truth that went beyond words and had the potential to free people from the tyranny of logic.[61] Twentieth-century writers, whether or not they engage history, are heirs to this tradition. Many of their readers have come to accept fiction as a vehicle for stretching and challenging their consciousness and understanding of the world in ways history does not.[62]

Historical counterfactuals have the potential to build bridges between history and fiction. They may be used to interrogate and offer critical perspectives on history and social science or their intellectual foundations. This is the avowed goal of my short story in chapter 7. It plays psycho-logic off against the laws of statistical inference to demonstrate the inherently conservative bias of the latter with respect to alternative worlds. My story takes place in an imaginary world in which Mozart has lived to the age of sixty-five, and as a result, neither world war nor the Holocaust occurred. My heroine and her partner try to imagine what the world would have been be like if Mozart had died at age thirty-five, her partner's age. The alternative world my characters invoke is a pale version of our twentieth-century world with all its unspeakable horrors, and is summarily dismissed by an imaginary critic who demonstrates its political and statistical improbability. My heroine concludes with a biting if humorous rejoinder. My story does double duty as a "long-shot" counterfactual and experimental instrument, which I use in chapter 6 as part of my effort to understand how historians and international relations scholars understand causation.

Chapter 8 examines more serious fiction in the form of two best-selling novels. It compares Sinclair Lewis's *It Can't Happen Here*, published in 1935, with Philip Roth's *The Plot Against America*, published in 2004.[63] The former looks ahead to the 1936 presidential election and the victory of the fictional fascist Senator Buzz Windrip over Franklin Roosevelt. The latter looks back to the 1940 presidential election to imagine Roosevelt's defeat by aviator Charles A. Lindbergh, in thrall to the Nazis, and whose administration is isolationist abroad and anti-Semitic at home. Strictly speaking, these novels only peripherally engage international relations. Novels about alternative worlds—especially those set in the past—are nevertheless the ultimate form of counterfactual unpacking. They speak to a fundamental goal of my book: exploring the ways in which fact and fiction work together to create a powerful impression on readers. They suggest that the binary between fact and fiction is to a great extent artificial and can creatively and usefully be bridged for analytical as well as artistic purposes. This understanding, I argue in the conclusion, has important implications for the study and practice of international relations.

Of the two novels, only *The Plot Against America* qualifies as counterfactual in that it remakes the past. Counterfactual fiction almost invariably uses an antecedent—some rewrite of history—to produce a consequent in the form of an altered present. The antecedent is intended to be amplifying in its effects, taking history farther away from the world we know. Roth changes history by changing the outcome of the 1940 election and making its winner subject to blackmail by Hitler, creating a sharp divergence from the history we know. Toward the end of the novel he introduces a deus ex machina to return history to its actual course once the alternative world he creates has served its purposes. Critics find his second order counterfactual unconvincing, but its credibility, I contend, is beside the point. Roth is a cut above other practitioners of the counterfactual novel genre, and not only by virtue of the quality of his writing. He is self-conscious and reflective about his use of history and counterhistory. There is much to learn from Roth about the ways in which counterfactual history can be used to offset inherent weaknesses of the genre of history and become an effective rhetorical vehicle for advancing cultural or political projects. More importantly for our purposes, his novel drives home just how much our emotional and intellectual anchors are the product of our circumstances, circumstances that we generally take for granted. Even if they are not as contingent as *The Plot Against America* appears to suggest, they are still parochial, not universal, and certainly not preordained. This realization has important consequences for our understanding of theory in the social sciences.

The last chapter, Conclusion, builds on the findings of the earlier chapters to make more general arguments about the nature of causation and the relationship between fact and fiction, and factual and counterfactual. Drawing on World War I and the Cold War cases, it expands upon the procedure outlined out in chapter 2 for determining the relative weight of systematic and nonsystematic causes in individual cases. It develops a strategy for using counterfactuals to explore nonlinear causation. It reviews the findings of my two experimental studies and their implications for international relations theory and the ability of scholars to meet the cognitive and ethical requirements Weber associates with good theory. A final section attempts to build bridges between literature and social science. It does so by revisiting the binary of fact and fiction. I argue that we should recognize the tensions and fuzziness that surround this binary and exploit them for creative ends, as do social scientists who conduct counterfactual research and novelists who write counterfactual fiction. Until now, these projects, often on parallel tracks, have had no switches connecting them. My book aspires to remedy this situation to the benefit, I believe, of both communities.

CHAPTER TWO

Counterfactual Thought Experiments

> A production without design would resemble more the ravings
> of a madman, than the sober efforts of genius and learning.
> —*David Hume*

THE ABILITY TO IMAGINE alternative scenarios is a ubiquitous, if not essential, part of human mental life.[1] It is a universal phenomenon, not a practice restricted to or more pronounced in Western culture.[2] Counterfactuals are routinely used by ordinary people and policymakers to work their way through problems, reach decisions, cope with anxiety, and make normative judgments. They are readily inspired by disconfirmed expectations and failed actions and the regrets they evoke.[3] In these circumstances, counterfactual scenarios can empower us by making us believe that we could have brought about better outcomes.[4] When people invent counterfactuals for any of these ends they are in effect running proxy experiments in their heads.[5] They imagine alternative worlds and features of it that generate different outcomes.[6] To understand the real world, past and present, we need to know when, why and how people evoke counterfactuals and their implications for their beliefs and behavior. This has become an increasingly important focus of research in cognitive psychology.

Counterfactuals are a powerful research tool. They are routinely used in the physical and biological sciences to develop and evaluate sophisticated nonlinear models.[7] They have been used with telling effect in psychology, economic history, and American politics.[8] To conduct counterfactual research in history and international relations, we require a clear understanding of the nature of counterfactuals, the circumstances in which they are appropriate, and robust protocols for conducting thought experiments. Tetlock and Belkin took an important step in this direction in their introductory essay to their 1996 edited volume, *Counterfactual Thought Experiments in World Politics*.[9] Tetlock and Parker have adapted these protocols to the study of history.[10] I accept most of their guidelines although I reformulate some and add additional ones.[11]

I begin this chapter with a discussion of the similarities and differences between counterfactual and so-called factual arguments and argue that the difference between these modes of inquiry has been greatly exaggerated; it is one of degree, not of kind. I then identify three kinds of counterfactuals—miracle, plausible world, and folk counterfactuals—and describe their respective uses. I go on to identify some of the different uses of counterfactuals for historians and international relations scholars. In the course of the discussion, I propose nine criteria to guide the choice and use of plausible world counterfactuals in international relations. I conclude by proposing a method of using counterfactuals to discriminate between the importance of systematic and nonsystematic factors in important historical outcomes. I use as my example the phenomenal success of Western civilization in the modern era.

COUNTERFACTUALS VERSUS FACTUALS

Counterfactual means contrary to facts.[12] A counterfactual describes an event that did not occur.[13] A prominent philosopher defines counterfactuals as "subjective conditionals" in which the antecedent is known to be false.[14] In everyday language counterfactuals can be characterized as "what if" statements. This description nicely captures the purpose of counterfactuals: to vary some aspect of the past to change some feature of the present. Some people use counterfactuals to impute different futures, although, strictly speaking, they only pertain to the past. Most counterfactuals in international relations are historical counterfactuals.[15]

In history and international relations counterfactual experiments generally involve some degree of speculation because, as Stephen J. Gould laments, we cannot rerun the tape of history to see what would actually happen in the new circumstances counterfactuals create. The inherently speculative nature of counterfactuals makes many scholars, especially historians, wary of them. We should nevertheless recognize that counterfactual experiments can sometimes be conducted in an evidence-rich environment. In the aftermath of Aldrich Ames's arrest as a Soviet spy, the Central Intelligence Agency convened a team of counterintelligence experts to figure out how he might have been unmasked earlier. The team imagined a series of procedures that could have been in place and asked which, if any of them, might have tripped Ames up. Their knowledge of Ames's personality, motives, and behavior, and of the modus operandi of his Soviet spy masters, allowed them to conduct their inquiry with what they believed to be a reasonable degree of precision.[16] In New York City authorities used the fear of widespread Y2K computer failures to test the ability of city agencies to respond to a complex emergency. Officials were confident that such breakdowns would not occur and used the scenarios as "future counterfactuals" to provide useful data to identify bottlenecks and improve performance.[17]

Whether we like it or not, counterfactuals lie at the core of almost all historical interpretations and their "lessons." The controversy surrounding the strategy of deterrence provides a good example. One of the principal policy "lessons" of the 1930s was that appeasement whets the appetites of dictators while military capability and resolve restrains them. The failure of Anglo-French efforts to appease Hitler is well established but the putative efficacy of deterrence rests on the counterfactual that Hitler *could* have been restrained *if* France and Britain had demonstrated willingness to go to war in defense of the European territorial status quo. German documents make this an eminently researchable question and historians have used them to try to determine at what point Hitler could no longer be deterred.[18] Their findings have important implications for the historical assessment of French and British policy and for the strategy of deterrence more generally.

The Cuban missile crisis is another evidence-rich environment and one in which the validity of counterfactuals drove policy and can now be tested. Nikita Khrushchev's decision to send and remove missiles from Cuba, and Kennedy's decision to impose a blockade were contingent upon hypothetical antecedents. Kennedy believed, incorrectly, it turned out, that Khrushchev sent missiles to Cuba because he doubted his resolve and would not have done so if he had taken a stronger stand at the Bay of Pigs or in Berlin. Kennedy reasoned that he had to compel Khrushchev to remove the missiles to convince him of his resolve and to deter a more serious Soviet challenge to the Western position in Berlin. Evidence from Soviet and American archives and interviews with former officials make it possible to explore the validity of most of these counterfactuals, and thus to evaluate the choices of Soviet and American leaders and subsequent scholarly analyses of the crisis.[19] This case also indicates how important counterfactuals are for policymakers attempting to reach and evaluate policy choices, making them an important component of any so-called factual history of the Cuban missile crisis.

Quantitative counterfactual analysis is another possibility. Jay Winter exploits counterfactual projections of mortality rates based on prewar data from Prudential Life Insurance policies to determine the age structure of British war losses. He combines data from the life tables for 1913 and 1915 in roughly two-to-one proportions, as the war did not begin until August 1914, to create a counterfactual table for 1914. On the basis of the life tables from the prewar decade he then calculates what the life tables would have been for the period 1914–18 in the absence of war. By comparing the death rates in each age group with the counterfactual estimates, he is able to determine the actual death rates by five year cohorts for each year of the war.[20]

Historical cases can be framed as counterfactuals and used to make comparisons. Victoria Tin-bor Hui uses this strategy to examine state formation in China and Europe. She identifies a series of processes common to both regions and uses China as a "real world counterfactual" to evaluate state formation in Europe, and vice versa.[21] Kenneth Pomeranz uses Europe as a counterfactual case to understand why China did not have an independent industrial revolution.[22] These experiments are based on the assumption that similar causal mechanisms operate in diverse contexts where they may have different consequences. By examining the differential impact of these mechanisms and the extent to which they were determined by local conditions, scholars in this instance attempt to identify different trajectories of historical development.[23]

Even when evidence is meager or absent, the difference between counterfactual and "factual" history is less than is commonly supposed. Documents are rarely "smoking guns" that allow researchers to establish motives or causes beyond a reasonable doubt. Actors only occasionally leave evidence about their motives, and historians rarely accept such testimony at face value. More often historians infer motives from what they know about actors' personalities and goals, their past behavior, and the constraints under which they operated. Janice Gross Stein and I spent several years researching a book on Cold War crises. We scoured archives in four countries, utilized documents collected or declassified by other researchers and conducted extensive interviews with former American, Soviet, Israeli, and Egyptian policymakers. We accumulated a mass of relevant information but still had no hard evidence about the reasons for some of the key decisions of Kennedy and Khrushchev. We suspect that Khrushchev was never clear in his own mind about the relative importance of the several goals that made a secret missile deployment in Cuba attractive to him. Given the delicate nature of many crisis decisions, neither leader was willing to confide his objectives and assumptions with even his most intimate advisors. Khrushchev further complicated the picture by telling various officials what they wanted to hear and thus what he thought most likely to garner their support.[24]

When we move from the level of analysis of individual actors to small groups, elites, societies, states, and regional and international systems, the balance between evidence and inference shifts decisively in the direction of the latter. Systemic arguments assume that behavior is a response to the constraints and opportunities generated by a set of domestic or international conditions. Mark Elvin's elegant study of China starts from the premise that empires expand to the point at which their technological superiority over their neighbors is approximately counterbalanced by the burdens of size. At this equilibrium imperial social institutions come under constant strain because of the high relative cost of security. Harsh taxation impoverishes peasant cultivators and leads to falling tax revenues. The ensuing decline in the number of free subjects makes military recruitment more difficult, and governments rely instead on barbarian auxiliaries, even for their main fighting forces. To save money, governments give up active defense policies and try to keep hostile barbarians at bay through diplomacy, bribery, and settlement on imperial lands. The inevitable outcome is a weakened economic base, barbarization from within, and, finally, partial or total collapse of the empire.[25] Elvin musters considerable evidence in support of his thesis, much of it from primary sources, but all of it in the way of illustration. Nowhere is he able to show that Chinese leaders took any of the policies he describes for any of the reasons he attributes to them.

This failure, understandable in the circumstances, is common to almost all systemic arguments, and often in instances where there is evidence about how actors in question understood the world and their situation. The end of the Cold War is a case in point. Realist scholars attribute Gorbachev's commitment to end the Cold War to an unfavorable balance of power. Some contend that Gorbachev felt comfortable making what were in effect unilateral concessions because the Soviet Union was secure by virtue of its nuclear arsenal.[26] Realists offer no evidence that Gorbachev or his closest advisors actually reasoned this way, but base their case on the claim that it would have been rational for them to do so. Nonsystemic accounts use Soviet documents, memoirs, and interviews with Gorbachev and other top Soviet leaders to make the case for the role of ideas in determining Gorbachev's foreign policy goals, and for domestic and organizational politics accounting for the pace and timing of his initiatives. All of these works are evidence rich, but in the end, their authors too must infer rather than document motives. Unlike systemic arguments that rely on a double chain of inference—from structural features of the situation to leaders' understandings of the world to their behavior—studies of domestic politics and leadership base their inferences directly on reconstructions of leaders' views of the world and *their* understanding of the constraints they face and the opportunities open to them, not those imputed to them on the basis of so-called structural imperatives.[27]

Systemic and nonsystemic arguments alike build on chains of inference that use behavioral "principles" as their anchor points. Empirical evidence, when available, is more likely to be exploited by nonsystemic explanations to suggest links between principles and behavior. But even in the best of cases these links are indirect and presumptive and can be corroborated only obliquely and incompletely. Readers must evaluate arguments and claims on the seeming "reasonableness" of the inferences, the quality and relevance of the evidence offered in support, and the extent to which that evidence permits or constrains alternative interpretations. Receptivity to arguments is significantly influenced by the nature of the underlying political and behavioral "principles" in which the inferences are anchored. When these "principles" run counter to the reigning orthodoxy the arguments may be dismissed out of hand regardless of the evidence.

Good counterfactual thought experiments differ little from "factual" modes of historical reconstruction. If we attempt to evaluate the importance of Mikhail Gorbachev for the end of the Cold War—as George Breslauer and I do in chapter 4—by considering the likely consequences of Chernenko being succeeded by someone else, we need to study the career and policies of other possible successors (e.g., Grishin, Romanov, Ligachev), and infer their policies on the basis of their past preferences and commitments, the political environment in 1985, and the general domestic and foreign situation of the Soviet Union. There is a lot of evidence that sustains informed arguments about the kind of domestic and foreign policies that these leaders might have pursued. Admittedly, unexpected events, like Mathias Rust's Cessna flight to Red Square in May 1987, which Gorbachev exploited to purge the military of many hardliners, can also have a significant influence on policy, its timing or success.

The difference between factual and counterfactual arguments is further blurred when we recognize that, as in the Cuban missile crisis, we often need to understand the factual *and* counterfactual beliefs of historical actors to account for their behavior. In the missile crisis beliefs shaped arguments: in the absence of hard evidence, they determined the motives the president and other American officials attributed to Khrushchev for deploying Soviet missiles in Cuba, the calculations and political conflicts they assumed to be taking place in Moscow, and the likely Soviet responses to a blockade, air strike, or invasion. The Soviets did the same. Some of these beliefs took the form of conditional expectations (e.g., if we don't withdraw the missiles, Kennedy will attack Cuba). With the passage of time they became historical counterfactuals (e.g., Kennedy would or would not have attacked Cuba if Khrushchev had not withdrawn the Soviet missiles).

Counterfactuals are frequently smuggled into so-called factual narratives. E. H. Carr, no friend of counterfactuals, does this in his treatment of the Soviet Union where he insists that the Bolshevik Revolution was highjacked by Stalin. The implication is that socialism would have developed differently without him.[28] John Lukacs, an even more vitriolic opponent of counterfactuals, does the same in his highly regarded study of the role Churchill played in preventing a British capitulation to Hitler. His argument rests on a series of unacknowledged counterfactuals, the principal one being no Churchill as prime minister, no allied victory in World War II.[29] Policymakers also succumb to this temptation. After the Cuban missile crisis, President Kennedy, administration officials, and subsequently many scholars maintained that Khrushchev would not have deployed missiles in Cuba had Kennedy behaved more decisively at the Bay of Pigs, the Vienna summit, and in Berlin. There was absolutely no evidence in support of this counterfactual but it quickly became the conventional wisdom and helped to shape a host of subsequent policy decisions, including the blockade of Cuba and disastrous intervention in Vietnam. The evidence that became available in the Gorbachev era suggested that Khrushchev decided to send missiles secretly to Cuba because he *overestimated* Kennedy's resolve; he feared that Kennedy was preparing to invade Cuba and would send the American navy to stop any ships carrying missiles to Cuba to deter that invasion.[30] Kennedy's counterfactual confirmed tautologically the policy lesson of the 1930s that strength and resolve deters aggression—when in fact it provoked it in the case of Cuba—a "lesson" that continues to guide American policymakers and most members of its national security community despite more compelling interpretations of Khrushchev's calculations and behavior in Cuba.

As the Kennedy counterfactual illustrates, counterfactual arguments, like their factual counterparts, will appeal to or fall flat with the policymakers, scholars, and the public for reasons that have little to do with their nature (i.e., factual or counterfactual) or evidence consistent with them. In both instances, their assumptions appear to be determining. When they are congruent or supportive of political or psychological needs—and both seem to have been in play in the case of the Kennedy and deterrence counterfactuals—they will be accepted uncritically. Arguments and evidence against them will have an uphill struggle, even within the scholarly community. This is a sobering truth and reflects the power of reinforcing motivational and cognitive biases.[31]

From a purely logical standpoint—as opposed to a political or psychological one—any historical argument should be only as compelling as its internal consistency and the quality of evidence that supports it, or is at least consistent with the hypothesized links between a stipulated cause and its effect. For this reason, every good counterfactual rests on multiple "factuals," just as every factual rests on counterfactual assumptions—assumptions that all too often go unexamined. Any sharp distinction between factuals and counterfactuals is based on questionable epistemological claims.

There is also the question of just what constitutes a "fact." Philosophers have come to "facts" as social constructions. They do not deny the existence of reality quite independently of any attempt to understand it by human beings. Stars, planets, mountains, rivers, and lakes are "brute" facts, to use Anscombe's terminology, because they do not require an institutional context to occur.[32] Our descriptions for them are nevertheless socially generated and often imprecise or arbitrary. Some of these understandings may transcend culture. Physical scientists may be correct in their claim that fundamental concepts like mass, volume, and temperature are essential to the study of nature, and that extraterrestrial scientists would have to possess the same concepts to understand the universe. This is simply not true of social concepts, which vary across and within cultures. There are many ways of describing social interactions, and the choice and utility of concepts depend largely on the purpose of the "knower."[33]

"Temperature" is undeniably a social construction, but is a measure of something observable and real: changes in temperature measure changes in the energy levels of molecules. Social and political concepts do not describe anything so concrete. There is no such thing as a balance of power, a social class, or a tolerant society. Social "facts" are reflections of the concepts we use to describe social reality, not of reality itself. They are ideational and subjective, and even the existence of "precise" measures for them—something we only rarely have—would not make them any less arbitrary. We must be careful and self-conscious in our use of terms like "fact," "case," and "evidence." Social facts, as noted above, are products of our conceptions and take on their character purely as a function of these conceptions. Cases are collections of social facts organized around a typology. Typologies are a higher level of social abstraction and construction. Cases—analyzed quantitatively or qualitatively—constitute or provide the "evidence" we use to evaluate propositions and theories. Models, propositions, and theories are also higher levels of social construction. They are *metafactual* in that they imagine an ensemble of generalized and related "facts." They often arise from or influence, if not dictate, the typologies we use to determine what counts as cases and by extension as evidence.

Evidence is not out there waiting to be scooped up like grains of sand—an image that seems to underlie King, Keohane, and Verbas's treatment of it in *Designing Social Inquiry*—but is a product of our theories, propositions, and typologies. Theories and evidence are thus part of the same chain of social construction that always verges on the tautological by virtue of the near impossibility of constructing categories of social facts and evidence independent of the interpretations, propositions, or theories we intend to evaluate or test. The manner in which facts, cases, evidence, interpretations, propositions, and theories are socially embedded does not make a mockery of social science and its methods but it compels us to recognize that the kind of knowledge it can generate (*epistēmē*) is to a high degree self-referential. Propositions and theories can only be "true" by convention because their terms, by definition, do not correspond to a world of first-order "facts." In practice, we may use categories of fact, case, and evidence, but with caution and full recognition of the extent to which they tell us more about our view of the world than about the world itself. We must be as much aware of what they *exclude* as we are of what they include.

If it is any consolation, this problem is not limited to the social sciences. Quine has shown that theoretical concepts insinuate themselves into the "data language" of even the hardest sciences.[34] Counterfactuals can be used to document his claim that there is no conceptually neutral data language. Chapter 5 reports an experiment Phil Tetlock and I conducted in which we asked a group of foreign policy experts to assess the contingency of the outcome of the Cuban missile crisis. One of their experiments used a "factual framing" of the question (at what point did some form of peaceful resolution of the Cuban missile crisis become inevitable?) and a counterfactual framing (at what point did all alternative, more violent outcomes become impossible?). Logically, the two questions are strictly complementary. If we know the answer to either, we should be able to deduce the answer to the other. Even though these two measures were obtained almost side by side in our questionnaire, the factual versus counterfactual framings of the historical question elicited systematically different responses, not just random variation that could be attributed to fatigue or boredom. Experts perceived substantially more contingency when they reflected on the counterfactually framed question. This is a good empirical demonstration of the importance of the benchmark against which the outcome is compared, and offers support for the constructivist claim that how we pose "purely empirical" questions systematically shapes the answers we find.

The social construction of facts does not mean, as a minority of poststructuralists contend, that all interpretations are equal. Like the sciences, history and social science have developed protocols to evaluate the competing claims of theories or interpretations. These protocols do not rest on any philosophical foundation but on the understandings respected practitioners within those fields have of what constitutes "good" physics, geology, history, or political science. Protocols vary from field to field, evolve over time and are often the subject of intense controversy, as they are in contemporary political science and international relations.[35] Science is best conceived of as a practice, and this book, as do many others, seeks to influence how we think about that practice and especially about what we consider legitimate modes of argumentation and ways of employing them. In the conclusion, I will return to this subject and argue that the constructions of "factual" history or international relations are largely imaginative exercises and should be thought of this way. The only claim to privilege of propositions, theories, and interpretations is that they tell us something useful or interesting about the social world. The same is true of counterfactual history.

WHY COUNTERFACTUALS?

In chapter 1 I noted the power of the certainty of hindsight bias and the strong human need to see the future as predictable. I suggested that the hindsight and various belief defenses combine to make this illusion possible. They allow people to upgrade retrospectively their predictive abilities and to explain away discrepant cases. Counterfactuals can combat both processes. They can make us see past and future alike as contingent, reveal contradictions in our belief systems and highlight double standards in our moral judgments. Counterfactuals are also an essential ingredient in theory formation. They help determine the research questions we deem important, not only the answers we find to them.

Receptivity to Contingency

Baruch Fischoff demonstrated that outcome knowledge affects our understanding of the past by making it difficult for us to recall that we were once unsure about what was going to happen. Events deemed improbable by experts (e.g., peace between Egypt and Israel, the end of the Cold War) are often considered overdetermined and all but inevitable after they have occurred.[36] By tracing the path that appears to have led to a known outcome, we diminish our sensitivity to alternative paths and outcomes. We may fail to recognize the uncertainty under which actors operated and the possibility that they could have made different choices that might have led to different outcomes.

Many psychologists regard the certainty of hindsight effect as deeply rooted and difficult to eliminate. But the experimental literature suggests that counterfactual intervention can assist people in retrieving and making explicit their massive but largely latent uncertainty about historical junctures—that is, to recognize that they once thought, perhaps correctly, that events could easily have taken a different turn. The proposed correctives use one cognitive bias to reduce the effect of another. Ross, Lepper, Strack, and Steinmetz exploited the tendency of people to inflate the perceived likelihood of vivid scenarios to make them more responsive to contingency. People they presented with scenarios describing possible life histories of post-therapy patients evaluated these possibilities as more likely than did members of the control group who were not given the scenarios. This effect persisted even when all the participants in the experiment were told that the post-therapy scenarios were entirely hypothetical.[37] The experiments reported in chapters 5 and 6 confirm this finding and suggest that scholars exposed to counterfactuals, and better yet, forced to grapple with their theoretical consequences, will also become more open to the role of contingency in key decisions and events.

Framing Research

Research questions arise when events strike us as interesting or anomalous. To conceive of an event as anomalous we need a benchmark that establishes what is normal. In the hard sciences, benchmarks can sometimes be derived from well-established laws or statistical generalizations; cold fusion would have been contrary to several of these laws and thus a strikingly anomalous event. There are few, if any, laws or universally valid statistical generalizations applicable to the social world, but we all hold to theories, or at least strong, if informal views, about how that world works. They give rise to expectations, and when these expectations are unfulfilled, to counterfactual worlds. These alternative worlds may appear more probable than the actual state of affairs. During the Cold War, the preeminent question in the security field was "the long peace" between the superpowers. In international political economy, a key question in the late 1970s and 1980s was the survival of the postwar international economic order in the face of America's seeming decline as a hegemon. Some security specialists considered it remarkable—that is, contrary to their theories and expectations—that the superpowers had avoided war, unlike rival hegemons of the past. Some political economists were equally surprised that neither Germany nor Japan had sought to restructure international economic relations to their advantage in response to the relative U.S. decline.[38] Both research agendas assumed that the status quo was an extraordinary anomaly that required an equally extraordinary explanation. For researchers who assumed that neither superpower was so unhappy with the existing state of affairs that it was willing to risk war to change it, or that Germany and Japan were not dissatisfied enough with the institutions that the United States had established at the end of World War II to manage the international economy to risk the disruption entailed in trying to change them, the seeming robustness of the postwar political and economic orders posed no intellectual puzzle.

On a larger scale, Western historians and social scientists have long taken the West as the norm and used it as the starting point for examining non-Western societies. Their differences—not ours—accordingly become the focus of attention. Students of state formation describe early modern Europe as composed of multiple political units, many with internal checks on the power of their leaders, something many of these scholars see as a highly likely, if not inevitable outcome.[39] China, by contrast, developed into a unitary empire, and even during periods of fragmentation, a universal empire was still recognized as the norm. Western scholars have sought to explain why China evolved differently. Not surprisingly, many Chinese historians assume that the development of a universal empire was all but inevitable and Chinese experience the norm.[40] Chang Kwang-chih suggests that it is time to consider building theories on the Chinese past, whose history and sources are "as formidable and massive as Western history."[41]

These examples indicate how ideology and culture provide the unspoken assumptions that shape our inquires of the social world. These understandings generate expectations, which if they are not met, in the future or historically, give rise to seeming anomalies and interesting research questions. Ideological and cultural biases, like their political counterparts, readily assume the guise of science and lend themselves to tautological confirmation. This tightens their hold on the minds of scholars, policymakers, and the public. Counterfactuals are a useful means of exposing the subjective foundations of beliefs and providing a possible means for scholars to step outside their own cultures and belief structures. Suppose we ask if there would have been a Cold War if the Soviet Union had been a liberal democracy in 1945, or if there had been no nuclear weapons? What if China had accessible coal reserves and iron deposits close to major commercial centers? Would it have begun its own industrial revolution and become a rival to Europe? These counterfactuals are utterly unrealistic but they compel us to examine the unspoken assumptions that guide our expectations about the real world.

Testing and Evaluation

All counterfactuals are causal assertions.[42] Although not all conditionals are causal.[43] Conversely, all causal assertions entail counterfactuals, making them fundamental to testing or evaluating theories and interpretations. If we hypothesize that "x" caused "y," we assume that "y" would not have happened, ceteris paribus, in the absence of "x." Quantitative research attempts to get around this problem, and the contrapositive form of the fallacy of affirmation, by constructing a sample of comparable cases large enough to contain adequate variation on dependent (what is to be explained) and independent (what allegedly explains it) variables.[44] This strategy is only effective if there are no causes beyond those considered that vary systematically with the error term.[45] To rule out this possibility, researchers need to pose the counterfactual of what would have happened if variables in the error term were altered. In actual experiments, this problem can only partially be solved by random assignment. In case studies and historical narratives this is not possible.

Historians typically attempt to establish causation by means of process tracing.[46] They try to document the links between a stated cause and a given outcome in lieu of establishing a statistical correlation. This works best at the individual level of analysis, but only when there is enough evidence to document the calculations and motives of actors—and this is generally not the case for reasons I have made clear. Even on the rare occasions when such evidence is available, it may still not be possible to determine the relative weight of the several hypothesized causes and which, if any, might have produced the outcome in the absence of others, or in combination with other causes not at work in the case. Like statistical analysis, process tracing is based on a prior set of beliefs about what is important, what makes for a case, and working assumptions about the causal nexus in the cases in question. Historians should, but rarely do, make these assumptions explicit. To sustain causal inference it is generally necessary to engage in comparative analysis.

Comparative analysis is also possible within a single case and can take two forms: intracase comparison and counterfactual analysis. Intracase comparison breaks a case down into a series of similar interactions that are treated as separate and independent cases for purposes of analysis. Numerous studies of arms control and superpower crises make use of this technique.[42] Like any form of comparative analysis, intracase comparisons try to obtain as much variation as possible on dependent (*explanandum*) and independent (the *explanans)* variables. This is sometimes more difficult to do than in cross-case comparisons. The independence of cases is also more problematic, as the process and outcome of past decisions are likely to have considerable influence on subsequent decisions about similar issues. But intracase comparison confers a singular benefit: it builds variation within a fundamentally similar political and cultural context, controlling better than intercase comparison for many factors that may be important but otherwise unrecognized. Unfortunately, not every case can be broken down into multiple decision points for purposes of comparison. This works only for those where actors have made multiple decisions about the same problem, and considered roughly similar options on these occasions.

When intracase comparison is impossible, variation can be generated within a case by counterfactual experimentation. This latter strategy lies at the core of many simulations where variables are given a wide range of counterfactual values to determine the sensitivity of the outcome to changes in one or more of them. Counterfactual simulation can identity key variables and the range of values in which they will have the most impact on the outcome. Information obtained this way, especially if it has counterintuitive implications, can guide subsequent empirical work intended to test the model or generate information necessary to make it a better representation of reality. Counterfactual simulation can evaluate theories more directly. Lars-Eric Cederman used this method to test the realist assumption that balancing is the inevitable consequence of international anarchy. It follows, Cederman reasoned, that global hegemons should rarely emerge in real or counterfactual worlds. He nevertheless found that they appear with regularity in counterfactual simulations, especially under conditions of defense dominance, the best case for neorealism.[48]

Counterfactual experiments and simulations can tease out the assumptions on which theories and historical interpretations rest. Apologists for the Soviet system insist that communism would have evolved differently if Lenin had lived longer or had been succeeded by someone other than Stalin.[49] Attempts to address this question have not resolved the controversy but have compelled historians to be more explicit about the underlying assumptions that guide and underpin contending interpretations of Stalin and the nature of the Communist party and the Soviet state. Those assumptions have now become the focus of controversy, and scholars have looked for evidence with which to evaluate them. This process has encouraged a more sophisticated historical debate. With this end in mind, Phil Tetlock, Geoffrey Parker, and I organized and carried out a counterfactual inquiry into the causes and contingency of Western civilization and its phenomenal success in the modern era.[50]

Because every causal argument has its associated counterfactual, critics of a particular theory or interpretation have two generic strategies open to them. They can offer a different and more compelling theory or interpretation—far and away the most common strategy—or show that the outcomes associated with the theory or interpretation would have happened in the absence of their hypothesized causes. John Mueller's study of the Cold War is a nice example of the second approach. In contrast to the conventional wisdom that attributes the long peace between the superpowers to nuclear deterrence, Mueller argues that Moscow and Washington were restrained by their general satisfaction with the status quo, by memories of the human and economic costs of World War II, and by their belief in the utter destructiveness of large-scale, conventional warfare. Mueller contends that nuclear weapons were redundant and possibly counterproductive to efforts to maintain the peace.[51]

Assessing Outcomes

Counterfactuals are a key component of evaluation in personal and political issues. Numerous psychological studies suggest that people invent counterfactuals to evaluate their choices and their outcomes, especially when they are negative.[52] Upward counterfactuals—which lead to better outcomes—improve affect, while downward counterfactuals can serve as "wake-up" calls that prompt or lead to calls for preparatory responses.[53]

Was the development of nuclear weapons a blessing or a curse for humankind? What about affirmative action, free trade, or the economic and political integration of Europe? Serious and thoughtful people can be found on all sides of these controversies. Their arguments have one thing in common: they use counterfactual benchmarks—most often, implicitly—to assess the merits of real-world policies, outcomes, or trends. Proponents of nuclear deterrence who claim that it restrained the superpowers during the Cold War imagine a superpower war, or at least a higher probability of one due to more acute crisis, in its absence. Some critics of nuclear weapons, like John Mueller, argue that self-deterrence based on memories of the horrors of conventional war would have kept the peace. Others—this author among them—contend that the strategy of nuclear deterrence, as opposed to the reality of nuclear deterrence, actually sustained and intensified the Cold War.[54] More recently, the Iraq War has spawned counterfactuals on both sides of the debate. Those opposed to the Anglo-American invasion of Iraq insist that it has provoked rather than minimized terrorism against the United Kingdom and United States. Their argument rests on an imaginary benchmark of what the level of terrorist attacks would have been like in the absence of the war. Conversely, supporters of the Bush administration contend that the president reduced the incidence of terrorism against the West by taking the war to the Islamic heartland "at low cost."[55]

Assessment can be significantly influenced, even determined, by the choice of counterfactual. The conventional wisdom holds that the Allied victory in World War I was a positive outcome: it prevented an expansionist Germany from achieving hegemony in continental Europe. This assessment makes sense from the vantage point of the corporate boardrooms and corridors of power in Paris, London, New York, and Washington. From the perspective of European Jewry, the outcome of the First World War was a disaster. If Germany had won, there almost certainly would have been no Hitler and no Holocaust. This counterfactual reveals the strikingly different interests of the groups in question and how they are drawn to different counterfactuals or evaluate the same ones differently. As with historical analogies, the interesting, and eminently researchable question becomes the extent to which counterfactuals guide evaluation or are chosen to justify positions that people have reached for quite different reasons.[56] Alessandro Portelli offers a telling example of the latter in his study of Italian communists. In interviews he conducted in the small city of Terni in Umbria he found that workers often told stories of how history *could* and *should* have gone. These narratives describe a better world that communist organizers believe might have come to pass if their leadership had endorsed more radical action between 1921 and 1925 or again between 1943 and 1953. Local leaders insist that they urged radical action at key meetings but there is no evidence to support their claims. Portelli reasons that they are ex post facto inventions to justify their lifelong sacrifices and commitments to a revolution that never occurred.[57]

Some psychologists maintain that human beings search for meaning in life, perhaps as a result of self-consciousness and awareness of mortality.[58] The Portelli example and experimental studies indicate that counterfactuals are an integral part of this process and are not infrequently used to buttress our self-esteem.[59]

Must counterfactuals be realistic?

The several uses of counterfactuals I have described employ a "plausible" and "miracle" world of counterfactuals.[60] Plausible world, or plausible rewrite, counterfactuals are intended to impress readers as realistic. As noted earlier, no social facts, propositions, or theories are real in the sense of providing an unmediated representation of the world. I use realistic here in a more subjective and psychological sense of not violating our understanding of what was technologically, culturally, temporally, or otherwise possible. In chapter 3, I imagine a world in which Archduke Franz Ferdinand and his wife, Countess Sophie, returned alive from their visit to Sarajevo. This counterfactual is eminently plausible because their assassination was such a near thing, and never would have happened if the archduke and those responsible for his security had acted sensibly either before the first, unsuccessful attempt on his life or in its immediate aftermath. A small, credible rewrite of history has the potential to bring about a different world. A more recent but equally compelling example concerns the survival of a young Cuban boy, Elián Gonzalez. In November 1999 Elián fled Cuba with his mother and twelve others in a small boat with a faulty engine; Elián's mother and ten other passengers died in the crossing. Floating in an inner tube, Elián was rescued at sea by two fisherman who handed him over to the U.S. Coast Guard. The subsequent decision by Attorney General Janet Reno to return Elián to his father in Cuba rather than letting him stay with his paternal great-uncle in Florida infuriated many Cuban Americans. As a result, many fewer Americans of Cuban descent voted Democratic in the 2000 presidential election. If Elián had drowned, Al Gore would have carried Florida and become president of the United States. His election would not have prevented 9/11 but almost certainly would have prevented the invasion of Iraq.

There are many plausible counterfactuals—historical near misses, if you like—that might have come to pass but probably would not have had any significance for outcomes we might want to mutate. Plausible counterfactuals must meet a second test: they must have a significant probability of leading to the alternative outcome—and one we want to bring about. To demonstrate the alleged link between antecedent (that aspect of the world we mutate) and consequent (its intended effect), we must construct a logical path between the counterfactual change and the hypothesized outcome. It must also meet additional tests I discuss later in this chapter.

Plausible world counterfactuals are thought by some researchers to be the only legitimate kind of counterfactual.[61] Other counterfactuals—what I call "miracle world" counterfactuals pace Tetlock and Belkin—make inherently implausible changes in reality. They violate our understanding of what is "realistic," or even conceivable, but they are valuable when they allow us to reason our way to the causes and contingency of real events, or the dynamics that govern them. Consider this miracle counterfactual: if the Black African population of Darfur had been bottle-nosed dolphins, the West would not have allowed their slaughter.[62] Even Dr. Seuss might find a landlocked region of aquatic mammals something of a stretch, but the analogy suggests other morally provocative counterfactuals. If the population of the southern Sudan were Caucasian and Christian, would the West have intervened? What if the United States had not intervened previously in Somalia, or had done so successfully, or if it had quickly and successfully restored order in Iraq after its 2003 invasion? Miracle counterfactuals can help us identify, highlight, and work through analytical as well as ethical problems. Suppose I hypothesize that Europe achieved its global military advantage in the nineteenth century because it was the only region of the world where no long-standing hegemony had been established. Prolonged competition among its leading political units made them lean and mean, better armed, and more efficient in the use of large-scale violence.[63] To advance this hypothesis I must posit a counterfactual world in which some state—perhaps a better organized and better led Spain in the sixteenth century—achieved something approaching continental hegemony. I must also reason through what a hegemonic Europe would have been like and how it would have differed from historical Europe in the dimensions relevant to my argument.

Miracle counterfactuals are essential tools in developing and evaluating competing historical and political interpretations and theories.

John Mueller's world without nuclear weapons involves a miracle counterfactual because it requires a massive rewrite of a century of scientific and political history to "uninvent" nuclear weapons, although the timing of their development might be altered by plausible world counterfactuals. As in this case, the utility of miracle counterfactuals does not depend on their realism but on the analytical utility of the alternative worlds they create. Counterfactuals of this kind have a distinguished lineage. Euclid used one to prove that there are an infinite number of prime numbers and Newton to demonstrate—incorrectly, as it turned out—that the universe could not be infinite, and with regularly distributed and fixed stars. If these conditions held, Newton reasoned, the sky would not be blue.[64] Philip Roth's remake of American history in *The Plot Against America*, the subject of chapter 8, also employs implausible counterfactuals to telling effect for quite different purposes.

It is useful to distinguish folk counterfactuals from plausible world and miracle counterfactuals used for scholarly purposes. Folk counterfactuals are embedded in popular culture and often influence how people frame and respond to problems. They may provide pithy and powerful statements of widely held beliefs that mobilize people for action. Throughout history, people have invoked such counterfactuals to explain disastrous storms, floods, plagues, and wars. A prominent American televangelist proclaimed that the Columbine school shootings would never have happened if Hollywood and the other media had not produced so many violent movies, television shows, video games, and so much profane popular music. Fundamentalist preachers have also interpreted the terrorist attacks of 9/11 as God's punishment on America for homosexuality and other practices of which they disapprove. This kind of counterfactual answers the age-old question: "where did we go wrong?" It assumes a turning point with a better real-world outcome if only we had acted differently. Regret and desire appear to be the principal motivating agents of such counterfactuals. My favorite example of this genre is not one to elicit the approval of fire-and-brimstone preachers. It is Andrew Marvel's poem that begins with the immortal lines: "Had we but World enough and time, This coyness, Lady, were no crime."[65]

Scholarly and folk counterfactuals not infrequently interact. Blaise Pascal invented the counterfactual of Cleopatra's nose to illustrate the power of human vanity, and it has since become folk wisdom.[66] A volume of *Astérix* is devoted to Cleopatra and her nose and there is even a Turkish saying, "to have a nose like Cleopatra's."[67] The counterfactual sensitizes and socializes listeners to a particular causal connection that finds expression in the English proverb "love makes the world go round." Folk counterfactuals, like history, encourage labeling and particular frames of reference. History in its academic and popular manifestations is a rhetorical strategy to get people to view the world or particular aspects of it in designated ways. Counterfactual history is perhaps an even more powerful rhetorical device toward this end. Even those who do not accept counterfactuals as a legitimate research tool cannot afford to ignore their utility, even centrality, as a means of persuasion and appeal in politics and social life.

Scholarly and folk counterfactuals shed light on how we work through more fundamental understandings of the world and how it works and relate them to our ethical beliefs and expectations. In this book I am more interested in the former so will not explore folk counterfactuals any further. We should note, however, that they are very much in the background of the Lewis and Roth novels. Like many works of literature, these novels derive at least part of their emotional power from playing off plot developments and their characters' responses to them against implicit folk counterfactuals about how one should behave and the likely consequences of not doing so. *The Plot Against America* interrogates the dominant Jewish American folk counterfactual: that our parents and grandparents were so smart when they left Europe for America because we would not have survived had they stayed put.

PLAUSIBLE WORLD COUNTERFACTUALS

Two publications by Niall Ferguson have sparked renewed interest in counterfactuals in the history discipline.[68] Unfortunately, neither work makes a good case for counterfactuals. In a long introduction to his edited volume, *Virtual History,* Ferguson offers no reasons for engaging in counterfactual history other than sensitizing readers to contingency, and only briefly addresses methods for conducting counterfactual experiments. He criticizes earlier counterfactual works for inferring momentous consequences from "simple, often trivial change[s]." With undisguised scorn, he cites as an example Pascal's intentionally provocative counterfactual about Cleopatra's nose: if it had been ugly, Anthony would not have fallen for her, and the history of Rome might have been different.[69] He objects to small changes having big effects, but on what grounds? Could anyone seriously doubt that the course of history would have been different if Pharaoh's daughter had not found a child in a basket in the reeds; if the Mongol invasion fleet had not encountered a destructive typhoon en route to Japan, if the Duke of Alba had not fallen sick in 1572, or if Hitler had died in trenches during World War I? When the Duke of Alba took to his bed, his inexperienced and arrogant son took command of the forces laying siege to Haarlem, rejected the town's offer of surrender, and prolonged the Dutch rebellion against Spanish rule. The sustained ability of the Dutch to resist infuriated Philip II and his nephew, Alexander Farnese, Duke of Parma. They convinced themselves that the Dutch only resisted because of English support and decided to deal with England directly. Geoffrey Parker suggests that the subsequent defeat of the Spanish Armada laid the American continent open to invasion and colonization by Northern Europeans and made possible the founding of the United States.[70] For want of aspirin, a continent may have been lost.

With reason, Max Weber insisted that the most plausible counter-factuals are those that make only "plausible rewrites" of history.[71] Suppose we want to evaluate Ronald Reagan's role in ending the Cold War by considering the likely course of that conflict in the late 1980s if he had not been president. It is more plausible to assume that Hinckley's bullet lodged a few millimeters closer to a vital organ than to concoct a complicated, multistep scenario to deprive Reagan of his overwhelming electoral triumph in 1980. As a general rule, the fewer and more trivial the changes we introduce in history, the fewer the steps linking them to the hypothesized consequent, and the less temporal distance between antecedent and consequent, the more plausible the counterfactual becomes. Not every small change will have significant, longer-term consequences; many, perhaps most, changes are likely to have consequences that are dampened over time. The real problem of counterfactual thought experimentation is determining which plausible rewrites will have lasting major effects on the course of history.

Let us return to Cleopatra's nose. An ugly proboscis might have remade world history. It could have dampened Anthony's ardor, with important consequences for the struggle for power among Caesars' successors. Roman history might also have been different if Anthony had been gay or had converted to a monotheistic religion. We do not object to such counterfactuals because they are trivial but because they are arbitrary and contrived. There is no particular reason why Cleopatra should have been less attractive or Anthony had a different sexual orientation or religion. Nor is it clear how the first of these changes would have been brought about in an era before cosmetic surgery or the second at all. Good counterfactuals arise from the context and require compelling mechanisms to bring them into being.

Ferguson wants to legitimate counterfactual research but his efforts to do so would put it into a straight jacket. He insists that we only consider counterfactual scenarios that contemporary actors considered and committed to paper, or some other form of record that is accepted by historians as a valid source.[72] These criteria would exclude entire categories of plausible-world counterfactuals. They would limit counterfactuals to elites who made written records, to contemplative decisions in which alternatives are likely to be carefully considered, and to political systems in which leaders and other important actors feel secure enough to write down their thoughts or share them with colleagues, journalists, family members, or friends. They would rule out all counterfactuals that were the result of impulsive behavior (or the lack of it); human accident, oversight, obtuseness, or unanticipated error; acts of nature or the confluence (or lack of it) of independent chains of causation. We could not contemplate a world in which the Duke of Alba remained healthy and did not relinquish command of his army to his son, Franz Ferdinand's touring car did not make a wrong turn, Hitler died in an automobile accident, or Hinckley assassinated Ronald Reagan. Ferguson's criteria would also rule out all miracle counterfactuals.

More thoughtful historians and social scientists have pondered the problem of plausible world counterfactuals and appropriate criteria for using them. In this connection, it is important to distinguish this objective from those of psychology and philosophy regarding counterfactuals. Most psychologists who study counterfactuals are interested in discovering why people invoke counterfactuals or consider them plausible. Philosophers primarily concern themselves with the question of what constitutes a true counterfactual.[73] There is no consensus among historians and social scientists about what constitutes a good counterfactual, but there is widespread recognition that it is extraordinarily difficult to construct a robust one: a counterfactual whose antecedent we can assert with confidence will result in the hypothesized consequent. Among the reasons for this well-warranted pessimism are the statistical improbability of multistep counterfactuals, the interconnectedness of events, and the unpredictable effects of second-order counterfactuals.

Compound probability

The probability of a consequent is a multiple of the probability of each counterfactual linking it to the hypothesized antecedent. In chapter 7 I contend that neither world war nor the Holocaust would have happened if Mozart had lived to the age of sixty-five. Having pushed classical form as far as it could go in the Jupiter Symphony, his last three operas, and the Requiem, his next dramatic works would have been the precursors of a new, "postclassicist" style. He would have created a viable alternative to Romanticism that would have been widely imitated by composers, writers, and artists. Postclassicism would have kept enlightenment political ideas alive and held Romanticism in check. Nationalism would have been more restrained, and thus Austria-Hungary and Germany would have undergone very different political evolution. This alternative and, I think, vastly preferable world has at least five counterfactual steps linking antecedent to consequent: Mozart must survive to old age, develop a new style of artistic expression; subsequent composers, artists, and writers must imitate and elaborate it; Romanticism must become to some degree marginalized; and artistic developments must have important political ramifications. This last counterfactual presupposes numerous other enabling counterfactuals about the nature of the political changes that will lead to the hypothesized consequent (e.g., internal reforms that resolve or reduce the threat of internal dissolution of Austria-Hungary, German unification under different terms, or at least a Germany satisfied with the status quo, no First World War, no Hitler, and no Holocaust without Germany's defeat in World War I). Suppose for the sake of the argument we grant every one of this long string of counterfactuals a probability of at least 50 percent, the overall probability of the consequent would be a mere .03 for five counterfactual steps and a frighteningly low .003 for eight steps. This particular counterfactual may appear far-fetched for this reason alone, but it is worth considering that our world was just as improbable from the vantage point of 1791. The really interesting, and ultimately unanswerable question, is not the probability of specific future worlds in 1791, but the probability of all worlds in which there was something like a World War I versus all those in which there was not. The probability of both sets may have been significant.

Interconnectedness

Scholars not infrequently assume that one aspect of the past can be changed and everything else kept constant. John Mueller's Cold War counterfactual is a case in point. He analyzes postwar history as it actually happened, including the Cuban missile crisis, to see if any major outcome would have been different in the absence of nuclear weapons. But what incentive would Khrushchev have had to deploy conventionally armed missiles in Cuba? The missiles could not have deterred an American invasion, and might well have invited one—the very event Khrushchev hoped to prevent.[74] Without a Cuban missile crisis, which had significant consequences for the future course of Soviet-American relations, the Cold War would have evolved differently, and the course of future superpower relations could have been more benign or malign. It is easy to make arguments in support of both outcomes but impossible to predict which—or some other scenario—would actually have prevailed.

Surgical counterfactuals are no more "realistic" than surgical air strikes. Causes are interdependent and have important interaction effects.

Even plausible rewrites of history may alter the context in such a way as to render the consequent moot or undercut the chain of events leading to it. Consider another missile crisis counterfactual: what if Richard Nixon, who lost by the narrowest of margins, had won the 1960 presidential election? It is highly likely that Nixon would have preferred an air strike to a blockade because he was more hawkish than Kennedy and would not have had a secretary of defense like Robert McNamara to make a strong case for restraint. For these same reasons Nixon, in contrast to Kennedy, might have committed American forces to the faltering Bay of Pigs invasion in April 1961. If Castro had been overthrown in 1961 there would have been no communist Cuba to which Khrushchev could send missiles a year later.

The second Nixon counterfactual renders the missile crisis moot by making the case for an alternative consequent arising from the antecedent, but outside the chain of logic leading from it to the intended consequent. If Nixon had been elected president in 1960 the world would have been different in many ways, some of them with implications that are impossible to grasp, let alone reason through. He would have appointed a different defense secretary who would have recommended appointment of a different chairman of the joint chiefs of staff. Personnel changes at the top would have had amplifying consequences for promotions and appointments farther down the line. To the extent that the behavior of individual officers could have important foreign policy implications—and it certainly did during the Berlin and Cuban missile crises—all kinds of alternative possibilities open up. Plausible rewrite counterfactuals are easy to create but extraordinarily difficult, if not impossible, to control.

Second-Order Counterfactuals

The problem of prediction is further complicated by the fact that history's clock does not stop if and when the hypothesized consequent is realized. Subsequent developments can return history to the course, or something close to it, from which the antecedent was intended to divert it.[75] Colin Martin and Geoffrey Parker demonstrate that the defeat of the Spanish Armada was a near event; they suggest that better communication, different decisions by local commanders, or better weather might have allowed the Spanish to land an invasion force in England. If Spain had put an army ashore it almost certainly would have conquered the country. To their credit, Martin and Parker go on to consider what would have happened next: Philip II was succeeded by Philip III, a far less capable ruler, who would have had enormous difficulty in maintaining an already overextended empire. In relatively short order, they maintain, England would have overthrown the Spanish yoke.[76]

Some counterfactuals are intended to work like the "butterfly effect"; they introduce small amplifying changes that have great long-term effects. Others, like a counterfactual Spanish victory in 1588, are major developments that seem to have equally major consequences, but the changes they introduce are dampened down over time and may end up having little lasting longer-term effects. It is nevertheless possible that second-order counterfactuals arising from a Spanish occupation of England, however brief that occupation, might have produced changes for European politics or in other realms (e.g., literature, the sciences) that Martin and Parker have not considered. Such outcomes are difficult to identify and trace and may well seem implausible when spun off from plausible rewrite counterfactuals, as in the case of Mozart living to sixty-five and Europe therefore avoiding the horrors of the twentieth century. The butterfly effect is unknowable in advance, difficult to recognize and document in retrospect, and even more difficult to establish counterfactually.[77]

Criteria for Use

Recognition that counterfactual arguments have indeterminate consequences has prompted scholars to propose restrictive criteria on their use. James Fearon advocates a proximity criterion. We should consider only those counterfactuals in which the antecedent appears likely to bring about the intended consequent and little else. Counterfactuals, he warns, must be limited to cases where "the proposed causes are temporally and, in some sense, spatially quite close to the consequents."[78] Robyn Dawes proposes more restrictive criteria: counterfactual inferences are warranted "if and only if they are embedded in a system of statistical contingency for which we have reasonable evidence."[79] Edgar Kiser and Margaret Levi suggest that counterfactuals are best used as substitutes for direct empirical analysis when data are limited or unavailable. These counterfactuals should be based on a general deductive theory with clear microfoundations and scope conditions.[80] Jon Elster, who also insists that good counterfactuals are derived from good theories, believes that there is only a narrow window for such experimentation: "the theory must be weak enough to admit the counterfactual assumption, and also strong enough to permit a clear-cut conclusion."[81]

Criteria that tie counterfactuals to established laws and statistical generalizations and attempt to limit second-order counterfactuals are superficially appealing. In practice, these conditions are impractical and would rule out some of the most important uses of counterfactual experimentation. The Fearon proximity criterion suffers from both defects. The requirement of a plausible cause that produces only a plausible effect is extraordinarily restrictive. Steven Weber rightly observes that "It rewards the psychologically easy and comfortable task of generating counterfactuals close to the margins of existing theories. It predisposes toward varying only the familiar variables, the ones that we think we know are tied into causal paths that we feel we know well." It also assumes that we know what plausible really means, and that requires a rather complete understanding of the behavior in question and its likely consequences. "If we knew this," Weber rightly points out, "we would no longer need counterfactuals."[82] Counterfactuals almost always have multiple consequences, and a counterfactual powerful enough to test a theory that makes only one small change in reality is an oxymoron.

The scholars most troubled by the inherent unpredictability of counterfactual outcomes are those who believe in the power of systemic explanations and want to use counterfactuals to test propositions and theories. They confront a serious problem: the less demonstrable the consequent, the less useful a counterfactual is for this purpose. Fearon proposes a fall-back position. Although it may not be possible to prove that "x" causes "y," he acknowledges, it may be within our power to demonstrate that without "x," whatever happened, would not have been "y."[83] I employ this strategy as part of my argument in chapter 3 to show why World War I was contingent. With respect to its immediate causes, I argue that this war required a special kind of catalyst, whose presence was problematic and whose causes were independent of any of the underlying causes of war.[84]

Seeming validation of a counterfactual is only important if the goal is to test a proposition or theory. Testing is only one part of the effort to convince others of a theory's plausibility. Theories also need to provide explanations for the phenomena they claim to explain. Also important are successful efforts to resolve existing anomalies in ways other theories cannot.[85] Counterfactuals can help with all of these goals by making scholars more sensitive to contingency, helping them work through the implications of existing theories and identify gaps and inconsistencies in them. Social science and history ultimately aim to broaden our intellectual horizons and to provide insight into contemporary problems and policy choices. Counterfactual experimentation is essential to these tasks and can be used effectively without the same degree of confidence that specific antecedents will lead to specific consequents. As Steven Weber put it, counterfactuals are better used as "mind-set changers" and "learning devices" than as "data points in explanation."[86] We should worry less about the uncertainty of counterfactual experiments and profit more from their mind-opening implications.

For most of the purposes described above, the clarity, completeness, and logical consistency of the arguments linking antecedent to consequents are more important than their external validity. I accordingly propose nine criteria for plausible world counterfactuals. Numbers 2, 3, 5, and 6 are drawn from, or are variants of, the list proposed by Tetlock and Belkin. Criterion number 6 on my list has been proposed independently by Tetlock. Numbers 1, 4, 8, and 9 are original.[87]

1. *Realism*: Niall Ferguson rightly ridiculed, although for the wrong reason, Pascal's counterfactual of Cleopatra's nose. It is objectionable because it is arbitrary and contrived. There is no particular reason why Cleopatra should have been less attractive. She might have broken and disfigured her nose in childhood accident, but it is not self-evident that this would have weakened the ardor of Anthony, who sought power as much as beauty and seems to have been taken in as much by Cleopatra's persona as her looks. Good counterfactuals ought to arise from the context. We must have compelling mechanisms to bring them into being that require only plausible rewrites of history. Moreover, these rewrites must be consistent with the pattern of decisions or behavior that follow from the counterfactuals themselves.

2. *Clarity*: All causal arguments should define as unambiguously as possible what is to be explained (the consequent in counterfactual arguments), what accounts for this outcome (the antecedent), and the chain of logic linking the two. Good counterfactuals should also specify the conditions that would have to be present for the antecedent to occur. Some historians have argued that timely public health measures could have significantly reduced the mortality in Europe associated with the Black Death pandemic of the fourteenth century. For European communities to have implemented these measures they would have had to recognize that human intervention could affect the spread of disease and had the authority and will to impose draconian measures on travel and trade over the likely objections of the wealthy and merchant classes.[88] These conditions, Geoffrey Hawthorn argues, are unrealistic given the values, knowledge, and political structure of the age; large-scale quarantines would not be implemented to combat infectious diseases until the eighteenth century.[89] Plausible world counterfactuals require not only antecedents that are understood to be realistic; the antecedents themselves must not require other, implausible conditions or counterfactuals.

3. *Logical consistency or cotenability*: Every counterfactual is a shorthand statement of a more complex argument that almost invariably requires a set of connecting conditions or principles. The antecedent

should not undercut any of the principles linking it to the consequent. A case in point is Robert Fogel's famous claim that if the railroads had not existed the American economy in the nineteenth century would have grown only slightly more slowly because there would have been a much stronger incentive to invent the internal combustion engine sooner.[90] John Elster rightly objects to this counterfactual on the grounds that if the technology was present to invent and produce automobiles it would almost certainly have also led to the prior invention and development of railroads.[91]

4. *Enabling counterfactuals should not undercut the antecedent*: Counterfactuals often require other counterfactuals to make them possible. For Germany to win World War II its armies would have had to defeat the Soviet Union and the United Kingdom, or at least have compelled both nations to sue for peace. In the aftermath of victory, Hitler would have had to rein in his aggressive impulses so as not to have provoked war with the United States and make Germany the target of American atomic bombs. For Hitler to have shown restraint he would have had to have become a very different person. If restraint and caution had been part of his character all along, he is unlikely to have come to power and even more unlikely to have gambled on occupying the Rhineland, *Anschluss* with Austria, challenging the British and French over Czechoslovakia, and invading the rump Czech state after gaining territorial concessions at Munich—the very successes that paved the way for a German invasion of Poland and subsequent challenge of the Soviet Union. To win World War II, Germany would have needed jet fighter planes and nuclear weapons, and here too, it has been well documented, Hitler's personality stood in the way of their effective development.[92]

5. *Historical consistency*: Max Weber insisted that plausible counterfactuals should make as few historical changes as possible on the grounds that the more we disturb the values, goals, and contexts in which actors operate, the less predictable their behavior becomes.[93] Counterfactual arguments that make a credible case for a dramatically different future on the basis of one small change in reality are very powerful and the plausible rewrite rule should be followed whenever possible. The *nature* of the changes made by the experiment are nevertheless more important than the *number* of changes. A plausible rewrite that makes only one alteration in reality may not qualify as a plausible world counterfactual if the counterfactual is unrealistic or if numerous subsequent counterfactual steps are necessary to reach the hypothesized consequent. A counterfactual based on several small changes, all of them appearing plausible, may be more plausible, especially if they lead more directly to the consequent. In chapter 3 I undo World War I by preventing the assassination of Franz Ferdinand. I could also use plausible rewrites to break, or at least

alter, the timing of the causal chains that led to gestalt shifts in Germany and Russia. By doing so I would dramatically increase the probability of preventing that conflict. Alternatively, I could break the Austrian chain by forestalling the Italian landing at Tripoli and remove the proximate cause of war by keeping Franz Ferdinand alive. Those who employ plausible rewrites of history should be explicit about the choices and why they fulfill this and other conditions better than alternative counterfactuals.

6. *Theoretical consistency*: There are few, if any, generally accepted theories in the social sciences, and none in international relations, comparative politics, or history. For purposes of counterfactual analysis, it is nevertheless useful to reference any theories, empirical findings, or historical interpretations on which the causal principles or connecting arguments are based. As assumptions are so critical for the plausibility of factual and counterfactual arguments, efforts to do this allow the researcher to prime readers to some degree about the assumptions in which the arguments in question are anchored.

7. *Avoid the conjunction fallacy*: There are good statistical grounds for the plausible rewrite rule, as the probability of a consequent is the multiple of the probability of each counterfactual step linking it to the antecedent. The laws of statistics suggest that the probability of any compound counterfactual is exceedingly low. This does not mean that our world is overdetermined, only that it is highly unlikely that hypothesized antecedents will produce *specific* consequences at any temporal remove. Social and political developments are highly contingent, and the future is undetermined—as was the past when it was still the future. The long-term consequences of change are almost always unpredictable. If Mozart had lived to sixty-five today's world could well have turned out to be strikingly different from the world we know. But many alternative worlds are possible, and the probability of any one of them coming to pass is exceedingly low. Counterfactuals might have changed the world, but in ways that become exponentially more difficult to track over time because of the additional branching points that enter the picture. As the probabilities associated with these outcomes will vary enormously, researchers need to specify if their counterfactuals are intended to produce a specific world, a set of worlds with particular characteristics, or *any* world (on a specific dimension) other than the one that actually came to pass.

8. *Recognize the interconnectedness of causes and outcomes*: Surgical counterfactuals are unrealistic because causes are interdependent and have important interaction effects. Changes we make in the past may require other changes to make them possible, and they in turn are almost certain to produce changes in addition to those we expect to produce the consequent. History is like a spring mattress. If one of the springs is cut, or simply subjected to extra pressure, the others will to varying degrees shift

their location and tension.[94] Good counterfactuals must specify, within reason, what else is likely to change as a result of a hypothesized antecedent, and consider how the change that appears the most important (a choice that also requires elaboration) might influence the probability of the consequent. In Holger Herwig's counterfactual probe of World War II, he reasons that even a Germany victory in the east would not have led to victory in World War II because it would have made Germany, not Japan, the target of the first American atomic weapons.[95] In the real world, German successes were the catalyst for an American crash effort to build nuclear weapons and now make it the preferred target for those weapons for the same reason. German victory is thus impossible unless some other plausible counterfactual can be devised to untrack the Manhattan Project.

9. *Consider second order counterfactuals*: Even when there is good to reason to believe that the antecedent will produce the desired consequent the possibility remains that subsequent developments will return history more or less to the course from which it was initially diverted by the antecedent. This might be the long-term result of enabling counterfactuals necessary to bring about the antecedent, of follow-on counterfactuals produced by the antecedent, of counterfactuals arising from the consequent—as in Martin and Parker's argument about the longer-term consequences of a Spanish conquest of Elizabethan England—or of interaction among any combination of these counterfactuals. Interaction effects among second-order counterfactuals might be considered "third order" counterfactuals, and they too can have profound consequences for the subsequent course of development.

Attempts to identify and analyze *all* of the counterfactuals arising from the antecedent and consequent would quickly lead to an infinite regress. Researchers should nevertheless try to identify what in their judgment is the most likely course(s) of events that could unravel their consequent or negate its value as an outcome. The last point entails the recognition that we choose a consequent because of some larger effect it is intended to produce. If other developments make it unlikely that the consequent will have the desired effect it loses its attractiveness. No counterfactual argument is complete without some argument about alternative, alternative futures, and some assessment of their likelihood and implications for both the consequent and its utility as a consequent.

These criteria will not allow researchers to validate plausible-world counterfactuals but they will help us weed out poor counterfactuals on the basis of clarity, logical, and substantive completeness. Counterfactuals that survive this rigorous set of tests are also likely to appear more plausible to readers. Most of these criteria are not applicable to miracle-world counterfactuals, which, by definition, are not required to meet any real-world tests. The value of a such counterfactuals is based entirely on their ability to provoke and inspire and compel researchers to think about issues and problems they would not otherwise recognize or address, or to look at them in a new light. For a field where careful technical work is increasingly valued over imagination, miracle-world counterfactuals have the potential to refocus our attention on a deeper set of important questions.

Unmaking the West

Having developed protocols for historical counterfactual thought experiments let us now turn to an interesting substantive problem: the development of Western civilization and its remarkable success in the modern era. How contingent were both developments? Could Western civilization or its political, economic, technological, and military primacy have been prevented by plausible rewrites of history? At what point did the success of the West become difficult to prevent? When did it become impossible to prevent? And what about the parallel development of other competitor civilizations: China, India, the Arabs, or the Ottoman Empire? Could plausible rewrites of their histories have made them more successful competitors with the West? At what point did that become unlikely or impossible?

I recently coedited a book on this subject: *Unmaking the West: "What-If" Counterfactuals that Remake World History.*[96] With the help of our contributors we sought to identify critical turning points in Western and non-Western history and probe their contingency through counterfactual experiments. We defined turning points as locations where causal chains converge—the sense in which I use the term in chapter 3—or at which developments in which one is interested undergo exponential amplification. The latter can be caused by converging chains or other phenomena that produce thresholds, tipping points, or even small changes that are amplifying, so in retrospect they give the appearance of being thresholds. Needless to say, none of these processes arise from the flow of events but from the categories we use for analysis. The historian participants for the most part do not use or invoke theories, but rather impose narratives on their subject. These narratives, like theories, are metafactual and highly abstract social constructions—more about this in the conclusion. So we need to acknowledge that any of the turning points we identified were the products of the narratives and interpretations embedded within them that our historians brought to their subjects. For our project, this was a defensible approach, in large part because it invited diversity in narratives and therefore choice in turning points.

Contributors relied on their historical knowledge and analytical instincts to identify and work through key counterfactuals. A more robust analysis requires protocols for assessing the contingency of each turning point and the aggregate implications of these turning points for the course of Western and non-Western history. With this end in mind, I propose six tests, all of which take the form of questions. They have relevance beyond this particular case and, I will argue, can help us determine the relative importance of systemic and nonsystemic factors in particular historical events or developments. Each of the counterfactuals used to answer these questions must in turn conform to the earlier protocols I laid out for using counterfactuals. These tests must be distinguished from the nine criteria for conducting plausible world counterfactuals. The latter are intended to enhance internal validity. These criteria are designed to give claims of contingency greater apparent external validity.

1. *What do we have to do to negate a turning point?* Turning points are important because of their consequences. Constantine's embrace of Christianity, his victory at Milvian Bridge in 312 and subsequent victories over Licinius in 323–24, made him sole ruler of the Roman Empire and in a position to impose Christianity on the Empire and repress other sects. A common religion and political tradition may have been essential for the long-term development of Western civilization. Had Constantine been decisively defeated in any of these campaigns, the religious life of Rome would have developed differently, and it is much less likely Christianity would have become the dominant religion of the Roman Empire.

Some of the events that made the West cohere as a culture or contributed to its success in the modern age may not need to be prevented. It may only be necessary to alter them in minor ways that render them innocuous much the way small mutations in the genes of pathogens can decisively reduce or increase their virulence. Suppose we allow the Greeks to win their crushing naval victory at Salamis in 480 BCE but introduce a small change in the events that followed. Sparta was asked to name a general to lead the Greek alliance against the Persians and nominated their King Pausanias. They recalled him about a year later, tried him on charges of corruption, and decided to withdraw from the alliance for fear that exposure to the life of richer city-states was too threatening to their way of life. Sparta's withdrawal opened the way for Athens to assume leadership of the alliance and ultimately to transform it into a powerful empire. A different and less corrupt Spartan leader might have forestalled Athenian leadership of the Delian League, and with it the wealth and self-confidence that produced the fifth-century cultural explosion that is widely acknowledged as another foundational pillar of Western civilization.

Mere postponement of a turning point may sometimes deprive it of its most important effects. In the next chapter I argue that World War I, or any conflict like it, might have been prevented if it could have been forestalled for another three years. The underlying conditions that moved Europe toward war were rapidly evolving, and any one of a number of changes would have made Austria, Germany, or Russia—or even all three—war averse. In our counterfactual probing of the end of the Cold War, George Breslauer and I alter the timing of contributing events and evaluate their consequences for the character and timing of the Cold War's demise. We find varying degrees of sensitivity on this score. Our first task, therefore, is to determine what kinds of changes we have to make in the events identified as turning points. Once we know whether they need to be prevented, altered, or merely forestalled, we can search for plausible rewrites capable of achieving these ends.

2. *How many plausible rewrites can be found that might prevent, alter, or stall the turning point?* Earlier I noted how easy it would have been to avert Franz Ferdinand's assassination if only his cavalcade had followed the planned route. Numerous other plausible rewrites could also have kept the archduke and his wife alive. Princip might have obeyed the order to abort the assassination sent to him by the military conspirators in Belgrade; Austrian authorities in Bosnia might have taken security as seriously as they did the menu and music for the banquets they planned in the archduke's honor; Franz Ferdinand might have canceled his trip in response to multiple warnings and his wife's fears, or he might have followed the advice of his advisors and left Sarajevo directly after the ceremony at city hall or have raced down Appel Quay past Princip. These plausible rewrites suggest contingency by virtue of their multiplicity. The first counterfactual removes the assassins, two others remove the target, and two more leave Franz Ferdinand on the scene but make him much more difficult to kill. As a general rule, the more different components of a turning point that can be removed by plausible rewrite counterfactuals, the more contingent the turning point.

3. *How far back must we go to find credible plausible rewrites?* We should try to avoid the conjunction fallacy, and the best way to do this is to keep the intervening steps between antecedent and consequent to a minimum. Temporal proximity, while not the same thing, is a rough equivalent. Most of the plausible rewrites I suggest in the example above meet this test. They would have prevented Franz Ferdinand's assassination with few intervening steps, and this is one reason they appear plausible. The farther back in time we go to find counterfactuals, the more steps there are likely to be between antecedent and consequent, and we must remember that the probability of any counterfactual is the multiple of the probabilities of every step in the chain. For this reason, readers of

my Mozart story understandably found it a much less credible means of untracking World War I than readers of the chapter that prevents the Sarajevo assassinations for the same end.

Plausible rewrite counterfactuals at a temporal remove invite a second problem: they allow more parallel chains of causation, one or more of which may lead by alternative routes to the outcome the plausible rewrite is intended to prevent. The failure of the bomb on the Appel Quay to kill the Archduke provided an incentive to Princip and his colleagues to look for another opportunity. Early public cancellation of the Archduke's visit to Sarajevo might have encouraged dedicated assassins to find some way of getting close him during the army maneuvers scheduled outside the city. This would have been more difficult but not impossible given the poor state of Austrian military security.

4. *At what level of analysis are our rewrites plausible?* Plausible rewrites of history require small, credible changes in the fabric of history that are likely to have big, or at least amplifying consequences. Surgical interventions at close proximity to the hypothesized consequent seriously constrain the choice of counterfactuals. For this reason, practitioners of counterfactual history often introduce changes in personnel due to assassinations (Hinkley kills Reagan), failed assassinations (Franz Ferdinand survives), the fortunes of war (William of Orange and Hitler die in battle), disease (Pericles survives the plague), and escaping the hangman (Jesus is not crucified and lives to old age). Almost as popular are changes in policy where the chosen course of action was a near thing, as was the Greek naval strategy at Salamis, or unintended deviations from plans arising from what Carl von Clausewitz called friction—the "countless minor incidents" including undelivered, garbled, or misinterpreted messages; the failure of key players or equipment to appear on time; and a host of other problems that degrade performance.[97] Other plausible rewrites rely on changes in the weather (the Mongol invasion fleet has a smooth crossing to Japan), timing (British forces advance in a more timely way and capture George Washington and most of his army before they can flee Long Island), or combinations of these changes.

To help assess contingency it is useful to employ the concept of levels of analysis. These levels have no ontological claim but have been found useful by social scientists for factoring problems and the answers we seek to them.[98] In our exercise, we look for explanations—or counterfactuals—at the system, unit, subunit, or individual level, or the environment in which the actors in question function. The individual level is usually the easiest place to construct plausible-rewrite counterfactuals, as there are often relatively simple and straightforward ways of changing, or at least removing, critical personnel. A generally accessible alternative is altering mutable features of context like weather, timing, and much of what comes under Clausewitz's rubric of friction. Many of the counterfactuals noted in the paragraphs above are of this sort. Changes in strategies can require intervention at the level of elites, bureaucracies or domestic politics, and more elaborate arguments linking antecedents to consequences.

When we change ideas, state structures, and the balance of power, the latter requiring intervention at the system level, plausible rewrites are out of the question unless we go back to a time when these ideas, structures, and balances had not jelled and might be significantly altered or sidetracked by small, plausible changes at the level of leaders or superficial context. We could readily imagine a different balance of power and set of alliances in seventeenth- or eighteenth-century Europe if we prevented or rearranged some of the marriages that Habsburgs, Bourbons, and other powerful families used to extend or consolidate their influence. But the farther back we introduce changes the less plausible the consequent, because our antecedent is almost certain to introduce other changes with unknown interaction effects and consequences. So for our purposes, a turning point should be considered contingent to the extent that it can be untracked by numerous, plausible counterfactuals at levels one and two.

5. *How redundant is the turning point?* Different causal paths have different implications for contingency. A turning point described by the simple, linear pathway of A + B + C (and only A + B + C) might be prevented by severing any link in the three-step chain. If A and B are themselves the products of other chains of causation, there may be many possible ways of using plausible rewrite counterfactuals to prevent the turning point by preventing preconditions A and B. There are few historical turning points that are the outcomes of simple linear chains. Most are likely to have many paths leading to them. If we prevent A + B + C, the possibility G + H + C, and perhaps of M + N + C, remain. To prevent a turning point with some certainty we need to know all the chains leading to it and something about their probability—and we can only guess at the answers to these questions. In situations of equifinality, where multiple paths lead to the same outcome, estimates of probability are likely to be complicated by interaction effects. The removal of any causal chain may significantly change the probability (in either direction) of other paths. Death is the best example of this phenomenon. If we eradicate child diseases, or inoculate people against them, reduce the incidence of other infectious diseases through public health measures, and gain the upper hand in the struggles against heart disease and cancer, the likelihood of dying from other causes (e.g., accident, stroke, kidney failure), including new ailments (e.g., Crohn's disease and HIV) will increase. One way or the other, the grim reaper will come for all of us.

Even multiple chains may fail to capture the causal complexity of some of the events identified by our authors as turning points in the rise of the West. Another causal model to consider is the confluence, in which a number of independent causal chains come together to produce an outcome. A house goes up in smoke. Investigation reveals that the fire spread from a lighted candle that was left unattended on a windowsill. The window was not completely sealed and a draft blew one of the curtains close enough to the flame for it to catch fire. The smoke alarm, connected to the house security system, did not function because its battery was dead and the fire department failed to receive a timely warning that might have permitted them to save the dwelling. What caused the house to burn down? The candle was the source of the fire but it would not have been lit or placed on the windowsill if it had not been the holiday season and had its owners not been following a neighborhood custom. If the window had not been warped, or the insulation around it had provided a better seal, the candle would not have started a fire. If the owners had been home, or if the smoke alarm had a charged battery, the house would not have burned down. No single factor was responsible for this disaster; it took a combination of them interacting in a particular way.[99] In *Unmaking the West*, contributing authors advance this kind of argument. They do not attribute industrialization to any single cause, but to complex interactions among a confluence of factors, most or all of which were necessary to bring about or prevent this critical development.[100]

An outcome that requires the confluence of many independent causes, but could be prevented, or transformed in magnitude, by removing any one of them with a plausible rewrite—like the fire in the house—is highly contingent. But other confluences may have multiple pathways that lead to them—and require multiple interventions to prevent them. Their contingency would depend on how many plausible rewrites were necessary to halt or deflect each possible pathway. Some authorities consider Western industrialization redundant for this reason.[101]

6. *What about second-order counterfactuals?* Up to this point we have tried to prevent, alter, or stall turning points. But we must also think about how they might come to pass despite our best efforts. Second-order counterfactuals, either by themselves or in interaction with one another, might produce the turning point, or some variant of it at a later date. Ross Hassig reasons that in some circumstances Cortés's defeat might have served as the catalyst for a renewed Spanish attempt at conquest. If disease had decimated the Aztec population, the Spanish might have succeeded the second time around and the history of Meso-America might have developed along strikingly similar lines.[102]

There are two other routes to turning points via the counterfactuals we have created to forestall them. The enabling counterfactuals necessary to bring about the antecedent can set in motion a different chain of events that leads to the same development that the counterfactual was intended to prevent. A rigorous attempt to assess contingency compels us to work though these possible pathways in search of the most likely ways that turning points could still come about. If secondary routes to turning points can be found, researchers need to find ways of stopping them with additional counterfactuals. Roughly speaking, the more alternative routes that are found, and the more likely each appears, the less contingent the turning point.

In this imaginary exercise, I have broken down the development and rise of the West into a set of smaller, more manageable problems through the use of turning points. By factoring our two big questions this way we allow a more fine-grained analysis of key components of key causal chains. When we work back to the larger picture, we confront the same set of problems we did with the individual turning points. There is no reason to suppose that Western civilization and its remarkable success in the modern era was the result of a single causal chain that could have been stopped by preventing any of its component turning points. It seems likely that outcomes so complex and with so many attributes were the result of multiple chains and, while not equifinal, are very hard to untrack once they progress to a certain point—say to the seventeenth or eighteenth century in the case of the West.[103]

The inescapable conclusion is that counterfactuals are like fractals. The defining characteristic of the latter is that its structure is the same at every level of magnification. So it is with counterfactuals. Enabling counterfactuals, turning point counterfactuals, and the use of turning points to prevent a larger outcome involve the same set of problems and require the same set of procedures to address them. And like fractals, the chain of connections could be extended further (but not infinitely, as in the case of fractals) in either the micro- or macrodirection. We could look at levels beneath enabling counterfactuals, or beyond the success of the West if we made it an antecedent to some other consequent.

Kasparov versus Deep Blue

The protocols for counterfactual experimentation and for assessing the contingency of turning points place extraordinary demands on researchers. They must determine the best strategy for negating a turning point and, in the process, consider and evaluate numerous other possible counterfactuals. Even the most promising counterfactuals can require additional, enabling counterfactuals, and researchers must then consider the most important implications of all these counterfactuals. They must also ask if the turning point could be produced by some other set of causal chains and, if so, find ways of untracking or slowing them down (or speeding them up) if the outcome in question is the result of a confluence. They must consider second-order counterfactuals and search for and untrack any that might lead to the turning point at some future time. Thorough execution of each of these tasks would make for more convincing counterfactuals but it is simply not feasible given the number of tasks involved, which increase exponentially with additional counterfactuals.

In February 1996 and May 1997, world chess champion Gary Kasparov played two matches against Deep Blue, a bank of refrigerator-size IBM SP 2 computers. Kasparov won the first match 4-2, but lost the second, 3.5-2.5 in what was hailed as a dramatic victory for artificial intelligence. The idea of a chess-playing machine dates back to the 1760s, when Wolfgang von Kempelen exhibited the Maezal Chess Automaton throughout Europe. His machine infuriated Napoleon when it beat him in nineteen moves. The emperor never guessed the nature of its mechanism: a diminutive Turkish chess master hidden inside the cabinet who operated the turbaned and mustachioed puppet to move pieces on the board above. Modern computers rely on elaborate algorithms to identify possible moves and the most likely responses of opponents, work through each line of play for a given number of turns, and evaluate all the outcomes to reach an informed choice.[104]

The principal advantage that computers have over people is their awesome ability to crunch numbers with phenomenal speed. Deep Blue analyzed a billion positions a second and this is why it was able to explore so many variations so many moves ahead. Counterfactual research demands a good search pattern, and here we can learn from chess. Like a chess master, historians and international relations scholars need to identify the most promising "moves," look at how reality might "counter" them (by having counterfactuals that follow or enable the plausible rewrite to cut the chain of developments leading to the consequent, or by putting events back on track through second-order counterfactuals) and how they can respond to these countermoves. The game of counterfactuals can become more complicated than chess because there is no limit to the size of the board, the number of players, or their possible moves. The analogy is also incomplete because in chess, two players engage in move and countermove. Each new move in the branching tree of analysis encompasses roughly thirty-eight times as many positions. In counterfactuals, there can be *multiple* interactions at every stage as antecedents, enabling counterfactuals, and the chains they set in motion interact with one another. In chess, the definition of a move is clear; each player moves a piece in turn. In counterfactuals, chains of consequence unfold simultaneously and continually.

Supercomputers are routinely used to conduct counterfactual simulations in the sciences. Until such time as the programmers of Deep Blue turn their attention to historical counterfactuals, historians must behave more like chess masters than computers. Gary Kasparov had the merest fraction of the processing speed and data storage capability of the simplest computer, but beat Deep Blue in their first tournament and lost the second by only one game. The most challenging task in chess is determination of which of the many branching points are most worth examining because no computer can analyze them all. Deep Blue was an improvement on its predecessors because it made use of more sophisticated tuning mechanisms to select promising lines of play. Human beings, especially chess masters, still have a considerable comparative advantage in this respect. They use their intuition and judgment to select one or two possible moves and project their likely consequences out to a limit of about eight turns ahead. At each turn, they are ruthless in eliminating possibilities and thus stay within the limiting data processing capabilities of the human mind by tracking only a few chains of moves. The best computer algorithm is crude in comparison to the still uncanny ability of a chess master to zero in on promising lines of play.

Scholars have no recourse but to follow the strategy of Gary Kasparov and substitute judgment for computing power, and limited for more comprehensive search. And this is what our contributors to *Unmaking the West* did. Collectively, we used our imagination to invent counterfactuals we thought capable of preventing or adding turning points and then selected a few chains of counterfactual interaction to analyze in detail and estimate the likely outcomes associated with each. In chess, there is a straightforward way to estimate performance: players win, lose, or draw their games. In counterfactual research this kind of resolution is not possible. The best players can do is to persuade by making absolutely explicit the logic connecting antecedent and consequent, and the assumptions on which all the chains of causation they consider are based. This exercise can be made more compelling when it is a collective one, bringing together people with different substantive expertise and even different starting estimates of the contingency of the event in question. Argument and counterargument can be brought to bear with respect to each step of the process and the implications of every counterfactual, reaching a consensus when possible, and bracketing disagreements when not. Such an exercise makes no pretense to be a science, only that it harnesses human intelligence with the goal of making informed individual and collective judgments about interesting and important problems. This is no different, although considerably more systematic, than the claims made by more conventional forms of history.

PART TWO

CHAPTER THREE

Franz Ferdinand Found Alive:
World War I Unnecessary

> If this war breaks out, then its duration and its end will be
> unforeseeable. The greatest powers of Europe, armed as never
> before, will be going into battle with each other, not one of
> them can be crushed so completely in one or two campaigns
> that it will admit defeat, be compelled to conclude peace under
> hard terms, and will not come back, even if it is a year later, to
> renew the struggle. Gentlemen, it may be a war of seven years'
> or thirty years' duration— and woe to him who sets Europe
> alight, who first puts the fuse to the powder keg.
> —*Helmuth von Moltke the Elder*

> If we must go under, we better go under decently.
> —*Emperor Franz Josef*

As THE TWENTIETH CENTURY RECEDES into history, it is useful to reflect
upon what may have been its most significant event: World War I. That
conflict was a cultural and political watershed; it marked the beginning
of Europe's political and cultural decline and set in motion a chain of
events that led to an even more destructive war. Without World War I
we might have been spared the horrors of communism, Auschwitz, and
the Cold War. Many historians nevertheless contend that World War I or
something like it would have been all but impossible to avoid. The distinguished British historian, F. H. Hinsley, insists that "If the Sarajevo crisis
had not precipitated a particular great war, some other crisis would have
precipitated a great war at no distant date."[1] The scholarly literature on
World War I is disproportionately devoted to its underlying causes; proximate causes are given short shrift and generally considered unproblematic. Is this emphasis warranted? Was a European war really inevitable?
Could the twentieth century have unfolded differently?

Before addressing these questions it is important to know why so
many scholars have lined up on the side of near inevitability. In chapter 1 I suggest a number of psychological reasons, ranging from the
hindsight bias to our need to use the past as a means of understanding
and controlling the future. There are additional reasons to consider in
the case of the July crisis. Many historians appear to have taken their

cue from leading actors who subsequently portrayed themselves as victims of earlier decisions and events with only the most limited ability to influence the course of the crisis.[2] Austrian chief of staff Conrad von Hötzendorf maintained that "the First World War came about inevitably and irresistibly as the result of the motive forces in the lives of states and people, like a thunderstorm which must by its nature discharge itself."[3] For Conrad, who pushed for war as soon as he received news of the archduke's assassination, this view of the conflict was patently self-serving. This is equally true of German chancellor Bethmann Hollweg's subsequent bewilderment at how it all happened and Princip's assertion that World War I would have broken out even if he had failed to shoot Franz Ferdinand.[4]

In reality, European political leaders, the media, and intelligentsia in 1914 considered war a remote possibility. In a country-by-country survey, Holger Afflerbach finds that few leaders saw any reason for concern in the summer of 1914. He argues that Friedrich von Bernhardi's *Deutschland und der nächste Krieg* (*Germany and the Next War*), often cited as evidence in the belief of the inevitability of war, is better understood as a conscious effort, actively supported by the German military, to stem the growing tide of antiwar sentiment.[5] In Germany, Roger Chickering documents how following the declaration of war in August 1914, reluctance, anxiety, panic, and opposition were just as pronounced as enthusiasm. War euphoria was largely a postwar myth created by right-wing politicians and propagandists during the Weimar era. They sought to foster an image of national fulfillment later destroyed by wartime betrayal and subversion culminating in the alleged *Dolchstoss* (stab in the back) of the army by socialists. War enthusiasm is more myth than fact.[6]

Historians have had political incentives to stress the underlying causes of World War I and how they made it all but impossible to avoid. In the 1920s and 1930s, German nationalists sought to tar France and Russia with responsibility for the war to challenge the "war guilt" clause of the Treaty of Versailles. Liberal internationalists wanted to show that the Great War had been the result of the balance of power and absence of international institutions to regulate interstate competition.[7] In the 1960s, the publication of Fritz Fischer's *Griff Nach der Weltmacht* (literally, grasping out for world power but prosaically translated as *Germany's Aims in the First World War*) touched off a new round of debate. Fischer privileged underlying causes to establish continuity in goals between Wilhelminian and Nazi Germany.[8] Much of his argument is based on the far-reaching war aims of the September 1914 Program and the Treaty of Brest-Litovsk, but they were a response to seeming military victory, not a cause of war. Unlike Fischer, we must be careful to distinguish between cause and effect and avoid the cognitive trap of believing that something that has monumental consequences must have had equally important and deep-seated causes.

Historians and international relations scholars have more general disciplinary reasons to see major events as overdetermined. Two distinct but reinforcing processes are at work. The first is nicely described by R. H. Tawney, who observed that historians give "an appearance of inevitableness" to an existing order by dragging into prominence the forces which have triumphed and thrusting into the background those which they have swallowed up."[9] Inevitability, Charles Tilly observes, is also an artifact of the "retrospective" approach that examines phenomena by working backward from them to discover their causes. When applied to the study of state formation it ignores the "hundreds of states that once flourished but then disappeared." Tilly proposes the "prospective" method to combat this bias; researchers would begin at the formative stages in history and search forward for alternative paths and outcomes.[10]

Historical interpretations, no matter how well documented or convincingly presented rarely achieve a consensus. They provoke critiques and contending interpretations, and the resulting controversy stimulates a search for additional documents. New evidence may require historians to reformulate their interpretations but rarely discredits them outright. As the historiography of the First World War indicates, new evidence often provides the basis for still more interpretations. Decades of controversy, or even centuries as in the case of the French Revolution or the collapse of the Roman Empire, give rise to a plethora of interpretations that attribute these developments to a wide range of intellectual, social, economic, and political causes.[11] Remove one or several putative causes and a half-dozen others remain. Historical debate encourages the belief that most major events and developments were massively "overdetermined."[12]

In contrast to the conventional wisdom, I contend that World War I was contingent with respect to both its underlying and immediate causes. What made Europe ripe for war was not the multitude of its alleged causes but the ways in which they combined to affect the willingness of policymakers to take risks. World War I is best understood as a nonlinear confluence of three largely independent chains of causation. These chains produced independent but more or less simultaneous gestalt shifts in Vienna and Berlin and a slightly earlier one in Russia.[13] Had the timing of the Austrian and German shifts been off by as little as two years, Austrian leaders would not have felt so intent on destroying Serbia, and German leaders would not have been so willing to urge them to do so. Most explanations for war—especially ones that attribute it to systemic factors—take catalysts for granted. If the right underlying conditions are present, some incident will sooner or later set armies on the march in the way the twin assassinations in Sarajevo did in 1914. But Sarajevo was not just any provocation. I will show that it met a diverse set of political and psychological requirements that were essential for Austrian and German leaders to risk war. It is possible, but extremely unlikely, that some other event would have met these conditions or that some other combination of great powers would have started a war for different reasons. In the absence of an appropriate catalyst, several more years of peace could have altered the strategic and domestic contexts of the great powers and made war less likely. There was a two- to three-year window when the leaders of at least two great powers thought their national or dynastic interests were better served by war than peace.

Before proceeding it is important to note that these three chains were not the only ones at work in 1914. One can readily construct causal chains leading Britain and France into alliance and close military cooperation (Fashoda, *Entente Cordiale*, First and Second Moroccan crises), promoting hostility between Britain and Germany (failure of alliance negotiations, Germany's naval buildup, the kaiser's bellicose rhetoric, the First and Second Moroccan crises, the failure of naval talks), Russia and Britain's rapprochement (Franco-Russe, colonial accommodation), and Serbia's radicalization (a confluence in its own right of Balkan wars and domestic developments). We can also construct chains that led to intellectual and social developments (e.g., belief in the inevitability of war by generals in Germany and Austria, preference for offensive strategies, belief in the legitimacy and even beneficial consequences of war among military elites, the influence of military officials in policymaking in central and eastern Europe). They are all relevant to understanding the origins of the war. Some of these outcomes, if not the chains themselves, are brought into the picture through the three causal chains I concentrate on, either as their products or enabling background conditions. I believe the three chains I have chosen are the most fundamental ones, and it would be difficult, if not impossible, to examine more than three, and their interactions, in a chapter.

Underlying Causes of War

To use counterfactual experiments to explore alternative worlds it helps to have as a starting point a generally accepted interpretation for why the world we live in has come about. Historians rarely agree about causes, but the degree of controversy surrounding the origins of World War I has been extreme. Scholars have disagreed about the causes of war, the appropriate level of analysis at which to search for them, which state or states were most responsible for the war, and the reasons their leaders acted as they did.

Many of these differences have narrowed in recent decades as the political controversies surrounding them have receded into history. Historians still disagree on specific points (e.g., German chancellor Theobald von Bethmann Hollweg's motives for risking war, the importance and rigidity of military plans, the relative importance of security versus other considerations) but there is widespread agreement that Austria-Hungary and Germany set in motion the chain of events that led to war; Austrian leaders exploited the assassination of Franz Ferdinand as the pretext for war with Serbia; and German leaders encouraged—even pushed—Austria toward decisive action.[14] Since the publication of Kurt Riezler's diaries, a near consensus has emerged among German historians that Bethmann Hollweg did not seek to provoke a European war but recognized that an Austrian conflict with Serbia would be difficult to contain. He was willing to run the risk of a continental war in the belief that such a war was sooner or later inevitable and that Germany's chance of winning it diminished with every year that passed.[15] The current controversy in German scholarship on the war arises from the publication of a series of articles and two books by Terence Zuber, a former American military officer turned historian. Making use of German military files that only became available after the end of the Cold War, Zuber claims there never was a Schlieffen Plan and that Chief of Staff Helmuth von Moltke and his colleagues recognized that their war plan—subsequently called the Schlieffen Plan as a way of hiding Moltke's responsibility for it—could not defeat France quickly but would provoke a protracted and costly conflict.[16] It has long been conventional wisdom that World War I was brought about at least in part by runaway escalation caused by the belief, most pronounced in Germany, that any delay in mobilization would diminish the chances of a rapid victory. Zuber's research and other recent writings constitute a serious challenge to this interpretation.[17]

Students of Austria-Hungary contended that its leaders acted for a combination of closely related foreign and domestic concerns.[18] More recently the motive of honor, national and personal, has gained prominence.[19] Russia's role has always been recognized as critical. The Austro-Serb Balkan conflict escalated into a European war because Russian leaders decided on 24–25 July to back Serbia. Recent scholarship indicates that the Russians supported Serbia in full recognition that it was almost certain to lead to war with Austria, and possibly with Germany as well.[20] The czar and his ministers nevertheless made the decision to mobilize without understanding its military consequences for Germany.[21] France has received less attention, and scholarly inquiry has focused on the extent to which French leaders strengthened Russian resolve in the Balkans before 1914 and during the July crisis.[22] Britain's role in the crisis has been more controversial and some students of the crisis have argued over the years that an earlier British commitment to support France might have encouraged Germany to restrain Austria.[23] More recent scholarship suggests that Foreign Secretary Edward Grey went as far as he could in signaling his country's intention to back France given the domestic constraints he faced and that a British commitment might not have had the desired effect on Germany.[24] Given the primary responsibility of Austria and Germany in initiating the chain of events that led to war in 1914, I will focus on their decisions but in full recognition that they are only part of the story.

Table 3.1 identifies some of the principal causes of war advanced in the literature by their level of analysis. The spate of diaries, memoirs, and documentary evidence that has emerged since 1914 has deepened our understanding of the origins of the war but has spawned more interpretations than it has ruled out. Some assertions have been discredited on the basis of this evidence (e.g., Harry Elmer Barnes's contention that France and Russia secretly planned the war, Fritz Fischer's claim that German leaders opted for war at the so-called War Council of 1912).[25] Many interpretations are not falsifiable in the Popperian sense of the term.[26] They are inadequately specified, so it is unclear what evidence, if any, would call their validity into question.

There has been no systematic effort to determine the relative importance of these hypothesized causes of war, the extent to which one or more of them could be subsumed by others, or what combination(s) of them were necessary and sufficient for war. Historians divide into hedgehogs and foxes on the latter question.[27] Fritz Fischer and Paul Schroeder represent the former and argue for a single, most important underlying cause for war. Foxes like James Joll, Imanuel Geiss, and Holger Herwig advance numerous causes for war without always discriminating among them. Geiss attributes World War I to imperialism, especially Wilhelminian *Weltpolitik*; national self-determination and its revolutionary potential; the determination of the German government to uphold conservative and monarchic forces by any means against the rising tide of social democracy; the containment policy of the Entente, and Germany's refusal to be contained.[28] Historical complexity is commendable; World War I certainly did not have a simple, single cause. But laundry lists are not explanations.

In fairness to historians, rank ordering of causes is difficult, often impossible, within the confines of a single case, especially one with nonlinear properties.[29] Historians typically try to establish causation through process tracing. They search for links between hypothesized causes and observed outcomes. Process tracing works best at the individual level of analysis, and only when there is enough evidence to document the calculations and the motives behind them of relevant actors. Even when such evidence is available, usually in the form of memoranda and recorded

TABLE 3.1
Underlying Causes of War

Deep causes
Industrial revolution (*war as escape from super ego constraints*)[1]
Modernization (*war as raison d'être for traditional classes and values*)[2]
Nationalism (*threatened survival of multinational empires*)[3]
Democratization (*threatened traditional political elites*)[4]

System level
Imperialism (*German "need" to acquire more colonies*)[5]
International anarchy (*struggle for relative gain*)[6] (*arms races*)[7]
Alliance structure (*alliances too tight*)[8] (*alliances too weak*)[9] (*need to preserve Austro-German alliance*)[10]
Shifts in the political balance (*encirclement of Austria*)[11] (*Russian fear of losing great power status*)[12]
Shifts in the military balance (*Russia growing stronger and Austria weaker*)[13]
Changes in rules of the game (*imperial competition in Europe*)[14]

Ideas
Social Darwinism (*international politics as a struggle for survival*)[15]
War is inevitable (*German fear of Franco-Russian intentions*)[16]
War is beneficial (*expected to temper the nation*)[17]
Code of honor (*required war in response to certain provocations*)[18]

State structure
Weak society and strong state (*domestic conflict is exported*)[19]

Domestic politics
Conservative desires to safeguard status quo (*German conservatives sought war to crush socialism*)[20] (*Austrian fear of Slavic nationalism*)[21] (*Russian fear of revolution*)[22]
Weak regimes (*Serbian sponsorship of Pan-Slavism*)[23]

Organization and bureaucracy
Military planning in a political vacuum (*The Schlieffen Plan*)[24] (*Russian failure to develop fully separate mobilization plans against Austria and Germany*)[25]
German military pressure for preemptive war[26]
Cult of the offensive (*preference for offensive over defensive strategies*)[27]
The short war illusion (*victory was possible at low cost to society*)[28]
Rigid organizational routines (*restricted freedom of political leaders*)[29]

Leaders
Poor German leadership after Bismarck (*led to German isolation and encirclement*)[30]
Poor German crisis management (*misread military balance*)[31] (*misread responses of other actors*)[32] (*fear and panic interfered with judgment*)[33]

(continued)

TABLE 3.1
(*Continued*)

Poor Austrian crisis management (*misread military balance and likely political consequences of war with Serbia*)[34] (*failed to convince Russia of Serbian complicity in the assassination*)[35] (*Conrad's purely personal motive for war*)[36]

Poor Russian crisis management (*failure to recognize consequences of partial mobilization*)[37]

Poor British crisis management (*belated recognition of Austro-German plans by Grey*)[38]

---

conversations, it may not permit scholars to determine the relative weight of contributing causes, and which, if any of them, might have produced the outcome in the absence of the others. This uncertainty is understandable when we consider that the actors themselves often had little idea at the time of the relative importance of the considerations responsible for their behavior.

Comparison is another method of establishing causation. Within the single case format, I noted in chapter 2, comparative analysis can take two forms: intracase comparison and counterfactual analysis. The former breaks out a case into a series of similar interactions and treats them as separate and independent cases for purposes of analysis. Austria-Hungary went to the brink of war four times between December 1912 and July 1914. Many important background factors remained constant across these cases (e.g., belief systems, the military balance, most leaders), while others varied (the political balance in the Balkans, the Austrian leadership). By asking why Austria rejected war in December 1912, April–May 1913 and October 1913, but not in July 1914, we can probe the 1914 decision in a semicontrolled manner. Such comparisons must nevertheless be made with caution because the cases are unlikely to be independent; the process and outcome of each one can influence that of its successors. Intracase comparison nevertheless confers a singular advantage: it builds variation within a fundamentally similar political and cultural context, controlling better than intercase comparison for many factors that may be important but unrecognized.

Counterfactual analysis allows researchers to use some of the controls normally only possible in a laboratory; we can try to add or remove causes or background conditions. Under ideal conditions, experiments can increase our confidence in the inferred consequent. Unlike experiments, we can never really know the consequences of variation counterfactuals introduce; the best we can do is to make a plausible case for the inferred consequent. For this reason, counterfactual experiments can rarely falsify explanations. They are nevertheless powerful vehicles for exploring relationships among hypothesized explanations. In the case of World War I, even a superficial counterfactual examination of its underlying causes reveals how tightly coupled they are. Counterfactual experiments also help us probe contingency. The most straightforward way to do this is to use minimal rewrite counterfactuals to remove putative causes of an event or development. Leaders can usually be changed by minimal rewrites, but to alter discourses, institutions, or the balance of power, it is usually necessary to go back to a time and place where these causes were malleable or still in the process of taking shape. I argued in chapter 2, the fewer counterfactuals necessary to remove putative causes, the more counterfactuals that can accomplish this end, and the more proximate they are to the consequent, the more contingent the consequent. In this chapter, I employ a variant of this strategy. I show that at least some of the more important underlying causes of war can be organized into independent chains of causation that produced war when they came into confluence, and that this confluence, if not the chains themselves, can readily be untracked by the use of minimal rewrite counterfactuals. By doing so, I make the case for contingency.

As I noted in chapter 2, a confluence envisages a multiple stream of independent causes that come together to produce an outcome. Such an outcome could be prevented by removing any one (or more) of its contributing causes with a minimal rewrite is contingent. Its degree of contingency depends on how easy it would be to prevent any one of its causes or their confluence. At the other end of the spectrum of contingency is an equifinal outcome, or one that can readily be produced through multiple pathways, so cannot be forestalled by untracking any one, or even several, of them. Some outcomes—death, for example—are so highly redundant as to make them all but inevitable.

World War I is best understood as a nonlinear confluence in which multiple, interrelated chains of causation had unanticipated interactions and unpredictable consequences. Three causal chains were critically important. First and foremost was Germany's security dilemma, caused by the prospect of a two-front war in which the general staff worried that it would soon be impossible to defeat their adversaries sequentially. The second causal chain consisted of all the Balkan developments that threatened the external security and internal stability of Austria-Hungary and encouraged influential opinion in Vienna to consider war with Serbia as a possible solution to these threats. The third chain centered on St. Petersburg and was itself a confluence of external setbacks (defeat in Russo-Japanese War of 1904–1905, humiliation in the Bosnian Annexation crisis of 1909) and internal weaknesses (the revolution of 1905, growing alienation of the middle classes, rise of a powerful revolutionary movement).

The combination of foreign and domestic concerns made Russian leaders fearful of the foreign and domestic costs of another foreign policy defeat.

Each of these three chains was contingent; they were the result of decisions, bad and generally avoidable ones, that had the unintended consequence of dividing Europe into two armed and hostile camps. If Bismarck had persuaded Wilhelm I not to annex Alsace-Lorraine, enduring French hostility might have been avoided. If Bismarck's successors had managed relations with Russia better St. Petersburg would not have had a strong incentive to ally with France. If Moltke and the German general staff had adopted a defensive strategy, which they knew to be superior, Germany would have been under no strategic pressure. If England and France had come to blows at Fashoda, if England had attacked Russia's fleet after the Dogger Bank incident, or if the French election of 1900 had not brought *la Défense Républicaine* to power, there would have been no *Entente Cordiale* and no Anglo-Russian colonial understanding, the latter having been brokered by France. The *Entente* might also have been prevented by a kaiser who knew how to keep his mouth shut and recognized the unnecessary expense and counterproductive nature of a naval race with England.

The point of no return in Austro-Serb relations was the Empire's annexation of Bosnia and Herzogovina in 1908. Austrian chief of staff Conrad von Hötzendorf had been pushing for annexation for some time and convinced Alois Lexa von Aehrenthal, who became foreign minister in 1906, to take this step as part of a new, assertive policy in the Balkans. Aehrenthal's poorly conceived initiative provoked a war-threatening crisis, humiliated Russia, and deeply embittered the Serbs. The annexation crisis destroyed a decade of Austro-Russian cooperation and put the two empires on a collision course. With more far-sighted foreign ministers in Vienna and St. Petersburg, this clash could easily have been avoided and Austro-Russian rivalry managed effectively as it had been in the past. If so, Russia would have been more restrained and probably would not have violated the tacit agreement between the two empires that neither would support dissident groups within the other's territory or sphere of influence. If St. Petersburg had not encouraged anti-Habsburg factions in Belgrade or stoked the fires of Romanian nationalism in Transylvania, the Austrian foreign office would have been much less threatened by the likely defection of Romania from its secret alliance with Austria. In the long run Slavic nationalism would almost certainly have asserted itself but that threat could have been managed for some time; as late as 1914 there were relatively few voices for independence within the Habsburg Empire. The division of Europe into two militarily powerful but insecure alliance systems was not inevitable nor did it make war unavoidable.

War was the outcome of the synergistic consequences of the confluence of these three chains of causation. Two features of nonlinear systems are particularly relevant in this connection. The first is how the effect of one variable (or cause) can depend on the presence of another, and when both present have a step level or phase transition effect. This means that the consequences of either cannot be predicted or understood independently.[30]

This phenomenon is well illustrated by the relationship between Russian armaments and railway construction and the Schlieffen Plan, by which Germany intended to invade and defeat France before Russian forces could penetrate too deeply into eastern Prussia. The former did not cause the latter. Germany was committed to an offensive against France before these Russian programs began, and its general staff had no confidence in their ability to defeat France, but nevertheless worried that Russian rearmament and railway construction would allow Russian forces to penetrate deep into Prussia while their army was engaged in France. Moltke consistently exaggerated his confidence in his war plan in conversations with the kaiser, chancellor, and foreign minister, and their belief that victory hinged on an early war significantly shaped the chancellor's response to Austria's request for support in July 1914.[31] France, which felt very much on the defensive vis-à-vis Germany after the 1905 Moroccan crisis, gave financial support to Russia in the hope of restraining Germany; French leaders reasoned that Berlin would become more cautious in proportion to its fear of the consequences of a two-front war. The French strategy of deterrence had the unintended consequence of provoking the German invasion of France it had been designed to prevent. It had the same effect in the July crisis when at least some Russian leaders favored mobilization in the hope that it might restrain Germany and Austria, not constitute a casus belli. In each instance the intensity and effects of individual causes of war were significantly influenced, and in some cases wholly determined, by the presence of other causes. In their absence, leaders might have made different choices, or the same choices might have had different consequences.

Game theorists who model strategic interactions have long recognized the need for actors to have a common framework, or at the very least have a common understanding of the kind of game they are playing. They assume that actors use a Bayesian process to update estimates of one another's preferences and that such learning helps them to move toward and establish a common bargaining framework.[32] In practice, new information is commonly assimilated to existing frameworks, and actors can continue to communicate for prolonged periods of time without realizing that they are playing different "games." "Signals" may be missed or their intended import grasped only after it is too late to respond appropriately.[33] Frameworks can change in the course of interactions and these changes can have profound consequences for behavior. The ability of actors to transform themselves and their understandings of their strategic interactions in the course of their interactions is a second fundamental characteristic of nonlinear, open systems central to understanding the events of July and August 1914.

Key Austrian and German leaders underwent independent gestalt shifts in 1913–14 that prompted dramatic reversals in their foreign policy preferences. In Berlin, Field Marshall Helmuth von Moltke, German chief of staff, and Chancellor Bethmann Hollweg had been troubled by Russia's seemingly growing military and mobilization capability for some time. But only in 1914, most likely as a result of the assassination of Franz Ferdinand, did the chancellor's concern—fueled by von Moltke's fear mongering—reach the level where he was willing to do something he had consistently rejected in the past: risk war in the hope of achieving a diplomatic triumph that might break up the Franco-Russian Alliance. Austrian leaders worried about a Balkan League directed against them that would constitute an external threat and fan the fissiparous tendencies within their empire. Conrad and Berchtold wanted to exploit the assassination of Franz Ferdinand as a pretext to attack Serbia, in large part to "show Serbia who was boss."[34] Franz Josef was persuaded to go along, largely for reasons of upholding Austria's honor, and Berlin was now willing to offer its support. The Russians knew nothing about these gestalt shifts and behaved in ways that exacerbated Austro-German insecurities and helped to provoke a war that none of their leaders wanted. Wilhelm, Bethmann Hollweg, and Foreign Secretary Gottlieb von Jagow were in turn victims of a Russian gestalt shift. They deluded themselves into thinking that they might repeat the success of 1909—when the German threat of mobilization forced Russia to back down in the Bosnian annexation crisis—and compel Russia to remain on the sidelines of an Austro-Serb war. But the humiliation of 1909 had led to a commitment not to back down again because leading Russian officials believed it would undermine their status as a great power. The Russian commitment to support Serbia was strengthened by a cabinet reshuffle in 1914. These several gestalt shifts entirely changed the nature and outcome of great power interactions.

One of the most remarkable features of 1914 was the coincidental timing of the German and Austrian security problems and gestalt shifts. Although Russia was a common threat, each ally's security problems had largely independent causes and there was no particular reason why they should have become acute at the same time. Germany's security dilemma was the result of its geographic position, prior policies that had encouraged its two most powerful neighbors to ally against it, and above all, its commitment to an offensive military strategy. Russia's improved military and mobilization capability, the developments that so threatened Germany in 1914, were the result of Russian industrialization and access to French capital markets. German willingness to risk war was also the result of the perceived decline of Austria-Hungary, Germany's principal military ally. German political and military authorities worried that failure to support Austria in 1914—indeed, to encourage it to take dramatic action—would only accelerate its decline and leave Germany at the mercy of Russia and France.

Austria-Hungary's insecurity was largely due to the precipitous decline of Ottoman power. This decline had many internal causes but was dramatically hastened by the Italian occupation of Tripoli in September 1911 and the war this triggered with the Ottoman Empire. It provided the opportunity for Serbia, Bulgaria, and Greece to take up arms, and to almost everyone's surprise, they succeeded in all but expelling Turkey from Europe. Serbia doubled its population and territory and, backed by Russia, sought to revive the Balkan League and transform in into an anti-Austrian alliance.

German leaders did not feel so threatened before 1914; German chancellors rejected military demands for war in 1905 and 1912 and supported diplomatic resolution of the 1912 and 1913 crises that threatened war between Austria and Serbia and Montenegro respectively. If the Italians had not occupied Tripoli or if the Balkan events that Austria-Hungary found so threatening had happened a few years earlier, the German kaiser and chancellor would probably not have encouraged Austria to draw its sword. Nor would they have felt so threatened if these events had occurred a few years later, an argument I will present later in the chapter. Timing was everything in 1914, and for this reason alone World War I was highly contingent.

IMMEDIATE CAUSES OF WAR

Like fires, wars need catalysts. Systematic theories of war assume an unproblematic relationship between underlying and immediate causes. If the underlying causes are present, an appropriate catalyst will come along or be manufactured by leaders.[35] This assumption is sometimes warranted. In February 1965, in the aftermath of a Vietcong attack on the American advisors' barracks at Pleiku, National Security Advisor McGeorge Bundy wrote a memorandum to President Lyndon Johnson urging the sustained bombing of North Vietnam. Bundy later acknowledged that Pleikus were like "streetcars." He could count on repeated Vietcong attacks against South Vietnamese forces or their American advisors to provide him with the pretext he needed at the opportune moment to sell escalation to the president.[36] Pretexts do not always resemble streetcars. They may be infrequent, inappropriate, or fail to materialize (as is sometimes also true of trams and buses); and without a catalyst, the predicted or intended behavior may not occur. In a matter of months or years, underlying conditions may evolve to make war less likely even if an otherwise appropriate catalyst ultimately comes along. The window of opportunity for war may be temporally narrow or broad depending on the nature and rate of changes in the underlying conditions. War may require a *conjunction* of underlying pressures and appropriate catalysts.

One of the most common metaphors used to describe Europe in 1914 is that of dry kindling waiting for a spark to set it aflame. As sparks are frequent in acute international conflicts this metaphor is appealing to those who emphasize the determining nature of systemic causes. Metaphors are no substitute for careful analysis, and historians and political scientists alike need to develop more precise conceptions of catalysts. We can begin by asking what about Sarajevo made it a successful catalyst and then inquire about other provocations or events that might have served the same end? Answers to these questions will provide a second perspective from which to estimate the contingency of war in 1914.

Joachim Remak insists that "Sarajevo was more than an excuse for war, it was one of its major causes."[37] Although he does not elaborate on this claim, many reasons can be offered and much evidence adduced in support. Arguably the most important reason was the political challenge the assassination appeared to create for Austria-Hungary. In June 1914 Austrian prime minister Berchtold, with Emperor Franz Josef's support, began a diplomatic offensive to arrest the decline of the Empire's position in the Balkans and to frustrate entente efforts to build a new Balkan League. There was no talk of war.[38] The assassination transformed the situation. Not only Conrad pushed for war but other officials in the foreign office and military argued that failure to respond forcibly would undermine, if not destroy, the Empire's standing as a great power and embolden its domestic and foreign enemies.[39] For Franz Josef there was an additional personal dimension to Sarajevo; he was outraged by the assassination of a member of the royal family and accepted the need to make war to preserve the honor of the Empire. He was by no means confident of the outcome and told Conrad: "If we must go under, we better go under decently."[40] Kaiser Wilhelm also grieved over the loss of Franz Ferdinand, whom he considered a friend and had spent time with only two weeks before.[41] He wanted Austria to take action against Serbia to show that actions against legitimate rulers would not be tolerated.[42]

Sarajevo shifted the balance of power of Vienna. Franz Ferdinand's views on defense matters were almost as important as those of the emperor. His influence derived from his official status as successor to the throne (*Thronfolger*), from his interest and knowledge about military affairs, and from the extensive network of contacts he had cultivated throughout the armed forces. His decidedly peaceful orientation evolved during the course of the Balkan wars.[43] The *Thronfolger* was intent on extending Austrian influence in the Balkans, but not at the risk of war with Russia. He warned that "A war between Austria and Russia would end either with the overthrow of the Romanovs or with the overthrow of the Habsburgs—or perhaps both."[44] He cherished the unrealistic idea of monarchical unity in the form of some revival of the Holy Alliance and had continually sought to cultivate good relations with Nicholas II. On a more practical level he took Russian military capability more seriously than either the war minister or chief of staff and was convinced that war against Serbia would draw in Russia. He did not believe that the Austro-Hungarian army was ready for war and worried that Italy would defect from the Triple Alliance and that Germany would find some reason to stand aloof. More fundamentally, Franz Ferdinand opposed war because it would make it impossible for him to impose fundamental changes in the structure of the Empire upon his accession to the throne.[45]

Samuel R. Williamson Jr. offers an intriguing counterfactual: if the governor-general of Bosnia-Herzogovina, Oskar Potiorek, had been killed at Sarajevo instead of Franz Ferdinand, Vienna would have responded differently.[46] Like Conrad, Potiorek was a charter member of the war party and his death would have removed another supporter of military action from the scene.[47] More importantly, Franz Ferdinand would have been influential in shaping Austria's response. His opposition to war, combined with that of Hungarian prime minister István Tisza, the senior voice against war in June and early July 1914, would have carried considerable weight because the two men were otherwise at odds. Tisza was the great defender of Hungary, and Franz Ferdinand made no secret of his dislike of Tisza and Hungarians more generally.[48] With Franz Ferdinand and Tisza urging moderation, Berchtold, a weak personality, would also have pursued a cautious line, and Franz Josef, cross-pressured in 1914, might well have sided with them instead of with Conrad. There would have been no Hoyos mission to seek German support for war against Serbia; Berlin would have been consulted with a diplomatic end in mind. The channel for communication with Germany would not have been the hawks in the foreign office but Franz Ferdinand, who had close personal relations with Kaiser Wilhelm and had been used in the past to sound out Berlin's intentions in the Balkans. Merely changing the victims of the terrorist attack in Sarajevo might have been enough to alter in a fundamental way Austria-Hungary's response.

Sarajevo provided a necessary incentive and opportunity for Germany. Moltke had pushed for war almost from the moment he became chief of staff because he was emotionally committed to fighting France and thought a successful war would give a boost to traditional values of honor and service within Germany. He wanted to go to war while Germany still had a chance of victory in a conflict that he knew would bring

Russia in on France's side.[49] Although the German general staff had a low regard for the military prowess of their Austrian ally, they were horrified at the prospect of an Austrian decline because it would leave Russia free to concentrate all of its forces against Germany in East Prussia. In Berlin, the assassination was perceived to threaten Austria's standing as a great power because it might expose Austria's lack of will to act like one. This additional consideration, when weighed along with the general concern for the deteriorating military balance, made Chancellor Bethmann Hollweg more receptive to Moltke's pleas for action later in the crisis. The assassination may well have been the catalyst for Bethmann Hollweg's gestalt shift described in the previous section.[50]

Bethmann Hollweg was more prescient than most of his contemporaries in recognizing, as he put it, that a European war was likely to topple more thrones than it would prop up. He accordingly deemed the backing of the Social Democrats, the largest and best organized working-class organization in Europe, the sine qua non of military action. Without confidence in the support of the Social Democrats, the chancellor would not have taken his "leap into the dark."[51] Moltke knew this and in February 1913 had discouraged Conrad from attacking Serbia on the grounds that the German people would not support a war that Austria provoked against a seemingly conciliatory adversary.[52] Sarajevo was a tailor-made provocation for Bethmann Hollweg. The assassinations aroused considerable sympathy for Austria throughout Europe, not the least among the German working class. Although the Austrian ultimatum was widely regarded as heavy-handed by the politically sophisticated, Germans perceived their country as a bystander in a Balkan conflict and then the innocent target of Russian aggression. The chancellor played up to these sentiments and benefited greatly from the general fear and dislike of Russia among Social Democrats, who regarded the czarist regime as barbaric because of its treatment of labor, dissident intellectuals, and minorities. The result was the *Burgfrieden* of 4 August in which the Social Democrats voted with near unanimity for war credits.

Sarajevo created the necessary psychological environment for the kaiser and chancellor to overcome their inhibitions about war. Admiral Alfred von Tirpitz observed that "When the Emperor did not consider the peace to be threatened he liked to give full play to his reminiscences of famous ancestors, [but] in moments which he realized to be critical he proceeded with extraordinary caution."[53] To his contemporaries the chancellor came across as a fatalist, as a man who had a deep revulsion of war but felt powerless to oppose the prevalent view that it was necessary. The kaiser and chancellor were caught on the horns of a dilemma: Germany would benefit from a diplomatic triumph that would break up the Franco-Russe, but this could only be achieved—if it could be achieved at all—by risking war. Neither man was willing to accept responsibility for starting a European war. Until July 1914, they procrastinated, a hallmark of defensive avoidance. By deferring a decision that was too difficult for them to make, the kaiser and chancellor preserved their psychological equilibrium. The July crises offered them a way out of their decisional dilemma.[54]

When Hoyos met Wilhelm and Bethmann Hollweg on 4 July in Potsdam he asked only for their support *if* Russia threatened intervention in support of Serbia. The kaiser and chancellor expected Russia to back down as it had in 1909, and this was also the expectation of their ambassador in St. Petersburg.[55] They doubted that France would come to Russia's assistance, or that Britain would intervene if it did. German support for Austria precipitated its ultimatum and declaration of war against Serbia, Russia's subsequent mobilization against Austria, German ultimatums to Russia, and France and German mobilization, which was the equivalent of war. When kaiser and chancellor confronted Russian mobilization, or more accurately, premature and exaggerated reports of Russian mobilization that flooded through the channels of German military intelligence, they convinced themselves that they were only reacting to Russian initiatives and that St. Petersburg, not they, bore the brunt of responsibility for the war they were about to unleash.[56]

To recapitulate, the Sarajevo assassinations changed the political and psychological environment in Vienna and Berlin in six important ways, all of which may have been necessary for the decisions that led to war. First, they constituted a political challenge to which Austrian leaders believed they had to respond forcefully; anything less was expected to encourage further challenges by domestic and foreign enemies. Second, they shocked and offended Franz Josef and Kaiser Wilhelm and made both emperors more receptive to calls for decisive measures to preserve Austria's honor and its standing as a great power. Third, they changed the policymaking context in Vienna by removing the principal spokesman for peace. Fourth, they may have been the catalyst for Bethmann Hollweg's gestalt shift. Fifth, they made it possible for Bethmann Hollweg to win the support of the socialists, without which he never would have risked war. Sixth, they created a psychological environment in which Wilhelm and Bethmann Hollweg could proceed in incremental steps toward war, convincing themselves at the outset that their actions were unlikely to provoke a European war and, at the end of the crisis, that others were responsible for war.

A striking feature of the July crisis was the tremendous psychological difficulty German leaders had in making a decision for war.[57] Given their unwillingness to accept responsibility for starting a great-power war, it is difficult to imagine how the kaiser and chancellor could have authorized mobilization if they had been compelled to recognize their share of responsibility for war from the outset. If the archduke had not been assassinated, giving rise to this unusual opportunity, Germany might have reached the fateful year of 1917 still at peace with its neighbors. Its leaders might have discovered that their fears of a window of vulnerability were greatly exaggerated, that their adversaries were constrained from attacking Germany for many of the same reasons that had prevented Germany from exploiting its military window of opportunity in the decade before 1914.

The double assassination was critical in its nature and timing but could easily have been avoided. Reports reached Vienna that Sarajevo was seething with discontent and a dangerous venue for a royal visit. Franz Ferdinand explored the possibility of postponing his trip and seems to have been encouraged by the emperor to do so. The Austrian high command nevertheless decided to proceed with its great maneuvers, and the archduke, who was inspector general of the armed forces, believed that he had no choice but to attend. Countess Sophie had come to Bosnia with dark misgivings that something dreadful was about to happen to her husband. She was aware that Dr. Josip Sunarić, one of the leaders of the Sabor, the Bosnian parliament, had urged General Potiorek to cancel their impending visit because of the hostility of the local population to the regime. The evening before the assassination Karl von Rumerskirch, the archduke's chamberlain, urged him to avoid Sarajevo for the same reason. General Potiorek's aide-de-camp, Lt.-Col. Eric von Merizzi, interceded and convinced Franz Ferdinand to proceed because cancellation would be a rebuke to his superior. The next morning the archduke and his wife were met at the Sarajevo train station by General Potiorek and the lord mayor and ushered into an open touring car to go to a nearby military camp for a quick inspection before going on to the city hall. The lead car in the procession was supposed to carry six specially trained security officers but had only three local policeman instead. On Appel Quay, a long street with houses on one side and an embankment on the other, a young man in a black coat asked a policeman which car carried the archduke and then stepped out into the street to throw a grenade at it. Franz Ferdinand's Czech driver saw the object coming his way and accelerated. The bomb fell on the folded roof, rolled off into the pavement and exploded under the rear wheel of the next car in the procession. The would-be assassin jumped over the embankment into the river.[58]

Lt.-Col. Merizzi and a second officer, in the car behind the archduke, were hit by bomb fragments and were rushed to a military hospital. Franz Ferdinand dismissed the attack as madness and insisted on proceeding to the city hall. Following the ceremony there the archduke asked General Potiorek if there were likely to be any more attacks. Potiorek advised taking a different route and skipping the planned visit to the museum.

Other members of the archduke's party urged him to leave Sarajevo immediately, but he insisted on visiting Lt.-Col. von Merizzi in the military hospital and then going on to the museum. The cars drove up Appel Quay, this time at high speed, but the lead car turned into Franz Josef Street by mistake and the next car with the police guard followed suit. Franz Ferdinand's driver, in the third car, was turning to follow when he was ordered by General Potiorek to stop, back up, and continue down Appel Quay. At that moment, Princip, standing at the intersection, took a revolver out of his coat and a nearby policeman reached out to grab his hand. An accomplice struck the policeman, and Princip fired twice at point-blank range into the car containing Franz Ferdinand and Sophie.[59]

Numerous minimal rewrites can prevent the assassinations: Princip might have obeyed the order to abort the mission sent to him by the military conspirators in Belgrade. Austrian authorities in Bosnia might have taken security as seriously as they did the menu and music for the banquets they planned in the archduke's honor, Franz Ferdinand might have canceled his trip in response to multiple warnings and his wife's fears, he might have followed the advice of his advisors and left Sarajevo directly after the ceremony at city hall, or his cavalcade could have adhered to the planned route and raced down Appel Quay past Princip. None of these changes strain our understanding of the world because most royal processions do not stray from their intended routes and most security details would have rushed the archduke and his wife to safety at the first sign of violence.

Was War Avoidable?

Without the assassinations there would have been no war in the summer of 1914. Could some other country, or combination of countries, have found a reason to start a war then or in the near future? Britain was committed to the status quo and was consumed with its Irish problem. France coveted Alsace-Lorraine but had been on the defensive in Europe since 1871 and perceived itself increasingly weaker militarily vis-à-vis Germany. The lynchpin of French security was the Franco-Russe, and France supported Russia in 1914 to preserve this alliance. France had also drawn closer to Britain and relied on British military assistance in case of a war with Germany, but the French knew this support would only materialize if they were attacked by Germany. Italy pursued an aggressive colonial policy that led to war with the Ottoman Empire and aspired to those parts of Austria-Hungary inhabited by Italian speakers. But before 1914 Italy was constrained by its alliance with Austria and Germany. The Ottoman Empire was everywhere on the defensive and not about to challenge any of the major powers or provide them with a pretext to intervene in support of any of its neighbors. Russia had more or less recovered from its defeat in the Russo-Japanese War and was intent on expanding its influence in the Balkans. But Russian leaders did not want war; they mobilized reluctantly in 1914 and hoped, although did not expect, that their action would deter Austria from attacking Serbia. Serbia had long-term aspirations to acquire Bosnia-Herzogovina but its energies were fully consumed with overcoming the resistance of its newly acquired subjects in Macedonia. In 1910 German foreign minister Alfred von Kiderlen-Wächter rightly observed that "If we do not conjure up a war into being, certainly no one else will do so."[60]

A failed assassination attempt would not have started a war; pre-1914 Europe was used to them, and Austria would have found much less sympathy in Europe if Franz Ferdinand had survived. A bungled assassination might have had beneficial consequences for the continent. Serbia's diplomatic humiliation in 1909 encouraged the formation of secret societies aimed at undermining Austrian rule in Bosnia-Herzogovina. Apis [a pseudonym for Col. Dragutin Dimitriević] was head of the "Black Hand" and at the center of many of these conspiracies, and supplied arms and other assistance to the archduke's assassins. Foreign Secretary Nikola Pašić was hostile to the conspirators but knew of their preparations; he felt constrained to provide only veiled warnings to the Austrian ambassador. Ironically, neither Apis nor the other conspirators wanted war with Austria, and Apis did not expect the assassination to provoke one. He hoped to strengthen his hand vis-à-vis civilian authorities, and sought to call off the assassination when he became convinced that it would not buttress his authority. From the perspective of those who mattered in Belgrade, the war was an unintended and undesired consequence of unwanted assassinations. A failed assassination attempt might have allowed the Serbian prime minister and Pašić to rein in Apis, which they finally did in the summer of 1915, when they dismissed him as chief of military intelligence. In December 1916 Apis was arrested and tried. He was executed the following year.

Historians who contend that a European war was inevitable root their argument in the deeper trends they see pushing the powers toward war. Would these systemic factors have become more or less pronounced after 1914? Structural determinists simply assume they would have intensified, although they offer no reasons why. We can certainly conjure up scenarios of more acute Austro-Russian competition in the Balkans, British-German economic competition in the Middle East, and even the breakup of the Triple Alliance due to Italy's defection. With no more imagination we can identify developments that would have muted underlying tensions and made war less likely.

The principal difference between the Balkan crises of 1908–1909 and 1914 was Russian willingness to go to war in support of Serbia in 1914. Some historians maintain that Russia was ripe for revolution in 1914 and that World War I postponed the upheaval for three years.[61] If revolution had broken out in the absence of war, Russia might have been consumed by domestic turmoil for several years afterward and not have been in any position to pursue an aggressive policy in the Balkans. This fate could also have overtaken Austria. Franz Josef died in 1916 and was succeeded by Prince Karl. If Franz Ferdinand had lived, he would have ascended to the throne. Motivated by hatred of Hungarians and the *Ausgleich* of 1867, Franz Ferdinand would have sought to reduce the power of Hungary. He had considered several strategies toward this end, including a triple rather than dual monarchy that would include southern Slavs as the third "pole" and a looser form of federalism. The documents he had prepared for his succession indicate that he probably would have introduced universal suffrage in Hungary at the outset of his reign in the hope of increasing the power of minorities at the expense of the Magyars. This would have provoked a strong reaction from Budapest and any further attempts by Franz Ferdinand to undercut the *Ausgleich* would have raised the prospect of civil war. Even short of such a conflict, the constitutional crisis provoked by any of these measures would have made a war with Serbia appear a serious and unwanted distraction, not a solution to the country's domestic problems.[62]

One of the principal causes of war in 1914 was the German military's belief that it was inevitable and had to be fought before 1916 or 1917 when improved Russian mobilization and armaments would have made victory in France via an offensive through Belgium even more remote, if not altogether impossible. One alternative, a direct onslaught on France across the Meuse and Moselle had little chance of success because of the terrain and French fortifications. Count Alfred von Schlieffen contemplated such a campaign in 1894 but quickly gave up the idea as unrealistic.[63] Could Germany have conducted an offensive in the East? Russian railway and fortress construction made an Austro-German offensive in Poland difficult, but not impossible. However, it could not produce the kind of decisive victory that Moltke sought. If the Germans broached the Narew River line, the Russians could withdraw with relative ease into their vast hinterland.[64]

If offensives against Russia or France were unrealistic, the most sensible strategy was a defensive posture on both fronts; German generals knew that France and Russia planned to march against Germany at the outbreak of war. With no German invasion of Belgium, Britain would almost certainly have remained neutral.[65] German war games indicated that the French army would exhaust itself—as indeed it began to do in

1914—in a series of unsuccessful and costly assaults against the strong German defensive position in Alsace.[66] In the east, the Russian offensive into Prussia was blunted by the meager forces Germany had left in the region. Reserve forces could have conducted a limited counteroffensive, after which Germany could have called for a restoration of peace on the basis of the status quo ante bellum. It seems improbable that there would have been much support in France or Russia for continuing the war after a series of disheartening defeats. Nor could these powers have resisted British, and perhaps American, pressures to lay down their arms and accept a reasonable peace. Austria-Hungary would have been preserved, although the Russian empire might have succumbed to revolution. German preeminence on the continent would not only have been maintained but immeasurably strengthened.

Moltke was willing to tinker with details of his offensive plan but unwilling to consider alternatives. Other members of the general staff doubted the likelihood of victory in 1914 but most clung to the existing "Moltke plan" because of their collective commitment to the offensive.[67] By 1917, according to the calculations of the general staff, Germany would have had no hope of waging successful, sequential offensives against France and Russia. If war had been avoided in 1914, the contradiction between strategy and reality would have become ever more pronounced. Moltke or his successor would have been compelled to abandon Moltke's war plan. As funds for additional troops were out of the question and the concept and technology of the blitzkrieg had not yet been developed, there was no viable alternative to the defensive. The German general staff might have been compelled to adopt such a strategy, or some variant of it by 1917 or shortly thereafter. They would no longer have had any military incentive to launch a preventive war or preempt in crisis, although it is important to remember that they were motivated more by considerations of honor than by strategy and tended to see war as an end in itself.[68]

Military considerations were only one cause of German willingness to risk war in 1914. Moltke and the kaiser were motivated by their hatred of France and Britain respectively and the kaiser was also moved by questions of honor. When he pledged German support to Count Hoyos at their luncheon meeting on 5 July—undoubtedly the most crucial German decision of the crisis—he acknowledged Austria's need to preserve its national dignity in the face of an intolerable affront by Serbia. More than two weeks later, he was still furious at Serbia, writing on the margin of a cable that "Serbia is nothing but a band of robbers that must be seized for its crimes! I will meddle in nothing of which the Emperor [Franz Josef] is alone competent to judge![69] The next day he penned yet another revealing comment: "in *vital* questions and those of honor, one does not consult with others."[70] On 6 July in Kiel, the kaiser made an interesting confession to his friend Krupp von Bohlen und Halbach. He told the steel magnate: "This time I shall not cave in"—and repeated himself three times.[71] Perhaps Sarajevo had also become a matter of internal honor for Wilhelm, anxious to convince himself and others that he was a man of courage. Moltke did not have the power or influence to bring about war his own, or even with the support of Bethmann Hollweg. The kaiser's position was critical, and it seems unlikely, given his caution in past crises, that he would have assumed the risk involved in issuing the so-called blank check to Austria in the absence of the assassinations that made honor foremost in his mind so that he framed his role in the crisis as serving as a "second" to Franz-Josef in his forthcoming duel with Serbia.[72]

I have asked if a European war could have been delayed in the absence of an appropriate catalyst. Could it have come *sooner*? I am inclined to discount the prospect of an earlier war. Austria considered and rejected going to war with Serbia in December 1912, April–May 1913, and October 1913. Between 1905 and 1914, the kaiser and his chancellors spurned Moltke's repeated pleas to exploit great-power crises as pretexts for war. Austrian and German swords remained sheathed because political leaders in Berlin and Vienna saw war as politically and militarily risky and did not feel threatened enough to assume these risks.

If war had come earlier there is no systemic reason to suppose it would have had a different outcome. The biggest military change between 1909 and 1914 was the Russian railway construction that so worried the Germans. The German general staff would have felt more confident about war in 1910–1912, but whether their confidence would have kept Moltke from panicking, as he did in 1914, and given him the courage to adhere to the original invasion plan, are open questions. Gerhard Ritter does not think it would have made any difference; the war plan, he insists, left too much to chance.[73] Gordon Craig believes that Germany sorely misjudged the military capability of its adversaries, and even if the German army had achieved a battlefield success, it would not necessarily have been decisive for the outcome of the war. As we have seen, this was also the view of Field Marshal Moltke, who was pessimistic about the chances of victory.

Alternative Europes

How different would Europe and the world have been if the major powers had peacefully negotiated the first several decades of the twentieth century? The Great War accelerated the relative political and economic decline of Europe.[74] It sapped the continent's strength demographically by killing off so many men and leaving its generally undernourished population vulnerable to the great influenza pandemic of 1919; undermined

French and British will to fight another war; created the conditions for Hitler's rise to power and the vastly more destructive war he and Stalin would unleash; led to the Russian revolution, the Bolshevik coup, civil war and communist triumph that kept Europe divided for seventy years; hastened the emergence of the United States as the world's leading economic and military power; and accelerated demands for independence by Europe's colonies. Could any or all of these outcomes have been averted?

Let me edge toward a conclusion by identifying two of many possible futures for Europe. I do not want to make an argument for the contingency of World War I and then insist that some alternative world was systemically determined.[75] In the optimistic scenario, Europe avoids a First World War and enjoys decades of sustained economic development. Eastern Europe, not held back by two world wars and communism, begins to pull abreast of the West sooner rather than later.[76] Russia undergoes a revolution, loses most of its empire, and is governed by a quasi-authoritarian but capitalist regime. Like the countries of the Pacific rim in the late twentieth century, Russia and most of its successor states gradually evolve into more stable and democratic regimes as the result of economic prosperity and the emergence of a large, educated middle class and export-oriented business elite. Austria-Hungary survives, but under pressure from dissident nationalities and a democratic Germany, concerned about the consequences of unrest along its southern border, adopts a looser, federal structure despite Magyar opposition. Later in the century, European powers confront demands for independence in Africa and Asia, but decolonization works itself out in largely peaceful ways, and in the absence of a Cold War and ideological competition, most newly independent countries maintain reasonably amicable relations with their former metropoles. Europe remains the political and economic center of the world but confronts stiff economic competition from the United States and Japan. In response, the continent develops various forms of supranational cooperation and organization, something facilitated by nearly universal knowledge of German by the region's political, business, and intellectual elites.

The pessimistic scenario also starts from the premise that war is avoided. But Russia is consumed by a revolution that leads to prolonged civil war, and these events destabilize Austria-Hungary, leading Vienna and Budapest to rely on increasingly repressive measures to retain their empire and hegemony in the Balkans. Germany remains the preeminent military and economic power, consolidates its economic hold on eastern Europe, and achieves something akin to superpower status. Within Germany, democratic reforms at the national level are frustrated, and during a period of sharp economic downturn—a version of the Great Depression—an authoritarian regime comes to power in France and develops a "special relationship" with its German counterpart. Great Britain is increasingly isolated from "illiberal" Europe and moves closer to the United States. Two power blocs emerge—Anglo-America and a German-dominated continent—and the ideological and interest-based divisions between them lead to a prolonged Cold War, made more threatening by their mutual development of nuclear arsenals. An authoritarian Japan holds the balance and exploits this situation to expand its territorial and economic influence throughout the Pacific Rim. As the century ends, the millennium is greeted with great pessimism throughout the developed world. The number one book on the American best-seller list, Paul Kennedy's *The Rise and Fall of the Great Powers*, argues that war is inevitable.

Either future, or others I have not described, could have come to pass—if World War I could have been avoided. Social scientists and historians of a deterministic persuasion err in thinking that major social and political developments are invariably specific instances of strong, or even weak, regularities in social behavior. These developments are sometimes the result of accidental conjunctions; they are events that might have had a low subjective probability. Conversely, events that seem highly likely may never happen. The concatenation of particular leaders with particular contexts, and of particular events with other events is always a matter of chance, never of necessity.[77]

CONTINGENCY AND CAUSATION

I have argued that the origins of World War I are best understood as a confluence of three largely independent chains of causation that came together in 1914. Their confluence and consequences are best envisaged as the results of a complex, nonlinear system. The value of important variables was not independent, but depended on the presence and value of other key variables. It also depended on the changing understandings actors had of their strategic interactions. A linear model that specified the presence of A (the set of variables associated with the German security dilemma), B (the set of variables relevant for Austria's security dilemma), and C (Russian willingness to risk war to support Serbia) would capture only part of the strategic picture. The values of A, B, and C were determined by gestalt shifts that took place in 1909 in Russia and in 1914 in Austria-Hungary and Germany. The presence of A + B + C prior to these gestalt shifts would not have produced a war. Nor, I have argued, would their coincidence have been likely to do so after 1916 or 1917 if the political alignment in the Balkans had changed, if Russia's domestic situation had become more acute, or if the German offensive war plan had been replaced by a more defense-oriented alternative. War required the coincidence of A + B + C *after* the gestalt shifts and *before* important underlying conditions changed to produce further shifts. The catalyst for the C gestalt shift was Russia's perception of its humiliation in the 1908–1909 Bosnian Annexation Crisis, and for the A and B shifts, the twin assassinations at Sarajevo.

World War I is not unique in its nonlinearity. World War II, which brought about the next transformation of the international system, was also the product of a highly contingent set of conditions. Aggressive as Hitler was, it is more difficult to imagine Germany starting a war in a less fortuitous context. In the 1930s, France was divided internally and Britain and France were loath to collaborate with the Soviet Union. Because his imperial policy in Africa had run afoul of Britain, Mussolini abandoned his opposition to German expansion and entered into an alliance with Hitler. In the Far East, Japan attacked China and posed a serious security threat to the Soviet Union and the Western powers. Isolationism guaranteed that the United States, whose intervention had determined the outcome of World War I, was no longer a player in the European balance of power. Hitler could attack his enemies piecemeal, while counting on the support of Italy and the neutrality of the Soviet Union and the United States. The end of the Cold War—which brought about the third system transformation of the century—can also be described as the result of complex, path dependent, nonlinear interactions, and I will do so in the next chapter.[78]

International relations theory needs to consider multiple paths of causation and their possible interactions. Current theories of international relations almost invariably focus on one chain of causation even if they acknowledge it is only one pathway to war.[79] Power transition theory, for example, attempts to explain the outbreak of wars responsible for system transformations in terms of the changing power balance between hegemons and challengers.[80] One power transition theorist, Robert Gilpin, describes responses other than war for declining hegemons and acknowledges that choice among these options depends on context.[81] Realist attempts to explain the end of the Cold War encounter the same problem of indeterminacy. They accordingly elicit the criticism that they are being used to explain ex post facto what they did not and could not have predicted. The indeterminacy problem arises from the fact that considerations independent of the power balance shape actors' responses to an actual or anticipated increase or decline in their power or that of others.[82]

In 1914 power was only part of the story; shifts in the political and military balance may have made German and Austrian leaders more willing to consider the use of force but were insufficient cause for them to draw their swords. Power transition theory—or any other systemic explanation for system transformation—may be a useful analytical starting point but it is unlikely to offer much analytical purchase in and of itself. Other factors and causal chains and their interactions must be taken into account. Contingencies in the form of random events and conjunctures of multiple chains of causation are difficult to deal with theoretically. Random events, by definition, lie outside our theories, as do conjunctures, which in turn may be caused by random events. For this reason alone prediction in individual cases is an unrealistic goal. Conditional forecasting may be a more appropriate strategy for attempting to cope with the manifold uncertainties associated with as complex events as those responsible for system transformations. Conditional forecasts use existing theories and behavioral regularities as a starting point to develop alternative scenarios of likely future developments, or of a system transformation. They consider multiple chains of causation and look at some of the possible interactions that might take place among them, as well as the paths that might lead from one scenario to another. They also stipulate the kind of information or events that will be used to determine the extent to which events track according to the expectations of any of the scenarios. As events unfold researchers repeatedly revise their scenarios and expectations in light of the new information. Such a process is messy and time consuming, but it is the only reasonable way of taking into account coincidence and random events. At the very least, it can provide early warning of major changes in a system or of the faulty expectations of those who are tracking its performance.[83]

In many physical processes catalysts are unproblematic. Chain reactions are triggered by the decay of atomic nuclei. Some of the neutrons they emit strike other nuclei prompting them to fission and emit more neutrons, which strike still more nuclei. Physicists can calculate how many kilograms of Uranium 235 or Plutonium at given pressures are necessary to produce a chain reaction. They can take it for granted that if a critical mass is achieved, a chain reaction will follow. This is because trillions of atoms are present, and at any given moment enough of them will decay to provide the neutrons needed to start the reaction. Wars and accommodations, and the system transformations they may bring about, involve relatively few actors. And unlike the weak force responsible for nuclear decay, political catalysts are not inherent properties of the interacting units. For both these reasons, we can never know if or when an appropriate political catalyst will occur.

Political catalysts differ from their physical counterparts in another important respect. They are often causes in their own right, as was Sarajevo. The twin assassinations caused the Austrian leadership to reframe the problem of Serbia. Risks that had been unacceptable in the past now became tolerable, even necessary. The independent role of catalysts creates another problem for theories and attempts to evaluate them. All the relevant underlying causes for an outcome may be present but absent a catalyst it will not occur. The uncertain and evolving relationship between underlying and immediate causes not only renders point prediction impossible, it renders problematic more general statements about the causes of war and system transformations—and many other international phenomena—because we have no way of knowing which of these events would have occurred in the presence of appropriate catalysts, and we cannot assume that their presence or absence can be treated as random. It is thus impossible to define the universe of such events or to construct a representative sample of them.

The independent role of catalysts in some classes of events also renders statistical tests meaningless because of the impossibility of coding outcomes. If war is the dependent variable, researchers will distinguish between cases or interactions that ended in war from those that did not, and look for association between these outcomes and their independent variables. Their results will be misleading if war would have occurred in the presence of their variables if a suitable catalyst had been present. Meaningful statistical studies would require two stage data sets that accounted for this variation.

Theorizing about catalysts is difficult because they are often situation specific. It is nevertheless useful to distinguish between situations in which actors are actively looking for an excuse for war and those in which the catalyst reshapes the way they think about the situation, making them more willing than they were previously to consider high-risk options because of the greater perceived costs of inaction. Classic examples of the former include Hitler in 1939, Lyndon Johnson in 1964, and George Bush in 2003; all three leaders invented pretexts to go to war when their adversaries failed to provide them.[84] Sarajevo may be the paradigmatic case of the situation in which catalysts play important, independent roles.

Once again, the best way to address the problem of catalysts in specific contexts is likely to be through some form of scenario generation. Analysts can reason forward and ask themselves what kind of event(s) would be required to prompt behavior likely to bring about war, accommodation, and system change. Or, they can reason backward by identifying the kind of events most likely to occur and asking themselves if any of these would serve as effective triggers.

Most models of political behavior assume instrumental rationality and this may also be the norm in everyday decision-making. The evidence from both world wars and from the end of the Cold War suggests that this is not true for the series of decisions responsible for system transformations. In all these cases, the behavior in question led to results diametrically opposed to those intended by key actors, and there was ample information available at the time to suggest that this would occur. The pathology of German decision-making in the two world wars has been extensively documented. The Austrian case in 1914 is less well known, and provides another striking example of deviance from instrumental rationality. In a seeming fit of emotion Austrian leaders went to war to uphold the honor of the royal family, crush Serbia and remove the domestic and foreign threats to the security of their empire. They had no appropriate mobilization plan for coping simultaneously with Serbia, and Russia, and could not fight the short war they deemed essential. In a longer war, they recognized they would become increasingly dependent upon Germany, and end up losing the very independence they were fighting to maintain. More enigmatic still was their crisis policy that maximized the likelihood that Russia would intervene and confront them with the two-front war they knew they were unprepared to wage.[85]

Unintended consequences are sometime the emergent properties of systems.[86] As presently used in the international relations literature, the concept of emergent properties elides two different phenomena. The first, and most common, are the kind of outcomes that are unanticipated by individual actors and are the result of behavior based on instrumentally rational calculations of self-interest. These outcomes arise from the complicated ways in which systems aggregate the behavior of individual actors to produce a system-level effect. Adam Smith coined the term "invisible hand," and Hegel, the "cunning of reason," to describe this process. Their examples were benign, and Smith's invisible hand unintentionally gave rise to a tradition of justifying greed on the basis of its allegedly beneficial consequences for the society. "Trickle down" economics is a recent example, and an interesting one because it attempted—without success—to exploit our understanding of emergent properties to bring one about. Negative examples, which are probably more common than positive ones, include arms races, runs on banks, and the 1990s Asian financial crisis. The second kind of phenomenon, and the one most directly relevant to the argument of this chapter, is *doubly* unintended. Here, behavior has unintended consequences for the actors and the system as a whole. It sets in motion a chain of events that leads to the system's transformation. The July crisis and the Cold War had such an effect.[87] None of our theories, as presently constituted, can account for this outcome. Nor, more fundamentally, can Humean causation with its commitment to regularity determinism.

Niklas Luhmann suggests that systems are repertories of codes and that outside influences must be translated by the logic of the system to have an effect upon its operation.[88] Outside influences in economics are translated into prices. Simple systemic theories in international relations ignore outside effects. More evolutionary approaches to systems—Robert Jervis makes a nice case for them—acknowledge that the structure and operating principles of systems undergo fundamental shifts in response to *outside* stimuli. World War I and the end of the Cold War indicate that systems can also be transformed through their *internal* operations. These cases point to the existence of a self-referential loop by which actors change their understanding of themselves, the system, and how it operates.

The possibility of system change through reflexivity—not merely adaptation to so-called structural imperatives—has important implications for the study of social systems and international relations in particular.

This finding directs our attention to the understandings actors have of each other and of their environments, and how these understandings evolve and sometimes become widely shared, giving rise to the kind of intersubjective understandings that lie at the core of constructivism. If the balance of power was important in 1914, it was not because it is an enduring, underlying mechanism of international relations, as many realists allege, but because it was common parlance among national security elites and had become to some degree "naturalized" by them and affected their calculations and behavior. Reconstructing a problem from the perspective of participants also encourages us to look at understandings that are *not* shared and perhaps highly idiosyncratic, as was Franz Ferdinand's, and what they have to tell us about the how system works—or why it does not work as a majority of important actors expect.

As John Stuart Mill warned, majority opinions are not necessarily correct opinions. The same phenomenon is evident in politics and international relations. Widely shared expectations can be unrealistic, with unrealism defined here as erroneous expectations about the likely consequences of specific kinds of behavior. The 1914 case gives vivid testimony of this kind of error, and the principal reason it unintentionally brought about a transformation of the European, if not the international system, was the degree to which the many widely shared assumptions about how the system worked were fundamentally wrong. There are several reasons for faulty expectations of this kind. They can always have represented misunderstandings of how the system worked but attained subjective validity by virtue of faulty or self-serving interpretations of the past encouraged by ideological commitments, self-interest, and motivated bias. Expectations can be based on more realistic assessments of past outcomes and their causes, but widespread knowledge of this kind can make such outcomes difficult or impossible to obtain in the future. The so-called January effect, noted in chapter 1, is a well-known example in economics.[89] Another possibility is that the dynamics of the system can have changed in ways that actors fail to recognize making behavior that may have been likely to produce a particular outcome in the past more likely to produce a different, even opposite outcome in the present. Reflexivity is deeply implicated in the first two causes, while the last more or less requires its absence, at least with respect to the causes or dynamics in question.

These several phenomena and their related dynamics highlight the need for more sophisticated approaches to policymaking and its consequences. We need to develop better understandings of the motives that guide actors, and not assume as most of our theories do, that they are motivated by fear (realism), interest (liberalism), or the implications of policy for their power or authority (domestic politics). These motives—and the quest for standing and honor—vary across leaders, elites, cultures, and epochs. They have profound implications for the logics that leaders use to make sense of the world, the lessons they learn about their past behavior and that of others and their propensity for risk taking.[90] Understanding actors does not mean we can understand or predict the consequences of their behavior. These outcomes, require knowledge of the systems in which they operate, but also their shared and idiosyncratic understandings of how they think the system works, as outcomes at the systems level are ultimately the result of the interactions of their actors. Insights into system-level dynamics do no better in helping us understand behavior and outcomes in the absence of reasonable knowledge about the motives and subjective understanding of actors. An understanding of how actors behave and the consequences of their behavior requires knowledge at both levels of analysis, and analytical tools for combining this knowledge in productive ways.

Notes for Table 3.1

1. Sigmund Freud, *Civilization and its Discontents*, trans. Joan Riviere (London, Hogarth Press, 1951 [1930]).

2. Joseph Schumpeter, *Imperialism and Social Classes*, trans. Heinz Norden, ed. Paul M. Sweezy (New York: A. M. Kelly, 1951); Fritz Stern, *The Politics of Cultural Despair: A Study in the Rise of German Ideology* (Berkeley: University of California Press, 1961); Kenneth D. Barkin, *The Controversy over German Industrialization, 1890–1902* (Chicago: University of Chicago Press, 1970).

3. Luigi Albertini, *The Origins of the War of 1914*, ed. and trans. Isabella M. Massey (London: Oxford University Press, 1953) I, passim; Imanuel Geiss, *Julikrise und Kriegsausbruch des Ersten Weltkrieges*, ch. 1, for a general argument. Herwig, *The First World War*, ch. 1, on Austrian fears. Williamson, "Influence, Power, and the Policy Process" and "The Origins of World War I," argues the decisive factor that led Hungarian minister president Istvan Tisza to support war against Serbia was the argument that failure to resolve the Serbian problem would exacerbate Rumanian agitation in Transylvania. Lieven, *Russia and the Origins of the First World War*, stresses Pan-Slavism, and the associated policy of prestige, as the core motivating factor behind Russia's decision to face war in 1914.

4. Schumpeter, *Imperialism and Social Classes*.

5. V. I. Lenin, *Imperialism: The Highest State of Capitalism* (New York: International Publishers, 1939); Fischer, *Germany's Aims in the First World War*; Geiss, *Julikrise und Kriegsausbruch des Ersten Weltkrieges*; Kaiser, "Germany and the Origins of the First World War."

6. Kenneth N. Waltz, *Theory of International Politics* (Reading, Mass.: Addison-Wesley, 1979); David Stevenson, *The First World War and International Politics* (Oxford: Oxford University Press, 1988).

7. James Joll, *The Origins of the First World War* (London: Longman, 1984); David G. Herrmann, *The Arming of Europe and the Making of the First World War* (Princeton: Princeton University Press, 1996); David Stevenson, *Armaments and the Coming of War: Europe 1904–1914* (Oxford: Oxford University Press, 1996).

8. Albertini, *The Origins of the War of 1914* I; , Joll, *The Origins of the First World War*, argues that because Europe was divided into two distinct camps it became more important to win or maintain the support of smaller powers.

9. Joachim Remak, "1914—The Third Balkan War: Origins Reconsidered," *Journal of Modern History* 43 (September 1971), pp. 353–66, and Stevenson, *The First World War*, contend that a balance of power promoted peace, as it did in the Bismarckian system, where all the major powers save France were bound, directly or indirectly, to Germany. After 1891, the balance of power was replaced by an unstable bipolarity between opposing coalition and became an engine for catastrophe.

10. Herwig, *The First World War*, pp. 18–19; Williamson, "Influence, Power, and the Policy Process," "The Origins of World War I," and *Austria-Hungary and the Coming of the First World War*.

11. Schroeder, "World War I as Galloping Gertie," depicts the encirclement of Austria by a Russian-led Balkan coalition as the principal incentive for Vienna to attack Serbia in 1914. F. R. Bridge, *From Sadowa to Sarajevo: The Foreign Policy of Austria-Hungary, 1866–1914* (London: Routledge and Kegan Paul, 1972), pp. 335–36; Stevenson, *The First World War*; Karl Dietrich Erdmann, "War Guilt 1914 Reconsidered: A Balance of New Research," in Koch, *The Origins of the First World War*, pp. 343–70; Williamson, "Influence, Power, and the Policy Process," "The Origins of World War I," and *Austria-Hungary and the Coming of the First World War*; Herwig, *The First World War*, p. 18, consider foreign policy concerns only one of the factors influencing Austrian decision-making.

12. D. W. Spring, "Russia and the Coming of War," in Evans and Pogge von Strandmann, *The Coming of the First World War*, pp. 57–86.

13. Fischer, *Germany's Aims in the First World War*, maintains that this consideration prompted Moltke to push for war since 1905. See also Hilgruber, "Riezlers Theorie des kalkulieren Risikos und Bethmann Hollwegs politische Konzeption in der Julikrise 1914"; Stern, "Bethmann Hollweg and the War"; Jarausch, "The Illusion of Limited War," and *The Enigmatic Chancellor*; Mommsen, *Das Zeitalter des Imperialismus* and "Domestic Factors in German Foreign Policy Before 1914"; Herwig, *The First World War*, p. 19.

14. Schroeder, "World War I as Galloping Gertie: A Reply to Joachim Remak," *Journal of Modern History*, 44, no. 2, (September 1972), pp. 319–44, and "Austria-Hungary in the International System Before 1914: What Changes?" Paper presented at a conference on "The Origins of the Great War," Oakland, Calif., 24–26 April 1988, argues that the rules of the great power game changed at the end of the nineteenth century. Previously, the focus of imperialism had been outside of Europe and helped to preserve the peace. Now its focus became European and it had destructive impact.

15. Gerhard Ritter, *The Sword and the Scepter: The Problem of Militarism in Germany*, trans. Heinz Norden (Coral Gables, Fl.: University of Miami Press, 1970) vol. 2, pp. 107–09; H. W. Koch, ed., *The Origins of the First World War* 2nd ed. (Oxford: Oxford University Press, 1984), Introduction; Erdmann, "War Guilt 1914 Reconsidered," pp. 343–70.

16. Wolfgang Mommsen, "The Debate on German War Aims," *Journal of Contemporary History* 1 (July 1966), pp. 47–74; Laurence Lafore, *The Long Fuse: An Interpretation of the Origins of World War I* (Philadelphia: Lippincott, 1966); Miles Kahler, "Rumors of War: The 1914 Analogy," *Foreign Affairs* 58 (Winter 1979), pp. 371–96; Gerhard Ritter, *The Sword and the Scepter*, vol. 2, pp. 107–109; Jarausch, "The Illusion of Limited War"; Joll, *The Origins of the First World War*, p. 235.

17. Fischer, *Origins of the First World War.*

18. Avner Offer, "Going to War in 1914: A Matter of Honor?" *Politics and Society* 23 (June 1995), pp. 213–41; Lebow, *A Cultural Theory of International Relations*, ch. 7.

19. Arthur Rosenberg, *Imperial Germany: The Birth of the German Republic, 1871–1918*, trans. Ian Morrow (Boston: Beacon Pres, 1964), 58; Michael R. Gordon, "Domestic Conflict and the Origins of the First World War: The British and the German Cases," *Journal of Modern History* 46 (June 1974), pp. 191–226.

20. Arthur Rosenberg, *Imperial Germany*; Fischer, *Germany's Aims in the First World War*; Geiss, *Julikrise und Kriegsausbruch des Ersten Weltkrieges*, ch. 1; Arno J. Mayer, "Domestic Causes of the First World War," in Krieger and Stern, *The Responsibility of Power*, pp. 286–93; Paul M. Kennedy, *The Rise of Anglo-German Antagonism, 1860–1914* (London: Allen and Unwin, 1980); Geoff Eley, *Reshaping the German Right: Radical Nationalism and Political Change after Bismarck* (New Haven: Yale University Press, 1980); Hans-Ulrich Wehler, *The German Empire, 1871–1989*, trans. Kim Traynor (Birmingham: Berg, 1985); Volker R. Berghahn, *Germany and the Approach of War in 1914*, 2nd ed. (New York: St. Martin's Press, 1993).

21. Albertini, *The Origins of the War of 1914*; D. Stevenson, *The First World War and International Politics*; Williamson, *Austria-Hungary and the Coming of the First World War*; Fritz Fellner, "Austria-Hungary," in Keith Wilson, ed., *Decisions for War, 1914* (New York: St. Martin's Press, 1995), pp. 9–25; Gabor Vermes, *István Tisza: The Liberal Vision and Conservative Statecraft of a Magyar Nationalist* (New York: Columbia University Press, 1985); Herwig, *The First World War*, pp. 8–18.

22. Hans, Rogger, "Russia in 1914," in Walter Laqueur and George L. Mosse, eds., *1914: The Coming of the First World War* (New York: Harper and Row, 1966), pp. 229–53; Mayer, "Domestic Causes of the First World War"; Lieven, *Russia and the Origins of the First World War*; D. W. Spring, "Russia and the Coming of War."

23. Vladimir Dedijer, *The Road to Sarajevo* (New York: Simon and Schuster, 1966); Remak, "1914—The Third Balkan War."

24. Albertini, *The Origins of the War of 1914*, I; Ritter, *The Sword and the Scepter*, vol. 2, pp. 119–36.

25. L.C.F. Turner, *Origins of the First World War* (New York: Norton, 1970), "The Role of the General Staffs in July 1914," *Australian Journal of Politics and History* 11 (1965), pp. 305–23, "The Russian Mobilization in 1914," *Journal of Contemporary History* 3 (1968), pp. 65–88.

26. Albertini, *The Origins of the War of 1914*, vol. 2, pp. 485–90; Fischer, *Germany's Aims in the First World War*; Stern, "Bethmann Hollweg and the War"; Jarausch, "The Illusion of Limited War," and *The Enigmatic Chancellor*; Herwig, *The First World War*, p. 19, argues that civilian leaders as well as military leaders were dominated by a "strike-now-better-than-later" mentality.

27. Jack Snyder, "Civil-Military Relations and the Cult of the Offensive, 1914 and 1984," *International Security* 9 (Summer 1984), pp. 108–46, and *The Ideology of the Offensive: Military Decision Making and the Disasters of 1914* (Ithaca: Cornell University Press, 1984); Stephen Van Evera, "The Cult of the Offensive and the Origins of the First World War," *International Security* 9 (Summer 1984), pp. 58–107, and *The Causes of War: Power and the Roots of Conflict* (Ithaca: Cornell University Press, 1999), esp. ch. 2.

28. Ritter, *The Sword and the Scepter*, vol. 2, p. 197, and "Eine neue Kriegsschuldthese?" *Historische Zeitschrift* 194 (June 1962), pp. 657–68; Lancelot L. Farrar, *The Short War Illusion: German Policy, Strategy, and Domestic Affairs, 1914* (Santa Barbara: ABC-Clio, 1973); Williamson, "Influence, Power, and the Policy Process," "The Origins of World War I," and *Austria-Hungary and the Coming of the First World War*.

29. A.J.P. Taylor, *War by Timetable* (London: MacDonald, 1969); Paul M. Kennedy, ed., *The War Plans of the Great Powers, 1880–1914* (London: Allen and Unwin, 1979); Jack S. Levy, "Organizational Routines and the Causes of War," *International Studies Quarterly* 30 (June 1986), pp.193–222.

30. Albertini, *The Origins of the War of 1914*, I, passim.

31. Remak, "1914—The Third Balkan War; Jarausch," "The Illusion of Limited War," and *The Enigmatic Chancellor*.

32. Stern, "Bethmann Hollweg and the War"; Ritter, *The Sword and the Scepter*, II, "Eine neue Kriegsschuldthese?" maintains that Bethmann Hollweg only belatedly realized that an Austro-Serb conflict could not be localized and then discovered that he was bound by the Schlieffen Plan to invade Belgium; Fischer, *Germany's Aims in the First World War*; Hilgruber, "Riezlers Theorie des kalkulieren Risikos und Bethmann Hollwegs politische Konzeption in der Julikrise 1914"; Zechlin, *Krieg und Kriegrisiko*, argues that Bethmann Hollweg counted on British neutrality from the beginning of the crisis; Berghahn, *Germany and the Approach of War in 1914*; Herwig, *The First World War*, ch. 1.

33. Turner, *Origins of the First World War*, "The Role of the General Staffs in July 1914," and "The Russian Mobilization in 1914;" Richard Ned Lebow, *Between Peace and War: The Nature of International Crisis* (Baltimore: Johns Hopkins University Press, 1981), ch. 5; Mommsen, *Das Zeitalter des Imperialismus*; John C. G. Röhl, "Germany," in Keith Wilson, ed., *Decisions for War, 1914* (New York: St. Martin's Press, 1995), pp. 27–54; Herwig, *The First World War*, ch. 1.

34. Albertini, *The Origins of the War of 1914*, vol. 2; Ritter, "Eine neue Kriegsschuldthese?"; Fellner, "Austria-Hungary."

35. Lieven, *Russia and the Origins of the First World War*, suggests that Russian foreign minister, S. D. Sazonov, might have looked for a way of distancing himself from Serbia and war, especially given revulsion at the assassination in Berlin and London. Austria's failure to provide any kind of dossier, combined with a history of prior Austrian lies about Serbia, led Austrian claims of complicity to be regarded with suspicion by the Russian leadership.

36. Williamson, "Influence, Power, and the Policy Process," "The Origins of World War I," and Austria-Hungary and the Coming of the First World War; Herwig, *The First World War*, pp. 10–11; Kronenbitter, *Krieg im Frieden*, p. 483; Tunstall, "Austria-Hungary"; Lawrence Sondhaus, *Franz Conrad von Hötzendorf: Architect of the Apocalypse* (Boston: Humanities Press, 2000).

37. Albertini, *The Origins of the War of 1914*, II; Turner, *Origins of the First World War*, "The Role of the General Staffs in July 1914," and "The Russian Mobilization in 1914."

38. Williamson, "Influence, Power, and the Policy Process," "The Origins of World War I," and *Austria-Hungary and the Coming of the First World War*.

CHAPTER FOUR

Leadership and the End of the Cold War: Did It Have to End This Way?

Coauthored with George W. Breslauer

> Hinckley's bullet still lodged in Reagan's brain. Doctors foresee little chance of recovery. Vice President Bush assumes presidential authority.
> —*AP Bulletin, 21 March 1981*

> Central Committee of the Communist Party of the Soviet Union has unanimously elected comrade Viktor Grishin as General Secretary.
> —*Pravda, 6 March 1985*

IF THE NEWS REPORTS above had been real, there might have been no "Gorbachev phenomenon," and glasnost and perestroika might not have become households words. Led by a cautious and conservative general secretary, Grishin, the Soviet Union might have pursued a variant of Brezhnevism. The United States, led by an equally cautious and conservative president, Bush, might not have sponsored dramatic initiatives to break through the stalemate in superpower relations. The Berlin Wall might still be in place and communist parties still in power in Moscow and eastern Europe. The Warsaw Pact and NATO might be preparing to deploy a new generation of weapons because of the continuing deadlock in their arms-control talks. The Cold War could have remained alive and well.

If this counterfactual—or some variant of it—seems plausible, it is because we recognize that leaders often make a difference, and sometimes make a huge difference. A Soviet Union without Gorbachev, and a Soviet-American relationship without the personal empathy and trust that developed between Reagan and Gorbachev, and between George Schultz and Eduard Shevardnadze, might not be identical to the world depicted above, but it almost certainly would have been very different from the world that actually took shape between 1985 and 1991. Nor are East-West relations an isolated case. The Soviet Union without Stalin, France without de Gaulle, the Middle East without Anwar el-Sadat, or South Africa without De Klerk or Mandela could have adopted very different policies and likely have taken very different paths to the future.

The willingness of most political analysts and commentators to recognize the importance of leaders stands in sharp contrast to theories of international relations. These theories typically rely on "structural" variables for their analytical power. To explain the Gorbachev foreign policy revolution, realists invoke the international balance of power, or expectations of impending shifts in that balance. Liberals attribute the change to the interaction between states, structures, and ideas, and downplay the independent role of leaders, contingencies, and accidents.[1] International relations theorists generally seek to understand the most critical driving forces behind events; they almost invariably do so after the fact, when the outcome is known. The process of backward reasoning tends to privilege theories that rely on a few key variables to account for the driving forces allegedly responsible for the outcomes in question. Since, for the sake of theoretical parsimony, the academic discipline generally favors independent variables that are "structural" in nature, the entire endeavor has a strong bias toward deterministic explanations, thus distorting our understanding of the causes of events or accounts that are products of complex, conjunctional causality.[2]

In retrospect, almost any outcome can be squared with any theory unless the theory is rigorously specified. The latter requirement is rarely met in the field of international relations, and its deleterious effect is readily observed in the ongoing debate over the end of the Cold War. Various scholars, none of whose theories predicted a peaceful end to that conflict, now assert that this was a nearly inevitable corollary of their respective theories.[3] We observe a similar phenomenon in studies of the Middle East. Developments that seemed almost unthinkable before they happened—Sadat's trip to Jerusalem, the Palestinian-Israeli moves toward peace—are subsequently described as having been overdetermined by structural causes, particularly shifts in the relative balance of power.[4]

The disciplinary tendency to privilege structural explanations is reinforced by the well-documented human bias to exaggerate in retrospect the probability of an observed outcome.[5] By working back from the outcome, and from the known path to that outcome, we diminish our sensitivity to alternative paths and consequences.

In our opinion, both structure and agency are important. The challenge for analysts and theorists alike is not to choose between them but to develop a better understanding of their interaction. With this end in mind, we examine the role of leadership in ending the Cold War and do so through the use of two counterfactual thought experiments that are based on a sober assessment of the strength of structural constraints. Thus, we do not claim that "anything was possible," for counterfactual speculation must be disciplined by a realistic appreciation of the historical context that helped shape the observed outcome. We categorically reject the claim, made by many realists, that the economic decline of the Soviet Union required an accommodation with the West, and that almost any leader would have been compelled to pursue some variant of accommodation. The theoretical basis for such a claim is weak, and there is little empirical evidence to support it.[6] We begin by asking if different leaders in Washington and Moscow, operating under the same domestic and international constraints as Gorbachev, Reagan, and Bush, would have adopted different foreign strategies and tactics. Would those choices have led to different patterns of interaction between the Soviet Union and the United States, and between both of them and important third parties? Would this have made any difference for the trajectory of evolution of the superpower relationship?

Our counterfactual thought experiment addresses only the short- to middle-term: the five years following the death of Konstantin Chernenko in March 1985. The longer-term prospects of a Soviet Union that avoided disintegration in 1990–91 are another matter. It is conceivable that the collapse of communism in eastern Europe, the dissolution of the Warsaw Pact, and even the breakup of the Soviet Union would ultimately have occurred regardless of the strategies of the post-Brezhnev-era leadership. But even structural determinists will concede that there was nothing inevitable about the way in which these developments occurred or about their timing. We believe that process and timing were critical for the peaceful transition that occurred and the nature of subsequent relations between Russia and the West.

METHOD

Our chapter relies on plausible world counterfactuals. We use minimal rewrites to give us different leaders in power in Washington and Moscow in the 1980s and early 1990s. We do our best to make our counterfactuals meet the nine tests of good counterfactuals elaborated in chapter 2. They must be realistic, clear, logically consistent, not undercut by enabling counterfactuals, historically consistent, theoretically consistent, they must avoid the conjunction fallacy, recognize the interconnectedness of causes and outcomes, and consider second-order counterfactuals. The first condition—realism—deserves additional comment and elaboration given the nature of our experiment. This is because we devote as much attention to exploring the follow-on consequences of our counterfactuals as establishing them. Rather than attempting to draw one path between antecedent and consequent, we are interested in multiple possible pathways—that is, in the variation they might produce. We rely extensively on second-order counterfactuals arising from the interactions of leaders to produce this variation.

Realism, by it nature, is always case specific. There are nevertheless certain requirements of realism that transcend cases and suggest the kinds of counterfactuals we must invent to meet this criterion in individual cases. Realistic political counterfactuals should meet three tests: intellectual availability, practicality, and political feasibility.

Intellectual Availability

Policymakers depend on the state of social knowledge at the time to make sense of the world and the information they receive about it. Since the industrial revolution, governments might have been able to spend their way out of recessions and depressions through a program of public works, selective investment, and tax cuts, but this strategy was not intellectually available until the twentieth century. Since the 1970s, many governments have been attempting to coordinate their policies to deal with looming threats to the global environment; the intellectual grounding for such efforts was not available in the 1950s. To be sure, such knowledge is rarely consensual, definitive, or universally accepted. Hence, the availability of a body of knowledge does not ensure its acceptability. But absent its availability, counterfactual thought experiments, to be plausible, cannot posit a rewrite of the historical context that stipulates the presence of social knowledge that does not yet exist.

Practicality

A strategy or policy might be intellectually available, but impractical in light of the resources available at the time. Those resources are technological, organizational, cultural, economic, and the like. Thus, to be plausible, counterfactual reconstructions must not be based on technological anachronism; for example, neither the Soviet Union nor the United States had the capability to deploy a space-based antimissile system in the 1980s. Organizational, cultural, and financial constraints are nicely illustrated by Norman Naimark's research on Soviet policy in eastern Germany after World War II. Stalin did not have the option of employing a strategy analogous to that which the West employed in western Germany: of winning the hearts and minds of the population through an expensive policy of economic assistance. Naimark contends that Stalin's reliance on coercion and brutality to establish and maintain Soviet influence was not a choice but a necessity given the political-economic limitations of the Soviet system.[7]

The observer can stipulate the limits of practicality only within general bounds. Some technological anachronisms are obvious; some economic limitations are also relatively "hard" constraints. But other technological and economic constraints may be less "hard," while many organizational and cultural constraints can be "softer" and more ambiguous, subject to being changed or avoided by policies crafted for that purpose. Bold campaigns to overcome alleged constraints may marshal resources and attain ends previously thought impractical. Soviet campaigns under Stalin and Khrushchev occasionally did precisely this. And John Kennedy launched a campaign—ultimately successful—to land a U.S. astronaut on the moon within the decade.

Such campaigns may also fail, and thereby demonstrate the intractability of the constraints in question. But it is important not to assume that policymakers will define what is practicable in the same way as will scientific observers. The "fact" that something is impractical does not mean that policymakers won't try it. Khrushchev misjudged the ability of the Soviet Union to deploy missiles in Cuba without their being detected by the United States. American and Soviet leaders miscalculated the ability of their respective armed forces to prevail in Vietnam and Afghanistan. Similarly, the fact that something is practical and desirable does not mean that policymakers will necessarily recognize its practicality. For example, early in the Berlin crisis of 1948–49, the White House and State Department thought there was no way an airlift to Berlin could deliver enough food, fuel, and medicine to support the city and were therefore prepared to give in to Stalin's demands. Only when the U.S. Air Force demonstrated its airlift capability did minds change about the limits of the practical.[8]

Thus, if our purpose is to explain how different policymakers might have behaved, or how the same policymakers might have behaved differently from the way they did, we have to consider both the limits of the "hard," practical constraints within their environment and the factors that might induce them to test the limits of hard constraints, to stretch the limits of the softer constraints, or to miscalculate by overestimating or underestimating their practical capabilities.

Political Feasibility

Many policies that are intellectually available and manifestly practical are impractical for political reasons. Most leaders will only sponsor major departures from established policies, or ways of conducting them, when they believe there is a real need to do so *and* think they have, or can muster, political support for these changes. The availability of political support may seem obvious to the outside observer in extreme circumstances: for example, it is likely that no American president could have sustained or built support for near-term conciliation of the Soviet Union following the invasion of Afghanistan; similarly, it would have been extremely difficult for any Soviet leader to justify a strategy of conciliating the United States following the bombing of Hanoi and the Americanization of the Vietnam War in 1965. But political feasibility is often a softer constraint than that, and can depend on the skills of the leader in building support for alternative policies. Moreover, a leader's ability to wield these resources can be affected by fortuitous circumstances, whether stochastic events (e.g., the Chernobyl meltdown) or changes in other policy realms (e.g., good economic news). When we posit different leaders pursuing different policies, we must ask whether the leader would have had the skills to exploit beneficial circumstances. And we must recognize that political factors may push leaders to undertake initiatives they would have otherwise not chosen to pursue. Thus, just as the judgment of practicality combines elements of the objective and subjective, so judgments of political feasibility are indeterminate *to some extent*.

The concept of political feasibility also encompasses the beliefs and personalities of the leaders in question. A leader's personal opposition to an initiative for which political support might have been (or been made) available will often doom such an initiative. For example, it is hard to imagine either Leonid Brezhnev or George Bush committing themselves to minimal deterrence and the radical reduction of nuclear weapons it would have involved, or to the strategy of "GRIT"[9] and the initial, unilateral concessions necessary to set it in play. Leaders will adopt policies because they are compatible with their goals, views of the world, and interests—or because they judge them tactically necessary to achieve more important goals like staying in power. They may or may not be able to create or sustain political support for their policies. Hence, that which is deemed politically feasible at a given point in time will depend on its acceptability to both the leaders in question and their actual or potential support bases.

Altering the Leadership Equation

To carry out our counterfactual experiment we need to substitute other leaders for Ronald Reagan and Mikhail Gorbachev. These leaders— George Bush or a Democratic president in the United States, and Viktor Grishin, Grigori Romanov, or Yegor Ligachev in the Soviet Union— cannot arbitrarily be inserted into power by us. We must introduce plausible rewrites of history to arrange for their accession to power. In the case of George Bush, this is a relatively straightforward matter. If

Hinckley had been "lucky" or had had better aim, Vice President Bush would have moved into the Oval Office in accord with the provisions of the Twenty-fifth Amendment to the Constitution. We would not have to introduce any changes in the domestic and foreign political context, although the domestic context would have evolved differently under a new, unelected president who assumed office almost at the outset of a new administration.

Substituting a Democrat for Reagan requires more serious political intervention. Walter Mondale, or some other prominent Democrat, would have to win the 1984 presidential election. Any number of developments could have led to this outcome, and the simplest scenario continues to rely on John Hinckley's bullet. A few millimeters difference in its trajectory might have brought Bush to office in March 1981 and three years in which to alienate enough of the electorate for a Democratic opponent to unseat him. Reagan might have survived, but have been seriously impaired and stepped down after one term, giving the voters a choice between a popular Democrat and a Republican who had spent four years in the relative obscurity of the vice presidency. Alternatively, Reagan might have decided to run for a second turn, but have been rejected by voters in favor of a younger, more vigorous challenger.

How might we imagine a Soviet Union more or less the same but without Gorbachev at the helm? The easiest counterfactual to imagine is extend to the life of Andropov or Chernenko another five or six years. But we can go beyond this pathway, and eliminate generational continuity from our counterfactual scenarios. Gorbachev could have been chosen general secretary but assassinated shortly thereafter. This is not farfetched; there were assassination attempts on several Soviet party leaders, including Gorbachev, and any one of them might have succeeded.[10]

The Politburo could also have chosen someone other than Gorbachev in March 1985. This is a bit more difficult to imagine in light of recent evidence. The Kremlinological literature of the late 1980s generally described the selection of Gorbachev as a close call, with Viktor Grishin and Grigori Romanov regarded as the main competitors. This judgment was based on the limited, indirect evidence available at the time, coupled with mistaken assumptions about voting norms and voting behavior within the Soviet leadership.[11] More recent literature, based on the extensive memoirs by Gorbachev's associates, tends toward the conclusion that Gorbachev won easily and quickly.[12] To change this outcome, we would probably have to change the participants in the process. Defense Minister Dmitri Ustinov, one of the most powerful members of the leadership in the early 1980s, died suddenly in December 1984. If we posit his survival and involvement in the decision-making processes of March 1985, we may plausibly change the equation sufficiently to produce another outcome. We can readily imagine a coalition of the aged prime minister Nikolai Tikhonov, Foreign Minister Andrei Gromyko, and Defense Minister Ustinov teaming up to block Gorbachev and to support someone from the "younger" generation whom they perceived as less likely to oust them from their jobs. In this circumstance, it is at least plausible that the Politburo could have been induced to choose Grishin or Romanov as a "neo-Brezhnevite" successor. Alternatively, they could have dipped down into the ranks of recently promoted regional secretaries for a "neo-Andropovite" successor like Yegor Ligachev, who had a reputation for being incorruptible. Any of these alternative leaders could have served as general secretary for at least five to ten years.

To run a controlled counterfactual experiment we need to hold domestic constraints and opportunities and the foreign environment constant and vary only the leaders in power. But any of the scenarios that would make a Democrat president in January 1985 or bring to office a different Soviet general secretary seven weeks later require changes, some of them significant, in the political context in the two countries. We need to acknowledge the nature of these changes and take them into account as best we can as we conduct our thought experiments. What other changes might our changes have brought about—second-order counterfactuals— and how might they have altered the domestic and foreign policy environment or the consequences of any of the alternative strategies chosen by our substitute leaders?

Moreover, the end of the Cold War was the product of interaction among numerous actors, not just the United States and the Soviet Union. When contemplating alternative strategies and scenarios, we must inquire how our minimal rewrite of a portion of the history would have affected interactions with these third parties. Sensitivity to second-order counterfactuals, including the implications of different strategies for both alliances, will help us estimate whether the factors that propelled accommodation were so powerful that it would have come about regardless of the strategies pursued by either superpower. Or, could even minimal changes have led to very different outcomes? Naturally, we can only address these concerns in part in an article, and therefore will not delve deeply into the roles of random events and third parties. But we will be as explicit as possible about the most important second-order counterfactuals that might arise as a result of the historical changes we introduce.

THE NATURE OF THE U.S. AND SOVIET SYSTEMS

To conduct our counterfactual thought experiment, we need a theory, or at least a more explicit understanding of the domestic and international structures within which the superpower interaction took place. This provides the context within which leadership processes take place. Our theory of the nature of the structural constraints will influence our conception both of their malleability and of the extent of leadership skill required to stretch them.[13] If we posit different leaders in power in Moscow and Washington, the question then becomes: would other leaders have been as capable of stretching those structural constraints and of bringing the Cold War to an end?

The Soviet Union and the United States stood at the center of militarized alliance systems that sought to deter and intimidate each other through the brandishing and bolstering of their nuclear capabilities, competed with each other for influence and allies throughout the world, yet regularly sought to reduce the level of tension in their relationship in order to avert nuclear war. Their relationship, then, was largely confrontational and competitive, but it contained as well an underlying collaborative dimension, once both political elites came to appreciate the dangers of an uncontrolled nuclear competition. The collaborative dimension periodically came to the fore in the form of summit meetings, arms control negotiations, and "détentes" (1955, 1959, 1963–64, 1971–75) of varying scope and length. Until the late 1980s, collaboration always remained subordinate to competition.[14]

The Cold War was neither static nor cyclical. Despite the repeated failure of efforts at comprehensive détentes, the conflict had changed significantly before Gorbachev came to power in 1985. Collective learning had taken place on both sides about the dangers of nuclear confrontation, the utility of arms control, the other side's approach to competition and collaboration, and the internal constraints affecting their own and their adversary's strategic and foreign policies.[15] Gorbachev's dramatic initiatives thus built upon prior achievements—both the substantial accomplishments in arms control and crisis-management and the evolution of views on both sides about their rivalry and its possible consequences. It is difficult to imagine that Gorbachev or any other Soviet leader would or could have embraced such a far-reaching agenda in the 1950s or 1960s. Neither the intellectual nor the political conditions were as yet propitious. Nevertheless, Gorbachev's efforts to conciliate the United States, end the Cold War, and transform the international system represented a quantum leap in accommodation. He sought to transcend manifold remaining constraints and to break out from almost fifty years of a competitive relationship. To make a difference, his initiatives had to be dramatic and far-reaching, for the international system remained polarized and fraught with distrust.

The Cold War international system reinforced or shaped the domestic politics in Moscow and Washington. The Soviet and American security establishments came to share some basic features, even though they differed sharply from each other in other ways. Common features included: (1) the nature of entrenched interests; (2) the structure of the dominant foreign policy ideology; and (3) the locus of policymaking authority. In both systems, the needs of the military and its associated industries usually received priority access to scarce resources, though to a far greater degree in the Soviet than in the American system. Although the American liberal and Soviet Leninist ideologies were diametrically opposed in content, they were, or became, strikingly parallel in form. They were progressive, optimistic, and missionary in seeking to influence others to reconstruct themselves in their image. In content, each ideology defined the other as its enemy; subsidiary, prescriptive ideologies of "anti-imperialism" and "anti-communism" justified struggle and competition and put the burden of proof on those who wanted to subordinate the competitive to the collaborative side of the relationship.[16] The locus of policymaking had always been highly centralized in the Soviet Union's Politburo or party leader. In the United States, the Cold War concentrated power over foreign and security policy in the executive branch and the office of the president.

To be sure, the differences between the systems were fundamental. The United States was an open society based on a commitment to individual freedoms, whereas the Soviet Union was a closed society that relied heavily on political repression. One political system dispersed political authority in the form of checks and balances among several branches of government, while the other concentrated authority in the highest levels of one institution (the Communist Party of the Soviet Union). Other differences are less obvious, but important to an appreciation of constraints on change in the relationship. In the United States, presidents were elected to fixed, but short (four-year) terms; in the Soviet Union, general Secretaries were chosen by a cabal of high-level officials for open-ended periods of office. Barring impeachment, incapacitation, or death, a U.S. president could govern in the certainty that he would remain in office until the end of his term, and might serve a second term if his electoral mandate was renewed. A Soviet party leader could *hope for* a very long period in power, but always had to worry about the possibility of being overthrown by an elite grouping. The difference in expected time-in-office, and in the nature and intensity of political insecurity, complicated efforts to coordinate superpower policies. Among other things, the authority-maintenance needs of the Soviet and American leaders were not always synchronized. For example, it was usually quite difficult for progress in U.S.-Soviet collaboration to take place before or during a presidential election campaign. Similarly, it was especially difficult to reach accommodations with Soviet leaders during the first year or two of a political succession struggle, when political opportunism ran high and the winning candidate was attempting to consolidate his power by placating hard-line constituencies.[17]

Ending the Cold War required a fundamental restructuring of the international system, and this could only be accomplished by overcoming manifold institutional, procedural, and ideational constraints. In short, it required *innovative, perhaps visionary, leadership.*[18] Absent Gorbachev and Reagan, would such leadership have been available?

The Superpowers' Policy Repertoires

To avoid embracing fanciful counterfactuals, we must explore the range of general options available to each superpower by the early 1980s. By that time, the Cold War had been raging for more than three decades. Many efforts at détente had been attempted and had collapsed, though with legacies that left certain agreements and institutions in place. By 1980–81, the United States had reverted to a posture of irreconcilable antagonism, while Soviet leaders, confused and concerned, were searching for a response. To understand what policies at the time were intellectually available, capable of being implemented, and politically feasible within each capital, we need to explore the general options or postures available at the time.

Realistic Soviet Options

When Ronald Reagan was elected president in November 1980, Mikhail Gorbachev was almost four and a half years away from being chosen general secretary. Indeed, Gorbachev would not become the Soviet leader until seven weeks into Reagan's second term. President Reagan's first term in office was marked instead by his having to deal with three aged and sickly Soviet leaders: Leonid Brezhnev (until November 1982); Yuri Andropov (until February 1984); and Konstantin Chernenko (until March 1985). During these years, Soviet leaders tried a series of approaches to parrying, countering, or defusing the threat from Reagan's conventional, nuclear, and space-based military buildup, his active support for anti-communist insurgencies in the Third World, and his apocalyptic rhetoric.[19] At various times, and in varying combinations, they pursued five types of policies:

1. *Confrontation*: Upping the ante by answering militancy with militancy and confronting the adversary with the potentially escalatory costs of intransigence. This may take the form of either threats or actions

or both. The Soviets repeatedly threatened to match Reagan's military buildup in kind or with offset measures. They boycotted arms-control talks beginning in November 1983. In spring 1984 they initiated a series of incidents with escalatory potential: maneuvers by the largest Soviet fleet ever seen assembled in the Norwegian Sea and North Atlantic; a buildup of missile-bearing submarines off the East Coast of the United States; ramming of an American naval vessel on the high seas; mugging of an American consular official in Leningrad; interference with air traffic in the Berlin corridor; and others.[20]

2. *Competition*: Avoidance of confrontation, but support for initiatives likely to undermine the adversary's positions, weaken and divide its coalitions, and undercut political support for its policies. During 1981–83 , for example, the Soviets sought to mobilize and sustain peace movements in western Europe in their opposition to the deployment of Pershing-II and cruise missile deployments.

3. *Temporization*: Watching and waiting while doing nothing likely to escalate or deescalate the confrontation. This strategy assumes that with time the situation may clarify or even turn to one's advantage. In the meantime, leaders do nothing that incurs great risks or costs. This was essentially the Brezhnev leadership's response in 1981–82 to the Reagan arms buildup.[21]

4. *Retrenchment*: Selectively cutting losses in realms that are not central to the conflict. Shortly after the Korean Airline incident in September 1983, Andropov imitated a behind-the-scenes review of Soviet foreign policy, especially policy toward the West. Although he did not live to implement the results of that review, Andropov intended to use it as a prelude to retrenchment.[22]

5. *Conciliation*: Offering concessions to the adversary in the main realms of superpower relations in order to break the confrontational deadlock and foster cooperation. The Brezhnev, Andropov, and Chernenko administrations all offered partial concessions in their terms for nuclear-arms-control agreements in hopes of inducing Western compromises. President Reagan still found their terms unacceptable.

Behind the scenes in Moscow during the early 1980s, all five options were being discussed and advocated by powerful political actors. These options were not mutually exclusive. One strategy could be pursued in one realm of foreign policy (e.g., retrenchment in the Third World) and another elsewhere (e.g., political competition in Europe and military confrontation in arms control). Strategies could also be sequenced within the same policy realm. A leader might consider following either retrenchment or confrontation with conciliation if the first strategy influenced the adversary to be more receptive to the proposed terms for cooperation.

By the time Chernenko lay dying in January–February 1985, none of these approaches had yielded fruit for Moscow. President Reagan had won reelection in a landslide; the deployment of new U.S. missiles in western Europe was proceeding apace, and the western European peace movement against deployment had failed; the more general Reagan military buildup had been financed and sustained by Congress, and the Strategic Defense Initiative ("Star Wars") remained in place; the Soviet Union was more deeply mired in Afghanistan, with no victory in sight; and Soviet policy in the Third World was increasingly controversial within the policymaking elite. Even the conciliation strategy, limited by the Brezhnevite premise of "offensive detente,"[23] had found no taker in Reagan. It would be reasonable to suppose that the Soviet establishment would be collectively primed for, and consensually receptive to, some new thinking.

This was not the case. In February 1985, Gorbachev and Politburomember Romanov engaged in polemics over what should come next in Soviet policy toward the United States. Gorbachev alluded to the necessity for, and the feasibility of cooperation; Romanov spoke of the irreconcilability of imperialism and the inevitability of confrontation.[24] Gorbachev's perspectives were consistent with a strategy of conciliation intended to break the dangerous deadlock in superpower relations. Romanov's perspectives implied some combinations of confrontation, competition, and retrenchment. Many others within the leadership were the fence-sitters, who shied away from either escalation or far-reaching conciliation, and who would likely have settled, at least in the near term, for a strategy of temporizing.

Realistically then, three, not five general strategies for dealing with the U.S.-Soviet deadlock were being advocated within the Soviet leadership in March 1985 when Gorbachev came to power. These were: (1) a hardline strategy of confrontation and competition, accompanied perhaps by selective cutting of losses (retrenchment) in some Third World hotspots; (2) an accommodative strategy that combined conciliation and retrenchment; and (3) a temporizing strategy of selectively cutting losses while avoiding any sharp turns toward either confrontation or conciliation in the principal theaters of confrontation: Europe and arms control. For ease of reference, we will refer to these three options as confrontation, conciliation, and temporization. These same general strategies were being debated in Washington at the time. Our first counterfactual thought experiment therefore will examine alternative scenarios based on the choice of different strategies by one or both superpowers.

The three foreign policy strategies we described were not unrelated to different orientations toward key domestic issues. In the Soviet Union, the confrontational strategy tended to correlate with advocacy of hardline policies on the domestic front: a continuing crackdown on political dissent, disciplinary-mobilizational policies toward labor, anticorruption campaigns among officials, and budgetary aggrandizement of the military-industrial complex. The conciliatory strategy tended to correlate with selective liberalization of the polity and economy. The temporizing strategy was consistent with a wide range of domestic policies. It could have been accompanied by a hold-the-line strategy in defense of central planning and party control, including the kinds of tinkering with the economic system that Brezhnev engaged in, but without a radical swing to either the "left" or the "right." Temporization could also have followed the "Chinese model," which combined partial liberalization and opening of the economy with the maintenance of tight political controls. Within the Soviet political establishment in 1984–85, advocates of all of these approaches could be found.[25]

Realistic American Options

Ronald Reagan was elected president in November 1980 promising to rebuild U.S. defense capability and to reassert the country's standing as a global superpower. His perspective on international affairs was a reaction against the so-called post-Vietnam "syndrome" of the 1970s. Nor was this sentiment confined to the Republican party. President Carter had already begun a defense buildup in 1980, embargoed grain sales to Moscow, and endorsed other confrontational and competitive initiatives in the wake of the Soviet invasion of Afghanistan in December 1979. With the exception of his reversal of the grain embargo, President Reagan continued and intensified his predecessor's policy of confrontation, initially kept diplomatic contacts limited, used more offensive rhetoric, accelerated the arms buildup, and publicly considered disavowing previous arms-control treaties and agreements.[26]

If our thought experiment is based on the plausible counterfactual that Hinckley's bullet ended Reagan's life or incapacitated him just two months after he became president,[27] we have to ask whether George H. W. Bush's policies of 1981–85 would have been any different from the determinedly confrontational line followed by Ronald Reagan. We noted that Brezhnev, Andropov, and Chernenko variously adopted five different policy postures in different policy realms at different times. It seems likely that Bush, whose temperament, beliefs, self-confidence, and political authority within the Republican party were quite different from Reagan's, would have responded in a more differentiated way than did Reagan. Like his Soviet counterparts, Bush would have had five strategies to choose among, or combine, at each point of decision: confrontation, competition, temporization, retrenchment, and conciliation. We view George Bush as more cautious and insecure, both personally and politically, than Ronald Reagan; as more ambivalent a personality; and as a more complex, but less visionary, thinker than Reagan (on which, more below).[28] Hence, we deduce that Bush would have been unlikely to initiate any major policy departure on his own, and slower than Reagan—which indeed was the case—in reciprocating a Soviet strategy of accommodation. It also follows that he would likely have responded in kind to a Soviet strategy of competition or temporization, but could have replied to Soviet retrenchment with a strategy of either competition or temporization. Each of these options was intellectually available and practical: they were all part of the repertoire of postures the United States had adopted in some policy realms at various stages of the Cold War. None of them exceeded U.S. capabilities in 1981–85. Their *political* availability, however, is less certain. Anti-Soviet sentiments surged among the U.S. public and Congress following the Soviet invasion of Afghanistan, and were further fanned by Carter's reaction to the invasion and Reagan's campaign rhetoric.[29] Reagan came into office after a landslide victory, while promising to turn the tide in world affairs. All this, plus the sentiment generated by Reagan's hypothetical death or incapacitation in March 1981, would have made it difficult, perhaps prohibitive, for his Republican successor to embrace a strategy of conciliation, even if he were so inclined.

But while the legacy probably ruled out, at least in the near term, most conciliatory U.S. initiatives, it did not determine which of the four alternatives to conciliation would be embraced. Reagan's personality, perspectives, and popularity inclined him toward extreme confrontation and competition in 1981–82; Bush's ambivalences, moderate Republicanism, and lesser popularity might have inclined him, in that same time period, toward a less sweeping strategy of confrontation, less extreme rhetoric ("evil empire") and policies (Star Wars), and even perhaps toward selective reciprocation of Soviet temporization. The latter choice might also have been made attractive by Brezhnev's death in November 1982, and his successor's initial softening of Soviet terms for an arms-control agreement and signaling that a reconsideration of Soviet Third World policy was under way. The growing strength of peace movements in western Europe and the related worries of key western-European leaders would have added another point of pressure on hypothetical President Bush to avoid confrontation, to temporize on matters like Euromissiles, and perhaps cautiously to explore the intent behind Soviet conciliatory gestures. By contrast, President Reagan dug in his heels in the face of all these obstacles and held out for maximal Soviet concessions. He announced his Strategic Defense Initiative only four months after Andropov came to power and pushed forward vigorously with deployment of the Pershing-2 and a new generation of cruise missiles in western Europe.

There was considerable diversity within the Republican party and the Reagan administration by the time Gorbachev came to power in early 1985. Like the Gorbachev Politburo, officials within the Reagan administration—and leading Republicans more generally—advanced quite different policy agendas and not infrequently worked at cross purposes with one another.[30] Gorbachev was perceived by some members of the Reagan administration as a skillful and dangerous master of public diplomacy whose goals were fundamentally similar to those of his predecessors. As "Gorbymania" swept Europe and North America, those officials worried that the Atlantic Alliance would weaken and that public support would diminish for nuclear weapons, large military budgets, and the hardline policies they thought essential to constrain and weaken the Soviet Union. Confrontation was also advocated by a minority of officials who acknowledged Gorbachev's interest in some kind of meaningful accommodation. Like Eisenhower and Dulles in 1953–54,[31] they read Soviet gestures as driven by weakness and considered it useful to hold out for more far-reaching Soviet concessions. Still another group of officials in the second Reagan administration, and much of the conservative media, doubted that Gorbachev's initiatives were "for real"; at best, they were temporary measures dictated by political circumstances and intended to strengthen the Soviet Union and permit renewed confrontation. These officials recommended a "wait and see" attitude—a strategy of temporization. And it took Ronald Reagan himself several years before he concluded that Gorbachev's foreign policy concessions and domestic liberalization had gone far enough to warrant treating them as significant changes.

The diversity of perspectives and personalities within the government would have provided a hypothetical President Bush with some wiggle room to pursue a less confrontational approach toward the Soviet Union in the years 1981–84. The temper of American politics, as well as Bush's personality, however, probably would have ruled out a substantially conciliatory U.S. response to Soviet gestures. Given the history of the Cold War to that point, it is also unlikely that any reduction of tensions—or mutual forbearance—in the early 1980s would have broken down the Cold War system or significantly altered the interests and ideologies in both countries that sustained that conflict. The Soviets under Brezhnev, Andropov, and Chernenko would not have abandoned "old thinking" or reduced the budget of the military-industrial complex. Nor would the United States, given the temper of the times. However, a president inclined toward conciliation—whether a reelected George Bush or a newly elected Walter Mondale—might increasingly have regained his freedom of action as a result of Gorbachev's domestic and foreign initiatives and the overwhelmingly favorable reaction they elicited from the American electorate and European leaders.

TABLE 4.1
Strategies and outcomes

Strategies	Short-term Outcomes
Soviet confrontation vs. U.S. confrontation Soviet confrontation vs. U.S. temporization Soviet temporization vs. U.S. confrontation	Possible intensification of the Cold War
Soviet temporization vs. U.S. temporization	No change
Soviet temporization vs. U.S. conciliation Soviet conciliation vs. U.S. temporization Soviet conciliation vs. U.S. conciliation	Amelioration of relations
Soviet conciliation vs. U.S. confrontation Soviet confrontation vs. U.S. conciliation	Unpredictable Fanciful Counterfactual

ALTERNATIVE SCENARIOS OF INTERACTION

We now formalize and extend some of these scenarios by looking beyond the specific strategies available to each superpower to examine alternative scenarios of bilateral interaction among them. For the sake of convenience, and because several strategies could be pursued simultaneously in different realms of policy, we collapse the five strategies into three: confrontation (a combination of confrontation and competition), temporization (a combination of temporization and retrenchment), and conciliation. We play off each of the three Soviet strategies with their three American counterparts, for a total of nine possible combinations (see table 4.1), and analyze the likely consequences of these different combinations for the course of East-West relations from 1985 to 1990. We also discuss how subtraction of Gorbachev or Reagan—or both—from the equation might have influenced the acceptability and political availability of each of the strategies. The stage is set by Reagan's (or, hypothetically, George Bush's) first term as president, and by the assumption that the American strategy during that term was, and would have been, largely confrontational. Our combinations therefore begin with Soviet policy following Chernenko's death in March 1985.

Soviet Confrontation and American Confrontation

Another Soviet leader—Romanov, for example—might have responded to "evil empire" Reagan or "enough is enough" George Bush with a strategy of confrontation based on a determination to confront the adversary, "tit-for-tat," with the costs of its intransigence.[32] Politically, this strategy would have been most appealing to a general secretary who considered Cold War tensions a useful means of building political support at home, keeping dissidents in line, and deflecting attention from the Soviet Union's many structural problems. Soviet confrontation could have taken many forms: an extension of the war in Afghanistan that included attacks against guerrilla training bases in Pakistan, increased harassment of domestic opponents and American media and diplomatic representatives, the use of force against nationalist and anticommunist movements in eastern Europe, acceleration of the arms race—all accompanied by a drum-beat of anti-American and "anti-imperialist" rhetoric.

Under this scenario, the Cold War almost certainly would have intensified, to the advantage of the military-defense establishments of both superpowers. There would have been few contacts between leaders of the superpowers—basically, the state of affairs during Reagan's first term—and certainly no arms-control negotiations, let alone agreements. Continued East-West confrontation, made more acute by mutual arms buildups, could have led to a crisis of the magnitude of Berlin in 1961 or Cuba in 1962. Suppose that Reagan had broken out of the ABM Treaty and that he or his successor had ignored stern warnings from Moscow and proceeded to deploy components of a space-based antimissile system. Even Gorbachev, who was publicly committed to oppose any such deployment, worried that such a challenge could lead to a missile crisis in reverse.[33]

A leader with the militarist perspectives of Romanov would likely have brought out the hard-line side of George Bush or Walter Mondale, making it politically almost impossible, and ideologically undesirable, for an American president to do anything but respond in kind, at least initially.

Soviet Confrontation and American Temporization

This is the flip side of Reagan's first term, when the Soviets generally temporized in the face of an American political-military challenge. Temporization might have been judged an appropriate response by a president who believed that reciprocal confrontation would only make the Cold War worse, strengthen hard-line forces in Moscow, and risk drawing the superpowers into a war-threatening crisis. At best, it would have bought time and facilitated the return of a more moderate leader to the Kremlin. Given the nature of American politics, temporizing in the face of repeated Soviet provocations would have been extremely difficult to justify to the American people.

Soviet Confrontation and American Conciliation

Some conflict-management strategies like GRIT recommend cooperation as a possible response to defection. But it seems implausible that a
president would have wanted to or could have pursued the strategy of
conciliation in a sustained way. A Democratic president would have been
accused of appeasement, and a Republican president would have confronted great opposition from within his own party and administration.

Soviet Temporization and American Confrontation

This was the reality of Reagan's first term. Relations deteriorated between
the superpowers and between the United States and its allies, particularly the Federal Republic of Germany. Soviet temporization was based
on the premise that little could be accomplished with a hard-line, hostile president. It also reflected the stasis of Brezhnev's last years and the
fragile health of his successors. If Gorbachev, or some other successor to
Chernenko, had continued to pursue a strategy of temporization, it seems
unlikely that much, if any progress would have been made in East-West
relations. As part of a strategy of temporization, Soviet leaders likely
would have sought to exploit politically growing disagreements within
the Western alliance, and might have selectively cut Soviet losses in Third
World hot spots. The net result might have been to raise the heat on an
intransigent American president from critics within Congress and western Europe, especially if the campaign were waged by a Soviet leader with
the public relations savvy of a Gorbachev.

In this scenario, the Cold War would have remained very much alive,
but its focus would have shifted to the political arena and could have put
a hard-line American administration with a penchant for bellicose rhetoric very much on the defensive. Given the political weight of Cold War
constituencies in the United States and western Europe at the time, however, it is difficult to imagine an American president—be it Reagan, Bush,
or Mondale—forced into unwanted, significant concessions on arms control and other issues central to the relationship in the absence of concrete
and far-reaching Soviet concessions in arms-control negotiations.

Soviet Temporization and American Temporization

This combination could have developed out of the previous scenario.
The political heat generated in Washington from a successful Soviet political campaign and selective retrenchment in the Third World might

have encouraged an American president to back away from confrontation when he came to realize that it played into his opponent's hand. Allied leaders, especially in western Europe, would undoubtedly have pushed for such a change when they found themselves stretched between their commitment to NATO and a public increasingly disenchanted with the United States. An American policy of temporization might have been the fall-back position after an American policy of confrontation in the face of Soviet temporizing.

Alternatively, both superpowers could simultaneously have chosen to pursue wait-and-see strategies in early 1985, motivated by domestic or foreign calculations. Leaders might have preferred to direct their time and energy to pressing domestic concerns unrelated to Cold War issues, and therefore might have attempted to keep foreign policy issues off the agenda. Leaders might also have chosen to temporize if they believed that the other side was uninterested in accommodation and that they could only lose politically at home by pursuing a strategy of conciliation. In this circumstance, arms competition and the struggle for influence would probably have continued in a muted way unless the independent action of third parties created some kind of undesired crisis. But such mutual temporization would likely have been temporary, as the growing costs of an arms race led to growing pressure on one or the other side to "do something" of either a confrontational or conciliatory nature to break the logjam.

Temporization could be the term to characterize much of Gorbachev's policy toward the United States in 1985. The response of the Reagan administration was to continue the policies of the first term until Moscow became conciliatory. It is conceivable, however, that a President Bush or Mondale would have been more inclined to temporize instead. But, as we have suggested, that in itself would have been insufficient to transform the relationship.

Soviet Temporization and American Conciliation

Soviet temporizing could have prompted an American strategy of conciliation. If the political heat from within western Europe threatened a crisis within the alliance, and that pressure was intensified by Soviet cutting of losses in the Third World, as well as the realization that the Soviets had not chosen to match the American military buildup of Reagan's first term, an American president might have chosen to respond to Soviet temporizing with genuinely conciliatory measures. The result of this interaction might have been Soviet adoption of a conciliatory strategy and a "virtuous circle" of mutual accommodation.

But American efforts at conciliation could have elicited other responses depending on the underlying reasons for Soviet temporization. If caution had been motivated by doubts about the United States being a willing or reliable partner, presidential efforts at conciliation could have reassured a Soviet leader and helped him to build domestic support for reciprocal gestures. If temporization was primarily a response to domestic consider- ations, conciliatory policies could have created something of a dilemma for a relatively new general secretary in the process of consolidating his power, all the more so if he derived support from more conservative ele- ments within the Communist party. For a general secretary committed to shifting resources from national security to other sectors of the economy, however, American efforts at conciliation would have been helpful.

Moreover, it is unclear whether, in the mid-1980s, a U.S. president would have been inclined to adopt a strategy of conciliation absent a So- viet conciliatory posture. On this score, we are challenged to demonstrate that a conciliatory counterfactual does not do violence to the history of the period. Perhaps it is plausible to contend that neither Bush nor Mondale would have had the self-confidence that Reagan had to stand fast until his maximal demands were met. Either of them might have responded to growing domestic and European demands for progress in U.S.-Soviet relations with a policy of conciliation in response to the growing political costs to the U.S. president of a successful Soviet strategy of temporization. Absent a rapid Soviet reciprocation of that conciliation, however, it is difficult to imagine this strategy being sustained.

The three remaining scenarios of interaction, all of which posit a So- viet strategy of conciliation, violate the premise with which we began this section: that, absent Gorbachev, Soviet policy would not have turned conciliatory to any great extent.

Soviet Conciliation and American Confrontation

This was the state of U.S.-Soviet relations in 1986–87. Soviet conciliation amounted to movement toward acceptance of unequal terms in arms- control treaties, liberalization of human rights policies, and movement toward retrenchment or cutting of losses in the Third World, including Afghanistan. If President Reagan had responded to Soviet conciliation by continuing to raise the ante in negotiations, by refusing to strike deals that would abandon U.S. military deployments, and by continuing to increase the military pressure on Soviet positions in the Third World— and some of his advisors urged him to do this—it seems unlikely that the Cold War would have moved rapidly toward resolution. Gorbachev might have found it difficult to maintain support within the Politburo for a sustained policy of unreciprocated conciliation. Hard-liners might have found it easier to mobilize support within the leadership against domestic changes that threatened to weaken the Soviet Union. In every way, Gorbachev would have been more constrained, and might have had to fall back on a foreign policy of temporization. Or, worse, he might have been replaced by a hard-line leadership that promptly abandoned both domestic reform and foreign accommodation.

It also seems clear that political opposition to an American posture of confrontation would have risen greatly and rapidly. The Reagan administration would have found it increasingly costly politically to continue its all-round confrontation of the Soviet Union in the face of Gorbachev's conciliatory behavior and clever public relations. "Gorbymania" would have put considerable pressure on first Reagan and then Bush to adopt more conciliatory policies.

This scenario is counterfactual in the sense that it alters the actual American response to Soviet conciliation. Another counterfactual alters the actual leadership equation by subtracting both Gorbachev and Reagan. It is difficult to imagine a Romanov or any other Soviet old-guard leader embracing a strategy of conciliation in 1986–87. It is easier—but still not easy—to imagine Bush or Mondale resisting the pressure to reciprocate Soviet conciliation, or at least to temporize in the face of it. If either man was insecure about his political authority and less than self-confident about his image within the United States, he might have been tempted to sustain a posture of American confrontation and deny the reality of Soviet conciliation. In that case, the explanation for Ronald Reagan's refusal to go this route, and to test the sincerity of Soviet conciliatory policies, would be his greater political security and sense of identity combined with his visionary urge to go down in history as a great peacemaker.

Soviet Conciliation and American Temporization

Soviet conciliation might have encouraged an American president to back away from a policy of confrontation in the expectation that a softer line would facilitate further Soviet retreat. There is evidence that Gorbachev's retrenchment and conciliation, coupled with his moves to liberalize the Soviet political system, had precisely this effect. Initially uncertain about Gorbachev's broader goals, and disinclined for domestic and foreign reasons to take many risks, the Reagan administration chose to temporize. The president became more forthcoming when given the prospect of a favorable arms-control treaty. If he had not done this, it might have been difficult for Gorbachev to continue his increasingly concessionary foreign policies. Gorbachev could have become more cautious about concessions in arms control, or simply drawn out the process of East-West accommodation for long enough that the German problem was still unresolved by the time his power waned.

Indeed, President Bush initially thought that Ronald Reagan had gone too far to accommodate Gorbachev; he accordingly temporized during 1989, his first year in office. Temporization is usually a short-term strategy, and Bush, like his predecessor, gradually moved toward conciliation. It is interesting to speculate about what would have happened had either president continued to temporize; it could have led to a very different end to the Cold War. It could have encouraged Gorbachev to try to cut a separate deal with Germany. Unification, even if it required a neutral Germany or special status for the East—as Gorbachev initially demanded—could have appealed to West German prime minister Helmut Kohl and his foreign minister, Hans-Dietrich Genscher.

Soviet Conciliation and American Conciliation

After the Geneva summit, Gorbachev's policy toward the West became increasingly conciliatory on all fronts. As noted, both American presidents temporized and then adopted conciliatory policies. This was the path through which the Cold War came to an end, at the time it did, and on the terms it did.

Our analysis of the likely interactions among these several Soviet and American strategies suggests a wide range of possible outcomes, from a rapid resolution of the Cold War to its intensification. In between lie a range of outcomes that represent continuation of the Cold War in one form or another (see table 4.1). Some of these combinations seem inherently unstable, given both the political pressures and the nuclear fears of the time. One or both sides would probably have switched to a less cooperative or less confrontational strategy. One combination—Soviet confrontation and American conciliation—seems fanciful, given the temper of American politics at the time.

It is entirely conceivable—perhaps, likely—that without Gorbachev and/or Reagan, the Cold War could have been alive and well for some time after 1989, the Berlin Wall still standing, the Soviet Union still in existence, and eastern Europe still run by communist regimes. A Soviet leader other than Gorbachev might have been inclined to respond to Star Wars with countermeasures or implacable opposition to further arms control. A Soviet leader other than Gorbachev might not have launched glasnost, perestroika, and democratization at home, thereby reducing the chance that antiregime forces within eastern Europe would eventually gain the upper hand. Of course, such a leader might also have been quite willing to use force in Poland and elsewhere in eastern Europe to hold the Warsaw Pact together; he would also have been more willing to counter challenges to the regime in the Soviet Union with the determined use of force.[34] A leader other than Reagan, facing a hard-line Soviet leader, might have sought and found ways to decrease the level of tension in the relationship. But he would not likely have achieved an accommodation that went beyond the kind of détente temporarily achieved by Nixon and Brezhnev in the early 1970s.

LEADER INDISPENSABILITY?[*]

The only peaceful route to resolution of the Cold War was through an iterative process of mutual conciliation. How essential were Mikhail Gorbachev and Ronald Reagan to the adoption of sustained, mutually conciliatory postures? We should be careful here not to equate the strategy of mutual conciliation with the kind of fragile, competitive, mutually "offensive détente" reached by Nixon and Brezhnev.[35] For the latter purpose, Gorbachev and Reagan were clearly dispensable. Earlier détentes did not break out of the Cold War pattern of combining selective collaboration with intense superpower competition; indeed, they may have unraveled for precisely that reason.

Gorbachev as Indispensable?

In the case of Gorbachev, we encounter a Soviet leader who made a conscious decision to reject the ideological assumptions that supported the "anti-imperialist" struggle, the Cold War international order, and the domestic Soviet institutions whose identities were defined by this approach to international politics. He came eventually to a conscious decision to transform Soviet domestic politics in a liberalizing, democratizing, and Westernizing direction.[36] He articulated a vision of a transformed domestic and international order and managed to justify his conciliatory posture with reference to that new way of thinking. He was able to sell the approach to key audiences within the political establishment, in part for political-intellectual reasons. His doctrinal innovations were ingenious syntheses of old and new precepts, in ways that appeared to retain fidelity to the Marxist revolutionary tradition, while rejecting core features of the

---

[*] The concept "leader dispensability" was first suggested by Alexander George.

Leninist approach to international relations.[37] In addition to these polit-ical-intellectual attributes, Gorbachev had the kind of self-confident and assertive personality that could dominate small-group decision-making processes. He also possessed the political skills to exploit opportunities created by stochastic events. At least from early 1985 through early 1989, before he lost control of events, he had an outstanding sense of timing, was highly articulate in small-group debate, and knew how to seize the initiative from prospective skeptics.[38] He used the Chernobyl accident as a springboard to rein in the censorship authorities, and exploited the landing on Red Square of Matthias Rust's Cessna as a pretext to purge the military command.

To be sure, Gorbachev was not a magician; he was operating in a con-text that facilitated his efforts. A good deal of individual and collective learning had been taking place behind the scenes of Soviet politics during the twenty years before Gorbachev came to power. By the 1980s, party intellectuals and officials in growing numbers had sensed that something fundamental had to give—that the Soviet Union was approaching a cul de sac in both its domestic evolution and foreign relations.[39] Their forebod-ing was far from a majority position, but it did provide an opening for an entrepreneurial political leader ready to exploit new ideas and build a new political base.[40] Then too, very large numbers of party officials who resisted this pessimistic conclusion had nonetheless lost confidence in their ability to justify their right to rule—to themselves and the populace at large—and worried about the sustainability of their domination under such conditions. Gorbachev was able to exploit these changes in both the intellectual and the psychological context, and to use his formidable political skills to maintain support—if only passive support in many in-stances—for the determined strategy of conciliation he had embraced.

There is no evidence to suggest that anyone else in the Soviet leadership possessed the flexible intellect, the personality, and the political skills that Gorbachev combined in his person. Reformist advisors such as Anatoliy Chernyayev and Georgy Shakhnazarov, along with other reformists in the journalistic and academic establishments, provided important ideas for Gorbachev to wield, but themselves could not have become party leaders at the time. Men like Aleksandr Yakovlev and Eduard Shevard-nadze matched Gorbachev in intellect; but neither was in a position to be elected general secretary in 1985, and neither had Gorbachev's personal-ity and political skills. Other supporters like Vadim Medvedev fell short on all three counts, and could not have been elected in any case. Other members of the Politburo did not display the inclination to heed the radi-cal advice being offered by "new thinkers" within the establishment or to conciliate the United States under the circumstances of the mid-1990s, though several of them might have been pragmatic enough to engage in retrenchment from positions of overextension in the Third World. In short, any counterfactual that eliminates Gorbachev from the scene in March 1985 leads to the conclusion that he was indispensable for the redirection of Soviet foreign policy toward a sustained and sustainable posture of conciliation.

Gorbachev's willingness simultaneously to transform Soviet domestic and foreign policy orientations and institutions lent much-needed credibility abroad to the rhetoric of "new thinking" in international relations. Foreign governments were understandably distrustful of changes in words alone; they wanted concrete evidence of changes in deeds. Changes in foreign policies that were not also accompanied by fundamental changes in domestic policies and institutions could be rationalized by foreign governments as mere efforts to gain a "breathing spell" abroad during a time of domestic weakness. This had been a time-honored Soviet strategy since the 1920s. Gorbachev's concomitant transformations largely undercut the political and intellectual grounding of the "enemy image" of the Soviet Union in Western governments.[41]

Reagan as Indispensable?

Was Ronald Reagan equally necessary for the realization of a virtuous circle of mutual conciliation? Did his personality and perspectives uniquely facilitate East-West accommodation? Reagan had a deep abhorrence of nuclear weapons and, with it, a growing commitment to find a way out of the East-West impasse. There is some evidence that Reagan's commitment intensified in early 1984 after his SIOP briefing (on the country's strategic nuclear options) and as a result of the Soviet Union's overreaction to the Able Archer nuclear exercise. These events seem to have "primed" Reagan to initiate efforts to reestablish better communications with Moscow and, possibly, to respond more favorably to the overtures toward accommodation that Gorbachev would later make.[42]

Ronald Reagan held strong views on many subjects and had little knowledge to back up those views. He repeatedly demonstrated his ignorance of the Soviet Union, in public and private. Reagan had a much less complex cognitive schema about the Soviet Union than did his advisors, or some other contenders for the presidency. Laboratory experiments indicate that people with different levels of complexity react differently to counterattitudinal information. People with less-developed schemas are initially more likely to maintain their schemas intact in the face of discrepant information, but to change them dramatically in the face of a consistent stream of discrepant information. People with more complex and developed schemas are more likely to find ways of interpreting discrepant information in a manner consistent with their schemas, or of making small, incremental changes in their schemas to accommodate this information.[43] Thus, it is not surprising that Reagan, who entered office with the most fervently anti-Soviet views, retired as the biggest dove in his administration. Reagan's advisors had far more elaborate schemas of the Soviet Union, and these schemas allowed them to explain away Gorbachev's reforms and interest in arms control and accommodation. They remained doubting and dubious longer than most Americans. As we have noted, Vice President Bush claimed to be still unconvinced of Gorbachev's sincerity when he assumed the presidency.

Reagan's dramatic about-face may also have been facilitated by his propensity—noted by many of his confidants—to reduce issues to personalities. If he liked and trusted someone, he was more prone to give credence to the policies they espoused. Reagan's closest advisors testify that his personal meetings with Gorbachev at Geneva in November 1985 and at Reykjavik in November 1986 made a big impact on him; he came away impressed by the general secretary and his seeming commitment to reduce the nuclear danger and tensions between the superpowers.[44] We can speculate that Reagan's assessment of Gorbachev created considerable cognitive dissonance for him. If many of his advisors interpreted Gorbachev's behavior in a manner consistent with their more complex schemas (i.e., that Gorbachev was clever, duplicitous, and seeking to weaken the West by appealing to the antiwar sentiments of European and American public opinion), Reagan, with his less developed schema, changed his view of the Soviet Union. Once he accepted Gorbachev as sincere, he worked with him to bring about the accommodation both men desired. By the time of the 1988 Moscow summit, when a newsman reminded Reagan of his earlier depiction of the Soviet Union as an "evil empire," the president chuckled and replied: "I was talking about another time, another era."[45] It seems unlikely another president, and certainly not George Bush, would have undergone such a transition.

The Reagan-Gorbachev Relationship

Was there something about the personal rapport between these two leaders that encouraged conciliation and helped them to sustain the momentum of that process once it had begun?[46] We think the answer is "yes." Gorbachev shared Reagan's horror of nuclear weapons.[47] The fact that both men happened to share a vision of a world without nuclear weapons was salutary to the process of mutual conciliation. That they were in power at the same time was a remarkable and perhaps even necessary coincidence.

The Cold War started as a struggle to fill a power vacuum in central Europe, and superpower competition ultimately spread to much of the Third World. Gradually and grudgingly, both the superpowers came to accept the political and territorial status quo in Europe, and even gave it something of a formal status in the 1975 Helsinki Accords. The Cold War had driven Washington and Moscow to acquire thermonuclear weapons and the arsenals to deliver them against each other's allies and homelands. By the early 1980s, cause and effect had become reversed, and the principal cause of superpower conflict had become weapons deployments and the insecurities they generated in both capitals. To end the Cold War, it was necessary first and foremost to reduce these insecurities by reducing the weapons. Previous arms-control agreements had done little to diminish nuclear arsenals; they were more a means of reducing uncertainty through regulated competition. Without Reagan's and Gorbachev's mutual commitment to deep cuts in strategic and theater-level forces, it is likely that whatever arms-control agreements their countries reached would have been along more traditional lines. They would not have cut the Gordian knot of the Cold War.

Moreover, Reagan and Gorbachev had the right chemistry. Both men were self-confident idealists unprepared to bow to political expediency. They "immediately sensed this" about each other, former foreign minister Aleksandr Bessmertnykh observed, and "this is why they made 'good partners.'"[48] Confronted with a different general secretary, who had neither Gorbachev's personality nor his commitment to reduce the nuclear threat, Reagan might well have remained a frustrated, anti-Soviet ideologue. Given his commitment to holding out for asymmetrical, indeed maximal, Soviet concessions in all realms, the Cold War might well have remained unresolved and a more complicated legacy for his successor. On the other hand, confronted with a different American president, Gorbachev might well have impressed and converted him with his willingness to make so many unilateral concessions. But the lesser resolve and greater political insecurity of a George Bush or Walter Mondale might have made it less attractive tactically and more difficult politically for Gorbachev to justify such far-reaching concessions. The perception that a Bush or Mondale would have settled for less could have led Gorbachev to demand a more balanced compromise. Had Gorbachev not transcended such a perspective, intellectually or politically, he might have participated in a more drawn-out process of negotiation that could have become the basis for mutual disillusionment—as it did in the 1970s—or, further down the line, a Cold War settlement different in scope and form. Paradoxically then, it is worth considering the proposition that it was Reagan's maximalism and resolve, coupled with his willingness to strike deals and abandon hostile rhetoric when his maximalist demands were being met, and fueled by the personal rapport and vision he shared with Gorbachev, that ended the Cold War when and how it did.

Thus, when we examine the process in finer detail, we discover that the mutual conciliation that led to the end of the Cold War was more than a simple, iterative process of strategic interaction. The results could not have been predicted by knowing only the strategies and preferences of the actors. We find that, after the first iteration, the adoption of follow-on strategies can be influenced, perhaps decisively, by the personal chemistry and trust—or lack of it—that develops between leaders and between negotiators. That chemistry and trust can reshape preferences, commitments, and expectations of reciprocity. It can, in other words, make the difference between breakdown and further iterations of the game. This highlights, in turn, the likely indispensability of both Gorbachev and Reagan to the ending of the Cold War in this time period.

CONCLUSIONS

In this chapter, we began by substituting other leaders for Gorbachev and Reagan to ask how Soviet-American relations might have evolved. To make our analysis as plausible as possible, we picked leaders (Grishin, Romanov, Ligachev, Bush, Mondale) who might have come to power in 1985, described scenarios by which this might have happened, and asked how the changed circumstances that would have brought these men into power would have affected the domestic and international constraints they faced. We identified five strategies toward superpower relations that other leaders might have pursued in different issue areas, and at different points in time. In order manageably to explore the dynamics of interaction between superpower strategies, we collapsed the five into three—confrontation, temporization, and conciliation. We examined the nine possible interactions among these strategies, but treated them only as starting points, and assumed that some of them were inherently unstable (e.g., Soviet conciliation vs. U.S. confrontation). We explored possible follow-on interactions and argued that many pathways led to three quasi-stable states for the near-term evolution of the Cold War: continuation, amelioration, and intensification.

Our thought experiment led us to the conclusion that the end of the Cold War was highly contingent. Without Gorbachev and Reagan, that conflict could have continued for some time, possibly in a more acute form. This is not only because of the strategies that Reagan and Gorbachev embraced. The end of the Cold War was more than an iterative process of strategic interaction. The personal interactions of the leaders, and of their most influential advisors, was also important for shaping their preferences, commitments, and expectations of reciprocity. The personal "chemistry" between Reagan and Gorbachev was especially critical in this regard.

By positing realistic changes in historical events, and by exploring their possible repercussions for the superpower relationship, our analysis attempts to assess the ongoing, not the static, malleability of the domestic and international orders in question. By using two men with extraordinary political skills and a deep commitment to change, it also provides an unusual opportunity to evaluate the power and limits of leadership. We believe that our provisional analysis proposes some tentative answers to important political questions and suggests a research program that could enrich our theoretical understanding of the relationship between agency and structure. However, our thought experiments beg the question of how events might have evolved in the longer term. One can acknowledge the contingent and diverse nature of short-term interactions and their outcomes, and still argue that in the course of time, by one means or another, the Cold War would have ended with a Soviet defeat, the collapse of communism in eastern Europe, dissolution of the Warsaw Pact, and the breakup of the Soviet Union.

We would not dismiss the utility of such speculation, but would emphasize that it is a very different kind of intellectual exercise. Counterfactual analysis is based on theories of politics that describe short-term interactions, whereas long-term prediction relies on broader, structural theories of evolution or interaction.[49] Grandiose, long-term theories are typically imprecise because they are open-ended in the temporal aspects of their predictions. More importantly for our purposes, the farther into the future we try to extend a counterfactual rewrite, the larger the number of intermediate effects ("consequents") we must control for in trying to fathom the long-term effects of an altered causal variable ("antecedent"). To take a concrete example, it is difficult enough to imagine what the Soviet Union would have looked like in 1939 if Nikolai Bukharin, not Joseph Stalin, had won the power struggle of the 1920s. Without a clear answer to this question we have no firm grounds to speculate on whether the Soviet Union would have won World War II—assuming there had been a World War II. And it is more difficult still to inquire as to whether there would have been a Cold War between the United States and the Soviet Union if the allies had won the war with Bukharin at the helm in Moscow. Counterfactual analysis is best employed as a tool for the short-term reconstruction of history, and is best complemented by short-term theories of continuity and change. Hence, whether the Cold War would have ended "anyway" in the subsequent ten to twenty years, or whether the Soviet Union would have eventually collapsed as well, are beyond the realm of our capacity to investigate using the analytic, theoretical, and methodological tools discussed in this chapter.

We do not challenge the importance of many of the underlying causes that scholars have identified as responsible for the end of the Cold War. But we have tried to demonstrate that underlying causes, no matter how numerous or deep-seated, do not make an event, or a sequence of events, inevitable. It is worth considering the somewhat counterintuitive proposition that there may be no relationship between the number and intensity of underlying causes and the probability of an outcome. One of us has made this case for World War I.[50] Social scientists err in thinking that major social and political developments are invariably specific instances of strong, or even weak, regularities in social behavior. These developments are sometimes the result of accidental conjunctions; they are events that might have had a low subjective probability. The concatenation of particular leaders with particular contexts, and of particular events with other events, is always a matter of chance, never of necessity.

PART THREE

CHAPTER FIVE

Scholars and Causation 1

Coauthored with Philip E. Tetlock

THIS CHAPTER EXPLORES a recurring source of disagreement between generalizers and particularizers: the soundness of close-call counterfactual scenarios that imply that, with only minimal rewriting of antecedent conditions, history could have been rerouted down different, sometimes radically different, event paths. Close-call counterfactuals are often focal points of disagreement for two reasons.

First, all causal inference from history ultimately rests on counterfactual claims about what would or could have happened in hypothetical worlds to which scholars have no direct empirical access.[1] This is not to say that evidence is irrelevant. Chapter 2 described counterfactuals where historical evidence could be brought to bear to differentiate more from less compelling counterfactual claims. However, disputes over the relative soundness of competing counterfactuals are often notoriously resistant to consensual resolution.

Second, close-call counterfactuals assign critical roles to causes that theorists committed to systematic accounts or covering laws tend to disparage as trivial, impossible to categorize, and best relegated to error variance.[2] The quest for parsimonious laws governing political processes becomes progressively more hopeless to the degree that the triumph of civilizations hinges on horseshoe-nail (or butterfly) effects in battles; the outbreak of world wars hinges on royal carriage drivers making a wrong turn in downtown Sarajevo or an emotionally unstable young man gaining admission to a Viennese art school; or the outcome of the Cuban missile crisis hinges on the interpersonal chemistry among presidential advisers.

We work from the uncontroversial premise that there is an ineradicable element of subjectivity in these debates over historical causality. Accordingly, a strong case can be made for rigorously scrutinizing potential cognitive biases in how historical observers go about evaluating the relative plausibility of competing what-if scenarios. We report two sets of empirical studies, one correlational and the other experimental. The correlational research explores the degree to which professional observers of world politics rely on abstract covering laws in assessing what was possible at specific times and places. These studies demonstrate that, across an array of contexts, the more credence observers place in relevant covering laws, and the stronger their cognitive-stylistic preferences for explanatory closure, the more likely they are to be guided by those covering laws in judging what could have been, and the less likely they are to make judgments of historical contingency on a case-by-case basis.

The correlational studies rely on naturally occurring variation in theoretical beliefs and cognitive-stylistic preferences to illustrate the deductive, top-down character of counterfactual reasoning and the power of theoretical preconceptions to shape the conclusions that experts draw about what was historically possible. The experimental studies encourage experts to perform what is, in effect, an unnatural cognitive act: to give more thought than they normally would to alternative pathways history could have followed. The goal is to test the notion that counterfactual reasoning can also take the form of inductive, bottom-up reasoning. In other words, the mental processes of imagining specific counterfactual scenarios can induce us to change our mind and become more circumspect about the power of our favorite causal generalizations to delimit the range of historical possibilities. Experiment 1 asks foreign policy experts to consider various scenarios, supported by varying amounts of detail, that "undo" the peaceful resolution of the Cuban missile crisis. The net effect was to increase their perceptions of the potential for alternative, more violent, endings. Experiment 2 shows that the manipulations need not be heavy handed and that no new information need even be presented. Experts were asked to draw on their own historical knowledge in searching for possible pathways to more violent endings of the crisis, and then to unpack these possibilities into progressively more differentiated subsets; the net effect was inflation of the subjective probabilities of those alternative outcomes. Moreover, consistent with Tversky and Fox's support theory, the more extensive the unpacking, the greater was the resulting inflation of subjective probabilities.[3] Experiment 3 demonstrates that these effects are not peculiar to the relatively recent and brief Cuban missile crisis. It provides a conceptual replication in the context of the debate about the rise of the West, the historical transformation over several centuries of western Europe from cultural backwater to global hegemon.

Taken together, the results give real-world empirical content to a cognitive account of the construction of historical knowledge that specifies the mental processes by which observers apply causal generalizations to history and judge the acceptability of close-call counterfactuals that circumscribe those generalizations. Historical observers may indeed often be prisoners of their preconceptions, but they hold the keys to their own release.[4] They are not constrained to explain only what happened. We are endowed with the imaginative capacity to envision alternative paths that history could have taken. The more energy we direct to elaborating dissonant alternatives, the weaker is the hold of our preconceptions (judging by the dwindling regression coefficients) on our judgments of contingency and possibility. But this liberation has a price. The more effort we devote to unpacking counterfactual scenarios, the more contradictory are our resulting judgments of history. Our findings suggest that historical observers of world politics confront an inescapable trade-off between being closed-minded but logically coherent or open-minded but logically incoherent.

Before proceding, we want to enter a caveat. Our binary of generalizers and particularizers does not reflect the range of cognitive styles of those who study history and international relations. On the evidence of the preceding chapters, we might identify inductive generalizers (perhaps the largest category of social scientists), deductive modelers (e.g., rational choice theorists), conceptually inclined sorters (e.g., many constructivists and one of the authors), and storytellers (most historians). These styles are not "types" in the sense of being defined on the basis of a single attribute. Our binary is only one of the ways of distinguishing among these different styles, although to some degree it also cuts across them. Deductive modelers are committed generalizers, but inductive modelers and conceptually inclined sorters also make generalizations. Storytellers come the closest to being particularizers, but even they may structure a narrative, as Thucydides certainly does, on the basis of a conceptual framework that rests, as all do, on a series of generalizations.[5] With few exceptions, all scholars generalize, they just go about it in a variety of different ways.

The distinction between generalizers and particularizers is nevertheless an interesting continuum to consider. A growing psychological literature on cognitive style reveals marked individual differences in the motivation to achieve simplicity and closure in the characterization and explanation of events.[6] Experimental and field research finds, for example, that people who score high on self-report measures of the need for closure tend to rely on prior beliefs in solving unfamiliar problems and in evaluating dissonant arguments, prefer parsimonious interpretations of evidence that invoke as few causal constructs as possible, and prefer deterministic accounts that downplay probabilistic qualifiers. This body of work suggests that professional observers of world politics with a strong need for closure should find close-call counterfactuals vexing to the degree that these imply that minor tinkering with antecedent conditions could have undone major outcomes that the observers felt they had already comfortably assimilated into favorite covering-law schemes.

The Correlational Studies

From a neopositivist perspective on historical explanation, theorists are under absolutely no logical obligation to apply covering laws to any specific event. Covering laws in social science are best viewed both as probabilistic and as applicable to sets of events, not individual occurrences.

Logical necessity to the side, however, there may well be considerable psychological pressure on observers to achieve closure in their historical explanations. Herbert Simon and his colleagues have shown that even highly trained experts function like boundedly rational satisficers who try to keep the number of variables and amount of information that must be integrated to a reasonable minimum.[7]

Exactly how do experts resist theoretically subversive counterfactuals? From a strictly logical perspective, there are three possible lines of defense.[8] From a psychological perspective, especially one grounded in cognitive consistency theory, there are good reasons for expecting experts to mobilize all three whenever experts feel core theoretical commitments are under siege (see Jervis on belief-system overkill).[9] The lines of defense are as follows.

First, challenge the mutability of the antecedent. For example, insist that it is hard to imagine Kennedy heeding his more hawkish advisers during the Cuban missile crisis. This defense often seems contrived, even to those who value closure. All but the most implacably La Placean determinists recognize that it is exceedingly implausible to insist that each and every microscopic detail surrounding key events had to take the form it did.

Second, challenge the connecting principles that bridge antecedent and consequent. Counterfactual arguments are inherently elliptical; it is impractical to spell out all the background assumptions that must be satisfied to sustain even the simplest antecedent-consequent linkages. Consider the claim that if Kennedy had heeded his hawkish advisers during the missile crisis and attacked Soviet bases in Cuba, World War III would have ensued. Deterrence theorists can counter that war was not inevitable because the Soviets recognized their strategic inferiority vis-à-vis the United States. They would have grudgingly acquiesced to the fait accompli and forbidden their ground forces in Cuba to use nuclear-tipped Luna missiles against the American armada.

Third, concede that the antecedents may be mutable and that connecting principles may be sound, but still insist that history would have been thrown off track only temporarily, and the proposed changes would have had little long-term significance. This defense is designated a second-order counterfactual because it undoes the undoing of history implied by the original scenario. For example, even if Genghis Khan had lived and the Mongols had mauled western Europe, the resilient Europeans would have bounced back quickly.

Hypothesis

The preceding argument lays the conceptual groundwork for the two hypotheses tested in each of the three correlational studies. The covering-law hypothesis predicts a main effect: the more confidence an expert places in any given causal generalization, the more likely he or she is to invoke all three lines of belief-system defense against close-call scenarios that undercut the applicability of the generalization to historical outcomes previously thought covered by that generalization. The cognitive-style hypothesis predicts an interactive effect: experts with a strong need for explanatory closure are likely to invoke all three defenses against dissonant scenarios.

Research Design and Logic of Analysis

The correlational studies probe reactions to close-call scenarios that undercut three categories of covering law. Study 1 targets variants of nuclear deterrence theory that stress the power of mutual assured destruction to induce even minimally rational actors to act with self-restraint.[10] Scenarios that imply we were on the brink of nuclear war at numerous junctures in the Cold War should seem far-fetched to theorists who posit the robustness of nuclear deterrence. Looking back on the Cold War, these theorists should find it hard to imagine that either superpower ever would have allowed a crisis to escalate into a nuclear war (just as, looking forward, they find it hard to worry about the dangers of nuclear proliferation).

Study 2 targets variants of the realist balancing hypothesis. That is, when one state threatens to become too powerful and to dominate the entire international system, other states—rational, self-preserving actors as they are posited to be—coalesce against it, thereby preserving the balance of power.[11] From this standpoint, the failure of aspiring hegemons, such as Philip II, Napoleon, or Hitler, is predetermined by a fundamental law of world politics, and close-call claims that these bids to dominate Europe might have succeeded are misinformed.

Study 3 targets a pair of covering laws that loom large in debates on the rise and fall of civilizations. The first is that history, in the long term, is an efficient process of winnowing out maladaptive forms of social organization. The second is that Western societies, with their emphasis on the rule of law, property rights, free markets, and the practical applications of science, are better adapted to prevail in long-term competition with other civilizations.[12] It is no accident that, between 1500 and 1800, Europeans came to wield global influence so disproportionate to their numbers. The rise of the West, at the expense of the "Rest," reveals the fundamental superiority of Western values and institutions. Close-call counterfactuals that purport to undo the rise of the West by minor mental mutations of antecedent conditions—more aggressive Islamic incursions into France in the eighth century or less isolationist Chinese emperors in the fifteenth century—are merely whimsical excursions into what-if history.

Methods and Measures

Participants were drawn from overlapping populations of scholars who specialize in diplomatic and military history, security studies, and international relations. The eighty-seven participants in correlational studies 1 and 2, which focus on realist balancing and nuclear deterrence, were randomly sampled from Division 18 (International Conflict) and Division 19 (International Security and Arms Control) of the American Political Science Association and from the Society of Diplomatic and Military Historians. The sixty-three participants for study 3, which focuses on the rise of the West, were randomly drawn from the membership roster of the World History Association. All respondents were contacted by either postal mail or e-mail, and they were promised both anonymity and detailed feedback on the purposes of the study. The response rate for studies 1 and 2 was 29 percent; for study 3, 31 percent. Assessing selection bias as a result of the relatively low response rates was problematic because of the limited information available on participating and nonparticipating individuals in our sample. Available results suggest, however, only slight overrepresentation of academics employed in large research universities.

Covering-Law Beliefs

These measures assessed endorsement of the covering laws on nine-point agree-disagree scales. For neorealist balancing there were four items: (a) "For all the talk about a new world order, world politics is still essentially anarchic—the strong do what they will and the weak accept what they must"; (b) "Whenever one state starts to become too powerful, other states find a way of combining forces and preventing it from dominating them"; (c) "The security policies of states are often driven by morality, not just by rational calculations of the impact of those policies on the balance of power"; (d) "It is naive to suppose that the failure of would-be conquerors such as Philip II, Napoleon, and Hitler to achieve lasting dominance in Europe was predetermined by balance-of-power politics—it might just have been an accident."

For nuclear deterrence there were three items: (a) "For all the talk about the risk of nuclear accidents, the U.S.A. and U.S.S.R. never really came close to nuclear war"; (b) "Nuclear weapons played a key role in moderating the behavior of both the American and Soviet governments during the Cold War"; (c) "It is unrealistic to assume that leaders working under great stress will always act with great restraint in crises that raise the risk of the use of nuclear weapons."

Two items dealt with the survival of the fittest civilizations: (a) "History is, in the long run, an efficient process of winnowing out maladaptive forms of social organization"; (b) "Western societies and institutions, with their greater emphasis on the rule of law, property rights, free markets, and the practical applications of science, were better adapted to prevail in long-term competition with other civilizations."

The Need for Explanatory Closure

Respondents gave answers on a nine-point agree-disagree scale to nine items: (a) "I think that having clear rules and order at work is essential for success"; (b) "Even after I have made up my mind about something, I am always eager to consider a different opinion"; (c) "I dislike questions that can be answered in many different ways"; (d) "I usually make important decisions quickly and confidently"; (e) "When considering most conflict situations, I can usually see how both sides could be right"; (f) "I prefer interacting with people whose opinions are very different from my own"; (g) "When trying to solve a problem I often see so many possible options that it is confusing"; (h) "Scholars are usually at greater risk of exaggerating the complexity of political processes than they are of underestimating the complexity of those processes"; (i) "Isaiah Berlin classified intellectuals as hedgehogs or foxes.[13] A hedgehog knows one big thing and tries to integrate the diversity of the world into a comprehensive and parsimonious vision whereas a fox knows many small things and tries to improvise explanations on a case-by-case basis. I would place myself toward the hedgehog or fox style of thinking about politics."

Beliefs about Close-Call Counterfactuals

The first set of scenarios undid the outcomes of either World War I or II: (a) "If Germany had proceeded with its invasion of France on August 2, 1914, but had respected the Belgian neutrality, Britain would not have entered the war, and France would have quickly fallen"; (b) "If the German High Command had implemented the Schlieffen Plan more aggressively in August 1914, the miracle of the Marne would have been impossible, and Paris would have fallen"; (c) "If Germany had avoided antagonizing the United States by meddling in Mexico and by initiating unrestricted submarine warfare, the United States would not have entered World War I and Germany would have prevailed against the French and British in its spring offensive of 1918"; (d) "If Hitler had not invaded the Soviet Union and concentrated German resources on defeating the British, Germany would have defeated Britain"; (e) "If Hitler had more consistently focused on taking Moscow in the summer of 1941, he could have knocked the Soviet Union out of the war"; (f) "If Hitler had not declared war on the United States on December 11, 1941, the British and the Soviets could never have defeated Nazi Germany."

The second set of counterfactuals explored the feasibility of the Cold War becoming thermonuclear: (a) "If Stalin had lived several years longer (surviving his stroke but in an irrational state of mind that encouraged high-risk adventures), World War III could easily have broken out in the mid-1950s"; (b) "If bad weather had delayed the discovery by U-2 reconnaissance planes of Soviet missiles in Cuba until the missiles were operational, the Soviets would have refused American demands to dismantle and withdraw the weapons"; (c) "If the Soviets had refused to withdraw their missiles, the U.S. would have launched air strikes against the Soviet bases"; (d) "If the U.S. had launched such air strikes, the Soviet commanders in Cuba would have launched at least some missiles at the eastern seaboard of the United States"; (e) "If the Soviets had fired Cuban-based nuclear missiles at American cities, retaliatory nuclear strikes would have been launched at Soviet cities"; (f) "If Soviet hard-liners had taken charge of the Communist party in the mid-1980s, the Cold War—far from ending peacefully and quickly—would have intensified."

The third set of counterfactuals explored the feasibility of unmaking the West through hypothetical interventions that either enfeebled Europe or empowered rival civilizations: (a) "If China had had, at key junctures, emperors more sympathetic to economic and technological development, it could have emerged as the world's first superpower"; (b) "If the Mongols had continued their advance into central and western Europe and not been distracted by the death of Genghis Khan, later European development would have been impossible"; (c) "If Islamic armies had made a serious attempt to conquer France and Italy in the eighth century, later European development could have been radically side-tracked"; (d) "If the Black Death had been even more lethal, killing, say, 70% of the population, Europe could not have arisen as the dominant region in the second half of the millennium."

For each scenario, experts were asked to make three judgments on nine-point scales. (1) "How plausible was the antecedent condition of the argument? (Do we have to 'rewrite' a little or a lot of history?)"; (2) "Assuming the plausibility of the antecedent, how likely was the hypothesized consequence?"; (3) "Assuming the plausibility of the hypothesized consequence, what would the long-term ramifications have been?"

Findings

Correlational analyses revealed that experts invoked all three belief-system defenses against dissonant close-calls but preferred certain defenses. Two of them— "challenge the logic of the connecting principles" and "generate second-order counterfactuals that put history back on track"—were widely employed and were tightly linked to the respondent's abstract orientation toward world politics (average r ~ 0.54 with the covering-law scales). The third defense—"challenge the mutability of historical antecedents"—was markedly less linked to abstract political orientation (average r ~ 0.29). There is no compelling reason one's theoretical position on the robustness of nuclear deterrence should predict whether one believes Stalin could have survived the cerebral hemorrhage of March 1953 or whether Cuba could have been cloudier on an October day in 1962. The plausibility of most antecedents hinges on specific facts tied to particular times, places, and events; if anything, it is disconcerting that abstract orientation predicts so much variance—8% to 10%—in judgments of the mutability of antecedents.

Table 5.1 summarizes ordinary-least-squares multiple regression results for a composite dependent variable that additively combines the two most correlated resistance strategies, challenges connecting principles, and invokes second-order counterfactuals. These regressions consistently show that the more committed the scholars were to a school of thought, the more dismissive they were of counterfactuals that undercut historical applications of favorite explanatory generalizations. The more experts believed in the reliability of the balancing hypothesis, the more they rejected the scenarios that implied Germany, with slightly sounder decision making, could have emerged victorious in either of the two world wars and achieved continental hegemony. The more experts believed in the robustness of nuclear deterrence, the more dismissive they were of close calls that implied the United States and the Soviet Union easily could have slipped into nuclear conflict during the Cold War. The more experts believed in the superiority of Western institutions, the less use they had for counterfactuals that implied other civilizations, with minor twists of fate, could have been contenders for geopolitical dominance.

Table 5.1 also shows that, as predicted, the interaction between theoretical belief and covering law emerged in all three domains of application: experts who most valued explanatory closure and parsimony mounted the stiffest resistance to dissonant scenarios. The interaction cannot, moreover, be attributed to a differential restriction of range. Hartley's Fmax test for heterogeneity of variance revealed only minimal differences in the variance of each theoretical belief scale among low versus high scorers on the cognitive-style scales (median split) and equally

TABLE 5.1
Predicting resistance to close-call counterfactuals

Covering law	b	SE	t
Neorealist balancing	0.96***	0.30	3.18
Cognitive style	0.35	0.29	1.20
Balancing ~ style	0.74**	0.36	2.07
n ~ 87	0.89**	0.34	2.65
R2 ~ 0.47	0.33	0.31	1.07
Nuclear deterrence	0.69**	0.33	2.06
Cognitive style	0.82**	0.36	2.27
Deterrence ~ style	0.23	0.28	0.83
n ~ 86	0.73*	0.36	2.10
R2 ~ 0.43			
Adaptive advantage of West			
Cognitive style			
West ~ style			
n ~ 63			
R2 ~ 0.41			

Note: The table presents the full ordinary-least-squares results for each of three separate multiple regressions. Each treats resistance to close-call counterfactuals as the dependent variable; independent variables are commitment to a particular school of thought (neorealist balancing, nuclear deterrence, and adaptive advantages of West), cognitive style (highly [r ~ .57]. *p ~ .05, **p ~ .01,***p ~ .001), need for closure, and a cross-product term designed to capture the degree to which resistance is greatest when both theoretical commitment and need for closure are high.

negligible differences in variation on the cognitive-style scale between low and high scorers on the three theoretical belief scales (no p value fell below .20). Differential reliability of measures also was not a factor. Cronbach alphas for the three theoretical belief scales were all in the relatively narrow range of 0.70 to 0.80 for both low and high scorers on the cognitive-style scale.

Discussion

Respondents with a high need for closure were not content just to claim that they had the right explanations of the past. They insisted that they "were not almost wrong," and that the historical outcomes they felt they had explained either were difficult to "undo" or were not undoable for long. As soon as one causal pathway to the theoretically predicted outcome was cut off, another pathway arose, hydralike, in a second-order counterfactual.[14]

These findings shed new light on some old observations: It is easy to extract lessons from history that reinforce our ideological or theoretical stance, and it is difficult to avoid the temptation of selection bias and theoretically self-serving reasoning in defense of that stance.[15] The data also put in new psychological perspective some old epistemological and methodological controversies. The patterns of counterfactual inference documented here can be viewed as integral parts of the cognitive mechanisms that produce selection bias in the use of historiography. Theoretically committed observers feel justified in giving short shrift to historical accounts that dwell on inconsequential contingencies and frivolous what-if scenarios.

The cognitive patterns documented here also encourage the conceptual stretching of theories that some scholars identify as signs of a degenerative research program.[16] Stretching can be facilitated either by dismissing dissonant scenarios ("my theory already explains x, so do not bother me with counterfactuals that imply I was almost wrong") or by embracing consonant close-calls ("my theory is admittedly hard-pressed to explain x, but ~x predicted by my theory almost occurred, so my theory should get some credit"). These arguments raise a fundamental challenge to the discipline: how can we avoid becoming prisoners of our preconceptions, trapped in a self-serving cycle of filling in the missing counterfactual control conditions of history with theory-scripted scenarios, and then deploying that same theory-driven content, in other contexts, to justify the theory itself?

EXPERIMENT 1: THEORY GUIDING INTERPRETATIONS

Although experts tend to dismiss dissonant close-call counterfactuals, hefty regression coefficients do not preclude the possibility that these scenarios have some measurable effect on their judgment of historical contingency. Indeed, the psychological literature suggests that causality operates in precisely this direction. Laboratory experiments repeatedly find support for the prediction—derived from Tversky and Kahneman's classic work on the availability and simulation heuristics—that merely imagining multi-event scenarios increases the perceived likelihood of the component events.[17] Scenarios tend to be mentally sticky: once they have been run through our "mental software," they leave psychological traces in the form of images, thoughts, and emotions that can shape a host of subsequent causal-propensity and subjective-probability judgments.

The literature on heuristics and biases also warns us to expect systematic logical inconsistencies when people judge complex event sequences that require integrating two or more probabilistic linkages. The textbook illustration is the conjunction fallacy.[18] Imagine that one randomly constituted group is asked to judge the likelihood of a plausible conjunction of events, such as an earthquake that ruptures a dam, which in turn causes a flood that kills more than five hundred people in California. Imagine that another randomly constituted group is asked to judge the likelihood of a flood (produced by any cause) killing more than five hundred people in California. The likelihood judgments of the former group typically will exceed those of the latter group by a substantial margin, even though the former group is judging a subset of the class of outcomes being judged by the latter group.

Building on this work, Tversky and Fox's support theory predicts systematic violations of the extensionality principle of probability theory.[19] The principle requires that if two sets of events have identical coverage, then they must have identical probabilities. Psycho-logic trumps logic here because most people can mobilize mental support more readily for highly specific possibilities than they can for the abstract sets that subsume these possibilities. As a result, people often judge the likelihood of an entire set of possibilities, such as a specific team from a given league winning the championship, to be substantially less likely than the sum of the likelihood values of that set's exclusive and exhaustive components (the probabilities of losses for individual teams that make up the league). In effect, people judge the whole to be less than the sum of its parts and give quite different answers to logically equivalent versions of the same question.

Hypotheses

Drawing on the literature on heuristics and biases as well as the work on cognitive styles, we designed experiment 1 to test two hypotheses. First, thinking about counterfactual scenarios (that pass some minimum plausibility threshold) should tend, on average, to increase the perception that those scenarios once had the potential to materialize and may even once have been more likely than the concatenation of events that actually materialized. Linking this prediction to research on cognitive style, we also expect that the effect should be more pronounced among respondents with low need for closure.

Second, Tetlock shows that there are two logically but not psychologically equivalent methods for scaling experts' perceptions of historical contingency.[20] One imposes a factual framing on the historical question and solicits inevitability-curve judgments. For example, in experiment 1, experts on the Cuban missile crisis were asked at what point some form of peaceful resolution became inevitable. They then were asked to trace how the subjective probability of that class of outcomes waxed or waned in the preceding days. The other method imposes a "counterfactual" framing on the historical question and solicits impossibility-curve judgments. In experiment 1, for example, experts also were asked at what point they believe all alternative, more violent endings of the crisis became impossible and then were asked to trace how the subjective likelihood of that class of outcomes waxed or waned in the preceding days.

It was not expected that experts would be blatantly inconsistent: their judgments of the retrospective likelihood of some form of peaceful outcome between October 16 and 29, 1962, should generally mirror their judgments of the retrospective likelihood of alternative, more violent, outcomes when those judgments are obtained back to back from the same respondents. Logic and psycho-logic should coincide when the principle or binary complementarity is transparently at stake, and experts can plainly see that they are assigning so much probability to both x and its complement that the sum will exceed 1.0. But logic and psycho-logic do not always coincide. Factual framings of historical questions effectively invite experts to engage in hypothesis-confirming searches for potent causal candidates that create an inexorable historical momentum toward outcome x. Analysts feel that they have answered the question when they have convinced themselves that x had to happen approximately when and in the manner it did.

By contrast, counterfactual framing of historical questions effectively invites analysts to look long and hard for causal candidates that have the potential to reroute events down radically different event paths. Accordingly, we expect systematic anomalies in retrospective likelihood judgments when we compare the judgments of two groups of experts, one of which completed the inevitability curve exercise and the other of which completed the logically redundant impossibility curve exercise, but neither of which had yet seen or worked through the other group's exercise.

We made two "anomaly" predictions. First, systematic violations of binary complementarity should arise at pre-inevitability and pre-impossibility dates. When we add the subjective probabilities assigned to peace by experts first asked to respond to inevitability curves and the subjective probabilities assigned to war by experts first asked to respond to impossibility curves, the sums will consistently exceed 1.0. Second, there will be a twilight-zone period during which experts who first complete inevitability curves will deem peace inevitable, but experts who first complete impossibility curves will judge war still to be possible. The rationale for the between-group nature of the comparisons is worth stating explicitly because it underscores the critical advantages of experimentation in this context. Given that the experimental groups were constitituted by random assignment and hence should not differ systematically in preexisting attitudes, there is no methodological reason to expect systematically different responses to the logically equivalent inevitability- and impossibility-curve questions. Across conditions, the error variance in responses should be normally distributed around the same "true" population mean of respondents' beliefs about the likelihood of peace or war.

Methods and Measures

Pilot groups for experiments 1 and 2 were informally drawn from faculty at two large American universities. Respondents for the actual treatment were then randomly selected from the membership lists of divisions 18 and 19 of the APSA, the Society for Military Historians, and the Society for Historians of American Foreign Relations. All respondents were contacted by mail and were promised complete anonymity and detailed feedback on the purposes of the survey. The response rate was 26 percent.

Experiment 1 randomly assigned the seventy-six participants to one of three conditions. First, in the control condition, respondents (n ~ 30) were asked (1) when some form of peaceful resolution of the Cuban missile crisis became inevitable and, having identified a point of no return, to estimate the likelihood of a peaceful resolution for each preceding day of the crisis (thereby creating inevitability curves). (2) They were also asked when all alternative (more violent) endings became impossible, and having identified an "impossibility" date, to estimate the likelihood of those alternative endings on each preceding day (thereby creating impossibility curves).

Second, in the moderate-salience condition, before making retrospective likelihood judgments, respondents (n ~ 23) judged the plausibility of three close-call scenarios. (1) "If Kennedy had heeded his more hawkish advisors in the initial meetings of October 16, there would have been an American air strike against Soviet missile bases in Cuba, and possibly a follow-up invasion of Cuba." (2) "If at least one Soviet ship either did not receive orders to stop before the blockade line (or, for some reason, disobeyed orders), there would have been a naval clash between American and Soviet forces in the Atlantic that would have resulted in military casualties, raising the possibility of tit-for-tat escalation." (3) "If, in the aftermath of the shooting down of a U.S. reconnaissance plane over Cuba on October 20, Kennedy had agreed to implement his standing order to carry out retaliatory air strikes against Soviet SAM (surface to air missile) sites in Cuba that shot down U.S. aircraft, then the U.S. Air Force would have attacked Soviet anti-aircraft installations, which might have set off tit-for-tat escalation." As in the correlational studies, respondents made three judgments of each scenario on nine-point scales: the ease of imagining that antecedent could have occurred; the likelihood of the hypothesized consequence if the antecedent had occurred; and the long-term effect on history if the hypothesized antecedent and consequence did occur.

Third, in the high-salience condition, respondents (n ~ 23) not only considered the three aforementioned situations but also judged a series of nine additional what-if scenarios that reinforced the antecedents in each of the three close calls. For example, counterfactual arguments 1, 2, and 3 reinforced the plausibility of the antecedents in the fourth counterfactual. (1) "If there had not been someone with the intellectual stature and credibility of Secretary of Defense McNamara to make a credible case for caution, then Kennedy would have followed the advice of his more hawkish advisors." (2) "If one of the newspapers to whom Kennedy had confided details of the Soviet placement of missiles in Cuba had leaked the story, there would have been irresistible public pressure on Kennedy to follow the advice of his more hawkish advisors." (3) "If Kennedy had believed that the United States Air Force could knock out all of the Soviet missiles in a single strike (with no need for a follow-up land invasion), he would have followed the advice of his more hawkish advisors." (4) "If Kennedy had followed the advice of his more hawkish advisors in the initial meetings of October 16, there would have been an American air strike against Soviet missile bases in Cuba, and possibly a follow-up invasion of Cuba." The full text and set-up for the presentation of the antecedent-bolstering arguments is available from the authors on request.

Retrospective Perceptions of Inevitability and Impossibility

The order of administration of these questions was always counterbalanced. The inevitability-curve exercise instructions were as follows:

"Let's define the crisis as having ended when, on October 29, Kennedy communicated to the Soviet leadership his agreement with Khrushchev's radio message of October 28. At that juncture, we could say that some form of peaceful resolution was a certainty—a subjective probability of 1.0. Going backward in time, day by day, from October 29 to October 16, trace on the graph your perceptions of how the likelihood of a peaceful resolution rose or fell during the 14 critical days of the crisis. If you think the U.S. and U.S.S.R. never came close to a military clash between October 16 and 29, then express that view by assigning consistently high probabilities to a peaceful resolution across all dates (indeed, as high as certainty, 1.0, if you wish). If you think the superpowers were very close to a military conflict throughout the crisis, then assign consistently low probabilities to a peaceful resolution across all dates. Finally, if you think the likelihood of a peaceful resolution waxed and waned day to day, then assign probabilities that rise or fall in accord with your intuitions about how close the U.S. and U.S.S.R. came to a military clash at various junctures. To start, we have set the subjective probability of peace at 1.0 (certainty) for October 29, marking the end of the crisis."

The impossibility-curve instructions were similar, except that the starting point was the subjective probability of 0.0 assigned to October 29 to signify that alternative, more violent outcomes had become impossible. Experts were then asked to go backward in time, day by day, from October 29 to October 16, and trace on the graph their perceptions of how the likelihood of those more violent outcomes waxed and waned.

Findings

The initial analyses involved a 3 ~ 2 ~ 13 fixed-effects, unweighted-means analysis of variance that crossed three levels of the between-subjects experimental manipulation (control, moderate, and high salience), two levels of the individual-difference classification variable (low versus high need for closure), and thirteen levels of the repeated-measures factor that corresponded to the days of the crisis. Contrary to expectation, the moderate and high conditions did not differ on either inevitability or impossibility curves (both Fs ~ 1). We attribute this null result to a methodological shortcoming: respondents reported being rather overwhelmed by the number of judgments required in the high-salience condition, and fatigue may have attenuated any further effect that exposure to additional counterfactual scenarios might have had.

To simplify analysis, therefore, we collapsed the moderate and high groups into a single salient condition. Follow-up analyses, now taking the form of a 2 ~ 2 ~ 13 analysis of variance, revealed the predicted second-order interaction: inevitability curves rose more slowly over time among those with lower need for closure assigned to the salient condition, $F(12, 908) ~ 6.74$, $p ~ .01$. The predicted mirror-image second-order interaction emerged on the impossibility curves $F(12, 908) ~ 5.33$, $p ~ .01$, which is not surprising, given that the measures were highly correlated, $r ~ 0.76$. Figures 5.1 and 5.2 clearly show that the distinctive functional forms of the inevitability and impossibility curves of low-need-closure respondents in the salient condition drive both interactions.

As expected, within-subjects comparisons reveal that when experts completed an inevitability curve and immediately thereafter an impossibility curve—that is, when binary complementarity was transparently

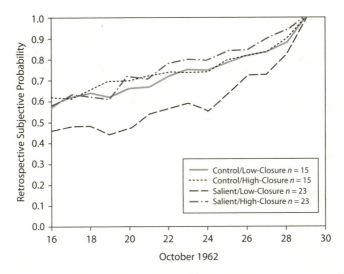

Figure 5.1. Inevitability curves from experiment 1

Note: The figure displays inevitability curves from experts with low and high need for closure in the control and salient conditions of experiment 1. The rate of rise toward 1.0 indicates the degree to which experts perceived the likelihood of some form of peaceful resolution of the Cuban missile crisis as increasingly likely with the passage of time, with the value of 1.0 signifying inevitability.

at stake—subjective probabilities of peace and war summed to approximately 1.0 (~ 1.04). Systematic violations of binary complementarity emerged, however, when we made more subtle between-group comparisons. For instance, when we add the subjective probability of peace assigned by experts who first completed inevitability curves to the subjective probability of war assigned by experts who first completed impossibility curves, the average sum across dates is 1.19. This value is significantly different from what we obtain by adding the probability of war and peace judgments of the two groups of experts who completed their inevitability or impossibility curves in the second position: the average sum across dates ~ 0.90, (F [1, 71] ~ 10.32, p ~ .01). There was, however, no evidence for the twilight-zone-period hypothesis that the experts who responded first to either inevitability or impossibility curves could be "lured" into assigning probability values that implied the existence of a period during which peace was inevitable (1.0) but war had not yet become impossible (0.0)—impossibility date of war (October 27.5) and inevitability date of peace (~ 26.9, F [1, 71] ~ 2.68, p ~ .15).

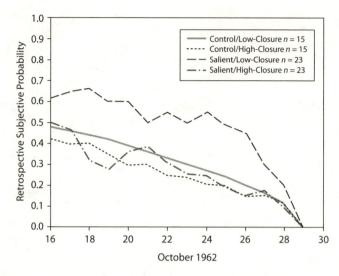

Figure 5.2. Impossibility curves from experiment 1

Note: The figure displays impossibility curves from experts with low and high need for closure in the control and salient conditions of Experiment 1. The rate of decline toward zero indicates the degree to which experts perceived the likelihood of alternative, more violent endings of the Cuban missile crisis as decreasingly likely with the passage of time, with zero signifying impossibility.

Experiment 2: Unpacking Alternative Outcomes

Skeptics can argue that in experiment 1 respondents were confronted with an elaborate battery of mutually reinforcing counterfactuals that made alternative histories unfairly vivid and left little room for deterministic rejoinders. It also can be argued that norms of politeness made experts reluctant to dismiss all the researchers' what-if scenarios as errant nonsense. Experiment 2 eliminates both objections by shifting the spotlight to the power of entirely self-generated counterfactual scenarios to alter perceptions of historical contingency.

Guiding Theory

Consider again forecasts of which league, division, or team will win a sports championship. Tversky and Fox demonstrate that the subjective probabilities people assign to binary complements at the league level (East versus West) generally sum to 1.0, but the subjective probabilities assigned to progressively more detailed or unpacked outcomes—the prospects of divisions within leagues and teams within divisions—typically exceed 1.0 and occasionally even 2.0.[21] Forecasters find it easier to generate evidential support for a particular team winning than for several different teams winning.

In support theory, it is the ease with which these reasons come to mind, their availability, that determines the subjective feeling of support for, and subjective probability of, outcomes. The result can be massive "subadditivity." The cumulative probabilities assigned to the exhaustive and exclusive components of the whole set exceed 1.0, which violates the extensionality axiom of probability theory. If people were to back up their unpacked bets with actual money, they would be quickly transformed into money pumps. It is, after all, logically impossible for each of four teams within an eight-team division to have a 0.4 chance of winning the championship the same year.

Unpacking manipulations are understandably viewed as sources of cognitive bias in subjective probability judgments of possible futures. They stimulate people to find too much support for too many possibilities. Yet, such manipulations may help reduce bias in subjective probability judgments of possible pasts via exactly the same mechanism. The key difference is that judgments of possible pasts, unlike those of possible futures, are already contaminated by the powerful certainty of hindsight. Experimental work shows that as soon as people learn which of a number of once deemed possible outcomes happened, they quickly assimilate that knowledge into their cognitive structure and have a hard time recapturing their ex ante state of uncertainty.[22] Mental exercises that involve unpacking sets of possible pasts should have the net effect of checking the hindsight bias by bringing back to psychological life counterfactual possibilities that people long ago buried with deterministic "I-knew-it-had-to-be" thinking.

Hypotheses

Drawing on support theory, we hypothesize that experts who are encouraged to unpack the set of more violent endings of the Cuban missile crisis into progressively more differentiated subsets will find support for those alternative outcomes. As a result, their inevitability curves will rise more slowly and their impossibility curves will fall less rapidly than those of experts who judge the entire set of possibilities as a whole. It is also expected that experts in the unpacking condition, especially those with low need for closure, will display stronger subadditivity effects (cumulative subjective probabilities exceeding 1.0) than the holistic group.

Research Design, Method, and Logic of Analysis

The sixty-four respondents in experiment 2 were drawn from the same subject population as experiment 1 and recruited in the same mail survey. Respondents were randomly assigned to one of two groups. The control group (n ~ 30) simply responded to the perceptions-of-inevitability and perceptions-of-impossibility items, as in experiment 1. The other group (n ~ 34) was asked to consider how the set of more violent endings of the Cuban missile crisis could be disaggregated (1) into subsets in which violence remained localized or spread outside the Caribbean, (2) in turn differentiated into subsets in which violence claimed fewer or more than one hundred casualties, and (3) for the higher casualty scenario, still more differentiated into a conflict either limited to conventional weaponry or extending to nuclear. Respondents generated impossibility curves for each of the six specific subsets of more violent scenarios as well as a single inevitability curve for the overall set of peaceful outcomes.

Findings

The results again reveal that how we pose historical questions shapes how we answer them. Figure 5.3 illustrates the power of unpacking questions. The shaded area represents the cumulative increase in the subjective probability that experts believe counterfactual alternatives once possessed, an increase that was produced by asking experts to generate impossibility curves not for the abstract set of more violent outcomes (lower curve) but for each of the six specific subsets of those outcomes (upper curve). The analysis of variance took the form of a fixed-effects, unweighted means 2 (control versus unpacking) ~ 2 (low versus high need for closure) ~ 13 (days of crisis) design.

Consider the impossibility-curve dependent variable. (Inevitability-curve results were again highly correlated, r ~ .71, and largely redundant for these hypothesis-testing purposes.) Analysis revealed the predicted main effects for unpacking (F [1, 58] ~ 7.89, p ~ .05) and need for closure (F [1, 58] ~ 5.05, p ~ .05), as well as the expected tendency for the impossibility curve of respondents with low need for closure to fall more slowly than that of high-need respondents in the unpacking condition (F [1, 58] ~ 4.35, p ~ .05). In addition, two unexpected tendencies emerged: unpacking effects diminished toward the end of the crisis (F [12, 718] ~ 7.31, p ~ .05), as did differences between low- and high-closure respondents (F [12, 718] ~ 5.02, p ~ .05). Experts, even low-need closure experts unpacking possibilities, saw less and less wiggle room for rewriting history as the end approached.

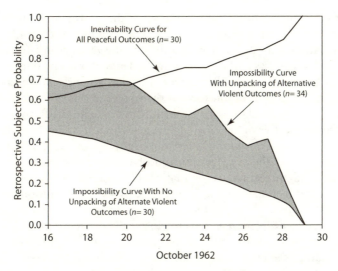

Figure 5.3. Inevitability and impossibility curves from experiment 2

Note: The figure presents inevitability and impossibility curves for the Cuban missile crisis. The inevitability curve displays gradually rising likelihood judgments of some form of peaceful resolution. The lower impossibility curve displays gradually declining likelihood judgments of all possible more violent endings. The higher impossibility curve was derived by adding the experts' likelihood judgments of six specific subsets of more violent possible endings. Adding value of the lower impossibility curve to the corresponding values of the inevitability curve yields sums only slightly above 1.0. Inserting values from the higher impossibility curve yields sums well above 1.0. The shaded area represents the cumulative effect of unpacking on the retrospective subjective probability of counterfactual alternatives to reality.

There was also support for the hypothesis that low-closure experts in the unpacking condition will exhibit the strongest subadditivity effects (probability judgments of exhaustive and exclusive sets of possibilities summing to more than 1.0). Averaged across dates, their combined inevitability and impossibility judgments summed to 1.38, which was significantly greater than the sum for low-closure experts in the control group (~~ ~ 1.12) or for high-closure experts in either the unpacking condition (~~ ~ 1.18) or control group (~~ ~ 1.04) (F [1, 58] ~ 9.89, p ~ .05). Again, there was little support for the twilight-zone-period hypothesis. The longest time during which experts judged peace inevitable (~~ inevitability date ~ Oct. 27.2) but war not yet impossible (~~ impossibility date ~ Oct. 28.1) emerged in judgments within the unpacking condition, and even this difference fell short statistically (F [1, 58] ~ 3.03, p ~ .10).

The curve-fitting results also underscore the power of counterfactual thought experiments to transform our understanding of the past. Simple linear equations capture large proportions of the variance in retrospective-likelihood judgments of the undifferentiated sets of peaceful outcomes (82 percent) and more violent alternatives (84 percent). The past appears to be a smooth linear progression toward the observed outcome. By contrast, the past looks more like a random walk, albeit around a discernible trend, from the perspective of low-closure experts who unpacked the set of more violent outcomes. A convoluted fourth-order polynomial equation is necessary to explain the same proportion of variance in their retrospective likelihood judgments, a function that rises and falls at three junctures.

The power of unpacking is also revealed by cross-condition comparisons of correlations between theoretical beliefs, such as the robustness of nuclear deterrence, and reactions to close-call counterfactuals that move the missile crisis toward war. The correlation is greater in the control condition than in the unpacking condition (r [28 df] ~ 0.61 versus r [32 df] ~ 0.27). This drop is consistent with the notion that, under unpacking, observers shift from a theory-driven, covering-law mode of thinking to a more idiographic, case-by-case mode.

EXPERIMENT 3: UNMAKING THE WEST

Guiding Theory

Scholars have long pondered how a small number of Europeans, working from the superficially unpromising starting point of AD 1000 or AD 1200 or even AD 1400, managed in a relatively few centuries to surpass all other peoples on the planet in wealth and power. Not surprisingly, there is a wide range of opinion. At one pole are determinists, who view history as an efficient process of winnowing out maladaptive forms of social organization and who believe that the triumph of capitalism has long been in the cards. The key advantages of European polities allegedly included more deeply rooted legal traditions of private property and individual rights, a religion that encouraged worldly achievement, and a fractious multistate system that prevented any single power from dominating all others and halting innovation at the reactionary whim of its ruling elite.[23]

At the other pole are the antideterminists. To adapt Gould's famous thought experiment,[24] they believe that if we could rerun world history thousands of times from the starting conditions that prevailed as recently as AD 1400, European dominance would be one of the least likely outcomes. These scholars decry "Eurocentric triumphalism" and depict the

European achievement as a precarious one that easily could have unraveled at countless junctures. Other civilizations could have checked the West and perhaps even been contenders themselves but for accidents of disease, weather, bad leadership, and other miscellaneous slings and arrows of outrageous fortune. As our third correlational study suggests, the list of "could-have-been-a-contender" counterfactuals is long. South Asia and perhaps East Africa might have been colonized by an invincible Chinese armada in the fifteenth century if only there had been more support in the imperial court for technological innovation and territorial expansion. Europe might have been Islamicized in the eighth century if the Moors had cared to launch a serious invasion of France. If not for Genghis Khan dying in the nick of time, European civilization might have been devastated by Mongol armies in the thirteenth century.

Within the antideterministic framework, thought experiments become exercises in ontological egalitarianism, an effort to restore dignity to those whom history has eclipsed by elevating possible worlds to the same moral and metaphysical status as the actual world.[25] Thought experiments are the only way left to even the score, an observation ironically reminiscent of the Marxist historian E. H. Carr's dismissal of anti-Bolsheviks as sore losers who, from dreary exile, contemplated counterfactuals that undid the Russian Revolution.[26] But now the gloaters, claiming historical vindication for their ideological principles, are on the Right, and the brooders, absorbed in wistful regret, are on the Left.

Hypotheses

The hypotheses parallel those for experiment 2, except now the focal issue is not the Cuban missile crisis but the rise of Western civilization to global hegemony (a massively complex historical transformation that stretches over centuries, not days). Once again, unpacking is expected to inflate the perceived likelihood of counterfactual possibilities and to produce subadditivity effects, especially for respondents with low need for closure.

Research Design, Methods, and Measures

Experiment 3 draws on the same respondents and uses the same mail survey as the third correlational study. The experiment has only two conditions. The no-unpacking control group (n ~ 27) generated inevitability curves for some form of Western geopolitical domination and impossibility curves for the set of all possible alternatives to that domination (order counterbalanced). The intensive unpacking group (n ~ 36) was first asked to unpack the set of all possible alternatives to Western domination into progressively more detailed subsets. These began with classes of possible worlds in which no region achieved global hegemony (either because of a weaker Europe or stiffer resistance from outside Europe) and moved on to classes of possible worlds in which a non-Western civilization achieved global hegemony (China, Islam, the Mongols, or a less familiar alternative). Experts then completed inevitability and impossibility curves that began with AD 1000 and moved by fifty-year increments to AD 1850 (for which the subjective probability of Western dominance was fixed at 1.0 and that of possible alternatives at 0.0).

Findings

The shaded area in figure 5.4[27] represents the cumulative increase in the subjective probability that experts believe counterfactual alternatives once possessed, an increase that was produced by asking experts to generate impossibility curves not for the abstract set of alternatives to Western domination (lower curve) but for each of the six specific subsets of alternatives (upper curve). The analysis of variance took the form of a fixed-effects, unweighted means 2 (no unpacking versus unpacking conditions) ~ 2 (low versus high closure) ~ 17 (fifty-year increments between 1000 and 1850) mixed-factorial design. It reveals a significant unpacking effect (F [1, 58] ~ 6.77, p ~ .05) and a significant interaction between unpacking and cognitive style: the differences between low- and high-closure respondents grew more pronounced when they were asked to perform the unpacking exercise (F [1, 58] ~ 4.88, p ~ .05). The same two unexpected but readily interpretable tendencies emerged as in experiment 2. That is, as dates approached the end of the time series, now 1800, experts who unpacked alternatives to Western dominance saw less potential for rewriting history (F [16, 1018] ~ 4.88, p ~ .01), and the gap between low- and high-closure respondents narrowed (F [16, 1018] ~ 4.02, p ~ .05). Again, observers saw less likelihood for counterfactually altering outcomes toward the end of the specified historical process.

Also as in experiment 2, low-closure experts in the unpacking condition were most likely to assign subjective probabilities that were subadditive, violated extensionality, and summed to well above 1.0. Averaged across dates, their judgments about inevitability and impossibility summed to 1.41, which was significantly greater than the sum for low-closure experts in the control group (~~ ~ 1.09) or for high-closure experts in the control group (~~ ~ 1.03) or unpacking condition (~~ ~ 1.21) (F [1, 58] ~ 4.67, p ~ .05). A twilight-zone period also emerged; in contrast to the

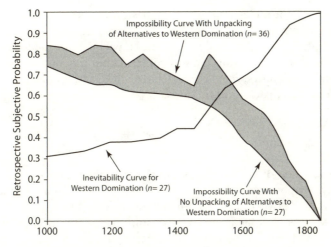

Figure 4. Inevitability and impossibility curves from experiment 3

Note: The figure presents inevitability and impossibility curves for the rise of the West. The inevitability curve displays gradually rising likelihood judgments of some form of Western geopolitical dominance. The lower impossibility curve displays gradually declining likelihood judgments of all possible alternatives to Western dominance. The upper impossibility curve was derived by adding experts' likelihood judgments of six subsets of alternatives to Western domination. Adding values of the lower impossibility curve to corresponding inevitability-curve values yields sums only slightly above 1.0. Inserting values from the upper impossibility curve yields sums well above 1.0. The shaded area represents the cumulative effect of unpacking on the retrospective subjective probability of counterfactual alternatives to reality.

temporally compacted missile crisis, there is now a sufficient range in responses to permit significant effects. Focusing just on the control condition, we compared the average date for the inevitability of Western dominance to the average date for the impossibility of alternatives to Western dominance. The result was a twilight-zone period bounded by the inevitability date of 1731 and the impossibility date of 1749 (F [1, 28] ~ 4.21, p ~ .05). This period for the unpacking condition was bounded, respectively, by 1751 and 1787, which not only is a significant difference in itself (F [1, 32] ~ 8.43, p ~ .01) but also is significantly longer (F [1, 58] ~ 4.36, p ~ .05).

In terms of curve fitting, a fifth-order polynomial equation was necessary to capture 80 percent of the variance in the numerous ups and downs in average perceptions of the likelihood of unpacked outcomes, whereas a simple linear equation sufficed for the undifferentiated set. Unpacking "messes up" our understanding of the past, transforming what had once been a smooth progression toward a preordained outcome into a far more erratic and unpredictable journey. Unpacking also undermines the power of abstract covering laws to constrain our perceptions of specific historical possibilities; correlations fell from 0.63 in the control condition to 0.25 in the unpacking conditions.

General Discussion

Our results do not tell us who is right about this or that historical controversy. Proponents of the covering-law approach can argue that high correlations between abstract theoretical beliefs and specific opinions about what is possible at given times and places are fully justified and that low-preference-for-parsimony experts who fail to make tight conceptual connections between the two levels are just confused and sloppy thinkers. As for the results of our experiments, these proponents can argue that unpacking manipulations simply lead historical observers into the inferential equivalent of wild goose chases that encourage them to assign far too much subjective probability to far too many scenarios. The end result is logical absurdities, such as "x is inevitable," but "alternatives to x remain possible." There is nothing admirably open-minded about incoherence.

Critics of the covering-law approach can respond that the high correlations between abstract theoretical beliefs and specific historical ones are a warning sign of an excessively theory-driven style of thinking about history. So much the better if unpacking manipulations prove an effective method of opening closed minds by reminding theory-driven thinkers of how riddled with indeterminacy history is. Unpacking reveals previously hidden cognitive contradictions and sets a constructive agenda for rethinking.

A cognitive approach to historical reasoning can never resolve the question of whether, in any given historical case, we have struck the right balance between theory-driven and imagination-driven modes of information processing. A cognitive approach can, however, enhance the quality of intellectual debate in four tangible ways.

First, it identifies systematic individual differences in the relative importance that observers place on achieving an integrative view of the past. Respondents with a preference for closure (who resemble the hedgehogs in Berlin's famous taxonomy) tried to assimilate the past into their favored deductive system. Those with less need for closure (who resemble Berlin's foxes) approached the past in a frame of mind open to the possibility that a potpourri of processes may have been involved, and an equally miscellaneous set of outcomes could have resulted. Moreover, these individual differences cut across disciplinary boundaries, a point underscored by the striking parallelism in the results of experiment 2 (which drew mostly on political scientists) and experiment 3 (which drew mostly on historians).

Second, a cognitive approach deepens our understanding of how the framing of historical questions can shape where and how we look for answers. Logically equivalent factual and counterfactual framings of the same historical issue elicit contradictory probabilistic intuitions about what had to be and what might have been. Our experiments also demonstrate the importance of the specificity of the question: the more detailed the unpacking of counterfactual alternatives, the greater is the tendency for the whole class of alternatives to be judged less likely than the sum of its exclusive and exhaustive components (subadditivity). The challenge that these findings pose to rationality should not be understated. Unpacking effects violate a core assumption not only of Bayesian but also of all formal logical models of belief, namely, the extensionality principle, which asserts that classes of events with the same content should be assigned the same probability.[28]

Third, a cognitive approach suggests methods of pitting cognitive biases against one another, the mental equivalent of fighting fire with fire, by checking the excesses of convergent, theory-driven thinking with divergent imagination-driven thinking, and vice versa. The preeminent theory-driven bias in historical reasoning is, as many laboratory studies now attest, certainty of hindsight.[29] Once people learn the outcome of a historical process—how the stock market finished the year or whether a crisis was resolved peacefully—they have difficulty recalling how uncertain they once were and exaggerate the degree to which "they knew it all along." The most influential cognitive explanation of the hindsight effect attributes it to the "automaticity" of theory-driven thought, to the rapidity with which people assimilate known outcomes into their favorite covering laws. In the process, they demote once possible, even probable, futures to the status of implausible historical counterfactuals.

Knowledge of past possibilities need not, however, be lost forever. The "debiasing" literature points to experimental interventions that can help people reconstruct latent knowledge of historical junctures at which they once thought events could have taken a different turn.[30] The potential correctives draw on two well-replicated effects widely considered judgmental biases themselves: the tendency to inflate the perceived likelihood of vivid, easily imagined, scenarios, coupled with the tendency to underestimate how rapidly subjective probabilities should diminish as a function of adding contingencies to scenarios.[31] The most effective manipulations for attenuating certainty of hindsight make use of these effects by asking people to imagine, in florid detail, alternative paths that history could have taken.

Fourth, a cognitive approach makes us aware of the trade-offs involved in the quest to open closed minds. Laboratory work on mental simulation shows that people can get carried away when they start imagining alternative "possible worlds."[32] To check runaway unpacking effects, people need plausibility pruners to cut off speculation that otherwise would grow like topsy beyond the bounds of probability. These elimination criteria inevitably reflect beliefs about what counts as a plausible cause-effect linkage. Indeed, the cognitive approach also warns us not to treat imagination as an alternative to theory-driven thinking. Alice in Wonderland scenarios aside, most imaginative thinking imports theory-driven schemes for understanding cause and effect in hypothetical worlds. The distinction between the two modes is a matter of degree: theory-driven cognition is convergent, relying on a single deductive framework to explain what actually happened, whereas imaginative cognition is divergent, drawing on a variety of frameworks to explore not only what happened but also what could have happened.

If this account is correct, historical observers confront a perplexing trade-off between theory-driven and imagination-driven modes of making sense of the past. Theory-driven strategies confer the benefits of explanatory closure and parsimony but desensitize us to nuance, complexity, contingency, and the possibility our theory is wrong. Imagination-driven strategies sensitize us to possible worlds that could have been, but desensitize us to patterns, regularities, and underlying causes. The challenge is to strike a reasonable balance, a reflective equilibrium, between the conflicting intuitions primed by factual framings of historical questions that activate narrowly theory-driven thinking and those primed by counterfactual framings that engage our imaginations and activate a wider range of theories.

Absent compelling grounds for preferring one or the other mode of information processing, the prudent stance is to define good judgment as an iterative process of checking convergent theory-driven thinking, which focuses on explaining why what was had to be, with divergent imagination-driven thinking, which focuses on what could have been, and then putting the whole procedure into reverse so that theory-driven thinking can be deployed to prevent us from spinning out of imaginative control. There will, of course, be no single, well-defined equilibrium solution. But it is reasonable to expect that the process—as it unfolds not just in the mind of one observer but in ostensibly self-correcting scholarly communities—will yield plausibility ranges of equilibrium solutions. These will be anchored at one end by those with the most hedgehoglike confidence in covering laws and at the other by those with the most foxlike curiosity about the paths events could have taken. This range of reflective equilibrium solutions should be preferred to lopsided solutions that give priority to either theory-driven or imaginative modes of thinking.

CHAPTER SIX

Scholars and Causation 2

CHAPTER 5 REVEALED a strong correlation between worldviews and openness to contingency. Across diverse contexts, the more credence foreign policy experts, historians and international relations scholars place in the ability of laws and generalizations to describe the social world, the stronger their cognitive-stylistic preference for explanatory closure. In making judgments about contingency, they are more likely to be guided by what they believe to be valid laws and generalizations than information provided to them on a case-by-case basis. Experts with a preference for lawlike understandings of history tend to resist counterfactuals that "undo" events or outcomes on which their preferred laws, theories, or generalization are based or which appear to sustain them. They are most open to counterfactuals that unmake events or outcomes that appear anomalous to these laws, theories, or generalizations. Foreign policy experts, historians, and international relations scholars who place little credence in the efficacy of laws and generalizations reveal less of a preference for explanatory closure. They are more likely to reason inductively and make judgments of contingency on a case-by-case basis. They are correspondingly less inclined to evaluate specific counterfactuals in terms of prior intellectual commitments.[1]

This chapter seeks to understand more about the ways in which historians and international relations scholars understand historical causation. There is, of course, a deep philosophical divide about causation as a conceptual category, going back to Hume and Kant's First Critique. I am not interested here in how we should understand causation, but rather in how experts understand it, in practice, not abstractly. My inquiry relates back to more philosophical inquiries because it illustrates the extent to which causation is cognitive in practice.

The novelty of this chapter lies in the nature of the questions I ask and the instruments I employ to try to get answers. Numerous studies of contingency, including those described in the last chapter, employ "close-call" counterfactuals to mutate events. Close-call counterfactuals have been used to test the relationship between counterfactual unpacking and estimates of contingency to, determine the characteristics of actors and environments that people think most susceptible to change, and to discover the conditions under which people are most likely to invoke counterfactuals without experimental priming. There is no similar research on how people respond to counterfactuals at considerable temporal remove from an outcome they are intended to mutate. The possibility and impossibility curves of the previous chapter indicate that foreign policy experts and historians lower their estimates of contingency the closer they approach an outcome in question. Conversely, the farther back we go from an event, the less determined it appears.

Counterfactuals are not just a laboratory tool. People invent their own counterfactuals for diverse cognitive and affective reasons. Are there significant differences in the kinds of counterfactuals people invent and those used by researchers to probe their understandings of causation? Are people more likely to give credence to the counterfactuals they invent than those that they confront in experiments? The first question is difficult to answer because people spontaneously engage in counterfactual thinking in a wide range of circumstances. It is something of an oxymoron to design a survey or experiment intended to encourage participants to spontaneously invent counterfactuals. The best we may we able to do is to encourage people to devise counterfactuals to mutate specific events and compare their counterfactuals and estimates of contingency with those of other participants who respond to counterfactuals devised by the researchers toward the same end.

The importance of belief systems helps to explain the resistance of experts to counterfactuals that violate their understandings of how the world works and their corresponding receptivity to those that make anomalous outcomes consistent with their beliefs. Even the most determinist foreign policy experts and scholars acknowledge some degree of contingency in the social world. One way for them to reconcile this acceptance with their overall commitment to determinism is to be more open to the antecedents of counterfactuals than to their consequents, especially in the case of outcomes dissonant with their belief systems. This suggests the broader proposition that how people respond to antecedents is not entirely independent of the consequences to which they are alleged to lead.

Experiment 1 makes use of a close-call counterfactual to undo World War I. Instrument one provides the outlines of an argument that World War I could have been avoided in the short- and longer-term if Archduke Franz Ferdinand and his wife Sophie had not been assassinated. Instrument two—chapter 3 in its entirety—offers, as the reader knows, a more comprehensive presentation of this argument. As expected, the more extensive unpacking of the same counterfactual in instrument two leads to greater estimates of contingency. Following the lead of Tversky and Kahneman, I surmise that the difference in estimates is due to its greater vividness.

Experiment 2 also seeks to unmake World War I. However, I do not provide participants—historians and international relations scholars—

with any information or arguments but rather ask them to devise their own counterfactuals to undo this event. Inventing a counterfactual requires more intellectual effort and imagination than merely responding to one and should make the resulting counterfactual more vivid and, hence, more credible, to its inventors. The evidence offers some support for this proposition.

Experiment 3 uses "long-shot" counterfactuals to untrack World War I. As noted earlier, long-shot counterfactuals are minimal rewrites of history at some temporal distance from the event they are intended to mutate. They require a longer and more elaborate chain of logic linking antecedent to consequent and more enabling counterfactuals. Enabling counterfactuals are additional minimal rewrites of history that sustain the chain of logic. Some enabling counterfactuals follow from the initial counterfactual and others must be invented de novo. Although people see events as more contingent the farther back from them in time one goes, I believe that long-shot counterfactuals should be judged less credible than their close-call counterparts because of their longer chain of logic and greater number of enabling counterfactuals. I further surmise that estimates of probability will be affected *negatively* by their vividness, an attribute of counterfactuals that is otherwise assumed to enhance their plausibility. The experimental results offer partial confirmation of this proposition.

A final experiment, experiment 4, is based on the robust finding of earlier studies that people are generally more willing to acknowledge the plausibility of counterfactual antecedents than the consequences to which they are intended to lead. This pattern is pronounced in the two instruments I use in experiment 1 to undo World War I. To explore the relationship between antecedent and consequent, and the extent to which estimates of one are dependent on the other, I had student participants evaluate the plausibility of sixteen counterfactuals that undid and created American triumphs and tragedies. I had a second sample of students evaluate these counterfactuals in reverse order; they were confronted first with the consequents, then with the chain of logic linking them to antecedents, and finally, with the antecedents. The experiment demonstrates the cognitive ability of people to reason backward and stop counterfactuals dead in their tracks if they consider them intellectually or psychologically objectionable.

The variation revealed by the correlational and experimental studies supports the general understanding in the psychological literature that causation must be understood as a distinctly perceptual category.[2] Historians and international relations scholars reveal an interesting mix of cognitive sophistication and naiveté. They have no difficulty recognizing the implications of counterfactuals and are strongly motivated to accept or reject them on the basis of their worldviews. Participants can nevertheless be encouraged by means of counterfactual priming to acknowledge more contingency than they otherwise would. Psycho-logic has the potential to render their judgments logically incoherent. This is most evident in the case of long-shot counterfactuals, which can *reduce* overall judgments of contingency by historians and international relations scholars despite surveys across cases that indicate they judge events and outcomes increasingly contingent the farther back in time from an event they are asked to make these assessments. These contradictions between beliefs and assessments might be reconciled with reference to the effects of vividness on estimates of contingency, but this in turn raises further questions about the ways in which scholars make assessments of historical contingency.

Experimental Study 1: "Close-Call" Counterfactuals

Guiding Theory

Several experiments have demonstrated the ability of counterfactual priming to shift experts' judgments of contingency. Ross, Lepper, Strack, and Steinmetz exploited the tendency of people to inflate the perceived likelihood of vivid scenarios to make them more responsive to contingency. People they presented with scenarios describing possible life histories of post-therapy patients evaluated these possibilities as more likely than did members of the control group who were not given the scenarios. This effect persisted even when participants in the experiment were told that the post-therapy scenarios were entirely hypothetical.[3] Tversky and Kahneman's studies of the availability and simulation heuristics suggest that merely imagining multi-event scenarios increases the perceived likelihood of the component events.[4] Close-call counterfactuals reveal that the human mind is not determinist. Even in hindsight we can recognize propensities that would have produced diverse outcomes.[5] Our three experiments in chapter five offer additional support to these propositions; we found that scholars exposed to the imputed consequences of reasonably plausible counterfactual scenarios become more open in general to the role of contingency in history and international relations.

Hypotheses

Thinking about plausible counterfactual scenarios should, on average, increase the perception that those scenarios once had the potential to materialize and may even have been more likely than events that came to pass.

The progressive unpacking of counterfactual scenarios should further increase estimates of contingency. The more information provided about plausible counterfactual scenarios in the form of argument and narrative detail, the more vivid they become, and hence, the more credible.[6]

Research Design

In chapter 2 I developed protocols for plausible close-call counterfactuals. Psychologists have conducted numerous experiments to discover what ordinary people consider to constitute plausible counterfactuals. They do this indirectly by asking them to devise counterfactuals of their own, on the assumption that they will alter reality by means they consider plausible. These studies indicate that people mutate aspects of reality that are close to the outcome they seek to change, are exceptional rather than normal features of the causal nexus, undo action rather than inaction, that can be altered with the most minor interventions. In effect, people make the counterfactual world work more in the way we think the real world should.[7] Preventing World War I by averting its catalyst—the assassinations of Franz Ferdinand and his wife on 28 June 1914—meets all these conditions. It was close to the consequent; war broke out six weeks later. It was an exceptional event; assassinations of royalty, presidents, and prime ministers are uncommon. It can readily be mutated by having the archduke and his wife leave Sarajevo after the first, failed assassination attempt that morning. The counterfactual makes the world function more the way we expect as security details are supposed to whisk away figures they protect at the slightest hint of danger. Research also indicates that people perceive events early in a causal chain as having the most significance and are correspondingly more responsive to counterfactuals that untrack them.[8] Averting the assassinations meets this condition because it sets in motion the chain of events that led to war.

World War I is nevertheless a special case. Historians and international relations scholars have been primed by an extensive literature that argues that this conflict was overdetermined. As we saw in chapter 3, historians and international relations scholars have offered a diverse set of reasons for why the continental war, and later world war that erupted in the second decade of the twentieth century was all but inevitable. They include the insecurity of the two major alliance systems, the commitment to offensive military doctrines, the domestic insecurity of Austria-Hungary and Russia, belief in the positive social and domestic political effects of war, and widespread expectations that it was inevitable. Some of these putative causes are questionable, as is the overall claim of near inevitability, but they have become the conventional wisdom for historians and international relations scholars alike.[9] For the latter, World War I has become the paradigmatic case in which to build and test theories of war, especially realist theories that attribute war to power transition or multipolarity. Laws and theories are based on underlying regularities and would be undercut if it could be shown that idiosyncratic elements of context have a determining effect on outcomes. Even scholars not committed to realist theories have been socialized into believing that World War I, or something like it, was all but inevitable. For these reasons, World War I thus represents a particularly "hard case"—arguably, the hardest case for historians and international relations scholars—in which to test the power of counterfactuals to increase estimates of contingency.

My first instrument requires respondents to read a two-and-a-half page document that maintains that if Franz Ferdinand had not been assassinated, there would have been no European war in the summer of 1914. It further contends that a European war more generally would have been averted because the confluence of events that made leaders in Vienna, Berlin, and St. Petersburg more risk accepting than they had been even the year before was short-lived. The second instrument—chapter 3 in its entirety—offers a more elaborate and more fully documented presentation of this argument that considers and attempts to rebut counterarguments. It also offers a brief sketch of the possible evolution of a Europe that escaped a continental war in the second decade of the twentieth century.

Participants for both instruments were randomly drawn from membership lists of professional organizations in history and international relations. I recruited participants from North America and Europe. The participating historians are members of the German history section of the American Historical Society, the Military History Society, and the Arbeitskreis Militaergeschichte Historisches Institut, the latter headquartered at the University of Bern. They specialize in diplomatic and military history of the nineteenth and twentieth centuries and the origins and conduct of war. The international relations participants come from the Section 34, International History and Politics, of the American Political Science Association. All respondents were contacted by e-mail and promised anonymity and feedback about the results of the study. They were asked to click on a URL that brought them to the website of surveymonkey.com, where they were randomly assigned to an instrument. Surveymonkey collected the data and sent it on to me with participants identified only by number. The response rate is difficult to determine because I do not know the total number of historians contacted. Two of the organizations in question gave me a list of members and their e-mail addresses, the third offered to forward my e-mail to their members. The total number of historians contacted was over 250. This suggests a response rate of at most 26 percent as only 54 historians participated in the online experiments. I contacted 300 international relations scholars, of whom 129 participated, giving a response rate of 43 percent. Although I attempted to recruit equally in Europe and North America, those who trained and work in North America (n = 137) are overrepresented in comparison to those who trained and work in Europe (n = 34) or elsewhere in the world.

Historians and international relations scholars were randomly assigned to the three experiments and the two instruments of experiment 1. Of the total sample (n = 173), the number participating in experiment 1 was (n = 90), with (n = 50) for instrument 1 and (n = 40) for instrument 2. Instrument 2 required reading an entire chapter, which may explain the lower response rate. Assessing selection bias is difficult because of absence of information of who participated and who did not. The control group (n = 54) consisted of participants who were asked to devise their own counterfactual. They were not presented with any documents to read and were asked the same questions about World War I at the outset of their survey, before they were asked to come up with their own counterfactual.

Methods and Measures

All participants were asked general questions about the contingency of World War I: (5) Did you find the overall argument about the contingency of World War I plausible?; (8) How likely was it that the assassination of Franz Ferdinand could have been prevented?; (9) If Franz Ferdinand had not been assassinated in June 1914, how likely is it that a major European war would have broken out sometime before 1918?; and (10) If there had been no European war between 1914 and 1918, what do you think the chances of one taking place in the course of the next ten years would have been?

Participants who received instruments 1 and 2 were asked six additional questions about the counterfactuals with which they were presented:

11. The text maintains that three independent causal chains led to greater willingness to take risks on the part of Austrian, German, and Russian leaders. It further argues that the Austrian causal chain was highly contingent and could easily have been untracked, slowed down, or speeded up by any number of possible events or nonevents. Do you think this likely?

12. The text maintains that Sarajevo was as much a cause as a trigger because of the ways it changed the balance of power in Vienna and made it easier for German leaders to assume risks. How likely is it that some other event or provocation could have met these conditions?

13. The text conducts several counterfactual thought experiments to probe causation and contingency. Do you consider this a useful strategy?

14. Counterfactuals consist of an antecedent (changing some aspect of the past), a consequent (the outcome it is to produce), and the chain of logic that connects the two. The text intervenes in history to return Franz Ferdinand safely to Vienna (antecedent) to prevent World War I from breaking out (consequent) by having him continue to oppose any policy likely to risk war with Russia. How credible do you find the antecedent?

15. How credible do you find the consequent?

16. How convincing do you find the chain of logic?

In each instrument, respondents were asked to judge plausibility on a standard five-point scale: highly likely, likely, possible, unlikely, highly unlikely.

Findings

The overall pattern of responses to instruments 1 and 2 is similar. Respondents find antecedents (questions 8 and 14) more plausible than their imputed consequents (questions 9 and 15). The comparison of questions 5 and 8 further indicates that participants in both samples found the antecedent more plausible than the consequent. The p values in each of these comparisons is less than .005 (see tables 6.1 and 6.2 below).

The data from the two instruments and the control group support the hypothesis that counterfactual unpacking prompts higher estimates of contingency. When asked to evaluate the overall contingency of World War I, the mean for the control group was ($x = 2.52$), for instrument 1 ($x = 2.29$), and for instrument 2 ($x = 1.39$). These differences are significant as the p values in paired samples tests are below .05 for each comparison. The differences between instrument 1 and 2 also hold true across the range of other questions asked in both surveys. Those who read the full article (instrument 1) versus the synopsis (instrument 2) were more willing to mutate the antecedent (questions 8 and 14) and consequent (questions 9 and 15) and less likely to believe that a second-order counterfactual (question 10) would have produced a war at a later point (see table 6.3 below). They were more likely find the chain of logic linking antecedent to consequent plausible, but not significantly so. There were some statistically significant differences between historians and international relations scholars. Historians gave more credence to the assertion (question 9) that preventing the assassinations would have prevented a world war. They were also more willing to believe (question 11) that any number of minimal rewrites of history could credibly have

TABLE 6.1
Franz Ferdinand paired samples test

		Paired Differences							
				Std. error mean	95% Confidence interval of the difference				Sig.
		Mean	Std. deviation		lower	upper	t	df	(2-tailed)
Pair 1	q8 - q9	2.361	1.437	.240	1.875	2.847	9.856	35	.000
Pair 2	q14 - q15	−.857	1.216	.206	−1.275	−.439	−4.170	34	.000
Pair 3	q5 - q8	−2.556	1.629	.272	−3.107	−2.004	−9.412	35	.000
Pair 4	q9 - q10	−.114	.718	.121	−.361	.132	−.941	34	.353
Pair 5	q9 - q12	−.029	.857	.145	−.323	.266	−.197	34	.845
Pair 6	q10 - q12	.086	.919	.155	−.230	.402	.552	34	.585

TABLE 6.2
Full Franz paired samples test

		Paired Differences							
				Std. error mean	95% Confidence interval of the difference				Sig.
		Mean	Std. deviation		lower	upper	t	df	(2-tailed)
Pair 1	q8 - q9	2.485	1.121	.195	2.087	2.882	12.729	32	.000
Pair 2	q14 - q15	−.667	.816	.142	−.956	−.377	−4.690	32	.000
Pair 3	q5 - q8	−4.029	1.000	.171	−4.378	−3.681	−23.506	33	.000
Pair 4	q9 - q10	.063	.878	.155	−.254	.379	.403	31	.690
Pair 5	q9 - q12	.303	.951	.166	−.034	.640	1.830	32	.077
Pair 6	q10 - q12	.250	.984	.174	−.105	.605	1.438	31	.161

untracked one or more of the causal chains that made Austrian, German and Russian leaders more risk prone in 1914.

Both instruments asked participants to identify the most plausible and implausible aspects of the counterfactual. Those who responded to instrument 1 put an equal emphasis on the assassinations as a trigger for war as they did on its underlying causes. Eight of the participants agreed that without the assassinations there would have been no war, and that the assassination brought about war by virtue of how it affected the political and psychological disposition of Austrian and German leaders. An equal number of participants stressed the narrow window of opportunity brought about by the confluence of interactive causes and how it made the war highly contingent. Respondents to instrument 2 placed less emphasis on the antecedent (the assassinations) and considerably more on the effects of open-ended systems and nonlinearity. Four participants noted the importance of the assassination as a cause in its own right, while eight emphasized nonlinearity and path dependence. Another eighteen offered variants of these arguments by noting the importance of path dependence, the confluence of independent chains of causation, or contingency in general. The most striking difference in the open-ended comments is the greater emphasis put by those who read instrument 2 on concepts (i.e., patterns of causality) as causes of war versus discrete historical events and their consequences, which were more likely to be stressed by those who read instrument 1.

With regard to implausibility, there are few differences across the instruments. Objections to the counterfactual in both instruments were more historical than conceptual. The most frequently voiced—indicative of a realist orientation—invoked the so-called structure of the European political system and how it would still be determining even in a slightly altered context. A number of participants pointed to the existence of other causal chains that could or would have led to war, most notably those associated with German *Weltpolitik*, and to other corrosive conflicts between the great powers. Some of those who judged the counterfactual implausible maintained that the psychological environment in which European policymaking elites operated was less important than the political and military conditions these leaders faced. Interestingly, several respondents argued that German aggressiveness would have made war unavoidable, while two others make just the opposite case: German insecurity made war unavoidable. The only noticeable difference between respondents to the two instruments was the former's attraction to second-order counterfactuals. Six respondents to instrument 1—but only two in instrument 2—argued that if war had been averted in 1914 something else would almost certainly have come along to trigger if off.

EXPERIMENT 2: MAKE YOUR OWN COUNTERFACTUAL

Guiding Theory

Ancient Greek sophists believed that the most convincing arguments were those that people considered their own. Their texts largely eschewed authorial statements, or used contradictions between them and narratives to lead readers to formulate their own conclusions—

conclusions, to be sure, that arose from text and how it was structured.[10] Thucydides uses this technique with telling effect, following the sophist insight that arguments and conclusions people reach, or think they reach, by themselves will have greater plausibility than those presented to them by others.[11] In this connection, I expect two processes to have reinforcing effects. The first is vividness, also known as "concreteness," which is assumed responsible for the principal effects of counterfactual priming since the pioneering work of Tversky and Kahneman.[12] Scenarios devised by respondents should be more vivid to them, in part because of the more extensive unpacking of the event and its putative causes they must go through to construct them. A second process builds more directly on the sophists and assumes greater commitment to one's own ideas than to those generated by others. The former give testimony to one's creativity and knowledge, something we can assume is dear to scholars. Participants with a high need for closure can find themselves cross-pressured: they may develop some degree of commitment to the counterfactuals they themselves devise but remain committed to the immutability of the outcome in question.

Hypotheses

I hypothesize that participants will devise counterfactuals similar in character to those most commonly devised by other people. They will be close to the event in question, remake social rather than physical attributes of context, undo what are perceived as extraordinary rather than normal features of the context, and unmake earlier rather than later events of causal chains. I further hypothesize that participants will offer higher estimates of the contingency of World War I than those of either the control group or instrument 1 of experiment 1. This instrument is the relevant one for purposes of comparison because respondents were asked to assess the contingency of World War I based on a relatively brief description of a counterfactual devised by the researcher.

Research Design

Participants for this experiment (n = 54) were drawn from the same overall sample of historians and international relations scholars described in the research design section of the previous experiment. The control groups (n = 90) consisted of historians and international relations scholars who were given instrument 1 of the Franz Ferdinand counterfactual.

Methods and Measures

At the outset, participants were told that "World War I, or something like it, has often been described as almost inevitable by some historians" and asked to assess its likelihood on a five-point scale. To provide participants with a template for making their own counterfactuals, they were given an example of one that had nothing to do with World War I.

On Thanksgiving 1999 a boat of Cuban refugees capsized and many drowned. One of the few survivors, Elian Gonzalez, became a cause célèbre when Attorney General Janet Reno repatriated the boy to his father in Cuba rather than allowing him to live with relatives in Florida. Many fewer Cuban Americans than usual voted Democratic in the 2000 presidential election. If Elian had drowned as his mother had, Cuban Americans would not have been so angry with the Clinton administration and would have given Democrats the same plurality in Dade County (Miami) as they had in previous elections. If so, Gore would have carried the state of Florida and become president of the United States.

Participants were asked (question 7) how likely is it that Elian could have drowned (the antecedent), and if Elian had drowned (question 8), how likely was it that Gore would have won the election (the consequent)? They were then told that "counterfactuals consist of an antecedent (changing some aspect of the past), a consequent (the outcome it is to produce), and a chain of logic that connects the two." They were asked: "Can you think of a counterfactual antecedent that would have prevented World War I or something like it during the second decade of the twentieth century? If so could you describe it below and briefly note why it might have prevented war?" Finally, they were presented with the Franz Ferdinand counterfactual and asked the same questions about its consequences as participants in instruments 1 and 2.

Findings

The first finding of note is the paired samples test of questions 8 (if Elian had drowned would Gore have won the election?) and 10 (if Franz Ferdinand had returned safely to Vienna, World War I would not have broken out). It is the most significant comparison between questions (see table 6.3) and supports my contention that World War I is a particularly hard event to mutate given the largely determinist understanding historians and international relations scholars have of it. Participants estimated (see

TABLE 6.3
Create your own counterfactual paired samples test

				Std. error mean	95% Confidence interval of the difference				Sig. (2-tailed)
		Mean	Std. deviation		lower	upper	t	df	
Pair 1	q10 - q11	.617	1.328	.194	.227	1.007	3.186	46	.003
Pair 2	q11 - q12	.128	.924	.135	−.143	.399	.948	46	.348
Pair 3	q5 - q6	.021	.978	.141	−.263	.305	.148	47	.883
Pair 4	q8 - q10	−.674	1.097	.162	−1.000	−.348	−4.168	45	.000
Pair 5	q8 - q11	−.043	1.074	.158	−.362	.275	−.275	45	.785

TABLE 6.4
Create your own counterfactual descriptive statistics

	N	Minimum	Maximum	Mean	Std. deviation
q10	47	2	5	3.13	.741
q11	47	1	4	2.51	.804
q12	47	1	5	2.38	.992
q5	48	1	4	2.52	.714
q6	48	1	4	2.50	.684
q8	48	1	4	2.52	.799
Valid N (listwise)	46				

table 6.4) that if Elian had drowned the chance of Gore winning the election was somewhere between possible and likely (x = 2.52), but that of avoiding World War I only between possible and unconvincing (x = 3.13). There were no significant differences in this assessment between historians and international relations scholars.

As in experiment 1, participants gave more credence to the antecedent than they did to the consequent. Their responses to counterfactuals about World War I—asked after they were asked to devise their own counterfactual—were not significantly different from those of participants who responded to instrument 1 but lower than those who responded to instrument 2. Participants made slightly higher—but statistically insignificant—evaluations of the contingency of World War I. In response to the question "If Franz Ferdinand had not been assassinated in June of 1914 how likely is it that a major European war would have broken out sometime before 1918," the means for respondents in this experiment (x = 2.51) and both instruments of experiment 1 (Franz x = 2.47) and (Full Franz = 2.97) came in between "likely" and "possible." With respect to the question about second-order counterfactuals—"If there had been no European war between 1914 and 1918, what do you think the chances of one taking place in the course of the next ten years would have been?"— participants in this instrument thought it more likely (x = 2.38) than those of instrument 1 (x = 2.6) or 2 (x = 2.91) that something else would have brought provoked a European war. The hypothesis about making one's own counterfactual cannot be considered proven.

When we turn to the counterfactuals devised by participants themselves, the first interesting finding is the apparent difficulty of the task— even for professional historians. Of the fifty-four respondents, seventeen volunteered no counterfactual and another five wrote in the allotted space that World War I was overdetermined or there were no plausible counterfactuals that could undo it. So 42.5 percent of the sample did not offer a counterfactual. Of the 57.5 percent that did, the most common counterfactual devised by historians and IR scholars alike was unmaking the Sarajevo assassinations (offered by six of the thirty-seven respondents). Second was better leaders in Austria and Germany (five respondents). Among the scholars who advanced the no-assassination counterfactual, only one offered a chain of logic linking it to the consequent of no European war. This participant wrote: "While the European powers were primed for war, the assassination created a 'spark'; given other factors (e.g., Russian capability for mobilisation, German war plans), the timing of this incident was incredibly important. Had it not happened, other developments might have intervened." The better-leaders counterfactual came in several variants. Participants suggested that war might have been averted if Bismarck had stayed in office and continued to maintain good relations with Austria and Russia or was allowed by Wilhelm to handpick his successor, presumably someone who would have followed his general foreign policy line. Several participants suggested that more astute leaders in Germany and Austria in 1914 would have done the trick, although they did not suggest how such leaders might have come to power.

By far the most striking finding is the distribution of close-call versus long-shot counterfactuals and minimal rewrites versus "miracle" counterfactuals. As table 6.5 indicates, of the thirty different counterfactuals devised by participants, only a little more than one-third qualify as close-call minimal rewrites.

Undoing the assassination, as noted earlier, accounts for six of these. Others made the kaiser more alert and in Berlin, not Potsdam, at the height of the crisis; gave the Russian army the possibility of mobilizing just against Austria (avoiding mobilization against Germany as well);

TABLE 6.5
Make your own counterfactuals

	Minimal rewrites	*Miracle cfs.*
Close call	11	6
Long shot	6	7

had Britain put Germany on notice in a timely way that they would go to war if it attacked Belgium or France; forestalled Germany's so-called blank check to Austria; and provided German and Austrian leaders better insight into the costliness and likely consequences of a war. By my reckoning these counterfactuals vary in their credibility for two reasons. Some require more than a minimal rewrite of history (e.g., forestalling the blank check, making German and Austrian leaders more prescient), and others do not necessarily produce the intended consequent of restraint and no war (e.g., making German and Austrian leaders more prescient, putting the Germans on notice that England would go to war).

There were six close-call "miracle" counterfactuals. They included no Russian mobilization, which seems unlikely in the circumstance of the July crisis, as does more astute Austrian and German leaders in 1914. Less realistic still was the deus ex machina of revolutions in Russia, Germany, or Russia and Germany. One international relations scholar proposed a natural disaster, such as a devastating pandemic, on the eve of the July crisis. The influenza pandemic that arrived in 1918 was such an event, but it struck Europe so hard because the resistance of the population had been weakened by four years of war, reduced caloric intake and the fact that so many young men—of the age group most susceptible to the disease—were living cheek and jowl due to their mobilization during the war. It is unclear how such a pandemic would have come about in 1914 or have had an immediate impact on the foreign policy of the great powers.

Altogether there are thirteen long-shot counterfactuals: seven miracle counterfactuals and six minimal rewrites of history. Several of the minimal rewrites involve Bismarck, as noted above, or the survival of Frederick III, which would have prevented Wilhelm from becoming emperor. One of the more imaginative counterfactuals did away with Wilhelm before he ascended to the throne. While touring with Buffalo Bill's Wild West Show in Europe, Annie Oakley accidently killed young Prince Wilhelm when he foolishly volunteered himself as a target for her shooting exploits. Changes in German leadership, several scholars note, might have avoided a rupture with Russia, and with it the Franco-Russe alliance and subsequent division of Europe into two hostile camps. One international relations scholar did away with Bismarck on the grounds that if he hadn't become chancellor Prussia would not have unified Germany through victorious wars against Denmark, Austria, and France. The same scholar suggested, somewhat less credibly in my view, that even in a unified Germany, the absence of Bismarck's social imperialism would have made for a stronger socialist movement and possibly, a revolution.

The seven long-shot miracle counterfactuals run the gamut from a French victory in the Franco-Prussian War to the undoing of the industrial revolution. Several called for a successful Bolshevik revolution in Russia in 1905; one of its proponents contended that a revolutionary Russia would have posed no threat to Austria in the Balkans. Almost all the counterfactuals—close call or long shot—attempted to change people, policy, or the institutional culture of Austria and Germany, although one German historian suggested that all would have been well if only Britain had not become such a successful imperial power.

Given the general belief that World War I or something like it was inevitable, it is not surprising that so many of our participants failed to offer counterfactuals to unmake this event or turned to miracle and long-shot counterfactuals to do so. The survey and follow-up telephone interviews with respondents indicate a tight correlation between the minority who believed in the contingency of World War I and their invention of close-call, minimal rewrite counterfactuals to prevent it. Conversely, those who see World War I as overdetermined are more likely to turn to long-shot and miracle counterfactuals, if they offer counterfactuals at all. Long-shot counterfactuals are a reasonable response to the belief that no small change in the short-term could have prevented war. The invocation of miracle counterfactuals is less explicable and could suggest a lack of imagination or interest in coming up with more credible rewrites of history, or simply opposition to the use of counterfactuals as a research tool.

I hypothesized that historians and international relations scholars alike would devise counterfactuals that meet the conditions that people in general associate with plausible counterfactuals. To do so they must be close to the event in question, remake social rather than physical attributes of context, undo what are perceived as extraordinary rather than normal features of the context, and unmake earlier rather than later events of causal chains. The evidence does not offer much support for this hypothesis as only eleven of the thirty counterfactuals were credible close-call counterfactuals. The counterfactuals I judge implausible, whether close-call or long-shot, violate one or more of the conditions noted above. This finding may also be an artefact of the case. It would be interesting to run a parallel experiment using an event that had few implications for international relations theory *and* was generally considered mutable by historians. In these conditions, it seems reasonable to suppose, that participants would offer more counterfactuals and that these counterfactuals would come closer to meeting the conditions people in general associate with good counterfactuals.

EXPERIMENT 3: "LONG-SHOT" COUNTERFACTUALS

Guiding Theory

The possibility and impossibility curves in chapter 5 indicate across an array of historical events that foreign policy experts, historians, and international relations scholars see outcomes as more determined the closer to the event in question they are asked to make an estimate. They are increasingly receptive to the contingency of outcomes at greater temporal distance. This pattern suggests inherent receptivity to what I call long-shot counterfactuals: minimal rewrites of history at considerable temporal remove from the outcome they are intended to mutate.

Long-shot counterfactuals require a longer and more elaborate chain of events and logic linking antecedent to consequent and thus many more enabling counterfactuals. Enabling counterfactuals are additional minimal rewrites of history that sustain the chain of logic. Some enabling counterfactuals follow from the initial counterfactual, while others must be invented de novo. Logically, long-shot counterfactuals should be inherently less credible than their close-call counterparts because of their distance from the event, longer chain of events, and logic and larger number of enabling counterfactuals.

Psycho-logic suggests that long-shot counterfactuals, like their close-call counterparts, ought to succeed in raising estimates of contingency to the extent that they evoke vividness in the minds of those exposed to them. Vividness depends on drawing participants into concrete details of a counterfactual scenario. There is no research on what constitutes a plausible long-shot counterfactual. By definition, counterfactuals of this kind violate one of the key conditions for their close-call counterparts: that the antecedent be temporally proximate to the consequent. It seems reasonable to assume that the other conditions for close-call counterfactuals apply to their long-shot counterparts: they should mutate social versus physical attributes and extraordinary versus normal features of context and earlier rather than later components of causal chains.

Hypotheses

Historical logic and earlier experiments suggest that scholars should be more receptive to long- than to short-term counterfactuals. Statistical logic indicates that the plausibility of any long-term counterfactual is low because its probability is a multiple of the probability of the antecedent and all subsequent enabling counterfactuals. Psycho-logic suggests that the plausibility of long-shot counterfactuals will depend on their vividness. I hypothesize that historical logic and psycho-logic will reinforce each other in counterfactual scenarios that appear historically plausible to participants and evoke vividness by virtue of their presentation. Scenarios of this kind should lead to higher estimates of contingency than might be warranted by statistical inference. Implausible scenarios that evoke vividness will have the reverse effect. Vividness in this condition will focus participant attention on a single narrative and the alternative world to which it leads. If that narrative or world is considered implausible, the event in question will appear less mutable.

Research Design, Methods, and Measures

Participants in this experiment (n = 29) were drawn from the same overall sample. They were randomly assigned to the long-shot counterfactual instrument. Control groups consisted of respondents to instruments 1 and 2, who evaluated close-call counterfactuals devised by the investigator. Participants were asked to read a story, written by the investigator, that takes place in an alternative world in which Mozart lived to the age of sixty-five and as a result neither world war nor the Holocaust took place. Inhabitants of this world attempt to imagine what the world would have been like if Mozart had died at thirty-five, the age of my heroine's partner and the age when Mozart actually died. The story as a whole is reproduced here as chapter 7. It has three parts: the initial story, a critique by an imaginary reviewer, and a short reply by my heroine. Participants were given only the first part, the story itself, to read.

Participants were asked to evaluate the plausibility of counterfactual about Mozart's longevity and its consequences for World War I. They were invited to comment on what they thought were the most and least credible components of the scenario. They were asked to evaluate each component part of the scenario: how likely was it (question 8) that Mozart could have lived to the age of sixty-five?; if Mozart had lived to sixty-five (question 9), how likely would he have been to invent something along the lines of postclassicism?; if postclassicism had been successful (question 10), would romanticism have remained a minor artistic movement?; if romanticism had remained a minor artistic movement (question 11), would Austria-Hungary have been any less subject to the centrifugal forces of nationalism?; if Austria-Hungary had been less subjected to the forces of nationalism (question 12), would its leaders have been less likely to seek war with Serbia? They were also asked (question 13) if counterfactual experiments were a useful strategy for probing causation and contingency, and to make an overall estimate of the contingency of World War I (question 14). Finally, participants were asked two follow-on questions about the consequences of World War I: if World War I had been averted—for whatever reason—(question 15), how likely would the Holocaust have been?; and assuming Germany had won World War I (question 16), how likely would the Holocaust have been?

There is no denying that the Mozart counterfactual is a roundabout, even far-fetched, way of untracking World War I. Its antecedent changes the physical world (Mozart survives his illness and lives in good health to a ripe old age for his era) rather than the social one, and it is far removed from the consequent, not only temporally but socially. It extends the life of a composer to alter the course of music and, consequently the arts in general, and assumes that these change will change the pattern of ethnic politics in what became the Austro-Hungarian Empire. The close coupling of art and politics, thought by many to be distinct domains, probably runs counter to the way in which many historians and most international relations scholars think the world works. The scenario also requires more enabling counterfactuals than one rooted entirely in the political realm. It mutates an event at the beginning of a causal chain, but it is by no means self-evident that the events the scenario links together actually constitute parts of a causal chain. The plausibility of an implausible counterfactual narrative rests entirely on its vividness. Vividness in this case is enhanced by packaging the scenario as a short story with palpably real characters living in an alternative world not so socially different from ours, making it easy to relate to its characters and their situation.

Findings

As expected, participants found the long-shot counterfactual less plausible than the close-call counterfactuals of experiment 1. On a five-point scale with 1 representing "very persuasive," the mean for respondents on question 5 was (x = 3.67) in comparison to (x = 2.29) and (x = 1.39) for instrument one of experiment 1. A t-test for the equality of means proved significant (p = ≤ .05).

Participants were asked to describe what they found most and least plausible about the scenario. Two participants wrote "nothing," while all the others found at least one or more elements of the scenario credible. Several acknowledged Mozart's influence on music and art more generally and agreed that it would have increased if he had lived to old age and that he might have developed something along the lines of postclassicism. Three participants accepted the connection between romanticism and aggressive nationalism but were not convinced that postclassicism would have held either in check. One historian noted that the more direct way of sidetracking romanticism was somehow to get rid of Rousseau. Three participants approved of the link the story makes between developments in the arts and politics and agreed that Austria-Hungary would have developed differently in the absence of romanticism. Another noted that different artistic developments might have had profound consequences for development for Germany too, perhaps allowing the constitution of the Frankfurt Parliament to survive and preventing unification of Germany by an authoritarian Prussia. The only direct link to foreign policy was the observation by one historian that in the absence of romanticism Germany might not have pursued a policy of *Weltpolitik*.

The comments about plausibility were usually limited to one aspect of the scenario. In contrast, participants often offered multiple reasons for rejecting it as implausible. One historian wrote that "every link in the counterfactual is dubious." In one form or another, ten participants rejected outright the possibility that one individual could profoundly affect the course of history. Some objected in principle, and others to the influence of Mozart's music on the growth and reception of the romantic movement. One historian, evidently a Marxist, attributed the war to capitalism, while another blamed the war on the ideology of the nation-state. Both doubted that artistic movements were in any way relevant to these developments. A third wrote: "Music reflects the spirit of the times far more than it influences it." Only a few participants raised conceptual objections to the scenario. According to one international relations specialist, "the causal arrows are too tightly drawn." Several put the same complaint a different way, arguing that important intellectual and political developments have multiple causes and that untracking any one of them is unlikely to prevent these developments. In applying this formulation directly to World War I, an international relations scholar insist that it was overdetermined and could not be untracked by any minimal rewrite of history.

These understandings are reflected in the assessments participants made of each component of the Mozart counterfactual. Not surprisingly, they found the initial antecedent—Mozart lives to the age of sixty-five (question 8)—the most plausible of the string of counterfactuals that constitute my scenario. It was considered somewhere between plausible and likely. Most of the other counterfactuals were judged between possible and unlikely. The distributions are relatively normal and there are no significant differences between historians and political scientists. Histograms indicate two outliers, both international relations scholars, who found the scenario persuasive (question 5).

Questions 15 and 16 address follow-on consequences of the counterfactual. Participants thought it closer to unlikely than possible (x = 3.76)

TABLE 6.6
Descriptive statistics

	N	Minimum	Maximum	Mean	Std. deviation
q5	21	2	5	3.67	.966
q8	20	2	6	4.20	1.105
q9	19	2	4	2.95	.524
q10	18	1	5	3.33	1.029
q11	20	2	5	3.70	.865
q12	20	1	5	2.50	1.051
q13	20	1	5	2.00	.973
q14	20	1	5	3.05	1.099
q15	21	2	5	3.76	.995
q16	21	2	5	3.81	.814
Valid N (listwise)	17				

that the Holocaust could have been avoided if World War I had been averted or (x = 3.81) or if Germany had emerged as the victor. These are two of the most common counterfactuals used to undo the Holocaust and also elicited high evaluations of plausibility in another survey I conducted.[13]

EXPERIMENT 4: ANTECEDENTS VERSUS CONSEQUENTS

Guiding Theory

In the surveys and experiments reported in chapter 5 and in a survey I conducted with Dartmouth undergraduates (Appendix 1), participants were asked to evaluate the plausibility of antecedents and consequents separately. In every counterfactual, participants found antecedents more plausible than their stipulated consequents.

There is a clear logic to this pattern. Many historians and international relations scholars are willing to accept some degree of contingency in politics but tend to draw the line at outcomes they deem consistent with their preferred theories or beliefs about the world. By accepting antecedents as to some degree plausible and rejecting their imputed consequences they can appear open-minded but still determinist in cases that matter. This implicit decision rule can nevertheless prompt dissonance if there is a reasonably plausible chain of logic connecting antecedent to consequent.

TABLE 6.7
Dartmouth students antecedents vs. consequents (all 16 questions)

	Mean	t-score	Significance
Antecedents	2.8382	−4.907	.000
Consequents	2.9942		

Hypotheses

My several hypotheses are based on the assumption that people act to reduce dissonance between components of their belief system.[14] I hypothesize that participants will respond differently to counterfactual antecedents when they know their intended consequences. Overall, they will lower their estimates of the plausibility of antecedents under this condition. Their estimates of antecedents will be more affected by their belief systems and psychological needs. They will be more likely to accept the plausibility of antecedents that support their beliefs or needs by unmaking anomalous cases, and less likely to judge as plausible those that run counter to them.

Research Design, Methods, and Measures

In April 2003 I presented undergraduate students (n = 131) with sixteen counterfactual scenarios that make and unmake real and imagined American triumphs and tragedies. There are four counterfactuals in each category. The questionnaire (instrument 1) is reproduced as Appendix 1. Each counterfactual begins with a paragraph describing history as it actually happened. It is followed by a "what if" (an antecedent), and a short description of the implications of the "what if" (the chain of logic), leading to a consequent. Participants were asked to evaluate the likelihood of the "what if" and the consequent on a standard five-point scale: highly likely (1), likely (2), even chance (3), not likely (4), highly unlikely (5).

A second sample of students (n = 30) was given the same questionnaire in January 2008 but with the order of individual counterfactuals reversed (instrument 2). They were presented with the consequent and then the chain of logic reaching backward to the "what if." They were asked to evaluate the likelihood of the consequent and then the "what if" on the same five-point scale. Being aware of the imputed consequences before considering the likelihood of the antecedent intensifies whatever dissonance the counterfactual generates and does so before and not after participants assess its plausibility.

I also asked experts (n = 20)—historians and political scientists with knowledge of American history—to rank order the plausibility of the antecedents. To reduce bias, I showed them all twenty of the antecedents without showing them the consequents or the chain of logic connecting them to the antecedent.

Findings

Independent samples tests indicate that there are statistically significant differences (p = < .05) on six of the sixteen counterfactuals between the original participants (instrument 1) and those who received the questions in reverse order (instrument 2). All but one participant made higher estimates of the plausibility of the antecedents (lower scores) than their counterparts who were primed by first reading and evaluating the consequent and the chain of logic leading to it (see tables 6.8 and 6.9 below).

The only case unmaking a tragedy in which students who responded to instrument 1 evaluated a counterfactual as less likely than those of instrument 2 was question 3. It prevents 9/11 on the basis of German warnings to the Federal Bureau of Investigation (FBI) of an impending terrorist attack that leads FBI officials in Washington to take seriously warnings from field offices that Middle Easterners are seeking security information and a peculiar kind of training from flight schools. In this counterfactual, the students who received instrument 1 evaluated the antecedent as less likely (x = 3.01) than did those of instrument 2 (x = 2.32), the instrument in which consequent and antecedent were presented in reverse order.

It may be that emotional needs account for this otherwise anomalous finding. Instrument 1 was given to Dartmouth students in April 2003, still in the shadow of 9/11. Research indicates two of the most common strategies people use to cope with tragedy is to (1) convince themselves that it is not as horrendous as they first thought; and (2) that it was inevitable and that accordingly there was nothing they could have done to have prevented it.[15] The belief in inevitability avoids retrospective counterfactuals that unmake the tragedy and the guilt this would provoke if they were deemed credible. The differences in the means of the two instruments may accordingly reflect proximity (instrument 1) and greater distance from (instrument 2) the events of 9/11.

When we compare the evaluations of experts with those of the students in the two samples, the differences are statistically significant in nine of sixteen counterfactuals (see table 6.10 below). Experts evaluated the plau-

Table 6.8
Descriptive statistics

	VAR00001	N	Mean	Std. deviation	Std. error mean
q13a	original	131	3.41	.867	.076
	reversed	19	3.53	.612	.140
q14a	original	131	2.67	1.056	.092
	reversed	19	2.79	.855	.196
q15a	original	131	3.17	1.104	.096
	reversed	16	3.69	.793	.198
q16a	original	131	2.85	.912	.080
	reversed	16	3.56	.964	.241
q9a	original	131	3.59	.902	.079
	reversed	23	4.35	.714	.149
q10a	original	130	2.63	.899	.079
	reversed	24	2.79	1.141	.233
q11a	original	131	2.21	1.036	.090
	reversed	24	3.08	1.060	.216
q12a	original	131	3.24	1.053	.092
	reversed	19	3.79	.976	.224
q5a	original	131	2.60	.883	.077
	reversed	28	2.36	.989	.187
q6a	original	131	2.70	.934	.082
	reversed	26	2.65	.846	.166
q7a	original	131	2.72	.971	.085
	reversed	25	2.56	.961	.192
q8a	original	131	2.16	.830	.073
	reversed	25	2.28	.891	.178
q1a	original	131	2.50	1.146	.100
	reversed	30	2.20	1.031	.188
q2a	original	131	2.82	1.011	.088
	reversed	29	2.55	1.183	.220
q3a	original	130	3.01	1.038	.091
	reversed	28	2.32	.723	.137
q4a	original	131	3.05	1.062	.093
	reversed	28	2.75	.928	.175

sibility of five (lower score) of these counterfactuals to be greater than did the students, and another four (higher score) to be less likely. Two of them unmake triumphs, four create tragedies, and three create triumphs. No patterns emerge with respect to the divergences between experts and students on the basis of the character of the counterfactual (real, imagined, tragedy, triumph) or the nature of the antecedents (individual, political,

TABLE 6.9
Independent samples test

Levene's test for equality of variances		F	Sig.	t-test for equality of means							
				t	df	Sig. (2-tailed)	Mean difference	Std. error difference	95% Confidence interval of the difference		
		Lower	Upper	Lower	Upper	Lower	Upper	Lower	Upper	Upper	Lower
q3a	Equal variances assumed	4.713	.031	3.325	156	.001	.686	.206		.279	1.094
	Equal variances not assumed			4.180	54.078	.000	.686	.164		.357	1.015
q9a	Equal variances assumed	1.815	.180	-3.833	152	.000	-.760	.198		-1.152	-.368
	Equal variances not assumed			-4.512	35.577	.000	-.760	.168		-1.102	-.418
q11a	Equal variances assumed	.404	.526	-3.801	153	.000	-.877	.231		-1.333	-.421
	Equal variances not assumed			-3.741	31.581	.001	-.877	.234		-1.355	-.399
q12a	Equal variances assumed	.932	.336	-2.127	148	.035	-.545	.256		-1.052	-.039
	Equal variances not assumed			-2.252	24.491	.034	-.545	.242		-1.044	-.046
q15a	Equal variances assumed	4.356	.039	-1.824	145	.070	-.520	.285		-1.083	.043
	Equal variances not assumed			-2.356	22.783	.027	-.520	.220		-.976	-.063
q16a	Equal variances assumed	.342	.559	-2.911	145	.004	-.708	.243		-1.188	-.227
	Equal variances not assumed			-2.787	18.438	.012	-.708	.254		-1.240	-.175

TABLE 6.10
Experts vs. students

Question	Sig. instruments	Expert score	Type of Cf.
Q6			Unmaking
Brown vs. Bd. of Ed	both	lower	triumph
Q8			Unmaking
Reagan shooting	both	lower	triumph
Q9			Creating
Union victory	1	higher	tragedy
Q10			Creating
Three Mile Island	1	lower	tragedy
Q11			Creating
Airliner explosion	both	lower	tragedy
Q12			Creating
WTO	1	higher	tragedy
Q14			Creating
HIV	1	higher	triumph
Q15			Creating
Fuel cells		both	higher
triumph			
Q16			Creating
Saddam Hussein	both	lower	triumph

technical, biological). It is interesting but not substantively significant that the experts differ with both instruments (n = 5) or with just instrument 1 (n = 4). There are no differences between experts and students in instrument 2.

General Discussion

My results offer more evidence for the key role of vividness in shaping estimates of contingency. As in the experiments in chapter 5, greater counterfactual unpacking in experiment 1 led to progressively greater estimates of contingency. Vividness appears to have had the opposite effect in my long-shot counterfactual in experiment 3. Participants in this experiment not only found the counterfactual unconvincing but afterward offered a lower estimate of the overall contingency of World War I than did participants in experiments 1 or 2.

Vividness is a concept that is poorly understood in psychology. Nisbet and Ross define vividness as information that is likely to attract and hold our attention because it is emotionally interesting, concrete, and image provoking, and proximate in a sensory, temporal, or spatial way.[16] Many studies confirm that vivid case-history information has a greater impact on judgment than pallid base-rate information.[17] It not self-evident that these results are attributable to vividness; Taylor and Thompson contend that many studies fail to distinguish between a vivid message and a vivid presentation. For a message to be vivid, they maintain, the message itself has to meet this condition, not merely the manner in which it is presented.[18]

Kiselius and Sternthal argue that the persuasive effect of vividness is affected by positive elaboration of the material it presents.[19] Drawing on Nisbet and Ross, they propose the availability-valence hypothesis, which argues that attitudinal judgments depend on the favorableness of information accessible in memory. Such information is more available and more likely to be elaborated.[20] In contrast to many earlier studies that stress the vividness of presentation, Kiselius and Sternthal contend that vividness can enhance, undermine, or have no effect on the persuasiveness of a message. The outcome will depend on the valence of the information that is elaborated. McGill and Anand offer experimental support for this proposition.[21]

The availability-valence hypothesis may help explain my findings. In the case of close-call counterfactuals, vividness of presentation not only makes a scenario come alive but it is more elaborated if it has inherent plausibility. When this latter condition is met, vividness combines with positive valence to effect judgments of plausibility in an upward direction. With long-shot counterfactuals, vividness can probably also produce this effect, but only if the counterfactual has positive valence. If not, vividness, according to the availability-valence hypothesis, can have the opposite effect. If they are vivid, counterfactuals focus the attention of participants on one scenario and reduce, even possibly exclude attention devoted to others. When other scenarios become less accessible, participants make higher overall estimates of contingency if they find counterfactual scenario plausible, and lower ones if it is not. Follow-on experiments that use more plausible long-shot and more implausible close-call counterfactuals could provide more convincing tests of this proposition.

Long-shot counterfactuals highlight a seeming cognitive paradox. The possibility and impossibility curves generated in experiments 1–3 of chapter 5 show that foreign policy experts, historians, and international relations scholars consider the contingency of an event to decrease the closer they approach it temporally. These curves, robust across professions and cases, suggest—ceteris paribus—that long-shot counterfactuals at greater temporal remove from an event ought to be even more effective than their close-call counterparts in increasing assessments of their contingency. All things, of course, are not equal. Long-shot counterfactuals require a longer chain of logic, connecting events, and more enabling counterfactuals. Like their close-call counterparts, they can also vary enormously in their inherent plausibility. My Mozart counterfactual was deliberately constructed to be implausible on both grounds. In addition to its long chain of logic and six multiple enabling counterfactuals, it requires participants, whose expertise is in politics and political history, to acknowledge that cultural developments can have profound consequences for politics and international relations. Not surprisingly, its plausibility was overwhelmingly rejected by participants; only 6.9 respondents thought this outcome highly likely and 13.8 percent, likely.

Close-call and long-shot counterfactuals pose different kinds of cognitive challenges. The former do not require great leaps of imagination, only recognition that small changes in the fabric of reality might have amplifying and large consequences. Even scholars with a great need for psychological closure, or those committed to relatively deterministic views of the world—and the two are clearly related—are still willing to acknowledge a degree of contingency arising from unanticipated events, domestic politics, differing assessments by leaders, and variation in their ability and independence. For such scholars, a plausible close-call counterfactual can be unsettling. The dissonance generated by acknowledging contingency can be reduced by invoking second-order counterfactuals, insisting that some other catalyst would sooner or later have led to roughly the same outcome. This is indeed the strategy invoked by many participants with respect to the First World War. They concede that the assassinations of Franz Ferdinand and Sophie could have prevented war from erupting in August 1914 but maintain that World War I was overdetermined and would have been triggered in relatively short order by some later provocation.

Long-shot counterfactuals drive home just how unlikely *any* outcome was from a suitably distant temporal perspective. Chains of logic leading from a distant present (1791 in the Mozart counterfactual) to the present or a less remote past (1914 in the case of World War I) involve many steps and enabling counterfactuals. The more elaborate the unpacking, the more the enabling counterfactuals are exposed, which can make the consequent appear less rather than more plausible. Counterfactual unpacking can accordingly make events looks less contingent. Long-shot counterfactuals ought to encourage participants to think about how remote and improbable *our* world would have been from the vantage point of the antecedent. Experiment three suggests that they do not affect retrospective judgments of the contingency of historical reality, although they significantly diminish judgments of the contingency of alternative worlds. The second part of my Mozart story—which was not read by participants in any of the surveys—maintains that to assess the probability of an alternative world we must direct our attention, not to any particular alternative world, but to all the possible worlds in which a specified outcome did or did not occur. Participants in my long-shot experiment are less likely to do this because of the degree to which their attention is drawn into a single narrative and the single alternative world to which it leads. It may be significant that none of the comments of any of the participants noted this critical distinction.

Counterfactuals devised by participants did not prompt any greater estimates of the contingency of World War I than those made in response to counterfactuals proposed by the investigator. It would be interesting to see if this finding holds in other cases, including those that respondents consider dissonant with their beliefs or expectations. The most anomalous finding of experiment 2 was the failure of the counterfactuals that participants devised to conform to the pattern documented by other researchers. Many of these counterfactuals were neither close-call nor minimal rewrites of history. This variation may have something to do with the nature of the case—which involved an overdetermined outcome in the judgment of so many respondents—or the fact that the outcome was historical and that many of the respondents were historians or international relations scholars steeped in history.

Experiment 4 offers additional confirmation of the finding, robust across experiments in chapters 5 and 6, that participants in surveys and experiments consistently find counterfactual antecedents more plausible than consequents. This experiment indicates that estimates of antecedent plausibility can to some degree be manipulated by providing or withholding information about the outcomes to which they are expected to lead and the chain of logic linking antecedents to consequents. As predicted, estimates of contingency are lower when participants are primed with this additional information. This result is in line with the overall finding of these surveys and experimental studies that there is a progression in deniability. Participants are least likely to deny the antecedent to close-call, or any kind of counterfactual, and more likely to deny the consequent by rejecting the chain of logic connecting it to the antecedent. If that is difficult to do, those unhappy with a mutated outcome for intellectual or psychological reasons will invoke second-order counterfactuals to put history back on track.

CONCLUSION

In chapter 1 I side with radical skeptics in rejecting the possibility of developing good predictive theories about social behavior. The principal reason for my pessimism is the open-ended, nonlinear nature of the social world. Critics of the behavioral revolution and its theory project also point to the seeming inability of social scientists to perform the cognitive tasks theory building and testing require. Thomas Kuhn levels a more fundamental objection against scientists: they are not nearly as open-minded as they think they are. The majority, he contends, are committed to the conceptual, theoretical, and methodological truths of their epoch and reject, often out of hand, the arguments and empirical findings of its critics.[22] Science still remains a self-correcting process, as Kuhn acknowledges, because dominant paradigms encounter anomalies, begin to break down when they resist explanation, and are ultimately replaced by new frameworks that provide more compelling explanations and predictions. This process is an uphill struggle, but facilitated by the increasing difficulty of denying the better correspondence between a new framework and the physical world, especially when it accounts for otherwise inexplicable anomalies and makes verifiable counterintuitive predictions. Social science does not work this way. As none of its theories—especially those in international relations—make successful predictions about any of the primary concerns of their fields, paradigms and theories endure despite repeated failures. In international relations they tend to gain and lose adherents as a function of events in the political world; these prompt shifts in attention, as did the end of the Cold War, drawing scholars to paradigms they consider more appropriate to their shifting agendas.

The surveys and experiments of chapters 5 and 6 lend some support to those who stress the cognitive limitations of historians and social scientists. They offer more support for the Kuhnian understanding of the belief systems of scientists. The majority of our respondents remain committed to the overdetermination of major international developments and the related belief that big events have big (i.e., structural or deep underlying) causes. For the most part they resist contingency, or when they acknowledge it, tend to deny its potential to restructure the international environment. At least some of the participants who resist contingency and its implications reveal a need for psychological closure or are committed to theory building. These orientations, as we saw in chapter 5, are not unrelated. Other participants may simply find recognition of the consequences of contingency and the extreme unpredictability of the social world threatening or intellectually disorienting. Whatever its causes, the rejection of contingency and the belief in structural causes serves to sustain, not only the behavioral project, but the deeper need to predict and control the future. As Max Weber noted, the demystification of the world and theory building are mutually supporting, if not mutually constitutive.

APPENDIX
EXPERIMENT 4, INSTRUMENT 1: UNMAKING AMERICAN TRAGEDIES

The following four COUNTERFACTUALS forestall events generally considered to be American tragedies.

1. FACT: Many Kennedy advisors assert that President Kennedy did not want a protracted conflict in Vietnam. Kennedy was assassinated by Lee Harvey Oswald on November 22, 1963. Vice President Lyndon B. Johnson assumed the presidency and escalated the war dramatically after winning reelection in 1964. As a result, 55,000 Americans lost their lives.

COUNTERFACTUAL: Kennedy is not assassinated, is reelected and refuses to escalate the war. He uses the blatant corruption of the Diem regime and its political and military failure as an excuse to back away from an American commitment. The United States withdraws its troops and reaches an uneasy political accommodation with Hanoi.

How likely is this outcome?

Highly likely___ Likely___ Even chance___ Not likely___ Highly unlikely___

MINIMAL REWRITE: Oswald's bullet only grazes Kennedy. The president is sped away from the scene and within a few weeks returns to the Oval Office.

How feasible is this counterfactual?

Highly likely___ Likely___ Even chance___ Not likely___ Highly unlikely___

2. FACT: Eric Harris, the ringleader of the Columbine High School shooting, took the anti-depressant *Luvox* to treat his obsessive-compulsive disorder. *Luvox* has been known to cause aggression in teens. The Marine Corps rejected Harris's application because of his use of *Luvox*.

COUNTERFACTUAL: Eric is accepted into the Marine Corps. Although he is still having problems with his classmates, he realizes that there will be life for him after high school. There is no shooting at Columbine High School.

How likely is this outcome?

Highly likely___ Likely___ Even chance___ Not likely___ Highly unlikely___

MINIMAL REWRITE: Eric Harris's doctor informs his parents of the side effects of *Luvox*. Together, they opt to treat his obsessive-compulsive disorder with behavioral therapy.

How feasible is this counterfactual?

Highly likely__ Likely__ Even chance__ Not likely__ Highly unlikely__

3. **FACT:** Terrorists hijacked four planes on September 11, 2001, and crashed them into the North and South Towers of the World Trade Center, the Pentagon, and a Pennsylvania field. A July 2001 memo from an Arizona FBI field office raised suspicions about some Middle Easterners seeking airport security information and limited pilot training from flight schools. In August 2001, the FBI received a warning from a Minnesota flight school instructor about a French citizen of Moroccan descent, Zacarias Moussaoui, who sought instruction in flying commercial planes. The Minnesota FBI arrested Moussaoui on immigration violations, but FBI headquarters in Washington did not allow further investigation.

COUNTERFACTUAL: The FBI finds inaccuracies in the visa and financial information of Moussaoui and other potential September 11 hijackers, detains them for questioning, and uncovers the Al-Qaeda plot. Neither September 11 nor any other large-scale terrorist attack occurs.

How likely is this outcome?

Highly likely__ Likely__ Even chance__ Not likely__ Highly unlikely__

MINIMAL REWRITE: In light of a warning from German authorities that a major terrorist incident against the United States was being planned by Arab terrorists, the FBI takes the Arizona and Minnesota warnings seriously. They implement a nationwide canvass of flight schools, checking the visa and financial information of all foreigners.

How feasible is this counterfactual?

Highly likely__ Likely__ Even chance__ Not likely__ Highly unlikely__

4. **FACT:** Enron was the largest bankruptcy in U.S. history. Countless thousands of investors and employees were hurt when Enron stock fell from $90 to under $1. Because President Bush was long-time friends with Kenneth Lay (Enron's CEO), he felt politically vulnerable and refused Lay's repeated requests for a bailout. The stock market as a whole suffered big losses.

COUNTERFACTUAL: Investor and consumer confidence increases and the economy improves.

How likely is this outcome?

Highly likely__ Likely__ Even chance__ Not likely__ Highly unlikely__

MINIMAL REWRITE: Al Gore narrowly wins the election. Having no personal connections with Enron executives, he asks Congress for a bailout to save Enron employees.

How feasible is this counterfactual?

Highly likely___ Likely___ Even chance___ Not likely___ Highly unlikely___

UNMAKING AMERICAN TRIUMPHS

The following four COUNTERFACTUALS forestall events generally considered to be American triumphs.

5. FACT: General George Washington led his troops through the miserable winter at Valley Forge with the help of General Nathaniel Greene, who secured necessary supplies for the troops. The American army went on to win independence from Britain. During Jefferson's presidency, the United States made the Louisiana Purchase, setting the stage for continental and, later, global hegemony.

COUNTERFACTUAL: The thirteen colonies do not gain independence from Britain until the later part of the nineteenth century. Like Canada, they become a Commonwealth. The Louisiana Purchase never occurs, precluding a United States that stretches from the Atlantic to the Pacific and ultimately includes Alaska and Hawaii. North America is regionally split among France, Spain, and Britain. The United States, limited to the eastern seaboard, does not attain global supremacy in the twentieth century.

How likely is this outcome?

Highly likely___ Likely___ Even chance___ Not likely___ Highly unlikely___

MINIMAL REWRITE: General Greene could not secure the supplies, and there are not enough troops to sustain the rebellion.

How feasible is this counterfactual?

Highly likely___ Likely___ Even chance___ Not likely___ Highly unlikely___

6. FACT: In 1954, in *Brown v. the Board of Education*, the Supreme Court declared the doctrine of "separate-but-equal" in school systems unconstitutional. Chief Justice Earl Warren, who was appointed chief justice after the death of Chief Justice Frederick Vinson in September 1953, pushed for this decision. While the vote was a unanimous 9-0, the true opinions of the justices were closer to a 5-4 split. Unanimity was achieved at the expense of compliance; the majority agreed not to put any "teeth" into the decision in the form of mandates or procedures required to achieve integration.

COUNTERFACTUAL: Segregation continues in public schools across the country. Because of the lack of progress, the civil rights movement becomes more radical and violent, polarizing race relations and leaving African Americans second-class citizens.

How likely is this outcome?

Highly likely___   Likely___   Even chance___   Not likely___   Highly unlikely___

MINIMAL REWRITE: Chief Justice Vinson remains healthy. With Vinson's more conservative orientation, the Supreme Court reaffirms "separate-but-equal" by a vote of 5-4.

How feasible is this counterfactual?

Highly likely___   Likely___   Even chance___   Not likely___   Highly unlikely___

7. **FACT:** In October 1962 American intelligence discovered that the Soviet Union was secretly deploying medium- and intermediate-range ballistic missiles in Cuba. President Kennedy ordered the navy to blockade Cuba, triggering the most severe crisis of the Cold War. A tense week ensued in which the United States prepared to launch air strikes against the missile sites and follow up with an invasion of Cuba. A Soviet missile brought down a U.S. spy plane over Cuba, killing its pilot and prompting the air force to demand a retaliatory strike. As events threatened to spin out of control, Soviet leader Nikita Khrushchev agreed to remove the missiles in return for a public pledge from President Kennedy not to invade Cuba and a private assurance that American missiles threatening to the Soviet Union would be removed from Turkey.

COUNTERFACTUAL: Although the American fleet action was intended to increase the pressure on Khrushchev to come to terms, the Cubans and Soviets interpret it as the prelude to an actual invasion. Soviet forces on the island are equipped with nuclear-tipped ground-to-ground missiles, as they in fact were. One missile battery, without authorization from Moscow, fires a missile at the American fleet. Several ships and the crews are destroyed in the resulting nuclear explosion. Kennedy and Khrushchev quickly reach a compromise settlement to forestall a full-scale nuclear war.

How likely is this outcome?

Highly likely___   Likely___   Even chance___   Not likely___   Highly unlikely___

MINIMAL REWRITE: Kennedy gives in to air force demands for a retaliatory strike against a Soviet missile battery in Cuba, leading to further escalation, when one of the attacking planes is shot down. The American military and public opinion demand action, and the president orders the invasion fleet to move toward the island of Cuba.

How feasible is this counterfactual?

Highly likely___ Likely___ Even chance___ Not likely___ Highly unlikely___

8. FACT: On March 30, 1981, John Hinckley Jr. shot and seriously wounded President Ronald Reagan. Within a month President Reagan recovered from his injuries. He was the principal official in his administration to push for an accommodation with Soviet president Mikhail Gorbachev, and the two men succeeded in winding down the Cold War.

COUNTERFACTUAL: The White House pursues an overly cautious policy with the Soviet Union, making little progress in arms control or the future of Eastern Europe and Germany. Hard-line communists, allied with the Soviet military, remove Gorbachev from office. The Cold War drags on.

How likely is this outcome?

Highly likely___ Likely___ Even chance___ Not likely___ Highly unlikely___

MINIMAL REWRITE: Hinckley's bullet enters the president's chest millimeters to the left of where it did. Doctors and nurses cannot revive the president, and Vice President George Bush, Sr., who doubts Gorbachev's sincerity, is sworn in as his successor.

How feasible is this counterfactual?

Highly likely___ Likely___ Even chance___ Not likely___ Highly unlikely___

CREATING AMERICAN TRAGEDIES

The following four COUNTERFACTUALS create outcomes that would probably be considered American tragedies.

9. FACT: On the night of November 7, 1862, President Lincoln relieved General George of command of the Union Army of the Potomac and its 100,000 troops. Some officers called on McClellan to march on Washington, but the general relinquished his command and went into retirement.

COUNTERFACTUAL: Lincoln recognizes the independence of the Confederate States of America.

How likely is this outcome?

Highly likely___ Likely___ Even chance___ Not likely___ Highly unlikely___

MINIMAL REWRITE: Not wishing any more of his men to die in battle, McClellan marches on Washington with his army. Their semioccupation of Washington compels Lincoln to seek a diplomatic solution to the Civil War.

How feasible is this counterfactual?

Highly likely___ Likely___ Even chance___ Not likely___ Highly unlikely___

10. **FACT:** On March 28, 1979, Three Mile Island power station suffered a minor malfunction in one of its reactors. No explosion occurred because the core was devoid of oxygen. Aside from serious damage to the core, no serious problems occurred as a result of the malfunction.

COUNTERFACTUAL: Hydrogen mixes with oxygen in the core. There is an explosion, hurling radioactive material miles in every direction. Hundreds of thousands of people are contaminated in a Chernobyl-like disaster.

How likely is this outcome?

Highly likely___ Likely___ Even chance___ Not likely___ Highly unlikely___

MINIMAL REWRITE: In addition to the dozen or so secondary malfunctions that actually occurred, one additional failure takes place: an O-ring deforms because of the intense heat and allows oxygen into the core.

How feasible is this counterfactual?

Highly likely___ Likely___ Even chance___ Not likely___ Highly unlikely___

11. **FACT:** On December 22, 2001, Richard Reid (the media-dubbed "Shoe Bomber") attempted, but failed, to ignite the C4 that he carried in his shoe while flying on a transatlantic flight. The FBI determined that he had enough C4 to blow a large hole in the fuselage, which would have caused the plane to crash.

COUNTERFACTUAL: Air travel to and from North America stops for several days, and American ports close for security checks. The sagging economy deteriorates further due to loss of trade, and the stock market continues to fall. Several major airlines declare bankruptcy.

How likely is this outcome?

Highly likely___ Likely___ Even chance___ Not likely___ Highly unlikely___

MINIMAL REWRITE: Richard Reid succeeds on his first attempt at ignition.

How feasible is this counterfactual?

Highly likely___ Likely___ Even chance___ Not likely___ Highly unlikely___

12. **FACT**: In November 1999 the World Trade Organization met in Seattle and was the focus of massive protests, some of which were violent.

COUNTERFACTUAL: Hoping to quell any violence at the outset, Seattle police fire rubber bullets at a group of raucous demonstrators. One of the bullets takes out the eye and later kills Kimberly Connor, a sixteen-year-old high school senior and nonviolent environmental activist. The American public becomes deeply involved in her struggle to survive and learns about her efforts on behalf of local recycling and wildlife and her opposition to SUVs.

How likely is this outcome?

Highly likely___ Likely___ Even chance___ Not likely___ Highly unlikely___

MINIMAL REWRITE: Kimberly's death triggers campus demonstrations, some of which become violent. The president of Ohio State University calls in riot police as a precaution at a planned "monster demo." Their presence and provocative behavior incites students to riot. In the ensuing melee, someone fires into the crowd—organizers insist it was the police—killing three students. Other campuses are swept by protests, and graduations in many institutions of higher learning are canceled out of sympathy for the dead students.

How feasible is this counterfactual?

Highly likely___ Likely___ Even chance___ Not likely___ Highly unlikely___

CREATING AMERICAN TRIUMPHS

The following four counterfactuals create outcomes that would probably be considered American triumphs.

13. **FACT**: In 1865 the Freedman's Bureau Act guarantees "forty acres and a mule" to former slaves. Bowing to pressure from former plantation owners, President Andrew Johnson vetoes the bill.

COUNTERFACTUAL: Former slaves are given a greater legal and economic foothold in the South, and sharecropping does not develop as a widespread institution. Race relations gradually improve throughout the twentieth century.

How likely is this outcome?

Highly likely___ Likely___ Even chance___ Not likely___ Highly unlikely___

MINIMAL REWRITE: Progressive and anti-Southern forces in the North did a better job of mobilizing support for this legislation, and, despite pressure from land owning Southern whites, Andrew Johnson does not exercise his veto.

How feasible is this counterfactual?

Highly likely___ Likely___ Even chance___ Not likely___ Highly unlikely___

14. **FACT**: We know now that the AIDS epidemic began in the early 1970s, but the Centers for Disease Control (CDC) did not diagnose AIDS and its sources of transmission until late in1982. President Reagan refused to ask Congress for major funding for research and patient care, and did not publicly acknowledge the existence of AIDS until 1987. By then over 19,000 Americans had died of AIDS, and many times that number were infected with the HIV virus.

COUNTERFACTUAL: These programs are in effect by 1980. Transmission of HIV throughout the United States is greatly reduced and much of the AIDS epidemic is averted.

How likely is this outcome?

Highly likely___ Likely___ Even chance___ Not likely___ Highly unlikely___

MINIMAL REWRITE: The CDC recognizes the existence of AIDS and HIV four years earlier in 1978, during the Carter administration. Carter calls for extensive research and health care, needle exchange, and sex education programs.

How feasible is this counterfactual?

Highly likely___ Likely___ Even chance___ Not likely___ Highly unlikely___

15. **FACT**: Emissions from gasoline-powered vehicles are one of the largest sources of pollution. Fuel cells, an alternative fuel source utilizing clean-burning hydrogen, will ultimately reduce dependence on foreign oil, improve the environment, and foster long-term economic growth. Recently, President George W. Bush proposed $1.7 billion in funding to research fuel cells to power automobiles.

COUNTERFACTUAL: The fuel-cell technology propels economic growth just as it was beginning to decline in late 2000. The American auto industry experiences a boom as world demand for American fuel-cell cars skyrockets. Oil prices also drop to compete with the fuel-cell technology, and by 2003 fuel cells power 10 percent of all cars on the road.

How likely is this outcome?

Highly likely___ Likely___ Even chance___ Not likely___ Highly unlikely___

MINIMAL REWRITE: The Clinton administration, inspired by the 1992 Rio Earth Summit and weary of the instability of oil prices, pushes $2 billion in funding for fuel-cell research through Congress in 1993. Developing fuel cells became for President Clinton what reaching the moon was for President Kennedy. The massive research effort leads to the development of a cheap, efficient fuel cell for vehicles by 2000.

How feasible is this counterfactual?

Highly likely___ Likely___ Even chance___ Not likely___ Highly unlikely___

16. **FACT:** The Bush administration regards Saddam Hussein, leader of Iraq, as a security threat. Fearful of his life, Saddam never sleeps in the same place two nights in a row. His movements are unpredictable.

COUNTERFACTUAL: In January 2003, the Bush administration uses a cruise missile to destroy the building in which Saddam Hussein is holding a meeting of his war council. Saddam, one son, and most of the senior members of his government are killed in the blast. A pro-Western regime comes to power in Baghdad and war with Iraq is averted.

Highly likely___ Likely___ Even chance___ Not likely___ Highly unlikely___

MINIMAL REWRITE: The United States receives good intelligence detailing Saddam's movements.

How feasible is this counterfactual?

Highly likely___ Likely___ Even chance___ Not likely___ Highly unlikely___

GENERAL QUESTIONS

QUESTION: How important is being an American to your identity?

Very important___ Somewhat important___ Not so important___ Not at all important___

QUESTION: Imagine a spectrum of views about the nature of the world. It is anchored on one end by the belief that the world is ordered and predictable, and on the other by the belief that it is utterly chaotic and unpredictable. Where would you place yourself along this continuum?

Predictable,   1 ____2 ____3 ____4 ____5 ____6 ____   Unpredictable,
   Ordered   Chaotic

CHAPTER SEVEN

If Mozart Had Died at Your Age:
Psycho-logic versus Statistical Inference

THE FOLLOWING TALE has three parts: a short story, a review by an imaginary critic, and a reply by the heroine of my story. The tale takes place in an imaginary world in which neither World War I or II nor the Shoah occurred because Mozart lived to the age of sixty-five. It seeks to dramatize the tensions between "psycho-logic"—exploited by the story—and the laws of statistical inference, which guide the imaginary critique. Psycho-logic describes the various cognitive and motivational biases that make estimates of probability and attributions of responsibility different from the expectations of so-called rational models. Biases and heuristics of all kinds can and have been described and documented by standard psychological studies and case studies of political decision-making. Understanding biases intellectually and "feeling" them emotionally are not the same thing, and the latter, I contend, is essential if we are to free ourselves from their grip. It is equally important to understand the conservative bias of the laws of statistical inference to avoid becoming their unwitting prisoner. Psycho-logic, which makes us more receptive to contingency by reason of the vividness of its narratives, is one way of preventing this.

A NIGHT AT THE OPERA

The woodwinds sounded a minor chord as Oedipus fell to his knees. Blind, overcome by pain and grief, he remained motionless several bars after the sound of the woodwinds died away. Slowly and unsteadily Oedipus rose and stared with unseeing eyes at the audience. Two violins quietly began the famous fugue that ends Act III. When the cellos introduced the second voice, Oedipus groped his way toward the far right of the dimly lit stage and made his final exit.

The applause began before the last notes of the fugue had sounded. Erika rose from her seat, propelled by her enthusiasm for the performance, and through the act of clapping sought release from the tension of the last act. Hans, in the seat alongside, had been deeply moved too but could not bring himself to express his feelings so unguardedly. He envied Erika her ability to do so. Three curtain calls later, her tension spent,

Erika turned to Hans, who took her hand and guided her gently through the crowd toward the exit.

The night was brisk but not uncomfortable, and the couple, still holding hands, walked down the Unter den Linden in the direction of the Brandenburger Tor. They stopped for a traffic light and Erika broke the silence between them.

"Wasn't I right?"

"It was stunning," Hans agreed. "I'm glad we went."

"What did you think of Sussmann?"

The pedestrian signal turned green, and Hans led Erika into the intersection. He waited to answer her question until they were safely across the street. "He's the perfect Mozartian hero. He has a powerful but controlled voice. I thought he made the transition from fiery youth to mature statesman very convincingly."

Erika nodded. "As I see it, *Oedipus* is about the parallel conflicts between man's desire to assert free will against the fate that he fears determines his destiny, and the striving for personal recognition and the need to feel an integrated part of a community. Oedipus unwittingly violates a communal taboo and punishes himself for this transgression. I like the way Mozart has the baritone sing *stonato* to convey Oedipus's internal conflict, and Sussmann does it as well as anybody I've heard."

"I sing off tune all the time, *Schatz*."

"Not deliberately!"

Hans gave her hand a squeeze.

The couple strolled along the perimeter of the Tiergarten. At Hans's suggestion, they entered a café and took a table within reach of the heat of the large, open hearth fire burning seasoned oak from one of the many forests surrounding the city. A waiter appeared and wrote down their orders: cappuccino for Erika, a *pils* for Hans.

Erika reached into her purse, pulled out a pack of cigarettes, put one in her mouth, and lit it with a small gold lighter that had also been stashed in her purse. Using both hands, she pushed her long blond hair back from her angular face. Hans recognized the gesture as a warning sign that Erika had something serious on her mind. He was nevertheless surprised when she leaned forward to ask what the world would have been like if Mozart had died a young man.

"What would the world be like?" Hans repeated her question.

"Yes. Would life be any different today? Would Mozart's premature death have changed things in any way? Would we be sitting here having a drink?"

"I've never given it any thought. I certainly hope I'd still be sitting here with you."

"I hope so too." Erika reached across to give his arm a squeeze.

"If Mozart had died young . . ." Hans paused to consider the problem. "Well, we wouldn't have any of his mature works. There would be no *Oedipus*, no *Werther*, and no late piano and violin sonatas or symphonies, including my favorite, fifty-seven."

"True enough, but that's not what I had in mind. I was thinking about the broader artistic and political ramifications."

"I can see another one of your zany ideas is about to sally forth."

"You're just a stick in the mud, Hans. Suppose Mozart had been run over by a carriage when he was your age, thirty-five. His last opera would have been *La Clemenza di Tito*, a wonderful score to be sure, but an old-fashioned *opera seria*, and a far cry from his mature, tragic works." Erika took a drag on her cigarette, and Hans lifted his mug of beer to his mouth. He waited for Erika to continue, as he knew she would.

"The postclassical movement would have been stillborn. Da Ponte, who wrote the libretti for *Cosi fan Tutte, Marriage of Figaro,* and *Don Giovanni,* had to flee Vienna after some count caught him in bed with his wife. Mozart did not find an equally gifted collaborator until he teamed up with Neuman in 1805. That's when he really began to explore the meaning of social justice and what kind of society would allow man to reconcile competing needs. *Oedipus, Orestes,* and *Luisa Miller* are vehicles for this analysis. Each opera examines some aspect of the problem in a more complex way, intellectually and artistically."

"Mozart wasn't alone in addressing these themes."

"That's my point, Hans. In the early nineteenth century, music was the most avant garde of the art forms. Mozart's mature compositions established a philosophical framework not only for music, but for literature and art, and even politics. Schubert's and Mendelsohn's music, Schiller's and Shelley's poetry, carried on and developed the postclassical tradition. Without Mozart, romanticism would have dominated the artistic life of Europe and the political consequences would have been profound and frightening."

"Come on, Erika. I know you despise romanticism, but that's an extraordinary allegation."

"Bear with me, Hans. Romanticism represents the untrammeled expression of individualism. Man ruled by his emotions, egoistic, self-indulgent, and unconcerned with the consequences of his actions for others. Beethoven, Byron, Siegfried—all the romantic heroes, real and fictional—are like this. Political leaders who were influenced by romantic ideals would have made conflict a virtue, compromise suspect, and passion in public life something to reward rather than constrain, and this at a time when rapid economic development and social change were creating great political strains. What if romanticism had become the crucible for strong nationalist movements whose leaders were not above using violence to achieve their goals? It would have been very difficult, maybe impossible, to accommodate the various struggles for reform or independence that developed in the last century."

"Your imagination never ceases to amaze me. But I don't buy your argument. All those mass movements were attempts by disenfranchised classes to gain a share of political and economic power. The Repeal Movement in Ireland was the prototype. In the 1840s Daniel O'Connell raised the prospect of political separation to compel the British to restore an Irish parliament with substantial autonomy from London. Other oppressed groups followed suit and met with varying degrees of success. The most serious confrontation was in the Habsburg Empire where the leadership's rigidity, suppression of dissent, and the late development of a middle class threatened to unleash chaos. Fortunately, cooler heads prevailed. Under the aegis of Germany, France, and Britain, a federal solution was worked out in 1878. Admittedly, it provoked a backlash by segments of the Empire's German and Hungarian communities, who until then had all but monopolized political and economic power."

"Don't minimize our country's problems, Hans. Remember the Vaterlandspartei that arose in the second half of the century and mobilized support from groups who had been marginalized by the industrial revolution. Beckstein, its leader until the great scandal, blamed the Jews for all of Germany's problems. He drew substantial support from the lower middle and artisan classes and disaffected intellectuals. As I recall, the Vaterlandspartei captured close to twenty percent of the vote in the 1894 elections; they were helped, of course, by the economic crisis. During the Great Depression we had a similar if less successful movement, led by that crazy Austrian, Hitler."

"He was a real flake." Hans raised his right arm in imitation of Hitler's signature salute.

"Ask yourself, Hans, why Beckstein and Hitler were flashes in the pan."

"That's pretty obvious. The 1849 constitution created the framework for a stable, decentralized, and democratic Germany. All the German states except for Austria sooner or later joined the confederation. Prussia, the most powerful and least democratic, was ultimately compelled to reform its electoral system. After that, it was only a matter of time before political power passed from the Junkers to the liberal industrialists. The more serious problem was labor unrest in northern Germany, Silesia, and the Rhineland. But once again, compromises were worked out, difficult as they were, and social democracy moderated its demands. German corporatism became the model for most of the rest of Europe. Because our political system was widely accepted as legitimate, neither Beckstein nor Hitler made much headway, even in times of economic crisis and widespread unemployment."

"You get honors in history, Hans. Now let me return to my counterfactual. Suppose in the absence of postclassicism, romanticism had come to dominate the artistic and political culture of the nineteenth century? Movements for reform would almost certainly have been movements for independence, and their leaders would not have sought independence as a means to an end but as an end in itself."

"I don't follow you?"

Erika brushed the hair back from around her cheeks and lit another cigarette. "In the latter half of the nineteenth century, many political movements demanded independence to extract political and economic concessions from governments. The threat usually worked, and the idea of independence, not very practical in most cases, was shelved. In Quebec, they still play this game. A unified Italy made sense, and Vienna accepted the inevitable, but think of what would have happened if the Habsburg Empire had been divided into a half-dozen so-called national states. None of these entities would have been viable economically. True "national" states would have been impossible in practice because the various language communities are so geographically intermingled throughout the region. Hungarians and Rumanians would have laid claim to Transylvania; Czechs and Germans to Bohemia; Poles and Germans to Silesia; Italians and Germans to Tirol; Slovenes, Croats, and Italians to Istria—*und so weiter*. The Habsburg successor states would have fragmented into still small units and fought one another over disputed territories. I shudder to think of the consequences, especially in the Balkans."

"It's a ridiculous predicament to contemplate, I admit. But you haven't answered my question."

"Sorry about the digression, *Schatz*. Have you ever read Herder?"

"We discussed him in *Gymnasium*, but I don't remember much. Some mystical nonsense about a nation being the organic expression of the soul of a people."

"That's the gist of it. The traditional concept of a nation included all of the inhabitants of a political unit organized in several estates. For Herder, a nation was a group of people who belonged to a specific language or cultural community, regardless of where they resided. They had a right— a duty actually—to organize themselves politically in a 'nation-state'. Some of Herder's successors carried his dangerous notion a step further by arguing that nations competed in a Darwinian world in which only the fittest would survive. To be one of history's winners, a nation had to become strong and carve out a niche for itself at the expense of its neighbors and competitors. Imagine a Europe of nation-states with foreign policies based on the narrowest calculations of self-interest!"

"It would have been grim."

"That's putting it mildly! Even in western Europe, so-called nation-states would have included substantial minorities who might have faced all kinds of discrimination. In Germany, the obvious target was the Jews. From the time of the Crusades they were the scapegoat for anything that went wrong. Beckstein and Hitler tried with only limited success to arouse hatred of Jews, but they might have succeeded in a different Germany."

"Now you're really getting carried away. France may have been the first country to tear down its ghettos, but Germany went much further than any of its neighbors in eradicating age-old prejudices. By the end of the nineteenth century, Jews, their religious practices aside, were indistinguishable from other citizens. Every schoolchild learns about the contributions they made to the scientific, cultural, and economic life of our country. They even gave us our sense of humor. We Germans are an enlightened and tolerant people. This is why Beckstein's and Hitler's hate-mongering fell on largely deaf ears."

"Don't be so smug! It didn't have to be that way. In the absence of post-classicism, the twentieth century could have turned out very differently. Germany, France, and Britain, the three great democracies, were an axis of stability in a Europe reeling from the consequences of rapid industrialization. Without a common liberal framework to unite them, the great powers could have been at each other's throats as they had always been in the past. Look at Asia. Modernization in the absence of a common political culture, mutual economic dependence, and accepted mechanisms for resolving international disputes led to a series of destructive wars. Romantic nationalism would have undermined the basis for international collaboration in Europe at the same time as it would have encouraged more aggressive postures by the great powers. If Russia, Austria-Hungary, and maybe even Germany had adopted expansionist foreign policies to cope with their domestic problems, a major European war would have been hard to avoid. Suppose Germany and Austria-Hungary had lost such a war. Afterward, some *mashuggene* like Hitler, who attributed the defeat to a Jewish-socialist conspiracy, might well have found a receptive audience."

"That's over the top!"

"Why?"

"Since the Age of Enlightenment, Europe has witnessed the steady advance of reason and progress. Education, science, and economic development have banished ignorance, superstition, and poverty to the remotest corners of the continent. These developments have deep, structural causes. They are not dependent on particular individuals. It's very unlikely that the premature death of any artist could have profound consequences for the cultural development of an entire civilization. And even if it did, the triumph of one mode of artistic expression over another could never have led to the kind of political consequences you describe. After a certain point, the development of a peaceful and prosperous Europe was all but inevitable."

"You're blinded by the hindsight bias."

"The what?"

"Did you ever read any psychology at university?"

"You must be kidding. Architecture students with time to read? But everybody knows about the cognitive revolution. Even *Leute von Heute* had a story about Tversky and Kahneman and their institute in Vienna."

"*Leute von Heute*? I didn't know you read such trash, Hans."

"It was in my dentist's office."

"Did the article say anything about the research of Baruch Fischoff? He's one of Tversky and Kahneman's Polish colleagues?"

"I don't think so."

"Fischoff discovered the hindsight bias. He found that once an event occurs, people upgrade their prior estimate of its probability. They see the outcome as almost inevitable and become correspondingly insensitive to the role of contingency. The hindsight bias is one of the most ubiquitous and best documented of all cognitive biases."

"And you think I've fallen victim to it!"

"I do, *Schatz*."

"Well, I think you've gone too far in the other direction. If small changes in the world can have such large effects, then almost anything is possible. One more hit of caffeine and you'll tell me how different European history would have been if Emperor Franz Josef had lived to be an old man, and his nephew, Franz Ferdinand, had never ascended to the throne. I can see the argument now. No Franz Ferdinand, no reforms, acute nationality problems in Austria-Hungary, and there's your European war."

"Who's getting carried away now!"

REVIEW OF MANUSCRIPT 98-248

The story examines a counterfactual world in which Wolfgang Amadeus Mozart died at the age of thirty-five. As a result, Europe became increasingly unstable and fought two destructive wars in the twentieth century. At the end of the first war, Austria-Hungary fragmented into a half-dozen unstable, independent states. Germany, the other big loser, also had to cede territory. A more fanatic version of Beckstein came to power, persecuted Germany's Jews, and started a second, unsuccessful war to regain Germany's lost territories.

The story is imaginative and reasonably well written, and the two protagonists, an opera-loving couple, are engaging characters. All the action is in the first paragraph, which describes the final scene of *Oedipus*. After the opera, Hans and Erika retire to a café where Erika poses the Mozart counterfactual and describes its political implications to a sensibly dubious Hans.

The counterfactual is unconvincing. I can best demonstrate why by unpacking its first several steps. The antecedent, step 1, Mozart's premature death in 1791, is an acceptable minimal rewrite of history because thirty-five was close to the normal life expectancy in the era before modern medicine. Step 2, in which the author contends that postclassicism never appeared, is highly problematic. Artistic styles capture or crystallize a society's mood. It is possible—I think likely—that some other composer, artist, or writer, or combination of them, would have developed postclassicism in the absence of Mozart. Artistic movements, like other human innovations, arise when the time is ripe. Physics offers a good example. At least a score of scientists struggled to understand the deeper meaning of the Michelson-Morley discovery that the speed of light in a vacuum was constant, regardless of its direction relative to the motion of the earth. If Poincaré and Lorentz had not come up with their theory of relativity, somebody else like Planck or Einstein almost certainly would have.

The most Mozart's premature death could have accomplished would have been to delay the emergence and ultimate triumph of postclassicism. At least some cultural historians of the period argue that Haydn, among others, was already moving in this direction, and might have developed postclassicism without the help of Mozart. If so, then cultural history would have been put "back on track" and the consequences of Mozart's death would have been dampened down rather quickly. Today's world would not be precisely the same; as Hans rightly observes, we would not enjoy *Oedipus* and other late Mozart works, but, *grosso modo*, the world would be the same in its general political and cultural outlines.

Let us nevertheless assume that postclassicism never developed and that romanticism became the dominant cultural movement. The author insists (step 3) that its triumph would have had profound consequences for European politics. Romanticism's celebration of imagination over reason and expression over argument would somehow have transformed moderate reform movements into extreme, even violent ones, that sought to break up the great multinational states that spanned Europe from the Rhine to the Urals. On the face of it, it is far-fetched to attribute such consequential political changes to variation in artistic style.

The political evolution of central and eastern Europe was largely determined by economics. Industrialization and trade produced a large and prosperous bourgeoisie, an educated and better-off working class and the widely recognized need for economies of scale. There were tensions between the aristocracy and the new, rising classes, and these tensions were a contributing cause of revolution in France. By the end of the nineteenth century the economic benefits of industrialization were apparent to nearly everyone and the transformation it wrought in the distribution of income and education compelled changes in the political structure. Even Erika, who makes the counterfactual case, recognizes that only economic and political chaos would have resulted from fragmentation of the Austro-Hungarian Empire. So did key political actors from all classes and language groups; it was the principal incentive for them, with Germany's assistance, to work out a more democratic and federal structure for the Empire. The Magyar aristocracy, the biggest losers from these reforms, ultimately recognized that they too had much to gain from a peaceful and prosperous Balkans. Enlightened self-interest motivated the political restructuring of Austria-Hungary. It had nothing to do with the music people listened to or the novels they read.

Counterfactual antecedents are linked to their consequents by a series of steps. Each of these steps is a development that is supposed to follow from the antecedent, and all of the steps are necessary to produce the consequent. The Mozart counterfactual contains at least six steps linking its antecedent (Mozart's death at age thirty-five) to the hypothesized consequent (an aggressive German regime in the twentieth century). Because Mozart dies young, (1) postclassicism fails to develop; (2) romanticism emerges as the dominant form of artistic expression; (3) reform movements in central Europe become nationalist; (4) Austria-Hungary and Germany go to war to cope with domestic and foreign threats; (5) they are defeated; and (6) in the aftermath, an anti-Semitic dictator hell-bent on a revisionist war comes to power in Germany. Each of these counterfactuals assumes other counterfactuals (e.g., romanticism becomes dominant because no other artist develop postclassicism; Austria-Hungary behaves aggressively in the Balkans because Germany encourages it to do so instead of pushing Austria to reach an accommodation with its various linguistic communities; the victors in the first war are short-sighted, and unlike their predecessors at the Congress of Vienna, dismember the losers and then stand aside and allow an obvious madman to come to power in Germany and bully its neighbors). The probability of the consequent is the product of the probabilities of every step. If we grant a probability of 0.5 for each step—and that is generous—the overall probability of the consequent is a mere .016.

There is admittedly something arbitrary about determining the number of steps in any counterfactual. Like a fractal—think of an ever longer coastline each time a map of it is enlarged to show more indentations—a counterfactual can usually be subdivided into an almost infinite number of steps. As a general rule, the more steps a counterfactual requires, the lower its probability. But the smaller the changes in history introduced by any counterfactual, the greater its likelihood. Conceivably, the overall probability of a counterfactual might not change significantly as we break it out into more and more steps.

There is nevertheless a difference, difficult as it may be to identify in practice, between the minimal requirements of a counterfactual (as I have tried to describe for the Mozart counterfactual) and the enabling requirements of each of these steps. Let me illustrate this with a counterfactual of my own. Marcel was injured in an accident while driving to work yesterday morning. I maintain this would not have happened if he had not listened to music instead of the news on the radio while eating his breakfast. Marcel took a different route to work because he heard the newscaster announce that the highway he normally takes was bumper-to-bumper in traffic. My counterfactual has two fundamental steps: Marcel does not listen to the radio and therefore does not change his route. There are many enabling steps: Marcel cannot slip on the ice while walking to the car, his car must start, and he must adhere to his regular route even when he discovers the highway ramp is backed up. The first two conditions have high probabilities. The third does not. Marcel might have responded to the tie-up by crossing town via an alternative route. But he would likely have reached his office without incident because he would have arrived at the intersection where the accident took place at a different time and would not have been hit by the truck that earlier had spun out of control. Adding these enabling steps does not significantly affect the probability of Marcel arriving safely at his office.

Despite the improbability of the Mozart counterfactual, many readers will still find it convincing. People respond positively to narratives, and numerous psychological experiments indicate that a story becomes more credible the more detail it contains. This is because probability judgments are not attached to events but to descriptions of events (Tversky and Kahneman, 1983; Tversky and Koehler, 1994). In a recent experiment, Lebow and Tetlock (2000) showed that counterfactual "unpacking" leads foreign policy experts to increase their estimate of the probability of historical events. The more details they provided about possible, alternative outcomes to 1962 Cuban Sugar crisis (triggered by the European Federation's decision to give trade preferences to Cuban sugar while imposing stiff tariffs on American marketed sugar) the more likely the experts considered these outcomes. Lebow and Tetlock made no attempt to manipulate the number of steps between antecedents and consequents, but there is no reason why experiments could not be designed to do this.

The laws of statistical inference suggest that the probability of *most* compound counterfactuals will be low, and almost all counterfactuals that hypothesize major changes in the course of history have multiple links between their antecedents and consequents. Does this mean that history is impervious to manipulation by counterfactual thought experimentation?

No, only that the past cannot be changed to produce at will some *specific* world at any temporal distance. There may be *many* alternative worlds in which great powers fight a war in the early twentieth century, but we cannot know with confidence what counterfactuals could generate them, and even less, the specific characteristics of the alternative worlds these counterfactuals, or a combination of them, would have. Because many alternative worlds are possible, the probability of producing any one of them is low. For the same reason it is all but impossible to predict the future. Imagine a group of scholars meeting in 1815 to consider the character of the world a hundred years hence. Any world they describe would depend on numerous intervening steps. From the vantage point of 1815, the world in which we live today had a vanishingly low probability.

When thinking about contingency it is useful to distinguish between *specific* worlds and general *sets* of worlds. A specific world, like our own, has many features, one of which is the absence of a great power war. More importantly for our purposes, it is the result of a particular pathway of history. Our world is one instantiation of the set of *all* possible worlds in which there was no European war. A world in which Mozart died a young man would be a different world but still, I believe, a member of this set. Any number of other counterfactuals might produce other members of this set. There is also a class of worlds in which the great powers *did* fight a war, and Lebow and Tetlock came up with some reasonable counterfactuals for producing such a world. None of their counterfactuals involve the arts, and some of them, I think, require more than minimal rewrites of history. The probability of producing a counterfactual world in either set of worlds is much greater than that of producing a specific member of either set. This is because there are more paths that lead to worlds in the set than to any one specific world.

The course of human events is admittedly more malleable than a superficial examination of probability would suggest. It may nevertheless be governed by something akin to Heisenberg's principle of uncertainty. There is an inverse relationship between the magnitude of change we want to produce in the world and our ability to know if any counterfactual(s) will produce this intended change. This is also true for changes we introduce in the real world to produce desired future consequences. The more radical the change (counterfactual or real), the more steps between the antecedent and its consequents, and the greater the temporal remove of these consequents, the more unpredictable the outcome of the experiment.

For the sake of simplicity, I assigned a 0.5 probability to every step in the Mozart counterfactual, but the probability of these steps will almost certainly vary. Some steps may be more likely than others. In a world in which "national movements" demanded independence, it would have been difficult to have reached a political accommodation in Austria-Hungary, and thus the probability of international conflict in the Balkans would also have been high. But I consider highly improbable the prior step on which the political stasis of Austria-Hungary depends: the determining influence of culture on the goals of reform movements in eastern Europe. If the probability of one or more steps of a counterfactual is low, as I contend they are in the Mozart story, the likelihood of the consequent will be close to zero. If we assign a 0.1 probability to this step, and retain the 0.5 for all the other steps, the overall probability of the consequent is an insignificant .0031. If we assign higher probabilities to this and other steps, say 0.75, the likelihood of the consequent rises to .178—still less than one in five. To raise the probability over 0.5, the average probability of each step has to be at least 0.9 (this gives a total probability of 0.53), and this is very unlikely. This simple thought experiment indicates that for multiple-step counterfactuals the probability of a consequent is more sensitive to the probability of individual steps than it is to the number of steps; even one step with a low probability will reduce significantly the probability of the consequent. While chains are only as strong as their weakest links, multiple counterfactuals are weaker than their weakest links.

The second assumption I made in calculating probability is that every fork leads to a meaningfully different alternative world. A six-step counterfactual like the Mozart story would generate sixty-four alternative worlds—assuming each step had two forks and each of these steps had two forks, and so on out to six steps. Many of the steps in this counterfactual could have multiple (more than two) forks. In the absence of Mozart, romanticism might entirely, largely, or only partially dominate the cultural life of Europe—or not at all if some other artist developed a version of postclassicism. The war Germany and Austria lost could have had multiple outcomes in terms of its human and territorial cost, and the particular mix of the two would surely have affected the probability of a dictator coming to power afterward. A six-step counterfactual could generate more than sixty-four alternative worlds. These worlds would all be different in at least some respects, but many of them would probably be the same with regard to the attributes that concern us. This is because "second order" consequences would lead some, perhaps, many, of the forks back to a few real or alternative worlds.

Counterfactuals track a specific chain of historical developments arising from an antecedent. Second-order consequences are developments outside this chain that might also follow on the antecedent and that could affect the probability of the hypothesized consequent. There is a prize-winning history of the Peloponnesian War that argues that Athens could have won a victory early on if somebody else other than Pericles had been in charge and had pursued a more aggressive strategy against Sparta. But it is also likely that without Pericles, the Athenian assembly would not have reversed itself and offered an alliance to Corcyra. Without this alliance, war would not have arisen, and the counterfactual would have been moot. If we do away with some individual or development we may also create a "niche" that other individuals or organizations fill. Earlier I suggested that without Mozart, some other composer, perhaps Haydn, might have developed postclassicism and put cultural history back on track. Second-order consequences can also affect the significance of the consequent, even if it does occur. Suppose we invent minimal rewrites that reverse the outcome of the Battle of Poitiers in 732, allowing Muslim invaders to penetrate France. If Muslim kingdoms in northern Spain continued their internecine fighting, weakening their overall power and drive to expand beyond the Pyrenées, then the benefits of their military success at Poitiers might have been short-lived. Second-order consequences would rather quickly have restored Christian political and religious dominance in France.

Only determinists will insist that second-order counterfactuals will ultimately make alternative worlds converge with the real one. Karl Marx insisted that the triumph of liberal democracy and rising standards of living for the working class were inevitable consequences of capitalism. If Disraeli had not introduced social legislation in Britain, and if Henry Ford had not pioneered profit sharing in America, other people would have done these things. Such claims are extreme, but they find an echo in biology, where ever since Darwin, it has been recognized that evolution produces morphological similitude because there is a best set of physical characteristics and strategy for grappling with the challenges of life. Diverse species have converged independently on the architectures and behaviors most suited to avoiding predators and exploiting food resources.

I think it reasonable to assume that societies, like organisms, have a limited number of stable states. Accidents of history, real or counterfactual, can move the path of history away from these states, but there will be strong pressures to bring them back to the original or another stable state. Viewed in this light, the Mozart counterfactual is wanting in two respects. For reasons I have already made clear, it is the wrong counterfactual to produce the desired political consequent: a great-power war in the early twentieth century. But even if some more appropriate counterfactual could produce that consequent, other developments—second-order counterfactuals—would sooner or later have brought about the peaceful, developed, democratic and closely integrated Europe that we enjoy today.

AUTHOR'S REPLY

The reviewer completely misses the point. Of course, the Mozart counterfactual is far-farfetched—that's the whole idea! Erika is Germany's answer to Rube Goldberg. She or I could easily have provoked a European war by rewriting snippets of political history; Lebow and Tetlock did this, and convincingly for at least some of the historians they surveyed. Erika wanted to show how small, seemingly insignificant changes in reality can have large, unanticipated consequences across different domains. By doing this, she hoped to make readers aware of just how contingent, interconnected, and unpredictable the real world is. None of the more prosaic, and admittedly, more convincing, paths to war would have accomplished this goal.

The reviewer claims to refute the Mozart counterfactual on scientific grounds. I shared his arguments with Erika, and she dismissed them as *Quatsch* (poppycock). After a long digression about the near impossibility of multistep counterfactuals, the reviewer concludes that what really matters is the probability of their individual steps, not their total number. The really telling question—and here we agree with the reviewer—is how to determine the probability of any step of any counterfactual. For some counterfactuals, this is pretty straightforward. Epidemiologists have robust equations that describe the factors responsible for the spread of infectious diseases. They routinely conduct counterfactual experiments by altering the values of one or more terms of the equation to see how it would retard or facilitate the spread of particular pathogens. For political counterfactuals, this is impossible; there are no general laws that we can apply to specific cases, or probabilities that we can calculate by observing the outcomes of a large number of similar events. Probability is a guessing game, and Erika's guesses are at least as good as the reviewer's.

When we strip away all the pseudoscience, the reviewer's prejudice is exposed. He or she is a crude determinist, no different from Karl Marx. The telling lines are the claims that culture could never influence economics or politics, but that economics determines politics. Does the reviewer offer any evidence for these assertions? None whatsoever. Many prominent historians believe that ideas determine the fundamental structure of any society's economics and politics, and that economics is a branch of political science devoted to analyzing how politics shapes economic decisions. Surely, there is room for different points of views—even in biology. At least one biologist, the American Stephen Jay Gould, argued for the determining role of accident in evolution. He insisted that if you could rewind the tape of life and run the program over again you would end up with a radically different set of organisms each time (Gould, 1989).

The reviewer makes an admittedly good point about second-order consequences. Changes in reality ripple through society in unpredictable ways—this is a core assumption of the story. In theory, some other composer could have invented postclassicism. I acknowledge the need to add a paragraph or two to consider this problem in general, and to explain why Haydn was not close to becoming a post-classicist.

The Mozart counterfactual was meant to provoke and make readers think about the contingent nature of our world. If Erika had wanted to be more "scientific," she could have invited numerous counterfactuals that did not reach so far back into history and involved only minimal rewrites to provoke a European war. The same Lebow and Tetlock—the reviewer cites them ad nauseum—developed ten counterfactuals that could have led to a great-power war in Europe in the first decades of the twentieth century. In their first counterfactual, the Congress of Vienna in 1815 awards Prussia land in Silesia and the Rhineland, where the industrial revolution got an early start and made possible Prussia's rise to great-power status. Germany becomes unified under Prussian leadership, assumes an authoritarian character, and later in the nineteenth century pursues an aggressive foreign policy. The other counterfactuals are scattered throughout the nineteenth century, and several of them take place during or on the eve of the crisis that supposedly led to a European war. The more proximate the counterfactual to the war, the fewer the steps between antecedent and consequent. Lebow and Tetlock surveyed historians and the later found some counterfactuals more plausible than others, and some of them likely to have produced the "desired" war. Most significantly, there was no correlation between their judgments and the number of steps these counterfactuals entailed.

I must warn you, Erika is very unhappy about this Luddite review and has threatened to write a story in which soccer, not baseball, becomes the most popular European sport in the late nineteenth century. Just think of the political consequences! Police—even those with helmets and leather jackets—were loath to mess with protesting students and workers. A stone in the hands of a fastball pitcher can be lethal. Police vulnerability encouraged concession and compromise, which in turn helped facilitate democratic transitions in France and Germany. If soccer had become the rage, Europeans would have been good at kicking but terrible at throwing. You can't kick cobblestones at police from behind barricades. European police and political authorities would never have been intimidated by students and workers, and we might still be living under repressive, authoritarian regimes! Reviewers like this one might not have had the ability—or the freedom—to throw their metaphorical stones.

Psycho-logic versus Statistics

Why did I develop such a seemingly far-fetched counterfactual in my story? For a start, it highlights just how improbable any scenario extended forward a hundred-plus years must be. Most of us tend to see our world as foreordained, or if not, at least highly probable for a range of reasons. Imagined in 1791 it would have been just as improbable as the alternative world of my story. It might have appeared more unlikely still to contemporaries who would have found it so far removed from any linear projection they could imagine of the world they knew. My critic is a stand-in for these naysayers. I give him the advantage of being our contemporary but a resident of the alternative world I have created. He mobilizes arguments—all of which represent the conventional scholarly wisdom in our world—to show why our world could never have come to pass. I gave the last word to my feisty heroine Erika who hastens to remind our critic that the relevant question is not the probability of her world or our world, but rather of *all* worlds in which World War I, or something like it, did or did not occur. The sum of the probability of both sets is 1.0, and variants of either set of worlds might have been presented in ways to make them realistic prospects to people even as far back as 1791. With a few minutes for reflection, I am certain Erika could have come up with a scenario far more compelling to present-day social scientists than one that begins with Mozart's longevity.

There is another striking anomaly Erika fails to point out. Events should get harder to untrack the closer we approach them. This belief is reflected in the impossibility and inevitability curves completed by historians, international relations scholars, and foreign policy experts in the surveys and experiments described in chapter 5. This belief holds true for sweeping developments on the scale of the rise of the West versus other cultures and regions and more discrete events like World War I. It follows that the farther back we go from an event like World War I, the easier it ought to be to untrack. Close to the event our only real choices are to change agents or other superficial, if at time critical, attributes of context. At considerable remove, it becomes easier to devise minimal rewrites to alter what would later become underlying causes or structural features of the situation that could only be removed by "miracle" counterfactuals. If we go back to 1815, with subtle interventions at the Congress of Vienna, as Erika observes, we could substitute some other territories for those Prussia received in the Rhineland. The Rhineland and Silesia were the core areas of German industrial development, and deprived of the Rhineland, Prussia would not have the military or geographical position to challenge France and unify Germany along authoritarian lines. The history of modern Europe—if not the world—would have been very different. Historical logic suggests that the contingency of an event is more probable the farther back we move in time from it, but statistical logic indicates that counterfactual scenarios to untrack it are increasingly improbable.

The two logics are not contradictory although they give the superficial appearance being just that. Psycho-logic relies on vividness, but also requires a chain of logic that connects antecedent to consequent. As the experiments of chapters 5 and 6 demonstrate, the more counterfactual unpacking we engage in, or require of participants, the more credible alternative futures become. Counterfactual unpacking increasingly narrows the parameters of alternative worlds, and the most vivid and credible counterfactuals are invariably those that involve a detailed story line about a single alternative world. Psycho-logic accordingly moves us toward the narrowest of pathways which, by definition, are the least likely of worlds statistically. Statistical inference, by contrast, tells us why such narrow pathways are highly improbable. Each is confining and liberating in opposite ways. To make reasonable inferences about contingency and its role in the world, we must experience, not just understand, psycho-logic and statistics and the tensions between them.

CHAPTER EIGHT

Heil to the Chief:
Sinclair Lewis, Philip Roth, and Fascism

> The terror of the unforeseen is what the science of history hides.
> —*Philip Roth*

IN THIS CHAPTER I compare Sinclair Lewis's *It Can't Happen Here*, published in 1935, with Philip Roth's *The Plot Against America*, published in 2004.[1] The former looks ahead to the 1936 presidential election and the victory of the fictional fascist Senator Buzz Windrip over President Franklin Roosevelt. The latter looks back to the 1940 election to imagine Roosevelt's defeat by aviator Charles A. Lindbergh, whose administration is isolationist abroad and anti-Semitic at home. The two authors conjure up "fascist" regimes for different purposes, and reviewers—and presumably readers—responded to them differently. The two novels only address international relations *en* passant. They are nevertheless relevant to my project because of the vivid and artful way they combine fact and fiction to create powerful impressions on readers. They suggest that the distinction between fact and fiction—so dear to the hearts of most social scientists—can readily be bridged and to good purpose. Their success in doing so pushes us to interrogate more closely the binaries of fact and fiction, and factual and counterfactual. A more profound, or at least more explicit, understanding of these relationships has important implications not only for international relations but for the social sciences more generally.

FACTUAL AND COUNTERFACTUAL NARRATIVES

Counterfactuals have been used to set up fictional narratives at least as far back as Homer's *Iliad*. Exasperated by years of stalemate, the Greeks were preparing to go home, and would have, Homer tells us, if Hera had not sent Athena down from Olympus to instruct Odysseus to prevent their departure.[2] The decision to stay sets in motion the events of the saga. Counterfactual novels are a more recent innovation, dating from the early nineteenth century. Geoffrey-Château's *Napoleon et la conquête de monde 1812–1823* (1836) is generally credited with being the first novel in this genre. In recent decades, counterfactual fiction has become a growth industry. *Uchronia* lists over 2,600 counterfactual novels, stories, and articles and another 130 works analyzing them. An Internet search for "alternative history" on Amazon.com gets 6,360 hits while "counterfactual fiction" gets 115,000 hits on Google and its own heading in Wikipedia.[3] Many of these novels remake wars; the U.S. Civil War and World War II are the most popular. Some imagine a divided America with an impoverished Union or a German-dominated Europe or world.[4] A recent best seller has Israel losing the 1947–48 War of Independence and Jews finding a homeland in Alaska, transforming them, one of the characters observes, from "the chosen" into "the frozen" people.[5] Most of these novels use counterfactuals for purposes of entertainment, although all of them, intentionally or not, highlight the contingency of events and, by doing so, problematize national, ethnic, and individual identities.

Some counterfactual novels are intentionally unsettling. In Philip K. Dick's *Fatherland*, the United States is governed by President Joseph P. Kennedy and an isolationist administration happy to do business with the Nazis. The Nazis see the Holocaust through to its completion in Europe. In its aftermath they destroy the death camps and succeed in keeping their extermination of the Jews a secret. Other counterfactual novels seek to reassure—at least targeted audiences. D. James Kennedy's *What If Jesus Had Never Been Born*, describes a miserable and unhappy world with the goal of demonstrating how Christ and Christianity are responsibility for economic development, cultural advancement, science, and even civil liberties.[6]

Of the two novels I am about to discuss, only one, *Plot Against America*, qualifies as counterfactual in that it remakes the past. Counterfactual fiction almost invariably does so to remake the present, and this Roth scrupulously avoids for reasons that will become clear. Toward the end of the novel he introduces a deus ex machina in the form of a second-order counterfactual to return history to its actual course once the alternative world he creates has served its purposes. Critics rightly find his second-order counterfactual unconvincing, but its credibility, I will argue, is beside the point. Roth is a cut above other practitioners of the genre, and not only by virtue of the quality of his writing. He is self-conscious and reflective about his use of history and counterhistory. There is much to learn about these binaries from reading Roth and much to learn about Roth, his art, and aims by comparing *Plot Against America* to *It Can't Happen Here*.

IT COULD HAPPEN HERE

Future history strikes us as an oxymoron. The future has not yet happened and we cannot write its history. However, past and future are logically equivalent as the past was once the future and the future will one day be the past. We harbor all kinds of expectations about the future. We routinely construct scenarios with good or bad outcomes based on the lessons we think we have learned from the past and use them to build imaginary futures that help us work our way through life and its choices. We also do this to sell our preferences to others. Proselytizers of religion and nationalism, and candidates for election, paint rosy and grim pictures of the future, the favorable outcomes allegedly dependent on the success of their missions. Artists and writers occasionally depict future outcomes as if they had already come to pass, or are in the process of happening. Hieronymus Bosch's *Last Judgment* triptych and Dante's *Inferno* do so quite graphically. They encourage viewers or readers to come away with memories of the future—future histories, if you will—that encode lessons for the present.

It Can't Happen Here is future history. Novels of this kind—Erskine Childer's *Riddle of the Sands* (1903), Jack London's *The Iron Heel* (1908), and H. G. Wells's *War in the Air* (1922), to cite prominent early examples, generally depict a bleak future in the hope that it will inspire us to act now to prevent it becoming a reality.[7] Their authors want to bring about a different future and transform what they fear is a likely, even probable, future into a counterfactual past. Some novels—for example, Edward Bellamy's *Looking Backward* (1889) and Theodor Herzl's *Altneuland* (1902)—portray a rosy future that they hope their fiction will help make a reality.[8] *It Can't Happen Here* is a jeremiad that paints a dark picture of the very near future. Its political agenda is transparent: democracy is threatened by fascism, and Roosevelt's victory in 1936 is critical to its preservation. On a deeper level, Lewis wants readers to recognize the importance of tolerance and respect for others, for a successful democratic order.

Lewis was sensitized to the Nazi threat by his wife, journalist Dorothy Parker. Within months of Hitler's accession to power she wrote a series of articles on the Nazi persecution of the Jews. In August 1934 she was expelled from Germany a few days after she arrived on a journalistic tour, an event that received wide coverage in the Western media. Parker's growing anger at the Nazis was shared by Lewis, who was appalled by their bullying and use of violence against Jews, radicals and political opponents. In due course, his novels would be burned publicly by the Nazis. In 1937, two years after the publication of *It Can't Happen Here*, a German producer bought the rights to his play, *Dodsworth* and wrote to Lewis and his agent Sidney Howard asking them for proof that they were not Jewish. An outraged Lewis wrote back asking that in future correspondence they be addressed by the real names: Sidney Horowitz and Sinclair Levy.[9]

Lewis later credited his wife with the idea of a novel exposing fascist tendencies in the United States. She suggested how a fascist triumph in America might come about in the book she rushed into print after her interview with Hitler. "Imagine," she wrote in *I Saw Hitler*, that "an orator with the tongue of the late Mr. [William Jennings] Bryan and the histrionic powers of Aimee Semple McPherson combined with the publicity gifts of Edward Bernays and Ivy Lee" who appeals to farmers, white-collar workers, the unemployed, and is backed by the likes of Henry Ford, the Daughters of the American Revolution and the Ku Klux Klan, then "you will have some idea of what the Hitler movement in Germany means."[10] In the spring of 1935, Parker went to Washington, D.C., on assignment for the *Saturday Evening Post* where she interviewed numerous politicians and administration officials and reported back to her husband that Roosevelt was in trouble. He is likely to win in 1936, she advised, but "if things move in the present tempo I think we may very easily have a Republican-fascist dictatorship in 1940."[11]

Parker's most disturbing interview was with Senator Huey Long of Louisiana. Known as the "Kingfish," the former governor was a corrupt populist and demagogue who had shrewdly built a powerful political base as governor by sponsoring public works programs to provide jobs for the unemployed, rewarded his supporters with patronage and graft, and punished his opponents by less than legal means.[12] As a senator he advocated a share-the-wealth plan, laid out in his book, *Every Man a King*.[13] Long was shifty when it came to discussing budget figures or his political ambitions, and Parker came away from the interview convinced that he was an impostor but one with enough innate shrewdness and popular appeal to make a successful run for the presidency on a third-party ticket. Many on the Left considered Long a serious threat to democracy, and Lewis, influenced by his wife and friends, made him something of the model for President Berzelius (Buzz) Windrip in his novel.[14]

In retrospect, it is apparent that the threat to democracy or to the Roosevelt administration in the mid-thirties was remote. In 1936 FDR won reelection in a landslide (523 to 8 electoral votes for Alf Landon), and was reelected handily for an unprecedented third term in 1940 (449 to 82 for Wendell Wilkie). At the time, of course, this was not so obvious. Unemployment remained high, the New Deal appeared to be struggling and was opposed by an array of opponents on the Left and Right. On the Left, the communists and socialists were both active and had widespread support among intellectuals. The forces on the Right ranged from traditional Republicans to nativist, protofascist, and anti-Semitic groups like Father Coughlin's Union of Social Justice, the Ku Klux Klan, the Silver Shirts, the German-American Bund, and the Black Legion, who blamed the country's ills on various combinations of Blacks, Catholics, Jews, and immigrants and were full of praise for Mussolini and Hitler. Roosevelt's astounding triumph in 1936 removed this threat, although his administration and the New Deal still faced opposition from the Supreme Court and later from isolationists desperate to avoid doing anything that raised the risk of war with Germany. *It Can't Happen Here* was the product of this relatively short-lived period of fear of home-grown fascism.

Senator "Buzz" Windrip, a rather vacuous windbag and author of *Zero Hour*, an American version of *Mein Kampf*, wins the 1936 election by making all kinds of promises to end the depression and punish those responsible for it. Windrip is a good-natured, poker-playing, whiskey-guzzling, and inept politician who more closely resembles Warren Harding than he does Huey Long. He has learned to play one role well: "Man-of-the-People." His strength derives from his corporate bankroll, political organization—the League of Forgotten Men—and his Minute Men storm troopers. Once in office he rewards business with all kinds of favors, packs the court with unknown and uncouth lawyers, consolidates and extends governmental control over the media, and compels newspapers, newsreels, and radio stations to become purveyors of propaganda and meaningless Hollywood gossip. His economic policies quickly lead to disaster and compel the administration to set up "labor camps" to control dissent. Windrip's election and presidency are managed by his principal advisor, Lee Sarason, who ultimately removes him by sending him off to France. Sarason in turn is murdered by the secretary of war, Colonel Dewey Haik, who reveals himself to be a power hungry-tyrant.

A stagnating economy and growing repression trigger a rebellion committed to the reestablishment of democratic government. The uprising receives support from General Emmanuel Coon who rallies regular forces to come to the aid of rebellious western farmers. It seeks to establish the American Cooperative Commonwealth under the leadership of liberal Republican senator Walt Trowbridge, the defeated Republican candidate for president in 1936, who has taken refuge in Canada. The central figure of the novel is Doremus Jessup, a small-town newspaper editor in Fort Beulah, Vermont. Jessup's fundamental goodness and tolerance at first give him a detached if analytical perspective on events. His editorials gradually become more outspoken and courageous. Refusing to be intimidated, he loses his newspaper and is subsequently arrested and sent off to a concentration camp for printing and distributing anti-Windrip flyers. His son-in-law is executed and his daughter, Mary, takes her revenge by diving her plane into the ship carrying the judge who tried and sentenced her husband. Jessup escapes from prison and is nursed back to health by his mistress, Lorinda Pike. He spurns a safe life in Canada to train as a resistance fighter.

Reviewers recognize that the intended lesson of the book is that it *can* happen here unless Americans act in a timely way to preserve democracy. They cannot afford to be as disinterested as Doremus Jessup initially was because by the time they are roused to action it could be too late.[15] Doremus explains to his communist friend Comrade Karl: "You see, we don't like murder as a way of argument—that's what really marks the Liberal." As the novel progresses, Doremus learns from Karl that liberals must also be willing to fight and die to preserve their faith.[16]

Even reviewers who shared Lewis's politics were on the whole critical of the novel as a work of art or politics. One of the most negative reviews calls it "a remarkably bad book" that "borrows so many *clichés* from popular fiction and so many episodes from the modern talking film, that his violence and obvious sincerity lose half their effect."[17] Another notes that the success of the book depends upon incidents and editorializing, not on character, representation, and the persuasiveness of language.[18] Reviewers were quick to pick up on the similarities between characters in the novel and American political figures. Some fail to find any of Lewis's politicians convincing because he devotes so little time to their development, or they object to the cardboard nature of the people surrounding Doremus Jessup.[19] Jessup himself comes across to them as a stand-in for the author. One reviewer finds him lovable but unconvincing.[20] Another confesses that he is drawn to Doremus as a character, but notes that he does not contribute much as a thinker. If fascism threatens us, "the Jessups can't stop it because they don't really stand for anything except a kindly twinkle and a sense of humor."[21] A Marxist critic describes him as "the petty bourgeois gone left in mortal combat with the Fascists, who are the petty bourgeois gone to the extreme right."[22]

By far the most common complaint is Lewis's model of fascism and how it comes to power. It is a wholesale importation of the Nazi and Bolshevik archetypes with little or no effort to differentiate his American fascist from theirs.[23] The homosexuality of the Brown Shirts, mapped onto their American counterparts, comes in for particular criticism.[24] Melvin Vincent writes, "By affecting to make a parallel Nazi regime happen in the United States, Lewis in reality shows how impossible the European pattern of dictatorship would be for us."[25] Geoffrey Stone finds the novel unconvincing because it "does not discover the truth about America, any more than the translation of a French book into English would transform it into a revealing picture of English life. There is a crude lack of imagination about this that might disturb even Mr. Lewis' most fervent admirers."[26] Writing in the *New York Times*, J. Donald Adams observes that the Corpos—the political party loyal to Windrip—is too closely modeled on Stalin's Communist party. He thinks it extremely unlikely that Buzz Windrip could disband the Congress and lock up Supreme Court judges without provoking a sizeable rebellion backed by many governors, the army, and at least several state militias. "Mr. Lewis transports his horrors to America too completely—to feel that though it might happen here, it could not happen in so completely the same way that it happened to Germany and Russia."[27]

The Bolsheviks grabbed power in a coup against the provisional revolutionary regime and imposed control through a long and bloody civil war. Hitler became prime minister legally in January 1933 through the back door of the constitution that gave the president of the Republic emergency powers in case the Reichstag was deadlocked. Hitler's consolidation of power, known as the *Gleichschaltung*, was largely extralegal. He called an election, and used his paramilitary forces—the S.A. or Brown Shirts—to intimidate the opposition. Taking advantage of a fire that burned down the Reichstag, he convinced the majority to pass the Enabling Act. He then proceeded to make his own laws, ban trade unions and opposition parties, set up the Gestapo, and murder or imprison key figures in his own party and the opposition on the "Night of the Long Knives" in July 1934.[28]

Even before coming to power Hitler had a powerful paramilitary organization that he used to attack communists, Jews, and other opponents. Lewis's critics are right in thinking it unlikely that any political leader could have possessed a private army and used it on the streets of American cities to beat up and murder opponents. Revulsion would have been nearly universal and law enforcement agencies, or the army, if necessary, would have been mobilized by mayors, governors, or the president to arrest the offenders and restore order. These very authorities, however, had little compunction about using private forces (notably, Pinkertons), de facto privatized sheriff's departments, national guard units to repress strikers and protesters. Under Douglas MacArthur's overall command, George Patton's cavalry used violence to put down and disperse "Bonus Marchers" peacefully camped out on the Mall in Washington, killing several and injuring hundreds of veterans. There was also mob violence against Blacks, which had a long history of toleration by authorities. Irruptions include the New York draft riots of 1863, the Tulsa race war of 1921, and the numerous lynchings before and between the world wars.[29] Such violence, while utterly reprehensible from our perspective, was rarely seen as a threat to those in power, and perhaps understood by some as an effective means of deflecting economic and political frustrations. The Prussian police, the most powerful force in Germany, allowed itself to be taken over without any resistance by the Nazi regime. As several reviewers note, the National Guard and law enforcement authorities in the more decentralized United States would have been unlikely to accept orders from what they and a majority of Americans regarded as an illegal regime.

One hundred years earlier, Tocqueville reasoned that any tyranny in America would take an entirely legal form and control dissent through the power of public opinion. As citizens become more equal and alike, they are less likely to follow blindly the opinions of another man or class. Their similarity with others gives them "an almost unlimited trust in the judgment of the public." The very equality that makes them independent of their fellow citizens leaves them "isolated and without defense against the action of the greatest number." In the absence of meaningful debate, they can easily be misled by politicians who advocate unlimited expansion of popular power. Instead of restraining officials, elections can become the vehicle for destroying democracy. Democracy, Tocqueville writes, has the potential to "extinguish the intellectual freedom that the democratic social state favors, so that the human spirit, having broken all the shackles that classes or men formerly imposed on it, would be tightly chained to the general will of the greatest number."[30] A more politically astute novelist would have introduced fascism into America by duplicitous but fully legal means.

There is, I suspect, another, less rational component to the concerns raised by reviewers. Critics who rightly object to the Corpos being directly modeled on their European counterparts nevertheless fail to tell us why an American variant of such a political party could not arise. Some of them may simply be unwilling to recognize this possibility and seek refuge in the rather artless way Lewis presents his case. Hints of this come across in various admissions of his critics, which include recognition of the growth of right-wing, antidemocratic forces with leaders who imitate or praise Hitler, the "herd instinct" so clearly manifest at conventions of the American legion or the Daughters of the American Revolution and the gullibility of many Americans to "all the awful 'gospel' truth dispensed by partisan radio programs, newspapers, magazines, soap-box demagogues and others."[31] Interestingly, none of the reviewers object to the future history format of the novel. One makes a comparison to H. G. Wells's book and film, *Things to Come* (1935), which is also set in the future and, like the Lewis scenario, has peace and progress arising from a temporary dictatorship whose "Boss" takes a thinly disguised America to war against next-door neighbors to consolidate his power.[32]

Could it have happened here? Not the way Lewis portrays it, the reviewers are convinced, and for good reasons. A minority agree that some American variant of fascism is conceivable given the growing popularity of demagogues and protofascist organizations.[33] This was certainly Lewis's view and, we observed, his principal incentive for writing the novel. To the extent that he thought it likely, or even probable, the novel fits nicely in the genre of future history. It describes a likely future, awareness of which gives agents the opportunity to prevent it from happening. I nevertheless suspect that Lewis, even more than Wells when he wrote *The Future to Come*, considered the future he described less than probable. Like Wells, he offered something close to a worst-case scenario with the goal of scaring people and, not incidentally, of selling a novel. By making fascism appear more likely than it was, making it so vivid in readers' minds, making them identify with its appealing hero and his travails and leaving the outcome and ultimate cost of the ensuing civil war in doubt, Lewis hoped to make people more proactive in the present. The immediate purpose of the novel is to get more people to vote for Roosevelt and the Democrats in 1936. If so, we should really think of *It Can't Happen Here* as a kind of future counterfactual history. It portrays a future that its author thinks unlikely and by doing so attempts to make it less likely still.

While there is nothing autobiographical in Lewis's novel, it seems clear that Doremus Jessup has the author's values and responds to personal challenges, including his unsatisfactory marriage and politics, the way the author does, or would like to think he would in the face of fascism. He conducts a satisfying and guiltless affair—much to the annoyance of one reviewer. Lorinda Pike becomes his soulmate and co-conspirator the way Dorothy, Lewis's second wife, did in real life. He has high professional standards and commitments, on the whole minds his own business, and, much more than Lewis, is tolerant of the cultural and other failings of small-town America. When finally aroused to fight against fascism he does so with courage and intelligence and shuns refuge in Canada after escaping from prison to remain active in the resistance. Could Doremus be intended as a role model for Lewis, to convince him that in the circumstances he would be willing to give up his comfortable lifestyle and act courageously? This putative link between character and author provides a nice segue to our second novel, where that connection is unambiguous and acknowledged.

It Did Happen Here

It Can't Happen Here was the product of a relatively short-lived fear of home-grown fascism that largely disappeared after Roosevelt's landslide reelection in 1936. The New Deal pushed ahead, the Supreme Court ultimately reversed itself and upheld legislation recognizing labor's right to collective bargaining and the administration's authority to create federal agencies and programs to respond to the economic crisis. Unemployment nevertheless remained high until the country entered the war in December 1941 and became the arsenal for democracy. Opposition to Roosevelt became increasingly focused on his foreign policy and seeming willingness to risk war on behalf of Britain. The isolationist movement sought to keep America out of war on the grounds that we had nothing to gain and everything to lose from entering the fray. The America First movement, which at its peak had 800,000 members, found numerous supporters within the business community and from political figures as diverse as right-wing senators Burton K. Wheeler and Gerald P. Nye and Socialist party leader Norman Thomas. Its most prominent spokesman was Charles A. Lindbergh, the decorated aviator, who had spent time in Germany, received a medal from Reichsmarshal Hermann Goering, and was friends with Henry Ford and other prominent anti-Semites.[34]

The Plot Against America is set against this background and envisages Lindbergh's nomination by acclamation at a deadlocked 1940 Republican convention. In leather flying suit and white scarf Lindbergh barnstorms around the country, promising peace and prosperity to a frightened electorate. He wins the election in a landslide, capturing forty-six states. The new president flies to Iceland for "cordial talks" with Hitler and the two leaders sign a nonaggression pact. Ten days later Lindbergh does the same with Japanese leaders in Hawaii, tacitly condoning Japanese military expansion in Asia. He invites Nazi foreign minister Ribbentrop to visit Washington and hosts a state dinner for him at the White House. He sets up the Office of American Absorption with the declared goal of hastening the assimilation of outsiders, specifically Jews. Local Reform rabbi Lionel Bengelsdorf becomes the head of the Office of American Absorption and together with his mistress, Bess, Philip's mother's sister, convinces Philip's brother Sandy to enlist in the "Just Folks" program. Sandy spends a summer on a Kentucky tobacco farm where he bulks up with the help of home-made sausages and cured ham and acquires a hint of a regional accent. The "Good Neighbor Project" comes next, and Jewish families are deported to the hinterland to break up their communities and isolate their members. Their former neighborhoods are repopulated with gentiles, all this allegedly done to "enrich" everyone's "Americanness."

The policies of the Lindbergh administration begin to affect the Roth family when Herman, Philip's father, takes them on a holiday to Washington, D.C. They visit the Lincoln Memorial, where seeing and touching the statue of Lincoln seems to provide psychological reassurance that the Constitution and Bill of Rights are still in place. Herman's idyll ends abruptly when another visitor denounces him as a "loudmouth Jew" for his criticism of President Lindbergh. Herman and his family are later expelled from their hotel when their ethnicity is discovered. At dinner that evening, Herman is denounced a second time as a "loudmouth Jew" by someone at another table, but other diners, including their local guide, come to his support, and the owner offers the Roths free coffee and their children as much ice cream as they can eat. Phil's cousin Alvin, disgusted with the course of events, enlists in the Canadian army to fight Hitler. He loses a leg in a commando operation and returns home a bag of bones full of bitterness and resentment with a stump that is not healing and a mouth rotten from tooth decay. Alvin shares a bedroom with a horrified and frightened Phil, who helps him regain his will to live. A local Jewish dentist drills his teeth and puts in seventeen gold inlays as his personal contribution to the fight against Hitler and fascism. Alvin goes on to a career as a successful mobster. Under the "Homestead 42" program, the Roths are selected for relocation to Kentucky, but Herman avoids this fate by resigning from his insurance job. He is forced to do manual labor at night for his brother Monty in his wholesale food market, but almost loses his job there because the FBI has it in for the Roth family because of Alvin's earlier stint in the Canadian army. Monty bribes the local FBI agent to look the other way and then deducts the bribe from Herman's meager salary. Phil tries to run away from home to escape from all the nastiness that is closing in around him, but gets kicked by a horse and ends up in the hospital. His precious stamp collection disappears in the process.

The most vocal resistance comes from Jewish journalist Walter Winchell who uses his weekly radio program to denounce "Adolf" Lindbergh, "the fascist in the White House." He receives little support outside of the Jewish community. Even the *New York Times*, owned by Jews, accuses him of "questionable taste" and praises Jergens Lotions for withdrawing its funding of his Sunday night program, causing it to be canceled. Winchell in turn denounces the proprietors of the *Times* as "ultracivilized Jewish Quislings" and declares his presidential candidacy as a Democrat. He is assassinated at a political rally in St. Louis. Fiorello La Guardia delivers a rousing oration at the memorial service, provoking Lindbergh to fly off in his plane after which he is never heard from again.

Lindbergh's disappearance makes matters worse. His successor, Vice President Burton K. Wheeler, is a more committed extremist and initiates a short-lived reign of terror. Riots break out and lead to violence against Jews and destruction of Jewish business establishments in Detroit and other cities. Wheeler sends in the National Guard only belatedly, after 122 people, most of them Jews, have been killed. In Newark, a self-proclaimed Jewish police force composed mostly of thugs organizes to defend their community and the police use the opportunity to gun three of them down. First Lady Anne Morrow Lindbergh condemns the riots and is taken into "protective custody" by the FBI, while local police arrest Mayor LaGuardia of New York, Supreme Court Justice Felix Frankfurter, former President Roosevelt, and some of the country's leading Jews in government, finance, and journalism. The army is sent into New York to close down its radio stations and newspapers. Martial law is imposed across the country, ports and airports are closed, and the borders with

Canada and Mexico are sealed. War against Canada becomes increasingly likely, in part because of the shelter it gives to American Jews.

At this point, things begin to right themselves. The First Lady escapes from Walter Reed hospital, where she is being held incommunicado, and broadcasts to the nation from a secret transmitter somewhere in Washington. In a gentle and calm voice she asks the New York police to end their occupation of radio stations and newspapers, the National Guard units to disarm, the army to leave American cities, and the FBI to release everyone they have arrested. She implores the Congress to impeach acting President Wheeler for the illegal behavior of his "seditious" administration. Wheeler's political opponents, who include La Guardia and Dorothy Thompson, help mobilize decent Americans from all walks of life and two-and-one-half weeks later Roosevelt returns to the White House by means of a special presidential election timed to coincide with the 1942 congressional election. Japan promptly bombs Pearl Harbor and history returns to its course. Roosevelt dies in office on 12 April 1945, the date of his actual death, but during his third rather than fourth term.

At the end of the novel Roth attempts to rehabilitate Lindbergh and Rabbi Bengelsdorf. The Lindbergh baby, it turns out, was not murdered by Bruno Hauptmann, but kidnapped by him and smuggled out of the country by Nazi agents. The Lindberghs were blackmailed by the Nazis, who allowed them to see but not speak to their child on a trip to Germany and promised to kill him unless they followed Berlin's instructions. Charles is ordered to become a prominent isolationist, run for the presidency, keep America neutral in the war, and begin a round-up of America's 3.5 million Jews as a prelude to their extermination. Mrs. Lindbergh confides all of this to Rabbi Bengelsdorf, who has become her spiritual advisor, and tells him that the president began to engage in passive resistance. The "Homestead 42" program was intended as a sop to Himmler, who is not fooled, derides Lindbergh as a mere "dinner party anti-Semite," and threatens to send their son to fight on the eastern front. The Nazis arrange for Lindbergh's flight to disappear, step up their blackmail against Mrs. Lindbergh, and try to arrange for Henry Ford—a real anti-Semite—to become Lindbergh's successor as president. Mrs. Lindbergh refuses to buckle under and saves the country. Rabbi Bengelsdorf reveals the real plot against America in his self-serving but enormously successful memoir. Mrs. Lindbergh, protective of her husband, and presumably of the country, denounces the book as a pack of lies.

There are striking parallels between *It Can't Happen Here* and *The Plot Against America*: FDR is defeated and retires to his estate above the Hudson, the new president is pro-German and manipulated by dark forces and disappears suddenly from the scene. Political repression accelerates and fascism threatens the country. Both novels center on the life of a family and how its members are affected by these developments. Both fathers, one a well-educated, prosperous member of the Protestant elite, the other the offspring of hardscrabble Jewish immigrants, rise to the challenge and become heroes and role models in the course of their courageous opposition to fascism. In excoriating the Lindberg administration in Roth's novel, Mayor LaGuardia exclaims: "It can't happen here? My friends, it *is* happening here."[35] Dorothy Parker, the catalyst for Lewis's novel, features prominently in *The Plot Against America*.

The similarities between the novels appear more than coincidental but Roth denies that he had any literary model for reimagining the past. He makes no mention of *It Can't Happen Here*, only of George Orwell's *1984*, written in 1948, which he read but did not reread before writing *The Plot Against America*. Roth insists that the inspiration for the book came to him while reading the bound proofs of Arthur Schlesinger Jr.'s autobiography. He was especially interested in Schlesinger's account of his life in the late 1930s and early 1940s because the same events had impinged on his life, although he was only a child at the time.

> The great world came into our house every day through the news reports on the radio that my father listened to regularly and the newspapers that he brought home with him at the end of the day and through his conversations with friends and family and their tremendous concern for what was going on in Europe and here in America. Even before I started school I knew something about Nazi anti-Semitism and about the American anti-Semitism that was being stoked, one way or another, by eminent figures like Henry Ford and Charles Lindbergh, who, in those years, along with movie stars like Chaplin and Valentino, were among the most famous international celebrities of the century.[36]

Roth came upon a sentence in which Schlesinger reports that some Republican isolationists hoped to persuade Lindbergh to run for president in 1940. "That's all there was, that one sentence with its reference to Lindbergh and to a fact about him I'd not known. It made me think, 'What if they had?' and I wrote the question in the margin. Between writing down that question and the fully evolved book there were three years of work, but that's how the idea came to me."[37]

There are, of course, many meaningful differences between the two novels. The narrator and central figure in *It Can't Happen Here* is Doremus Jessup, a middle-aged man, while in *The Plot against America*, it is "Phil," who represents the author as an eight-year-old boy. Doremus's is a largely personal story, although one in which other members of his family feature prominently. Phil is not shy about his personal aspirations and reactions to what goes on around him, but tells a collective tale about his family. Most of the relationships that matter in *It Can't Happen Here* are outside the family, between Doremus and other characters in the novel, notably his mistress and his nemesis, a former gardener who becomes a sadistic local Gauleiter under the new regime. In *The Plot Against America*, family relations are far and away the dominant theme and include the extended not just the nuclear family and others who live in the building and neighborhood. *It Can't Happen Here* ends while a civil war is under way, but readers sense that ultimately the forces of democracy will triumph. Judging from the name of the resistance movement—The American Cooperative Commonwealth—it is unlikely to be a restoration of the traditional American republic but something with a more socialist orientation. In *The Plot Against America* everything returns to normal after Roosevelt regains the White House.

Fear pervades both novels—it is the opening word of *The Plot Against America*—but it has different origins, threatens the two families in somewhat different ways, and ends up shattering one of them while reinforcing the unity of the other. The Jessups are financially and socially secure. Doremus is a highly regarded member of the local elite and secure in his New England roots. He has a strong sense of himself as a New Englander and is proud of the values of hard work, self-reliance, tolerance and pragmatism that he associates with the region. He worries that his children, who have grown up in an America increasingly focused on material acquisition and pleasure, are losing touch with these values. Fear enters the picture from outside, due to the rise of the Corpo regime. The Jessup family is slow to see the threat, and Mrs. Jessup—apolitical, family oriented, and utterly conventional—never really develops any understanding or political consciousness. Ineluctably the noose tightens around the Jessup family, leading to the death of their son-in-law and daughter, Doremus's expulsion from the newspaper, imprisonment, and later his desertion of his wife for his mistress.

The Roths are fearful from the outset because of their marginal position as Jews and members of the lower middle class in depression-ridden America. In one of the opening scenes we learn how one status impacts negatively on the other. Herman has been offered a promotion that will increase, possibly double, his income and allow his family to escape their cramped apartment, in which Phil and Sandy share a room, for a detached one-family house in the suburbs. They are thrilled by the prospect and on a Sunday afternoon drive to the nearby town they would have to move to if Herman accepts the promotion. They pass comfortable homes with porches and neatly manicured lawns, but with nobody in sight, and they wonder aloud if there are any other Jews in the community. Bess remembers her childhood, when she was one of only a few Jews in her neighborhood, and thinks how awkward it would be for Sandy and Phil to grow up as outsiders in this community. The clincher is a picnic they come upon of the German-American Bund in one of the town's beer gardens. Herman turns down the promotion and chooses to remain in a poorer, crowded urban setting surrounded by other Jews where his children can be themselves. Herman is also quick to pick up on the dangers of the Lindbergh administration, but refuses to emigrate. He chooses to stay and fight in whatever way he can for his rights and the preservation of democracy. Herman and Doremus have the same civic values.

The differences between the two families prove more important than their similarities, and reflect cultural and economic differences between Wasps and Jews, and a fundamental difference in the interests of the two authors. Lewis conjures up a fascist regime to make its consequences palpable for America readers and, by doing so, to mobilize them to support the New Deal and Franklin Roosevelt. The Jessup family is a means to this political end, although Doremus also serves to showcase the best side of small-town America and its values and how critical they are to democracy. Doremus is a corrective to Dodsworth and Elmer Gantry, and perhaps a response to the criticism Lewis received from so many small-town residents, including those in the Minnesota town in which he grew up. Roth's novel is above all else about his family. The deteriorating political situation in America is intended to intensify their vulnerability and sharpen the choices the family, and Jews more generally, have to make. Roth's parents rise to the occasion. They respond to a series of crises with insight, maturity, and courage and do their best to shelter Phil and Sandy from the diverse threats that descend on their community and family. Conflict nevertheless erupts: Herman has a punch-up with his nephew Alvin, and expels his wife's sister Evelyn from their house for trying to convert their son Sandy into a supporter of Lindbergh. Sandy and Phil are slapped by their parents for the first time in their lives. In real life, anti-Semitism and economic hardship took their toll on Herman Roth. A counterfactual novel gives Herman the opportunity to display his courage and regain, at least metaphorically, his dignity and manhood. Bessie is a dedicated and loving wife and mother who in her own quiet way holds the family together under increasingly difficult circumstances. Both parents demonstrate, their son explains, how "to remain strong when you are not welcome."[38]

Roth has warm feelings about his entire family and tells us how emotionally satisfying it was to write a novel about them:

The writing, then, put me in touch with my dead parents no less than with the period, and in touch eventually with the kind of little boy I myself was, because I've tried to portray him faithfully too. But the deepest reward in the writing and what lends the story its pathos wasn't the resurrection of my family circa 1941 but the invention of the family downstairs, of the tragic Wishnows, on whom the full brunt of the anti-Semitism falls—the invention particularly of the Wishnow's little boy, Seldon, that nice, lonely little kid in your class whom you run away from when you're yourself a kid because he demands to be befriended by you in ways that another child cannot stand. He's the responsibility that you can't get rid of. The more you want to get rid of him, the less you can, and the less you can, the more you want to get rid of him. And that the little Roth child wants to get rid of him is what leads to the tragedy of the book.[39]

In the first instance, the novel gives Roth the opportunity to put himself in closer touch with his parents and to honor them. It would have been easy and appealing for him to conduct imaginary conversations with family members as memories of them emerged from the recesses of his mind making them more accessible. Bakhtinian dialogue of a sort draws father and son closer together and puts Philip more in touch with what his parents might have thought and felt at the time. Their fears, by no means successfully veiled from the historical and fictional Phil, become positively palpable. Philip understands something Phil cannot: just how humiliated and emasculated Herman must have felt when subjected to the kind of anti-Semitism he faces in Washington and Newark in front of his family. These encounters are fictional but as this author knows from his own childhood experiences, being turned away from hotels and called a "loudmouth Jew" were regular occurrences in the more benign America of Roosevelt and Truman.

It is enigmatic and revealing that Roth describes the invention of the Wishnow family, and particularly their son Seldon, Phil's cloying contemporary, as "the deepest reward in the writing." Why should the author of an autobiographical novel derive the most satisfaction from a fictional family, and one, moreover, that suffers so terribly? I think the answer is to be found in Roth's earlier novels and what they reveal about his struggle to understand the Holocaust and its meaning for himself and American Jewry.

Roth's early stories were about Jews who move to the suburbs and attempt to remake themselves as full-fledged "White" Americans in the postwar era when this first became possible. Their Jewish identities, which they previously took for granted, now become problematic. In "Goodbye, Columbus," one of the characters who understands this dilemma exclaims: "Since when do Jewish people live in the suburbs? They couldn't be real Jews, believe me."[40] In "Eli the Fanatic," a secularized Jewish lawyer is unsettled and threatened by the arrival of an immigrant Hasidic community in his suburban New Jersey town. He encounters one of them, Leo Tzuref, a Holocaust survivor whose very name evokes the Yiddish word for trouble (*tsuris*). Eli gives Leo his suit in the hope of Americanizing him, in the tradition of German Jews who used charity as a strategy to assimilate earlier immigrants from eastern Europe. This being Roth, there is, of course, a twist. The Hasid accepts his clothes and in return gives Eli his caftan, yarmulke and religious paraphernalia. Both men change character and begin to lead counterlives, and in the process Eli appears to free himself of self-hate and the need to escape his past. He nevertheless shocks his fellow assimilated Jews, and when, in his Hasidic garb, he visits his wife in the hospital after she has just given birth to their first child, he is taken away to the mental ward. As in *The Plot Against America*, it is not gentiles who pose the greatest threat to Jews, but Jews who begin to think of themselves as all but gentiles.[41]

Later Roth novels also ask what it means to be a Jew and how this identity can be maintained. Many of their characters use Eli's strategy of "doubling"—of assuming another identity to get outside of themselves. They also indulge the traditional Jewish penchant for self-mockery, parody, and criticism. In *Operation Shylock*, Smilesberger recognizes how these several responses are reinforcing: Jews talk a lot, he suggests, because words are the medium in which a doppelgänger can be created and interrogated.[42] As students of Roth have long recognized, he is fascinated by identity and how it is constantly being revised and reinvented. No identity is fixed, but his characters are fierce in asserting and defending the most temporary ones. Sons routinely confront their fathers and suggest that identities are developed through transgressive acts. There are also limits to self-invention, and these Roth explores in *The Human Stain* (2000) in which a black Christian passes for a white Jew. Unlike Bernard Malamud's Jews, who are archetypes from the Lower East Side facing time-honored tribulations, Roth's suburban Jews are quintessentially American and always being transformed by life in this wonderful country.[43]

Roth's early fiction is set in the United States. From the outset, however, he plays the European Jewish experience off against the American one by bringing into his stories and novels real and imaginary European characters like Leo Tzuref, Franz Kafka, and an imagined Anne Frank.[44] In his more mature novels, Roth turns to the Holocaust as a counternarrative to American Jewish life. This development comes at a time when Americans are beginning to confront the Shoah through such vehicles as the first Anne Frank movie, the Eichmann trial, the mini-series *Holocaust*, and later, the opening of the Holocaust Museum and *Schindler's List*.[45] Roth's more mature novels rest on the premise that American Jewish life cannot be understood in isolation and that the key to much of this understanding is the Holocaust, a subject nearly taboo during the first few decades of the postwar world.

In his novels set outside the United States—notably *Counterlife* (1986) and *Operation Shylock* (1993)—Jewish past and present, America, Europe, and Israel come together. In *Counterlife* Nathan Zuckerman's brother dies during heart surgery. In a variant that follows in the same novel, his brother survives and makes aliyah to Israel where he takes up residence in Judea with a rabid nationalist group. This gives Nathan the opportunity to visit Israel and confront him and through his arguments with his brother and the leader of the sect to explore the merits and meaning of Jewish life in Israel and America. In subsequent variants, Nathan dies and survives. In the latter, he moves to London with his new English wife. The anti-Semitism he encounters there, so markedly different from his more tolerant experiences in the States, compels him to examine the extent to which his identity and behavior reflect his Jewishness.

In *Operation Shylock*, the author travels to Israel for the *New York Times* to interview novelist and Holocaust survivor Aharon Appelfeld. Appelfeld tells him (more fiction) that he has just spoken to former Solidarity leader Lech Wałesa who wants all European Jews to return to their former homelands, including Poland. The European Diaspora is now examined as the authentic homeland of the Jews, where their rabbinic culture and so much else of meaning to them developed. The return to Europe is also espoused by a "fake" Philip Roth, also in Israel, where he has been preaching a religiously inspired anti-Zionism. Roth confronts his doppelgänger only to discover that he is a virtual twin who categorically refuses to give up his impersonation. In the course of an exceedingly complicated plot, the real Philip Roth finds it increasingly difficult to distinguish reality from subterfuge, as do the Israeli and Palestinian intelligence agencies with whom he becomes involved. As a high-profile Jewish figure, Roth begins to suspect that both Israeli and Palestinian intelligence are trying to corral him into working for their respective causes. The admittedly "crazy idea" (Roth's description) of a return of Israel's Jews to Europe lets Roth examine Israel as a "counterlife," which indeed it was for European Jews in Theodor Herzl's day. It also allows him to pose critical questions about present-day Israel, and to use his answers to look at American Jews in comparative perspective and their love-hate relationship with Israel.

Both novels reveal how different life is at almost every level for Jews in America and those in Israel and Europe. Roth acknowledges that *The Plot Against America* represents an effort to bridge the deep chasm of security and prosperity that divides American Jews from all other Jewish communities, past and present. He chooses Lindbergh for his counterfactual president because "I wanted America's Jews to feel the pressure of a genuine anti-Semitic threat." Although Lindbergh did not pursue exclusionary measures and ethnic cleansing as president, he was a white supremacist, anti-Semite, and isolationist. Under his fictive presidency, Roth maintains, it becomes possible for Jews "to imagine how they might have conducted themselves under the enormous pressure of a Jewish crisis such as they never really had to encounter as native born New Jerseyans."[46]

Weeequahic is the Jewish equivalent of Rousseau's state of nature. Its Jews take their Judaism for granted and act on it unreflexively. Late in the novel, looking back with nostalgia on this world as Rousseau did on the state of nature, Roth opines: "Neither was their being Jews a mishap or a misfortune or an achievement to be 'proud' of. What they were was what they couldn't get rid of. Their being Jews issued from their being themselves, as did their being American. It was as it was, in the nature of things, as fundamental as having arteries and veins, and they never manifested the slightest desire to change it or deny it, regardless of the consequences." In early Roth novels, the state of nature in which America's Jews live is corrupted by wealth and the social acceptance it brings in postwar America. Jews are allowed to "whiten" themselves, making their Jewishness an identity of choice, and for some, problematic. The state of nature is always insecure, and the consequences of this are also explored in *The Plot Against America*. American Jews are forced to make the kinds of choices they never had to face in practice. By compelling them to do so, Roth exposes the generally unpredictable ways in which character and chance interact. As in *Counterlife*, character dictates the choices people make, but chance determines the outcomes to which they lead. At the end of *The Plot Against* America Phil describes three key choices: "My father chooses resistance, Rabbi Bengelsdorf chooses collaboration, and Uncle Monty chooses himself."[47] This is by no means an exhaustive list. Shepsie Tirschwell and his wife choose flight (to Canada), and Phil himself tries to flee when events became too much for him, although he does not get very far.

Only in retrospect do the consequences of these choices become apparent. Herman's early recognition of the dangers posed by Lindbergh, his refusal to emigrate to Canada or accept internal resettlement in Kentucky, and his unwavering resistance to the regime make him the hero of the book. However, his success is a near thing. If Herman and Sandy had made one too many wrong turns in their marathon drive to Kentucky to bring Seldon home, or if Mr. Cucuzza had not rushed Herman, suffering from pneumonia, to the hospital, the story would have had a different ending. Herman's brother Monty appears untouched by political developments. He carries on as usual during the Lindbergh administration and remains accommodating to the mob and FBI. Had anti-Semitism progressed further—and at this point in the novel Himmler is trying to arrange for Henry Ford to become president and impose a "Final Solution"—Monty and his businesses would have come to a grievous end.

Given his connections, he probably would have denied the possibility of his fate until it was too late to avert. A Ford presidency represents counterfactual speculation within a counterfactual world and is enough in tune with plot developments to make us ponder its consequences for at least one of the characters of the novel.

The more interesting peripheral figure is Rabbi Bengelsdorf. He is the archetypical assimilated German Jew who is slow to see danger and opportunist in his response. He naively puts his trust in friends in high places. He associates himself early on with Lindbergh when he is running for office, and as Alvin so nicely puts it, tries to "kosher him" for the Jews. When Lindbergh becomes president, the rabbi is put in charge of the "Homestead 42" Program, invited to the White House for dinner with his fiancée, Evelyn, Bess's big-breasted, social-climbing, and manipulative sister. Their wedding is attended by leading representatives of New Jersey's Jewish and non-Jewish establishments, and the couple receive congratulations from the White House. After the Wheeler putsch, the rabbi's fortunes rapidly change. The FBI breaks into his Washington hotel room and takes him away in handcuffs. Evelyn flees to Newark but is afraid to return home lest the FBI is waiting for her. She seeks refuge from her sister who turns her away in disgust. Phil takes pity on Evelyn and hides her in their dank basement and, worried that she will have no place to relieve herself, sneaks downstairs with a bedpan. Bess discovers what is afoot, relents, and invites her upstairs to eat. Rabbi Bengelsdorf is released after the coup fails and, because of his close relationship with Mrs. Lindbergh is let in on the otherwise closely guarded secret of her child's kidnapping by the Nazis and their subsequent efforts to bribe the family. He makes a small fortune by telling all in his memoirs, but his reputation is seriously tarnished when a spokesman for the former first lady condemns his revelation as a "reprehensible calumny."[48]

Rabbi Bengelsdorf's reversal of fortune is one of the few developments in the book that brings a smile to our face, and the subplot that surrounds him comes close to being comedy. It represents a stunningly successful mixing of genres by Roth. *The Plot Against America* is presented as a tragedy, as the plot moves ineluctably toward a horrible but seemingly unavoidable fate for American Jews. It avoids tragedy because the logical outcome—extermination of American Jewry—is averted. A deus ex machina intervenes in the form of an unconvincing countercoup inspired by the first lady. Phil serves as the chorus, commenting on the behavior and character of the actors, but here too Roth violates convention by making him a principal actor as well. Roth's comedy violates other conventions. The rabbi gets married, as everyone is supposed to in a comedy, but the wedding comes in the middle of the story, not the end, and the subplot continues to unfold and ultimately to mix with the tragedy. The

Roth family is reunited, a seemingly happy ending, but the reunion puts Phil in even closer touch with Seldon, the very person from whom he has been trying desperately to escape. The adoption, violation, and mixing of genres allows Roth to foreground the quixotic nature of fate, regardless of the character of the actors and the choices they make.

Writing *The Plot Against America* not only put Philip in closer touch with his parents and younger brother but with himself. The Phil-Philip dichotomy allows the author to write a novel about himself as a boy, but the act of writing partially overcomes this separation and allows the man to recapture and experience the feelings of the boy—in his real and counterfactual life.[49] The fictive life gives Philip the opportunity to expose his younger self to a muted version of the horrors faced by millions of his less fortunate contemporaries. Phil behaves as might be expected: he displays a mix of fear, denial, bravery, loyalty to friends and family, and self-protection, some of which have little to do with the larger political threat. In October 1942, after the family stayed awake all night awaiting the pogrom that failed to materialize, he comes to the awful recognition that Jews and Americans are no longer compatible. He imagines himself an immigrant, like the Tershwells and so many European Jewish children. "I wept all the way to school," Phil reports. "Our incomparable American childhood was ended. Soon my homeland would be nothing more than my birthplace. Even Seldon in Kentucky was better off now," although we know he is not. Phil has faced the twin threats of loss of self from without and within, and danger can be removed, and indeed needs to be removed, if the novel is to serve its purpose. And this is what happens. The very next sentence tells us: "But then it was over." In the pages that follow, Roth restores democracy, brings Herman, Sandy, and Seldon safely back to Newark and his readers back to our America.[50]

What purpose does all of this serve? Why does Philip immerse himself, and his younger alter ego in a fictional world of violent, government-supported anti-Semitism? To the extent that we remember a happy childhood, we look back on our early years with a certain nostalgia. At the very least, these years appear to have been less complicated and filled with the intense emotions that go with discovery and novelty. Roth makes nostalgic references to such a happy youth in his Zuckerman novels. It is reasonable that someone in his seventies would want to reacquaint himself with his past self, and a good novelist has the option not available to most of us for doing so through his writing. This would not account for the counterfactual conceit around which the novel is structured, which seems to work against this goal because it creates a more difficult and painful youth for his alter ego. We must look elsewhere for the explanation of why the author imagines such a threatening childhood in its place.

Maybe the answer is to be found in Philip's exceptionally happy childhood and, by extension, the carefree childhood, at least in a political sense, of American-born Jews of his generation. While their European contemporaries were being hunted down and murdered, Phil and his friends played imaginary games of war with rubber balls on the street until called home by their parents for snacks or dinner. Roth ponders the meaning of such security in other novels but most directly in this one and in his commentary about it. In *The Counterlife* and *Operation Shylock* Roth articulates his belief that American Jews need to understand and appreciate their extraordinary good fortune in living in what really is the Promised Land. One way to drive this truth home is to expose them to an alternative America in which fear is the most pervasive emotion of childhood. Early in *The Plot Against America*, Philip—not Phil—tells us that Lindbergh's nomination "assaulted, as nothing ever had before, that huge endowment of personal security that I had taken for granted as an American child of American parents in an American school in an American city in an America at peace with the world."[51]

Tragedy draws spectators, or readers in this instance, into the drama emotionally while distancing them from it intellectually, thereby encouraging a more profound understanding of its dynamics and meaning. Aristotle invokes the concept of catharsis to show how the emotional anguish aroused by tragedy can promote knowledge.[52] Literally meaning "to purge" or "to purify," catharsis allows all kinds of otherwise repressed emotions to surface. In ancient Athens, under the protective umbrella of the Great Dionysia festival, tragedies brought citizens to emotional states that were otherwise taboo or avoided. These included loss of control, the breakdown of conventions, and the release of primal human passions.[53] Tragedy works in a manner similar to vaccination. The audience or readers experience the powerful emotions of tragedy second hand and in a stylized and less virulent form. They are not overwhelmed by these emotions and their consequences the way the characters in the drama are and are thus in a position to use reason to reflect upon their meaning. They can learn from what they have seen and experienced. In tragedy, confrontation with chaos is intended to be a profoundly civilizing experience.

Shakespeare's tragedies aim for this effect, and so to some degree does *The Plot Against America*. The Holocaust was taboo for several decades, not only in gentile America but in Jewish America as well. Holocaust survivors, many with visible markers of their experience in the form of tattooed numbers on their arms, were seen as an embarrassment, but even more, as a threat. They reminded American Jews of what could have happened to them—another counterfactual—if their parents or grandparents had not left the Old Country for the New World. The *Diary of Anne Frank*, the play and the movie about it that followed in the 1950s, and the trial in Israel of Adolf Eichmann in 1961, brought the Holocaust to the attention of publics in North American and Europe. The Holocaust taboo was more effectively breached in the late 1970s and 1980s by a spate of television shows, movies, memoirs, and historical studies. By the 1990s, it had become part of the school curriculum in many states, and there were Holocaust museums and memorials, not only in Washington, D.C., but in other American cities. Roth appears to suggest that Holocaust survivor guilt is greatly abetted by counterfactual imagining.

The Holocaust has been brought into the American consciousness in dramatic ways but little effort has been made to address the fear and even guilt it has the potential to provoke. On one level, Americans appear to be more willing now to address the Holocaust than they were in the decades immediately following war, when it was too close and too painful, but greater visibility of the Holocaust today may make the need to repress the emotions it triggers that much greater. There is always a gap between trauma and its explicit public discussion. One to three generations appears to be the norm.[54] In this connection, *The Plot Against America* can usefully be read against two nearly contemporary German novels: W. G. Sebald's *Austerlitz* and Günther Grass's *Im Krebsgang* (Crab Walk).[55]

Trauma, and the difficulty of addressing it, brings us full circle to Seldon Wishnow and his relationship to Phil and Philip Roth. Phil has three roommates in the course of the novel: his brother, Sandy; his cousin Alvin; and, after his return from Kentucky, his neighbor Seldon. Phil worships Sandy at the outset of the novel but becomes increasingly distant from him as Sandy becomes a supporter of Lindbergh and speaks disparagingly of his family as Jews with a ghetto mentality who are afraid of their own shadows. Sandy unwittingly strengthens Phil's Jewish identity. Cousin Alvin returns home from the war with only one leg, enormous anger, and little will to live. Phil at first recoils from the sight of Alvin and his stump, but rises to the challenge of helping him look after it and matures in the process. Alvin also deserts the Roth family, for money and respect in a gangster family. Seldon, by contrast, cannot get close enough to Phil and the Roth family, much to Phil's annoyance—he considers him a nuisance and an embarrassment. Philip describes Seldon as "a trusting American kid who suffers something like the European Jewish experience. He is not the child who survives the confusion to tell the tale but the one whose childhood is destroyed by it."[56] In the last sentence of the book, Phil contrasts him to Alvin: "There was no stump for me to care for this time. The boy himself was the stump, and I was the "prosthesis" until he was taken to live with his mother's married sister in Brooklyn ten months later.[57]

Seldon is a stand-in for Phil, or another internal counterfactual. The Roths are scheduled to be sent to Danville, Kentucky, an assignment Herman ultimately spurns even though it means giving up his job with Metropolitan Life Insurance. Seldon and his mother end up going instead, because Phil, in an attempt to keep his family in Newark, intervenes with his aunt Evelyn, fiancée of Rabbi Bengelsdorf, the director of the relocation program. He falsely represents Seldon as his best friend, with the result that both families are selected for relocation to Kentucky. Seldon's mother is summoned from Danville to Louisville by her boss, presumably to be fired. En route, she is attacked and burned to death in her car by the KKK on an anti-Semitic rampage. Seldon and his family had previously lived in the basement of the Roth home. In Aeschylus's *Oresteia*, the threatening furies are transformed into the "well wishers" and led to their new home beneath the city of Athens. They are sublimated and repressed by relocating them underground. As Freud understood, the underground is a stand-in for the unconscious. In the course of the novel then Seldon moves from Phil's subconscious to Kentucky and finally to his tiny, cramped bedroom. So, in a way, does the Holocaust. It is something that Philip has struggled with and, like so many Americans, has repressed or kept at arm's length from his life and that of America's Jews. The novel does not confront the Holocaust directly, but it certainly allows the author to acknowledge through the Wishnow's persecution and ill-fortune whatever guilt he feels for living such a comfortable life in the 1940s.

By bringing a pale and temporary version of Nazi Germany to America, the novel attempts to make American Jews understand their extraordinarily privileged position and how their individual and collective angst about who they are and what it means to be Jewish is a by-product of their security and acceptance. Here, too, Seldon and his family play the critical role by imparting verisimilitude to the threat posed by the Lindbergh administration. They suffer in a way the Roths do not. Mrs. Wishnow is murdered, and Seldon is left the shell of a normal youth. In this connection it is interesting to compare *The Plot Against America* with Stephen Spielberg's film *Schindler's List*. Spielberg recognizes that the Holocaust was so horrendous that any accurate portrayal of the camps would be so painful to his audience that it would limit the film's appeal and undercut its message. For the same reason, most of the film's characters had to survive. Roth must tread more carefully when it comes to violence and suffering, and the Wishnows' fate evokes the required emotions without overwhelming readers—as it might if Phil suffered such a fate, or if Mrs. Wishnow's murder had been depicted more graphically. Philip has every reason to be satisfied with his creation of Seldon.

Let us conclude by looking at the interesting links the novel creates between Newark and the White House. Rabbi Bengelsdorf has the most direct connection through the position he occupies in the Lindbergh administration. Phil is metaphorically connected to the previous occupant of the White House by his hobby of stamp collecting. When Roosevelt is defeated and returns to his home in Hyde Park, Phil imagines him inspecting and mounting in albums the stamps he accumulated while president. Phil spends the little money he has on his stamps and takes his most precious stamps to Washington with him. When he flees home to escape the consequences of Lindbergh's victory, he takes his stamp album along but loses it when he is kicked unconscious by a horse. His nightmare also involves stamps as he imagines the Yosemite commemorative with a black swastika overprint. The importance of the stamps and the dream is highlighted by making a stamp a central part of the dust jacket design, something presumably approved, or even suggested, by Roth.

Roosevelt, who personally commissioned the national park commemorative series, of which the Yosemite stamp is one, is a kind of surrogate father for Phil, as he was for many of Newark's Jews. When Lindbergh defeats Roosevelt, Phil is deprived of that father, although he tries to take him with him when he flees by bringing his stamp album. Events force Phil to grow up and distance himself from his real and surrogate father, which in turn allows him to show them the deference and respect they deserve. The author acknowledges, "It's the children of the book who join the trivial to the tragic; far from constraining me, their presence was what allowed my latitude."[58]

POLITICS

It Can't Happen Here is an avowedly political novel. Sinclair Lewis made no attempt to hide his purpose and spoke frequently, as did his wife, of the dangers of fascism and the need to convince Americans of the danger. Roth cautions readers not to interpret *The Plot Against America* as a roman à clef. "My every imaginative effort," he insists, "was directed toward making the effect of that reality as strong as I could, not so much to illuminate the present through the past but illuminate the past through the past."[59] Some critics refuse to take him at his word and insist that *The Plot Against America* is a not so veiled attack on the Bush administration, or at the very least, inspired by the events of 9/11.[60] *London Times* reviewer Michael Gorra maintains, "It is impossible to read this book, in which an election plunges the nation into an alternative universe, without America's current condition in mind."[61] In *Newsweek*, David Gates observes that Roth does not oversell the parallels, but the rise of right-wing, Christian America in the 1930s has a creepy resemblance to the contemporary ascendancy of today's Christian right.[62] Writing in the *New York Times*, Michiko Kakutani contends that the novel can readily be read as a warning of either the dangers of isolationism or of the Patriot Act.[63]

Nor would it be the first time, J. M. Coetzee observes, that Roth has invited us to think about fascism being imposed top down from the White House. In Roth's *American Pastoral* (1997), the hero's father watches the Watergate hearings on television and says about the Nixon administration: "These so-called patriots . . . would take this country and make Nazi Germany out of it.[64]

There are certainly characters and passages in *The Plot Against America* that cannot help but focus our attention on contemporary politics. George Bush is reminiscent of Charles Lindbergh in his boyish manner, use of stock phrases, short, canned remarks, and seeming manipulation by evil powers behind the throne. After Ribbentrop is greeted by the president in the White House, an angry Herman Roth exclaims: "every day I ask myself the same question: how can this be happening in America? How can people like this be in charge of our country?" Later in the novel, Herman sputters: "The man is unfit. He shouldn't be there. He shouldn't be there, and it's as simple as that!" Many of us, Roth included, have been prompted to ask the same question about George W. Bush. In another angry remark that must strike readers as ironical, Herman tells Bess, but really himself: "There is still a Supreme Court in this country. Thanks to Franklin Roosevelt, it is a liberal court, and it is there to look after our rights."[65]

After many of her husband's colleagues are deported to the hinterlands, Bess, in tears, cries out to her husband, but within earshot of Phil: "Well, like it or not, Lindbergh is teaching us what it is to be Jews. . . . We only think we're Americans." Herman is unwilling to choose between being Jewish and American. Being American "is not up for negotiation." "He dares to call *us others? He's* the other. The one who looks most American—and he's the one who is least American!"[66] Herman's assertion that honest, patriotic Jews, respectful of the rights of others and worshipful of the Constitution, are the real Americans is reinforced by the plot of *The Plot Against America*. In what Aristotle would have admired as a clever *peripeteia* (reversal), the real plot against America is not being hatched by the Jews—as anti-Semites and the Lindbergh administration contend—but by the administration itself. The plot is foiled by the first lady, but revealed to America by a rabbi, of all people, who has helped to buttress Mrs. Lindbergh's courage through her difficult ordeal. In Newark, the city's Jews are protected by Mayor Murphy, who mobilizes every available policeman to protect Jewish neighborhoods. On Summit Avenue, the Roth's new downstairs neighbors—an Italian family brought in to "Americanize" the Jewish ghetto—rally to their support. Mr. Cucuzza, who fled Mussolini, gives Herman a gun and stays up all night covering the windows with his own weapon to keep any mob of anti-Semites at bay. In Danfield, the Mawhinny family goes to the aid of

Seldon Wishnow, alone in their rented house in Danville after his mother has been killed. After Herman and Sandy return from their grueling drive to Kentucky to retrieve Seldon, Mr. Cucuzza rushes Herman to Beth Israel Hospital when he collapses on the dining room table from the effects of pneumonia. Good and evil are independent of ethnicity or a family's arrival in America.

A more appropriate political analogy might be to Watergate, where most of the major perpetrators—Nixon, his advisors, and some members of his cabinet—were WASPS, many of them, although not Nixon, drawn from the establishment. The administration was brought down and the Constitution preserved by a mix of courageous WASPS (e.g., Attorney General Eliot Richardson, Special Prosecutor Archibald Cox, Senator Sam Ervin) and equally committed figures of minority backgrounds (e.g., Special Prosecutor Leon Jaworski, Judge John Sirica, Senator Barbara Jordan, Representative Elizabeth Holtzman). If there is a broader political message intended for Roth's readers it is that commitment to the ideals of the Constitution are shared by America's blacks and ethnics and decent WASPS, and that the preservation of these ideals depends on close cooperation across ethnic, racial, and economic divides.

To the extent that there is any analogy to the Bush administration, it arises more subtly from the quasi-tragic structure of the novel. Tragic plots are narratives that link ethical decisions to an unintended negative consequence by means of an agon, or contest between actors. Their denouement comes when surviving actors recognize what has happened and are overwhelmed by grief. In their efforts to protect what is important to them, they destroy it. This reversal or *peripeteia* provides the irony that Aristotle thought deepened the sense of tragedy.[67] Viewed in this light, Charles Lindbergh is the tragic hero of *The Plot Against America*. He is driven to save his child and America, but by collaborating with the Nazis puts both at greater risk. His electoral contest with Roosevelt sets in motion a chain of events that lead to his own destruction, and might have led to America's as well, if not for the deus ex machina introduced by Roth. Intended or not, the tragedy of Lindbergh brings to mind the tragedy of George Bush. Like his counterfactual predecessor, his administration embarked on a crusade to keep America safe, but his war on terror and invasions of Afghanistan and Iraq made the country more insecure, and did so at enormous physical and human cost.

These and other possible evocations of the present turn the novel into something of a Rorschach Test. They highlight the potential of any work of fiction—or of nonfiction—to take on meanings that go beyond the intentions of its author. Roth is fully cognizant of this phenomenon and in some ways encourages it. In the same *New York Times* article in which he discusses *The Plot Against America* he observes that Franz Kafka did not intend his novels to be political allegories, but that they were read this way by eastern Europeans under communism.[68] Works take on lives of their own because of the different concerns, beliefs, and experiences readers bring to them. The gap between authors and readers in this regard is likely to increase over time. Later readers, as eastern Europeans did during the Cold War, bring to a text knowledge of subsequent events that may suggest meanings that were not available to the author. A counterfactual novel works differently in that it is the author who uses his knowledge of the present to bring new meaning to the past. This intervention is intended to bring new sensitivities and insights to the present. Readers play the same game, of course, and can come away with quite a different set of meanings for the present. With the passage of time, we can reflect back on author and readers alike, putting their intentions, understandings, conflicts, and dialogues into still different and enlightening perspectives.

COUNTERFACTUALS

Reviewers responded more favorably to *The Plot Against America* than they did to *It Can't Happen Here*. A few critics, however, found it overly sentimental and derided "its air of popeyed tabloid melodrama." An English reviewer, incapable of hiding his antagonism to Israel, dismissed it as an unconvincing restatement of the case for Zionism.[69] Most critics consider it among Roth's best novels.[70] Even those who find his counterfactual far-fetched are impressed by the character, plot development, the tightness of the structure, and the verisimilitude of the dialogue. One critic writes: "The family is intimately portrayed, and every character who enters the story gets a good portrait. There are no throwaway parts in *The Plot Against America*. Everything is seamlessly, gracefully told in a series of reminiscences. All the meals, the trips, the movies, the bus rides have shades of meaning and inform the movement of the book. There is where Roth's talent shines."[71]

Roth's reliance on counterfactuals is extensively discussed by critics. None of them object to their use to set up a novel. A minority find Lindbergh's election a plausible conceit. Timothy Parrish, a prominent Philip Roth scholar, contends that widespread concern about a Roosevelt third term, the continuing depression, and the prospect of a populist hero as president make a Lindbergh victory in 1940 seem "not so far-fetched."[72] Other reviewers are less persuaded. Writing in the *Atlantic Monthly*, Clive James describes Roth's intervention in American history as "a rearrangement of the furniture" that could have been done much more adroitly.[73] Ross Douthat finds the political plot unconvincing and consistently at odds with the drama of persecution. There is no catastrophe or other development to explain what would have to be the key to a Republican victory: the unraveling of the New Deal coalition. Douthat reasons that Roth "has set himself a nearly impossible task—the creation of an American Diary of Anne Frank.[74] The most troublesome part of the plot for many critics is its sudden, happy denouement. One critic calls it "a curious fizzling of a bold enterprise."[75] Another finds the finale so unrealistic that it only confirms "that it can't happen here," and raises the question of whether the novel should be regarded as an exercise in political paranoia.[76]

Counterfactuals are not new to Roth. He experimented with them in earlier works, but always at the purely individual level, leaving the general fabric of history untouched. In "I always Wanted You to Admire my Fasting; or Looking at Kafka" (1973), Franz Kafka emigrates to America and becomes the author's Hebrew school teacher in Newark. In *The Ghost Writer* (1979), Anne Frank, who would have just turned fifty, has survived Bergen-Belsen and lives in America where she is a writer, or so Nathan Zuckerman, Roth's alter ego, fantasizes. *The Plot Against America* is a far more ambitious counterfactual enterprise because the entire novel hangs on a Lindbergh presidency that transforms America's politics and ethnic relations. The country that emerges is less like Nazi Germany—the model for *It Can't Happen Here*—and closer to Vichy France, an authoritarian regime under the thumb of Hitler whose leaders willingly support his foreign policy goals and war against the Jews. Vichy drew support from the old aristocracy, army, church, and middle classes in more traditional towns, none of whom were reconciled to the French Revolution and the values it propagated. The Third Republic (1871–1940) had held these forces in check, although the Dreyfus affair at the end of the nineteenth century gave some indication of their enduring influence. In the 1930s, the cry of the French right became "Better Hitler than Blum." Leon Blum was Jewish, twice prime minister in the 1930s and leader of the popular front that united the parties of the Left against Hitler. For the French Right, antisocialism and anti-Semitism trumped any commitment they might have felt toward the nation.[77]

The United States never had an aristocracy, army, or formally established church around which an antimodern movement could form. Nor are the Italian and German models any more relevant. Mussolini and Hitler rose to power on the backs of powerful paramilitary movements that were held together by their leaders' charisma and ruthlessness. They appealed to voters who were disenchanted with the seeming paralysis of democratic government and deeply aggrieved by military defeat and its consequences in the case of Germany, or failure to profit from victory in the case of Italy. The economic situation was worse in both countries, and with the possible exception of President Hindenburg in Germany, who helped to bring Hitler to power, there was no democratic leader with the mass appeal of Franklin Roosevelt.[78]

Much of American history needs to be changed to make any fascist regime plausible. To his credit, Roth wants to introduce as few changes as possible, relying on what Max Weber called "minimal rewrites" of history.[79] Roth told an interviewer: "Once I was going to give American history a little turn and have Lindbergh run and win in 1940, then I decided everything else should be as it was, [with] only one change. It's a false memoir that takes the form of a real memoir."[80] He contrasts himself with George Orwell, who conjured up a vastly different future world in *1984*. "I tried to imagine a small change in the past with horrendous consequences for a relative few. Orwell imagined a dystopia, I imaged a uchronia." "My talent," he insists, "isn't for imagining events on the grand scale.

> I imagined something small, really, small enough to be credible. I hoped that could easily have happened in an American presidential election in 1940, when the country was angrily divided between the Republican isolationists, who, not without reason, wanted no part of a second European war—and who probably represented a slight majority of the populace—and the Democratic interventionists, who didn't necessarily want to go to war either but who believed that Hitler had to be stopped before he invaded and conquered England and Europe was entirely fascist and totally his.[81]

Roth reasons, correctly in my view, that Wilkie could not have defeated Roosevelt in 1940 because he was also an interventionist. "But if Lindbergh had run?" he asks. "With that boyish manly aura of his? With all that glamor and celebrity, with his being virtually the first great American hero to delight America's emerging entertainment society? And with his unshakeable isolationist convictions that committed him to keeping our country out of this horrible war? I don't think it's far-fetched to imagine the election outcome as I do in the book, to imagine Lindbergh's depriving Roosevelt of a third term."[82]

Roth can be faulted for focusing solely on Lindbergh's appeal to voters. It is nevertheless hard to unseat an incumbent, especially a much loved one who won the previous election in a landslide. For Lindbergh to have a serious shot at the White House, let alone win 57 percent of the popular vote and carry forty-six states, as he does in the novel, Roosevelt must not only lose support, but his New Deal coalition of labor unions, ethnics, African Americans, intellectuals, and Southern Democrats must fall apart. That coalition began to crack in the late 1960s when presidential advocacy for civil rights alienated southern Democrats and many members of the working class. It broke apart when Republicans were successful in making social issues and security prominent, which further eroded support for the Democrats among the working and middle classes. In the 1930s, economics was far and away the dominant issue and the glue that bonded the different groups that constituted the New Deal coalition. In the absence of other interventions in the history of the period that would seriously discredit the administration and its economic policies, it is difficult to imagine a Roosevelt defeat. To be sure, there were voters who were shocked by his court-packing scheme, those who opposed a third term on principle, and still others, represented by America First, who feared entry into the European war. Roosevelt was a clever enough politician to defuse some of this opposition, and proceeded very cautiously on the war issue. The destroyer deal that he concluded with Churchill in the summer of 1940 is a case in point. He described it to the American people as the sale of fifty "over-age" destroyers in return for valuable bases in the Caribbean. Only after his reelection as a quasi–peace candidate did Roosevelt submit the Lend Lease bill to Congress and use his executive authority to order the navy to provide convoy escort so that by mid-1941 the United States and Germany were fighting an undeclared naval war in the North Atlantic.

Roth uses two key enabling counterfactuals to get Lindbergh nominated. The first, the real whopper, is his decision to run for office, given that he lived the private life of an exile in the 1930s. We learn at the end of the novel that this dramatic change of life plan was the result of Nazi blackmail. The more credible counterfactual is a deadlocked Republican convention that embraces the enormously popular Lindbergh as its standard bearer. The Nazi scheme to kidnap the Lindbergh child in 1932 and then turn the aviator and his wife into their agents is admittedly far-fetched. Hitler only came to power in January 1933 and, before that, had no spy ring in America or access to the German planes and submarines (there were none of the latter at the time) that Roth's plot requires. Nor is it reasonable to suppose that Himmler or anyone else in the Nazi hierarchy had much interest in American politics in 1933, let alone the prescience to identify Lindbergh as a likely "Manchurian candidate."

To be persuasive, Roth would require clever, enabling counterfactuals to weaken Roosevelt and his electoral coalition. As the economy did not substantially improve until the country became the arsenal of democracy, and Roosevelt still prevailed handily in 1940, some kind of really dramatic downturn seems necessary to loosen his grip on the electorate. A couple of scandals would come in handy, and evidence credibly linking him—at least in the eyes of enough voters—to some secret and underhanded deal with Churchill promising to come to Britain's aid after the election.

This discussion makes clear that minimal rewrites of history often require other prior rewrites of history to make them possible. The more such interventions and more elaborate changes they require, the more we move away from "minimal" rewrites of history to "miracle" counter-factuals. Lindbergh's election does not ineluctably lead to fascism, so the need for counterfactuals continues. He must remain in the thrall of the Nazis, sell out his country to protect a son he has not seen since he was an infant (and may not even be alive), and be removed from the scene when he begins to resist Himmler's more extreme demands regarding the Jews. Acting President Wheeler must jettison the Constitution and Bill of Rights and appear to get away with it. In Roth's account, there are no riots on the streets when martial law is declared and leading politi-cal figures arrested. The army, the Federal Bureau of Investigation, and governors—who control the national guard—inexplicably obey the act-ing president as do the New York City police, under control of Mayor LaGuardia of New York, whom they arrest along with former President Roosevelt. While not quite on the order of giving Napoleon stealth bomb-ers at Waterloo, bringing dictatorship and the Final Solution to America comes close to being a miracle, not a minimal rewrite counterfactual.

Even more problematic is the rabbit that Roth pulls out of his hat to terminate his conceit. The first lady, having escaped from Walter Reed, calls upon the Congress to remove him from office and asks the army, national guard, and police to release their prisoners and terminate their role as occupation forces. They comply as readily as they did to the or-ders instructing them to violate the Constitution although in this case their orders come "solely on her authority as 'spouse of the thirty-third president of the United States.'"[83] Two weeks later FDR is back in the White House and a week later the Japanese attack. None of this is plau-sible. Surely, there would have been Democratic governors, and some Re-publicans as well, who would have resisted illegal orders from an acting president. The New York City police are more likely to have protected La Guardia and Roosevelt than to have taken them into custody. And if the army, national guard, and FBI followed the orders of the acting president, why would they suddenly reverse themselves in response to a plea from a woman with absolutely no constitutional standing? The Japanese attack on Pearl Harbor is equally unrealistic. Tokyo had no incentive to attack before Roosevelt's reelection, as they profited in every way from benign American neutrality and would have needed more than a week after his reelection to gather, provision, and dispatch a carrier task force halfway across the Pacific.

The antecedent (Lindbergh wins the presidency) and the consequent (fascism comes to America) are both questionable, as is the chain of logic that connects them. Roth nevertheless makes a serious attempt to estab-lish the antecedent and even includes a twenty-six-page postscript replete with bibliography to provide historical background for readers and to

document the anti-Semitism and opportunism of some of the key actors in his drama. By contrast, the return to democracy and history as
we know it is abrupt and very sketchy in its outlines. We are given no
reasons why such a complacent and antiwar American public did such
an abrupt about-face and voted for Roosevelt or how a special election
for the presidency was held without a constitutional amendment. Roth
does not consider what else might have changed by virtue of his initial
counterfactuals that could have interfered with, or at least complicated,
his attempt to bring quick closure to his alternative history. Nor does
he consider "second-order" counterfactuals that might have confounded
the return of history to its known course. Franklin Roosevelt still dies of
a stroke at Warm Springs on 12 April 1945. It seems possible, perhaps
likely, that without a third term and the stress it generated, and with two
years of previous rest at his Hyde Park estate, that his health would have
deteriorated more slowly. More importantly, as I argue below, World
War II would have become a more difficult and uncertain struggle for the
United States.

Roth's counterfactuals suggest three possible scenarios for the course
of history once Roosevelt returns to the White House. The first and
probably most realistic is that the changes Roth has introduced continue
to amplify in their effects, taking America and the world of the 1940s
farther away from history as we know it. Lindbergh's accommodation
with Germany, Italy, and Japan would have made it extremely difficult
for Britain and the Soviet Union to survive the German onslaught. Deprived not only of Lend Lease aid, but of all American products, and certainly without the benefit of American naval and air cover for convoys,
it is doubtful that Britain could have kept the North Atlantic sea lanes
open. The Churchill government would have found it difficult, if not impossible, to feed its people and keep the RAF in the air. Without America
and the enormous resources behind it, Britain could not have spared
the men, armor, and fuel to stop Rommel in North Africa, and Egypt
and the Suez Canal would likely have fallen to the Germans. If Britain
had been knocked out of the war, Hitler could have directed all of his
military resources against the Soviet Union, and lacking the trucks, lo-
comotives, and other supplies delivered under Lend Lease, the Red army
would have found it much harder going. It is possible, even probable,
that Lindbergh, unlike Roosevelt, would have ignored the letter written to him by Albert Einstein and Leo Szilard—two Jewish refugees—
warning of a possible German program to develop an atomic weapon.
Einstein and Szilard, not types to tolerate fascism or anti-Semitism,
might have emigrated to Canada and addressed their letter to Churchill.
Britain and Canada, even if still independent, lacked the resources to
sponsor a crash program along the lines of the Manhattan Project. At

the same time, Roth tells us, Hitler began a serious program to develop atomic weapons—another counterfactual—which, if successful, might have made Germany unbeatable.

The Pacific War would also have been different. By December 1942, when the Japanese attack Pearl Harbor in the novel, they would have been in control of all Southeast Asia and the Asian rimland as far as the Indian border. Japanese forces would have been in a much stronger position to follow up an air attack on Pearl Harbor with an invasion of Hawaii. If successful, and this seems likely given the incompetence of American military leadership in the Pacific before Pearl Harbor, Japan would have become significantly more difficult to defeat.

With no Roosevelt and no democracy in America, and possibly no Jews, Phil might not have survived. If he had, he might have been in a concentration camp and he would hardly have been in a position to write, let alone publish *The Plot Against America* or any of his other novels. At best, he and his readers would, at great risk, be circulating *Samizdat* furtively among themselves. Even emigration to Canada might not have helped, because with the fascists victorious everywhere, it too would have come under the heel of Berlin and Washington. Such an outcome to the novel—or any variant even approaching an Axis victory—would undermine its purposes by totally dominating it. No longer a conceit to intensify pressures on the Jews and the Roth family, the counterfactual story line would overwhelm the Jews, the Roths, and the novel. Phil's fate would be incidental to the political developments responsible for this unspeakable tragedy, and on these events our attention would be focused—whether or not the novel adequately dealt with them.

The second outcome, and the one that Roth chooses, is to dampen the effects of Lindbergh's election and accommodation with the dictators. As we have seen, Roosevelt is restored to power in a special election in 1942, the Japanese attack Pearl Harbor, and World War II resumes its actual course, only one year behind schedule. As the critics note, Roth's return to history is less credible and developed than his departure from it. Fascism has almost come to America, and his family has lived through their nightmare. At age forty-one Herman Roth has fought his Guadalcanal or Battle of the Bulge—as Philip (not Phil) describes his trip to Kentucky— and is on the brink of death from pneumonia. It is time to restore the sanity, physical and mental, of the Roths, the Jews, and America. Like the cavalry coming over the hill in a B-grade movie, the first lady blows her bugle and FDR comes riding out of retirement into the White House to rescue us all. For purposes of the novel, this may be the most satisfactory outcome even if it is the least realistic.

A third outcome, and the most plausible, is for history to work out somewhat differently, even if Roosevelt is reelected in 1942. Surgical counterfactuals are no more realistic then surgical air strikes. They often have unintended consequences—collateral historical damage, if you like—that lie outside the chain of logic that connects antecedent to consequent. I explored several possibilities that would have prolonged World War II and made an American victory less certain and far more costly had they occurred. It seems likely that victory under these circumstances would have come about differently, perhaps as a result of the atomic bombing of Germany.[84] Such an outcome encourages us to think about second-order counterfactuals—in particular, the ways in which the postwar world would have been different from the one we know. If the Soviet Union had been defeated or waging a desperate rear-guard defense when Germany surrendered, it would not have fought its way to Berlin. There would have been no Cold War and no divided Europe. Having fought a more costly war, the Truman administration (if there was one—there is no mention in the novel of FDR's running mate in 1942) and the American people might not have been in the mood or the position to sponsor the Marshall Plan and the rebuilding of western Europe and Japan. Without a Soviet threat there would have been no NATO and probably no efforts at European integration, the precursor of the European Union. The world of 2004 would have been a very different place.

Sinclair Lewis had the good sense to choose this third kind of scenario. In *It Can't Happen Here*, victory against the fascists in the civil war remains uncertain, but even if the republican side wins, it is clear that the United States will be a different country and political system than it was before Dewey Haik's dictatorship. For Lewis, this open-endedness is unproblematic because his novel is about politics and only secondarily about the Jessup family. It is appropriate, not counterproductive, for them to recede in importance and their future to be clouded with uncertainty, as it is by Doremus's refusal to accept security in Canada as a member of the government in exile.

Counterfactuals are like playing with fire. They are exciting but difficult to control once they really get going. Roth's attempt to light a bright flame and then extinguish it after it illuminates his family prove difficult to do in a convincing manner. His failure to put out the fire in a credible way encourages readers to look beyond his family to other objects and events it might illuminate. It is easy for counterfactual novels to go beyond their authors' intentions.

POETRY AND HISTORY

Aristotle reasons that poetry speaks a higher truth than history because it does not recount the jumble of what actually happened, but what should have happened according to the laws of order or necessity. The Renaissance witnessed a complex series of shifts that reversed this rank ordering, favoring history over poetry on the grounds that it described certain kinds of necessity.[85] In the nineteenth century, Hegel and Marx built on this foundation and gained wide acceptance for the superiority of history.

Twentieth-century writers have reasserted the primacy of poetry. Philip Roth is very much in this tradition. Echoing Aristotle, he contends that history describes reality. It "is everything that happens everywhere. Even here in Newark. Even here on Summit Avenue. Even what happens in his house to an ordinary man—that'll be history too someday." History nevertheless does injustice to reality because "Lindbergh's election couldn't have made it clearer to me, the unfolding of the unforeseen was everything. Turned the wrong way around, the relentless unforeseen was what we schoolchildren studied as 'History,' harmless history, where everything unexpected in its own time is chronicled on the page as inevitable. The terror of the unforeseen is what the science of history hides, and turns a disaster into an epic." As Alvin puts it: "There's pain where you are, and there is pain where you ain't."[86]

Roth refers to the history he read in school, and textbooks of this kind are notorious for their determinism and dry recitation of facts in politically acceptable narratives. Even professional history has tendency to be deterministic, and, if it does not always ignore or downplay the role of emotion, it is decidedly detached in its presentation of decisions and human actions. Fiction, by contrast, "aims to give us the truth of lived experience, the truth of emotional and psychological effect, rather than a cool appraisal of past events."[87] History tends to reduce uncertainty, while fiction, for which uncertainty is often essential, tries to expand it. Fiction reminds us, as do both novels, that history could have turned out differently. Roth understands that uncertainty is itself a source of emotion, and has the potential to intensify existing ones like hope and fear. These emotions are just as important as the behavior that gets chronicled and are often its underlying cause.

Counterfactual fiction adds another element to the mix. As we have seen, Aristotle thinks poetry a superior art form because it has the potential to expose a higher truth. Its structure does not depend on what actually happened but on a deeper understanding of human nature and social necessity. Roth uses his counterfactuals for the same purpose. By exposing his parents to situations they never had to confront, the novel brings out the true characters of Bess and Herman. The choices they make are not arbitrary but an expression of their characters. They would remain imperfectly understood in the absence of poetic license in the form of counterfactual history. Roth's counterfactuals also demonstrate how unlikely a fascist regime was in America. By doing so, they serve the Aristotelian project of helping us distinguish necessity from chance.

Both novels challenge the divide between fact and fiction. Yet novels, like history, are founded on this binary. Fiction is, by definition, nonfactual and imaginary, just as history purports to be the opposite. Fiction nevertheless depends on fact, and vice versa. Fiction must be rooted in some factual context for us to make sense of it. Its narratives must also operate in accord with consistent laws that strike readers in the real world as plausible. Even science fiction novels, often set in different worlds far off in the future and populated by diverse species, make enough connection with our world to allow us to make sense of their characters and situations. Fiction that fails to do this is difficult, if not impossible to understand, and must, like the absurdist *Finnegans Wake*, be approached through other keys like language. For the same reason, we find counterfactual fiction more convincing if it connects to "facts" we know through minimal, plausible rewrites of history and unfolds in ways that strike us as consistent with these "facts," our assumptions about the actors, and the context in which they operate.

History requires narrative. In the language of G.E.M. Ansombe, narratives transform "brute" facts into "social" facts and give meaning to both.[88] Confronted with a chaos of "facts," Hayden White contends, historians must "choose, sever and carve them up." The narratives they create usually present these "facts" in chronological sequences with a beginning, middle, and end, unencumbered by questions regarding the suitability of such a form. White shows that many historians adapt their narratives from fiction, imposing well-established plot lines like tragedy and comedy.[89] Elsewhere, I have shown how both Herodotus and Thucydides make use of tragedy, establishing a tradition that would significantly influence historical writing down to modern times.[90]

Fact and fiction are essential categories not just for writing, but for negotiating life. Efforts to keep them separate—ontologically, analytically, and normatively—are intended to justify genres of scholarship and fiction and, more importantly, to make life easier, more comprehensive and predictable. These efforts are to some degree problematic because fiction and nonfiction are co-constitutive. This does not means that we should strop trying to sustain this binary, only that we need to have a better understanding of it in theory and practice. The one can inform the other, and I will expand on this theme in the concluding chapter.

Conclusions

Writers are "valuable allies . . . [who in] their knowledge of
the mind . . . are far in advance of us everyday people, for they
draw upon sources which have not yet opened up for science."
—*Sigmund Freud*[1]

CAUSE AND CHANCE have been traditionally thought of as antonyms.
This understanding goes back to the Greeks who held that knowledge
of a cause ruled out the operation of chance, and vice versa. In early
modern Europe, Calvin and Spinoza did their best to define contingency
out of existence. In the eighteenth century, Leibniz, Montesquieu, and
Hume followed suit. Outcomes that appear to be the result of chance,
Hume wrote, may be the product of "the secret operation of contrary
causes."[1] Montesquieu makes a more extreme claim, insisting, "If the fortune of a battle, that is, a particular case, has ruined a State, a general
cause was always responsible for the fact that this State had to be ruined
by a single battle."[2] *Forbidden Fruit* starts from the opposite premise:
that contingency is the norm, not the exception; that chance, confluence,
and accident often play a determining role in the social world and that
all claims about causation accordingly require careful consideration of
counterfactuals.

In this book I use counterfactuals to advance three parallel projects:
the exploration of nonlinear causation in open-ended systems; the ways
in which expert understandings of causation are influenced by beliefs
and psychological needs; and the relationship factual and counterfactual,
and fact and fiction. Toward these ends, I have employed historical case
studies, surveys, experiments, a short story, and literary criticism. Although these three projects are distinct, they are reinforcing in a double
sense. Findings in each domain have important theoretical and substantive implications for the others. One of the more interesting—and
ironic—findings in this regard is the degree to which a commitment to
science and scientific methods by international relations scholars can
constitute a major impediment to their practice of science. International
relations scholars with the strongest commitments to science appear to
have the strongest need for psychological closure, manifested in the belief that the world is ordered and predictable. Scholars who score high
on the closure scale resist counterfactuals that demonstrate contingency,
especially if they mutate events that are constitutive or supportive of their

preferred theories. They are nevertheless more open than other international relations scholars to counterfactuals that unmake cases they otherwise regard as anomalous for these theories. Historians are involved in a different kind of contradiction. Those most scornful of counterfactuals do not hesitate to smuggle them into their works where they are foundational to their arguments or essential to the dramatic structure of their narratives. Done furtively, they are used poorly.

My findings in all three domains expose and highlight tensions in theory building in international relations. In this, the final chapter, I want to begin by addressing some of these problems. My treatment is divided into two parts: the negative implications of my findings for the epistemology on which most international relations theories are constructed, followed by an effort to develop an alternative approach that recognizes and builds on the contingency of so many important historical outcomes. This approach is intended to complement, not substitute for, existing approaches to theory. I conclude with a discussion of the relationship between fact and fiction. The latter question may appear to some readers as remote from international relations theory, but it grows out of and ties together the diverse chapters of this volume. It also has some important implications for social science.

THE LIMITS OF THEORY

Counterfactual probing of the origins of World War I and the end of the Cold War reveals how contingent these events were and in turn raises questions about the ability of our theories to explain, let alone predict, developments of this kind. Theories in international relations are systemic or structural—I use the terms interchangeably. They rely on some condition or set of conditions (e.g., balance of power, type of regime, nature and implications of military technology) or process (equilibria, or their absence) to explain and predict outcomes. They assume that selection effects are strong enough to shape behavior over time or that actors are sufficiently rational and self-interested to grasp the imperatives generated by these structures or bargaining games and respond as theorists expect they should. Theories of this kind in international relations, I argue in chapter 1, are notoriously unsuccessful in explaining much of the variance in cases where they claim to be the most applicable.

Critics attribute their failure to a variety of ontological and psychological causes. The key ontological objections are the open-ended, nonlinear, path-dependent, and reflexive nature of the social world. Systemic theories and formal models invariably ignore the cognitive limitations and emotional commitments of actors and the attention, even priority, they can give to other domestic and foreign problems they confront. Models of bargaining impose a format of move and countermove on interstate relations that often bear only a passing relationship to the understanding actors have of their interactions. They also assume that "moves" convey signals that are generally understood as intended.[3] More fundamentally, both kinds of approaches assume that there is something called strategic logic that is independent of culture. In *A Cultural Theory of International Relations* I mobilize evidence across countries and cultures to show that conceptions of reason and risk taking are culturally determined, making the character of strategic logic situationally specific.[4]

My case studies in this book raise a different objection to theory in international relations: the failure to consider enabling or immediate causes. These theories take for granted that appropriate catalysts will come along when the underlying conditions for whatever they are trying to account for are present. The origins of World War I indicate that this is an unwarranted assumption; underlying and immediate causes are not necessarily linked, and the latter may be every bit as complicated and problematic. Sarajevo met a series of conditions without which war would have been unthinkable for German and Austrian leaders. It removed the principal Austrian opponent to war; angered Emperor Franz Josef and Kaiser Wilhelm in ways that made them more receptive to strong action against Serbia; made it possible for German Chancellor Bethmann Hollweg to win over the Social Democrats by making Russia appear responsible for any war, allowing the German kaiser and chancellor—men unwilling to accept responsibility for war—to convince themselves at the outset that support for Austria would not escalate into a continental war, and that if it did, responsibility would lie elsewhere. Sarajevo was not a match that set the dry kindling of Europe alight—the metaphor routinely invoked by historians and international relations scholars. It was more like a permissive action link on a nuclear weapon, a trigger as complicated as the weapon itself that requires a specific code without which the warhead cannot be detonated.

The independence and importance of immediate causes is subject to empirical investigation and I expect the future research will find considerable variation across categories and cases. In the case of war, I am confident that the independent importance of immediate causes will be shown to vary as a function of the kind of crisis that so often precedes and often triggers military confrontations. In *Between Peace and War*, I describe four generic kinds of international crises: justification of hostility, brinkmanship, chain of events, and accidents.[5] In justification of hostility crises, war is the goal of the initiator from the outset, and the crisis is intended to mobilize support at home and abroad. Precipitants are pretexts for war, and when they do not arise, leaders invent them as

Hitler did in 1939 (a staged attack on a border post falsely blamed on Poland) and George Bush (Saddam's alleged possession of weapons of mass destruction) in 2003. The July crisis of 1914 was only a justification of hostility for Austria, and in Vienna and Budapest, there were important actors opposed to war at the outset. For Germany, Russia, and France it was a brinkmanship crisis, in which their leaders hoped to achieve their objectives by raising the risk of war without actually provoking one, and certainly not a multifront continental war. Crisis management is the critical determinant of the outcome of brinkmanship crises, and European crisis management in all capitals in 1914 was woefully inadequate for reasons that are well known. It is important to bear in mind that there would have been no crisis in the absence of the assassinations. If subsequent events had triggered a crisis, for the reasons I have made apparent, it would have been more likely to resemble earlier European crises in which all the great powers sought to make gains *and* avoid war. A continental war required at least one great power committed to starting a local war and another committed to coming to the aid of that state it attacked by another great power. If Archduke Franz Ferdinand had survived, neither he nor the emperor would have allowed Austria to start a war in the Balkans.

If catalysts fail to materialize, war is unlikely to occur in any kind of crisis other than a justification of hostility. By not taking the independent and problematic causation of immediate causes into account, existing theories are incomplete and data sets used to test them of questionable utility. Even if all the underlying causes for war are present, no war will occur in the absence of an appropriate precipitant, and the case will is likely to taken as disconfirming. The problem of causation and theory testing is further complicated by incontrovertible evidence that events that are described as mere catalysts—like the assassinations at Sarajevo— may be important causes in their own right, with origins independent of any underlying causes.[6]

Underlying causes are equally problematic for existing theories. My case studies demonstrate that the origins of the First World War and the end of the Cold War were the result of nonlinear confluences. In 1914 the intersection of several independent chains of causation brought about dramatic shifts in risk taking that would not otherwise have occurred. There is no reason to think that World War I is atypical in this regard. A strong case can be made that what are commonly considered the three transformations of the international system in the twentieth century— those arising from World War I, World War II, and the end of the Cold War—were all the result of nonlinear confluences. If so, theories that attempt to account for hegemonic wars and other transformative events in terms of single factors (e.g., power transition, offensive-defensive balance), or even combinations of them, must be considered inadequate. To the extent that many major international developments are nonlinear in nature—another question open to empirical investigation—we must search for *multiple* causes *and* the synergistic ways in which they interact.

Events like World War I and the end of the Cold War are particularly interesting to theorists because of their consequences for the future of international relations. Theories that seek to explain them, or the transformations they bring about, assume that the latter follow ineluctably from the former. There is nevertheless every reason to think that the consequences of events of this kind are as contingent as the events themselves. Because the Austro-Russian conflict over Serbia escalated into a continental and then a world war, it is commonly assumed that any European war of this period would also have done so. A different kind of provocation, or a similar one at another time, could have led to a different kind of war, even one that remained localized in the east. If we mutate leaders or military strategies, all kinds of variation becomes possible and leads to very different postwar worlds. World War I—the war that was actually fought—could have ended by means of a diplomatic settlement or even a victory by the Central Powers as Germany came close to winning on more than one occasion.[7] World War II—or at least its opening round—could have been ended by a diplomatic settlement in 1940 or 1941 if Britain had responded favorably, as many conservatives wished, to Hitler's peace overtures following the fall of France, or if Hitler had taken up Stalin's peace feelers after the Red Army's initial and catastrophic defeats.[8] George Breslauer and I demonstrate that the Cold War could have ended in different ways at different times. When and how the Cold War was resolved was all-important for the character of post–Cold War international relations. Even theories that might alert us to the possibility of a European war or an end of the Cold War—valuable as they would be—could tell us only part of what we want to know. To make more meaningful statements about transformations—to link events to outcomes—we must take nonsystematic factors into account. We must devise theories about precipitants, not only about underlying causes.

The origins of World War I and the end of the Cold War were both sensitive to timing. For reasons that I made clear in chapter 3, World War I, or something like it, would have become much harder to start after 1917. By then Archduke Franz Ferdinand would have been emperor and unlikely to travel to Sarajevo or any destination where his security would be at risk. Austria-Hungary would almost certainly have been in the throes of a serious constitutional crisis, touched off by the new emperor's extension of the universal franchise to those parts of the empire controlled by the Hungarian minority. Germany would have been compelled to adopt a defensive military strategy, as even Moltke was on record that an offensive against France would not work by 1917. A defensive strategy, perhaps devised by his successor, or one based on an initial defense followed by counteroffensives on either or both fronts, would have undercut Moltke's argument that strategic pressure compelled Germany to go to war. According to some authorities Russia might have faced a revolution, or at least a serious domestic crisis, even in the absence of the setbacks and suffering of World War I. If a great-power war did start in 1917 or sometime afterward, it might have had different antagonists and a different outcome.

The end of the Cold War and the way it was resolved were equally dependent on timing. If Andropov or Chernenko had lived a few years longer, Gorbachev might have had George Bush instead of Ronald Reagan as his initial American interlocutor. We know that when Bush assumed the presidency in 1988, he was still not convinced that Gorbachev was sincere and was inclined to slow down, if not halt altogether, Soviet-American rapprochement. Bush's view was shared by a significant fraction of the official national security community. In the absence of Reagan, who was more committed to responding positively to Gorbachev's overtures than any of his advisors, it could have proven difficult to wind down the Cold War while Gorbachev was still in power. If Saddam had still invaded Kuwait in August 1990—or anytime in the 1990s—the Soviet Union would almost certainly not have been as supportive of the United States as it was under Gorbachev. The American response might also have been different, and if not, war in the Persian Gulf might have intensified the Cold War. If the Cold War had dragged on into the twenty-first century, even in muted form, there is no reason to think that the attacks of 11 September against the World Trade Center and the Pentagon would not have occurred, as the United States would still have had a close relationship with Saudi Arabia. How the American response would have played out against the background of an ongoing Cold War is difficult to predict. The international environment in which an American president acted and sought to cobble together a coalition of allies and local powers—critical for any invasion of Kuwait and Iraq—would have been very different than it was in 1991. In the absence of the Gulf War, subsequent relations between the United States and Iraq would also have developed differently.

Timing effects are by no means limited to these cases. Consider the fate of divided nations (the two Germanies, Koreas, Chinas, and Vietnams) and partitioned countries (Ireland, Cyprus, Palestine-Israel, India-Pakistan), two great sources of conflict in the second half of the twentieth century. India and South Korea consistently sought to isolate and undermine Pakistan and North Korea respectively. Their goals changed in the aftermath of the unification of Germany. Observing how much money it cost the Federal Republic to begin to integrate the people and territory of the former German Democratic Republic, Indian and South Korean politicians and business leaders grew fearful of the consequences of the possible collapse of their long-standing rivals. They envisaged themselves swamped with refugees and burdened with costs of occupation and reconstruction.[9] Their policies have undergone an observable shift in favor of doing what they can to keep their rivals in business. If North Korea had collapsed first with absolutely chaotic consequences for the South, it is entirely conceivable the German government would have responded differently to the prospect of unification.

Counterfactual thought experiments prompt a radical but inescapable conclusion. Variation across time, due to changing conditions and human reflection, the openness of social systems, and the complexity of the interaction among stipulated causes make the likelihood of predictive theory—even of a probabilistic kind—extraordinarily low.[10] Multivariate theories run into the problem of negative degrees of freedom, and in international relations it is rare to have data sets in the high double digits. Where larger data sets can be constructed, they invariably group together cases that differ from one another in theoretically important ways. Complexity in the form of multiple causation and equifinality makes simple statistical comparisons misleading. But it is hard to elaborate more sophisticated statistical tests until one has a deeper understanding of the nature of the phenomenon in question, as well as the categories and variables that make up candidate causes.[11] In the case of wars and many other events of interest to international relations scholars, this is probably impossible given the relatively small number of comparable and independent events in any of these categories. As Milja Kurki argues, international relations theorists must free themselves of the limitations of Humean causation.[12]

In a practical sense, all social systems (and many physical and biological systems) are open. Empirical invariance does not exist in such systems and seeming probabilistic invariance may be causally unrelated.[13] Evolution is the quintessential open system. It is the result of biological change and natural selection. The former is a function of random genetic mutation and mating. The latter depends on the nature and variety of ecological niches and the competition for them. These niches are in turn shaped by such factors as continental drift, the varying output of the sun, changes in the earth's orbit, and local conditions that are difficult to specify. Biologists recognize that all the primary causes of evolution are random, or if not, interact in complex nonlinear ways that make prediction impossible. Certain kinds of outcomes can be ruled out in a probabilistic sense but almost never absolutely. Biologists have attempted to document the course of evolution and explain the ways in which natural selection works. Historical and theoretical work has resulted in a robust theory of evolution that permits scientific reconstruction of the past in the context of a logic that explains why things turned out the way they did. As the social world is open ended and nonlinear, efforts to build parsimonious, predictive theories of international relations are misguided for all the same reasons. We would be better off to accept these limitations, focus more on explanation than prediction, and recognize that any theory in the social world is nothing more than a starting point for working through a policy problem or making a provisional forecast.

THEORY BUILDING

We are predisposed to think of big events as having big causes, a bias routinely reflected in historical narratives and social science theories.[14] Ever since Thucydides, historians and international relations scholars have almost invariably privileged underlying over immediate causes. In the case of World War I, as we have seen, the conventional wisdom holds that if the assassinations Sarajevo had not taken place, some other event would have triggered a European war. The end of the Cold War is also attributed to deep structural causes, most notably the failure of communism as a social-economic system and, with it, the loss of communism's appeal and the relative decline of the Soviet Union vis-à-vis the West.

Counterfactual priming and case studies have the potential to make us aware of the extent to which our theories build on and reinforce our proclivity to see history as a linear progression from which deviation was improbable. They can alert us to the shortcomings of linear models, so central to existing approaches to the study of international relations and, more fundamentally, to Humean causation and its search for regularities across cases. By loosening the hold of this approach to causation, counterfactuals can make us more receptive to complex, nonlinear models that recognize that international relations is an open system whose outcomes are sensitive to—if not always the result of—chance, agency, and confluence.

Theory building in international relations might start from the premise that wars and other events (e.g., economic crises) that have the potential to transform the international system or behavior of actors are likely to be the result of multiple reinforcing causes. Such events can require catalysts with independent causes. The underlying and immediate causes of such events accordingly need to be addressed separately and in sequence. The problem of causation can be set up as a decision tree that encourages us to explore different branches, or lines of inquiry, depending on our answers to successive sets of questions. I used this method to work my way through the causes and contingency of World War I. I describe it below and show how it can be deployed to understand other wars. In principle, it is applicable to any complex international event or development.

With respect to war, we begin by asking about its immediate causes: the incident, provocation, or crisis from which it arose. Was this situation novel or repetitive in the sense that it had occurred on more than one occasion in the past without leading to war? If novel, what might have brought it about? Was the incident, provocation, or crisis the result of a causal chain that can be traced back to underlying causes and enabling conditions? If the behavior was repetitive, or the situation in which it arose recurrent, it may be possible to conduct intracase comparisons. We could then ask how many times the behavior or situation in question occurred and why it failed to produce war in these instances. Can these failures be attributed to the absence of an appropriate catalyst, or did war require the presence of other behaviors or conditions that might have been the product of other causal chains? If multiple causal chains are involved, to what degree were they independent of one another? The greater their independence, the more the war must be understood as the result of a confluence.

Even satisfactory answers to these questions will provide only a partial account of the underlying causes of war. We must go on to consider background conditions that were essential for these causes to have their effects. These conditions are sometimes difficult to identify because they do not necessarily show variation in the short term. In the 1914 case, one of the critical background conditions was the belief among German policymakers that sooner or later war was inevitable. It made the kaiser, chancellor, and chief of staff more willing to exploit the opportunity that arose as a result of the twin assassinations. In other war-threatening crises (e.g., Fashoda, 1898; Berlin, 1958–59 and 1961; and Cuba, 1962), policymakers believed and hoped that resolution of the crisis might enhance the prospects of a longer-term peace.[15] Another important background condition in 1914 was the nearly universal commitment to offensive strategies by European general staffs. I attributed this orientation to the hold of traditional aristocratic and warrior values, commitments more intense in Germany by virtue of the difficulties the Junker class had in response to the political, economic, and social challenges of modernity.[16] These examples indicate the extent to which critical background conditions in turn have deeper causes that must be traced and considered more fundamental underlying causes of war.

Immediate causes of war are catalysts that trigger hostilities. Sometimes they are unproblematic in the sense that they are almost certain to arise when the underlying conditions for war are present. It is useful for purposes of analysis to recognize four classes of catalysts or immediate causes (see table 9.1). Type I catalysts are common occurrences linked to the underlying causes of the event we are trying to explain. "Fender benders" are minor road accidents; they are more likely in cities where there is lots of vehicular traffic. In this instance the increase in traffic—the underlying cause—brings with it an increase in accidents. Border incidents might also fit in this category. They are generally outgrowths of deeper conflicts between countries and historically have served to trigger wars. They have sometimes been arranged with this end in mind.

Type II catalysts are events with independent causes but occur frequently and can serve as catalysts when the appropriate conditions are present. Rainfall is independent of traffic but a regular event in temperate climates. It will almost certainly bring about an increase in fender benders on heavily trafficked and slick streets, and more so still in aggressive driving cultures or in countries like India where one does not need a license to purchase or drive a car.

Type III catalysts consist of events that are not only independent of underlying causes but infrequent. Staying with our illustration of road accidents, this might include fatalities caused by a bridge collapse, as happened in August 2007 on Interstate 35 where it crosses the Mississippi River in Minneapolis. The collapse occurred during the rush hour and at dusk, a time of poor visibility, which increased the number of fatalities, but the timing was unconnected to the causes of the collapse. Bridge failures are relatively infrequent and their distribution is entirely independent of the underlying causes of the events in which we are primarily interested.[17]

Type IV catalysts are also independent of underlying causes. Like viruses that require a specific surface architecture to penetrate a target cell, they must meet a set of additional requirements to serve as catalysts. Sarajevo is the quintessential example. The assassinations were the outgrowth of an internal struggle for power in Serbia, and their timing was entirely independent of the confluences that made leaders in Vienna, Berlin, and Petersburg more risk prone. I noted earlier that Sarajevo created or helped to bring about four critical changes without which Austria would not have declared war on Serbia. This is one of the reasons World War I was so contingent.

The likelihood of a catalyst appearing when underlying causes and enabling conditions of context are present varies as a function of type. Type I catalysts are the most common and can more or less be assumed to occur in these conditions. Type II–IV catalysts are increasingly problematic, type III and IV especially so. We must treat them as causes with probabilities different from and independent of underlying causes. To the extent that they can readily be untracked by minimal rewrites we must consider the wars that they triggered highly contingent.

My approach for probing the causes of events like wars is more or less the reverse of how scholars usually attempt to analyze such events. It is far more common to start with a theory or propositions about causes

Table 9.1
Immediate causes

Type of Catalyst	Characteristics
1	Linked to underlying causes
2	Independent but frequent
3	Independent and infrequent
4	Independent and rare

and to test or evaluate them against an appropriate data set or in selected case studies. Instead of working deductively from theory to data, I have worked inductively from data to theory—with the understanding, of course, that what we select as relevant data is inevitably conditioned by the theoretical assumptions we bring to the problem. The advantage of this strategy, I believe, is that it is capable of capturing the richness of the causal nexus responsible for transformative events like some wars. In contrast to approaches that test for the presence or absence of a single cause, or even multiple causes, and ignore other possible causes and enabling conditions, my approach foregrounds them, making it possible to account for the effects of open-ended systems and nonlinear effects. It also stands in sharp contrast to historical narratives that may propose multiple causes for war and even describe key enabling conditions, but do so in an atheoretical way that makes it difficult to see the connections among the many hypothesized causes and between these causes and relevant enabling conditions.

In social science, rigor always needs to be balanced against richness. This is not infrequently done by excluding so-called contextual features from consideration and treating cases as fully comparable when they are not. This is bad science, and uses the claim of rigor as a rhetorical fig leaf. My strategy leads us to consider multiple causes and the importance of context. Admittedly, it can lead to a proliferation of causes that makes theorizing difficult in the absence of any way of ranking their importance and of distinguishing those that were critical from those that were not. In an ideal world, we would do this by constructing a data set of independent but comparable cases that was large enough and contained sufficient variation on its independent and dependent variables to allow us to run appropriate statistical tests. For reasons that have been made clear, this is simply not feasible with respect to wars and many other kinds of major international events. And if it were, it would still be stymied by cases where proximate causes were necessary and independent of underlying ones.

An admittedly less rigorous, but generally more feasible strategy, is counterfactual probing. We remove one by one hypothesized causes of war and enabling conditions and ask ourselves if the outcome would have been any different. Would policymakers have behaved in similar ways in the absence of one or more of these causes and conditions? Answers to these questions invariably involve a degree of speculation, but there is often considerable evidence available that allows us to make informed and empirically defensible inferences. Suppose, for example, the German military had not been committed to an offensive strategy but had had plans for conducting a defensive strategy on both fronts intended to draw advancing French and Russian armies into traps where they could be repulsed, perhaps even destroyed, with relatively moderate German losses in carefully prepared counteroffensives. Would the kaiser and chancellor have given a "blank check" to Austria in these circumstances? Would they have felt the need to stiffen the spine of their Austrian ally? If it can be demonstrated from the documents—as I think it can—that the kaiser framed the question as one of honor, not of security, and felt compelled to act, as he put it, as Franz Joseph's "second" in his duel with Serbia, then he would probably still have acted aggressively even though security concerns were not determinant. This was not true for his chancellor, who had been convinced by Chief of Staff Moltke that war had to be fought before 1917 when the offensive Schlieffen Plan—really the Moltke plan—would no longer have any chance of success.[18] With a good defensive strategy, the chancellor would have been relatively immune to Moltke's blandishments. However, the kaiser might well have ignored his chancellor's pleas for caution in this circumstance, as he did in January 1917 when he supported his admirals' demand for unrestricted submarine warfare.[19] This counterfactual thought experiment suggests that an offensive military plan, while contributing to war, was not a decisive cause, as the Germans might have issued the blank check to Austria in its absence. They would have been less likely to have mobilized when they did, as they would not have been under the same strategic pressure. However, German support for Austria would still not have prevented Russian mobilization, which, in retrospect, would have remained the point of no return.

Surgical counterfactuals are a misnomer, so we must also consider what else would have been different—or the same—when we remove a cause or enabling condition. As I noted above, a German defensive strategy would have obviated the need for rapid mobilization and an unacceptable ultimatum to France demanding that key border fortresses be handed over to Germany. War on two fronts was inevitable once Germany and Russia went to war. However, a German defensive strategy would have preserved Belgian neutrality and in all likelihood kept Britain neutral. Germany would have been much more likely to have emerged victorious in these circumstances. But how plausible was a defensive strategy? It is difficult to imagine Germany adopting such a military plan as long as Moltke was chief of staff. If the kaiser had not appointed him—and military authorities thought Moltke an unusual choice at the time—other generals would have favored an offensive strategy, although they may have been less outspoken in demanding war in every crisis from 1905 to 1914. Even this brief excursus indicates that offensive military doctrines, while not a decisive cause of war, were still important and would have been difficult to remove before 1916–17 with only minimal rewrites of history.

Similar thought experiments with other causes and enabling conditions can within reason allow us to make some judgments about the extent to which they were necessary for war, how contingent they were and how linked they were to other causes and conditions. If we remove a cause or condition, and other causes and conditions drop out as well by virtue of the counterfactuals we must introduce to do this, they can said to be coupled. By this means we can build up a causal map of the event in question that can help eliminate some causes as unnecessary or redundant and identify those that appear to be the most important and perhaps some that can be traced to similar origins. An example of the latter was the intense desire of so many Austrian military and political officials for war with Serbia even though they recognized that it put Austria's security at risk because it almost certainly entailed war with Russia in circumstances where little military help could be expected from Germany. For these officials and the emperor, Austria's honor demanded a military response almost regardless of the consequences. Austrian motives for war, and those of the German kaiser and his chief of staff, can be traced back to the same source: an aristocratic honor code. It was kept alive by leading officials in both countries and adhered to with a vengeance because of the perceived threat of modernity and, with it, the spread of bourgeois values throughout society.[20]

A causal map has the additional benefit of helping us identify multiple chains of causation, make judgments about their independence from one another and the extent to which war was the result of a confluence. Chains of causation also lend themselves to counterfactual analysis. In *Ending the Cold War*, contributors were asked to study events we all agreed constituted important links in the causal chain that resolved the Cold War. They were Gorbachev's election as general secretary, his withdrawal of Soviet forces from Afghanistan, arms-control agreements with the West, the political independence of eastern Europe, and the unification of Germany. To explain the end of the Cold War we need to know how many of these turning points were necessary, how independent they were of one another and how many other pathways could have led to the same outcome.

There was a consensus among our authors that *all* five turning points were necessary to end the Cold War but that they could have come about in a different order. Most of our contributors agreed that the Soviet retreat from Afghanistan, arms control and troop withdrawals, and encouragement of political reform in eastern Europe were all linked and manifestations of "new thinking." But a change in policy toward Afghanistan would have been possible without any of the other initiatives; it could have been initiated by a conservative leadership anxious to cut losses and shore up support at home. We can also imagine major changes in eastern Europe leading to the collapse of communism and the unification of Germany prior to withdrawal from Afghanistan or any arms-control agreements. Breslauer and I describe this scenario as one of many that might have followed a Reagan assassination and the presidency of a far more cautious and suspicious George Bush. In our judgment, the end of the Cold War required a resolution of Afghanistan, some kind of arms-control agreements in Europe, and a decline in competition in the Third World—all major sources of East-West tensions. Presumably, an end to Europe's division could have come before Afghanistan and other Third World flash points were addressed and would have created strong pressures to deal with these problems.[21]

What about a different set of turning points leading to more or less the same outcome? Or, could the same turning points have led to a different outcome? It is relatively easy to conceive of different routes to political change in eastern Europe and the unification of Germany within NATO. Gorbachev or some other Soviet leader could have offered to let their eastern European allies reform politically without Soviet interference in return for promises that they would remain members of the Warsaw Pact and continue to allow Soviet forces to be stationed on their territories. The United States might even have become a co-guarantor of such an agreement if an American president thought it necessary to bring about liberalization in eastern Europe. In December 1988 Henry Kissinger pleaded with the incoming Bush administration to propose such a deal to Moscow.[22] It seems unlikely that such an arrangement could have endured in the long term—although Gorbachev might readily have convinced himself that it could have. When it began to unravel, the Soviet Union might have faced a situation roughly comparable to the one it did in 1990–91. In retrospect, historians and political scientists would undoubtedly have argued that the de-Sovietization of eastern Europe and the unification of Germany within NATO would have been unlikely without this intermediary agreement.

It is possible to construct an alternative context in which many of the turning points we identified would have taken place but not moved the Cold War toward resolution. Breslauer and I suggest that the most likely alternative to Gorbachev was a more conservative and cautious leader who would have pursued "a kinder, gentler form of Brezhnevism."

A leader such as Yigor Ligachev could have sought arms-control agreements with the West and a broader disengagement from the Third World as a means of reducing tension, saving money, and building domestic support. Accommodation with the West might have stopped there, without major changes in eastern Europe, in which case neither the retreat from Afghanistan nor arms control would have constituted turning points in a chain leading to the end of the Cold War.

How independent were our five turning points? Proponents of both the material- and idea-based explanations for the end of the Cold War insist that they were tightly coupled and to varying degrees an expression of underlying changes in material capabilities or ideology. Even if this argument is persuasive, it says little about possible interaction effects among the turning points and the extent to which the presence of one or more of them made others more or less likely. Taking our first turning point—Gorbachev's accession to power "A"—as a given, there are strong links between this turning point and all the developments that followed, but none of these turning points were inevitable after "A." Withdrawal from Afghanistan "B" and arms control "C" could not have happened without "A." They might be described as part of a coincidental chain, one in which events in a chain were not dependent on prior events in the chain.[23] "B" and "C" were turning points in part because they helped to establish Gorbachev's bona fides in the West, but they did not directly lead to "D," political change in eastern Europe, or "E," Germany's unification within NATO. There are very strong links between "D" and "E"; it is inconceivable that German reunification—especially within NATO— would have occurred without the prior collapse of communist regimes in eastern Europe and the ensuing dissolution of the Warsaw Pact. They can be described as part of an "unfolding chain" in which events are not switchable in time because of their relationship.[24] "D" and "E" were set in motion by "A," but required other independent and contributing causes. So too was the particular shape of these outcomes significantly influenced but not determined by Gorbachev's policies.

The preceding analysis suggests that there is little evidence for a monocausal explanation for the end of the Cold War. "A" was a necessary but insufficient condition for this outcome, but A + B + C + D + E combined in additive *and* interactive ways to produce that outcome. Our counterfactual exploration suggests that A, B, C, and D might have been ordered differently and, more importantly, that there were other causal pathways that could have led to the same generic resolution of the Cold War. If we are addressing an outcome that was at some point highly likely but could have been reached through multiple, additive pathways, we must consider the possibility that the pathway A + B + C + D + E was an accident of history.

The hindsight bias and historical scholarship encourage us to regard major developments as overdetermined. We know this is not the case and that there is considerable variation in the contingency of all important social outcomes. Anchoring one end of the continuum is the so-called butterfly effect, where small changes have amplifying effects, moving the course of developments far from the path they would otherwise have taken. Butterflies of this kind might have prevented events that were otherwise probable or have been responsible for others that appeared at the time to have a low probability. The determinist end of the continuum might be compared to a freight train highballing down the track. In the absence of switches it takes enormous counter-forces to alter its path. Counterfactuals can be used to make a reasonable determination of where along this continuum a particular event lies. In chapter 2 I propose a multistep process for determining the contingency of an event, which I applied to the rise of the West and, later, to World War I and the end of the Cold War. I offer a brief recapitulation of these steps below:

1. *What do we have to do to negate a cause or confluence?* Causes or confluences should be mutated in ways that are readily credible and render them innocuous much the way small mutations in the genes of pathogens can eliminate or significantly reduce their virulence.

2. *How many credible minimal rewrites can be found that might prevent, alter or stall the turning point?* As a general rule, the more different components of a turning point that can be removed by minimal rewrite counterfactuals, the more contingent the turning point.

3. *How far back must we go to find credible minimal rewrites?* The further back in time we go to find a minimal rewrite counterfactual, the more steps there are likely to be between antecedent and consequent, and the lower its probability, as the probability of any counterfactual is the multiple of the probabilities of every step in the chain. Multiple-step counterfactuals also increase the possibility that other developments set in motion by the initial counterfactuals could sever the chain of causation leading to the desired alternative outcome.

4. *At what level of analysis are our minimal rewrites?* Minimal rewrites of history require small, plausible changes in reality that are likely to have big consequences. For this reason practitioners of counterfactual history most often invoke changes in personnel, policy, or the fortunes of war. Changes sometimes require intervention at the level of elites, bureaucracies, or domestic politics, and more elaborate arguments linking antecedents to consequences. When we change ideas, state structures, and the balance of power, the latter requiring intervention at the system level, minimal rewrites are out of the question unless we go back to a point in time when those ideas, structures, and balances had not jelled and might

be significantly affected by small, plausible changes at levels 1 and 2. The farther back we introduce changes, the less plausible the consequent becomes because our antecedent is likely to introduce other changes with unknown interaction effects and consequences. So a turning point can be considered contingent if it can be untracked by numerous, plausible counterfactuals involving agents, confluence, or chance, and much less so if it requires intervention at the level of elites, bureaucracies, or ideas.

5. *How redundant is the turning point?* Different causal paths have different implications for contingency. A turning point described by the simple linear pathway of A + B + C (and only A + B + C) might be prevented by severing any link in the three-step chain. If A and B are themselves the products of other chains of causation, there may be many possible way of using minimal rewrite counterfactuals to prevent the turning point by preventing preconditions "A" and "B." There are turning points that are the outcomes of simple linear chains. Others are likely to have one or more paths leading to them. If we prevent A + B + C, the possibility of G + H + C and perhaps of M + N + C remain. To prevent a turning point with a minimal rewrite counterfactual, we need to know all the principal chains leading to it and something about their probability. In situations where multiple paths lead to the same outcome, estimates of probability are likely to be complicated by interaction effects. The removal of any causal chain may significantly change the probability (in either direction) of other paths. An outcome that requires the confluence of many independent causes, but could be prevented or transformed in magnitude by removing any one of them with a minimal is highly contingent. But other confluences can have multiple pathways that lead to "C" and require multiple interventions to prevent them. Their contingency would depend on how many minimal rewrites were necessary to halt or deflect each possible pathway.

6. *What about second-order counterfactuals?* Up to this point we have tried to prevent, alter, or delay turning points. But we must also consider how they might still come to pass in the aftermath of successful counterfactual intervention. Second-order counterfactuals, either by themselves or in interaction with one another, might produce the turning point, or some variant of it, at a later date. The enabling counterfactuals necessary to bring about the antecedent can set in motion a chain of events that lead to the turning point, as can events arising from the antecedent itself. A rigorous attempt to assess contingency compels us to work through these possible pathways in search of the most likely ways that turning points could still come about. If secondary routes to turning points can be found, researchers need to find ways of stopping or delaying them with additional counterfactuals. Roughly speaking, the more alternatives we find, and the more likely they appear, the less contingent the turning point.

Counterfactual thought experiments are a powerful experimental tool. They allow us to probe the causes and contingency of discrete events and by doing so formulate more sophisticated understandings of how the world works. The methods I propose for conducting such experiments are not intended to replace traditional approaches but rather to supplement them. If theories and propositions work from the general to the particular, my approach progresses from the particular to the general. It is more inductive than deductive, but complementary not antagonistic. By tacking back and forth between deductive theory and inductive counterfactual probes of empirical cases, we can develop better theories and better understandings of both their potential and their limitations.

This project could be made more compelling if it was made collaborative and brought together scholars with different substantive expertise and different initial estimates of the contingency of the event in question. Argument and counterargument over counterfactuals and their implications have the potential to bring about a consensus or bracket disagreement when that is not possible. Such an exercise is not necessarily limited to the past. It is equally appropriate to forecasting, which makes use of many of the same techniques. It establishes possible branching points in scenarios and engages in speculative inquiry about how much (or how little) the alternative paths they create diverge from the main narrative.[25]

FACT AND FICTION

Philip Roth is sensitive to the ways in which representations of the past shape how we think about the present and the communities with which we affiliate. He considers fiction an important, if not necessary, corrective to the determinism of standard history and its proclivity to reshape the past in accord with politically acceptable narratives. History in his view narrows the horizons of even the most intelligent and thoughtful people. Roth has set himself the task of stretching the horizons of the American Jewish community and Americans more generally by confronting them with a counternarrative of their history.

Roth has another grievance against history: it ignores or downplays the role of emotions and generally aspires to offer a detached analysis of human decisions and behavior. Fiction, by contrast, "aims to give us the truth of lived experience, the truth of emotional and psychological effect, rather than a cool appraisal of past events."[26] Roth's characters mimic real people in responding emotionally to uncertainty. Uncertainty intensifies their hopes and fears, leading to all kinds of behavior that cannot easily be understood as strategic. If history reduces uncertainty, fiction, especially counterfactual fiction, has the potential to expand it. It reminds us, as does *The Plot Against America*, that events could have unfolded differently and, by doing so, encourages us to explore the likelihood and consequences of alternative worlds and especially how they might have affected us. Counterfactual history offers a vantage point to assess our own world, our identities, and the roles we perform and often take for granted.

It *Can't Happen Here* and *The Plot Against America* challenge the divide between fact and fiction. Fact is assumed to have some truth content, although this claim is controversial. In his dispute with Hayden White and Pierre Vidal-Naquet over how best to refute Holocaust denials, Carlo Ginzburg argues for distinguishing the performative efficacy of historical narrative from its factuality. Truth is relative, he acknowledges, but fact is not.[27] Ginzburg makes the case for objective constraints on representation, difficult as they are to recognize. Fact is ultimately an ontological question, but one that can be finessed if we accept a pragmatic working definition. Rhetorical theory is helpful in this regard as it defines as the area of consensus in a dispute that about which we need not argue.[28] Any datum loses its status as fact the moment it becomes open to question. An alternative working definition is provided by philosopher of science John Ziman, who distinguishes the content of scientific knowledge not by its actual consensuality but by its consensibility—its susceptibility to agreed-upon empirical procedures of verification.[29] Underlying both procedures is the evidence of the senses. Insofar as the organs of perception are common to humans, perception in the empirical realm is consensible and not necessarily restricted by culture or epoch. We may accordingly define a fact, in Tullio Maranhão's words, as "an ostensive reference capable of generating agreement."[30]

Novels, like history, rest on the distinction between fact and fiction. Fiction is supposed to be nonfactual, and history factual. In practice, this distinction is hard to sustain, as David Hume noted back in the eighteenth century.[31] In our era, Paul Ricoeur makes a similar argument; he characterizes fiction as "quasi historical" and history as "quasi fictional." The former explores the "unrealized potentialities of the historical past" while the latter "requires the mediations of fiction in its treatment of the past."[32] To make sense to its readers, fiction must connect in some way to the real world, usually through its characters, their environments, and the situations they confront. Fiction tries to make itself look real and factual, and its essential fictiveness lies not in its characters, objects, or situations, but in how it assembles them in its own phenomenological world.[33] For this reason, the rules of fiction generally correspond closely with those that we think govern the real world and refer us back to that world. Fantastic fiction, a category to which some counterfactual fiction belongs, constructs alternative worlds that take liberties with the social or physical world (e.g., changing gravity, conferring immortality, introducing aliens, or supraliminal travel). The conspicuous violation of real-world conditions, limitations or social practices in such fiction ironically requires the emphatic continuity of other real-world givens (e.g., gender, bodies, eating, death, politics, ethics). To a lesser degree, this is true of all fiction.

Writers can take considerable leeway with reality—in substance and language—and still expect readers to make appropriate connections to the real world. In Lewis Carroll's "Jabberwocky" almost every noun and verb is an invention, but they are assembled in a familiar narrative pattern that gives us expectations of what they are and how actors are likely to behave. We do not really know what a Jabberwocky is, but we are capable of understanding the kind of thing it is. This is because it has a stable and definable set of features familiar to us from literature about monsters, which itself is based on the observed form and behavior of wild, ferocious animals.[34]

Modern fiction is heavily psychological, which puts a greater burden on authors. The inner conflicts and feelings of characters must bear some resemblance to actual people for fiction to impress readers with its verisimilitude, and fiction is most appealing when the anxiety and conflicts of its characters resemble those that readers confront. History for its part requires narratives that transform "brute" facts into "institutional" facts, giving meaning to both.[35] Narratives usually order events in chronological sequence, making history into a story with a beginning, middle, and end. They often draw on literary conventions to do this and make use of well-established plot lines like tragedy and comedy.[36] Roth, I suggest in chapter 8, uses both genres in his counterfactual history and plays one off the other with telling effect.

Perhaps the most useful way of thinking about the differences between fact and fiction is in terms of two other binaries: observable reality versus its representation, and narrative that represents itself as truthful versus that which acknowledges itself as imaginary. Reality impinges on us through our sensory organs and, as Locke and Hume note, makes impressions on us.[37] We use our intellect to organize these impressions and, according to Hume, impose notions of causality on the social and physical worlds. Cognitive psychology describes such impressions as schemas and has elaborated the dynamics and biases associated with image formation, retention, and revision.[38] Schemas are abstract and much condensed representations of reality that range from the very simple to the very complex, and often incorporate, à la Hume, notions of causation. They allow us to make sense of reality and respond rapidly in a generally efficient way to sensory stimuli. While attempting to represent reality, they are imaginary creations, as no two observers are likely to share exactly the same schemas even if they share numerous common experiences. So even the most direct efforts to make sense of the world require a notable degree of fictional representation.

The more meaningful binary may be the volitional one between narratives that purport to describe real versus fictional worlds. All forms of social science are committed to the former. Counterfactual history makes no pretence about its fictive nature, although its authors usually do their best to make the alternative worlds they create as real as possible. They are generally careful about policing the boundary, as they understand it, between fact and counterfact. Practitioners of this genre conform to John Searle's dictum that "The author of a work of fiction pretends to perform a series of illocutionary acts . . . without any intention to deceive."[39] This is not necessarily true of historical novels, whose authors routinely mix fact and fantasy and not infrequently keep readers in the dark about which is which. They rewrite history, sometimes with finesse, to make their characters more appealing, evil, romantic, clever, or innocent. Novels about Caesar, Napoleon, Hitler, the Kennedy assassination, and John Lennon's murder sell well and attract at least as many readers as serious biographies.[40] Like biographies, they invariably focus on individuals and exaggerate the role of agency. Pulp fiction and comic books—even more influential with the general public—do the same. Even serious novels and opera play their part. Boris Godunov's reputation has never recovered from his treatment at the hands of Pushkin and Mussorgsky. A benign contrast is the ex post facto integration of World War II army platoons by American war comics of the 1960s and 1970s.

Social science and historical fiction deceive in similar ways. They emphasize what is tellable versus what is complicated. Social science lauds the value of Occam's razor and the need to make trade-offs between rigor and richness in favor of the former. Such a choice is also practical. A simple story gets its point across; black-and-white is always more memorable than gray-and-nuance, whether in social science, fiction, or political rhetoric. Philip Tetlock finds that hedgehogs (who know one thing) are worse predictors than foxes (who know many things) but more successful professionally.[41] This may be because what is communicable is memorable and easier to explain to others. Narratibility, alas, is also the quality that gives power to historical lies. They are simple but consequential stories that override for many people the question of their nonfactual basis.

The binary between "truthful" and "fictional" narratives is frequently transgressed by those who purport to write in one modality but actually write in another. Various gospels trace Christ's lineage back to Moses and Adam, and Augustus had himself described as the son of a god. The literature of chivalry transforms Charlemagne and Roland (allegedly one of Charlemagne's warriors) from bloodthirsty marauders into saintly knights, and their booty-seeking expedition against Spanish Christians into a holy crusade against infidels. David Hume and Thomas Macaulay give credence to fictional accounts of atrocities to make the Irish appear responsible for all the bloodshed and disorder in that colonized country.[42] Combatants in wars routinely rewrite their history to make themselves innocent victims of foreign aggression. During World War II, Henry Luce's *Time-Life* empire, reported battles between Chinese Nationalists and Japanese that never took place. Soviet authorities rewrote their history to insert Stalin into key meetings or events at which he was not present or played only a minor role. They subsequently rewrote history to discredit Stalin but continued the Stalinist tradition of removing players from history, as Stalin had with Trotsky, when they became political "nonpersons." David Irving repeatedly denied the historicity of the Holocaust and a French anti-Semite published a best-selling popular book in the aftermath of 9/11 falsely alleging that the terrorist attack on the World Trade Center was planned by Israel and that Jews working in the Twin Towers were warned in advance to stay home on the day of the attack.[43] Former officials of the Reagan administration and their fellow travelers in the media and academic world have successfully perpetrated the fiction that Star Wars and the Reagan arms buildup brought the Soviet Union to its knees and ended the Cold War.[44] As history is what people believe it to be, propaganda, self-serving memoirs, conspiracy theories, and counterfactual history have the potential to be accepted as factual history for entire peoples and nations.

Even the most casual examination of official history, popular literature, and film reveals that the distinction between fact and fiction is often stressed in these several genres to the degree that it is being distorted. Oliver Stone claims to be acting in the role of a historian in depicting Kennedy's assassination, as does Don DeLillo in his novel on the subject.[45] Both give credence to unsubstantiated conspiracy theories in which Lee Harvey Oswald is only the tip of the iceberg. Like most conspiracy theorists, they make much of facts. They pile fact on top of fact to bolster sketchy arguments. Many of their "facts" have little or no connection with reality, and when they do, they are unconnected by logical arguments, or rest on the most dubious assumptions. Polls nevertheless indicate that conspiracy theories resonate with the public. Three years after the assassination in 1966, fully half of the American people believed that Lee Harvey Oswald had not acted alone. By 1976, presumably in response to all the publicity given to books advocating conspiracies, 81 percent of the public believed that Oswald had accomplices. This figure only dropped to 70 percent by 2003.[46] False beliefs become political facts and feed back into reality, influencing, if not changing, the course of history. A well-known example is the infamous "stab in the back" (*Dolchstoss*) thesis that alleged that Germany was not defeated on the battlefield in World War I but betrayed at home by socialists and Jews. Propagated by Field Marshal Paul von Hindenburg and right-wing nationalists, it helped to undermine the authority of the postwar Weimar Republic and bring Hitler to power.[47] In a variant of Gresham's law, bad history—in the form of conspiracy theories, novels, films, and Internet websites and blogs—has the potential to drive out the good and appears in many instances to have done so.

Western modernity has created and fetishized the concept of the "fact." Not surprisingly, some philosophers, social scientists, and even humanists have struggled to find ways of keeping fact and fiction apart. Bertrand Russell was committed to a robust realism. He insisted that there was only one world, the real one. In the realm of fiction, only the thoughts of authors and their readers could be considered real.[48] Gottlob Frege distinguished meaning or reference (*Bedeutung*) from sense (*Sinn*). His system had no place for fiction because its names and narratives lack reference and without it they have no truth value.[49] Other philosophers have been more open to alternative or possible worlds, a concept that dates back to Leibniz. Saul Kripke proposes a "model structure" for modal logic, which he interprets in terms of possible worlds. His successors have reformulated his model structure on the assumption that our actual world is surrounded by an infinity of other possible worlds.[50]

Positivist social science has on the whole treated the distinction between fact and fiction as unproblematic. Reality is out there and independent of our thoughts or conceptions and can be organized as evidence, incorporated into data sets, and analyzed with appropriate statistical tools. King, Keohane, and Verba's *Designing Social Inquiry* is a prominent exemplar of this long-since discredited epistemology. It defines data as "systematically collected elements of information about the world," and limits its discussion to procedures for collecting such data. Validity "refers to measuring what we think we are measuring," and is assumed to be a function of respondents understanding our questions and answering them honestly. There is no understanding that evidence is a problematic category or that the categories we use to define and organize it in the social sciences are products of our mind, not reflections of some external reality that would be understood the same way by all intelligent and informed observers.[51] In practice, the persuasiveness of social science texts generally rests at least as much with their rhetoric as it does with their so-called science. Dierdre McCloskey notes that mainstream economists market their articles as the products of top-of-the line econometric models and statistical methods but they appeal to readers on the basis of their often implicit references to popular wisdom, myths, and established authorities, whose claims to fame rest on similar rhetorical moves.[52]

Some humanists are engaged in mirror efforts to distinguish fiction from fact, with the goal of legitimizing the former. The starting point for some literary theorists is rebellion against Aristotle's conception of mimesis, which understands fiction as an imitation or representation of real life.[53] Lubomír Doležel condemns mimesis as "One of the most reductive operations of which the human mind is capable: the vast, open, and inviting fictional universe is shrunk to the model of one single world, actual human experience." At the same time, the concept of fiction also suffers, as Doležel recognizes, from the claim by some philosophers and social scientists that so-called facts incorporate elements of fiction. "If reality is called fiction," he reasons, a new word for fiction has to be invented."[54] To date, literary theorists drawing on either their analysis of texts or of possible worlds have found no convincing way of categorically distinguishing fiction from fact.

The majority of humanists show relatively little interest in the fact-fiction binary or in truth claims. Poststructuralists aside, they understand that narratives are more or less accurate; they are more concerned with how they work and the projects they serve. They are interested in fact and fiction as labels. There is a large and growing literature on how genres shape messages and on how narratives are constructed. Genres marked as fact carry different expectations than those marked as fiction. Perhaps because of these expectations, scholars and reviewers alike become agitated by works of fiction that deceptively blur genres. Recent examples include James Frey's *A Thousand Little Pieces*, a fake but moving memoir about a young man who overcomes alcohol and crack addictions.[55] Before that, there was a major fuss over the discovery of fictional elements in the autobiography of Nobelist Rigoberta Menchu.[56]

Pure narratology is concerned exclusively with fiction. It *largely* ignores the problem of recalcitrant content, although recalcitrant content and messages that escape the intent or control of their shapers are matters of interest to contemporary scholarship on the novel. More historically oriented humanists, including many feminists and scholars committed to a postcolonial agenda, are interested in the tensions between the represented and their representations. Influenced by poststructuralists, they recognize that there is no transparent access to reality, which is another reason why they are more focused on its representations.

Other social scientists and most humanists are prepared to live with the fuzziness of fact and fiction as categories and the difficulty, if not the impossibility, of effectively distinguishing one from the other. Some social scientists continue to deny or ignore this imprecision and overlap. Counterfactual research in psychology and political science attempts to exploit the imprecision and overlap between these binaries for creative ends, as do historical and counterfactual novels. Until now these projects in social science and literature have been largely uninformed by each other. Both could profit from awareness of the other's goals, methods, and products. I offer this volume as a small step in this direction.

Counterfactuals, Identity and Scholarship

Let me return to my starting point: the central role of World War I for international relations, ideas, and the arts of the twentieth century. I suggested that so much of how we think of modernity, not only of international relations, is the product of that war and its outcome. Counterfactuals that attempt to show the contingency of the war and an allied victory met considerable resistance, and not only among scholars with a high need for psychological closure and a commitment to lawlike explanations for both events. Experiments and interviews with participants indicate that scholars, like ordinary mortals, tend to believe that big events have big causes. This belief biases them in favor of systematic theories and against agency, accident, and confluence. Counterfactual priming nevertheless makes scholars, at least in the short term, more responsive to contingency and the corresponding importance of small events, even accidents, in bringing about big changes in the world. In conversations, many participants admit to feeling uneasy about the implications of contingency. As I noted in chapter 6, some look for ways of squaring their belief in determinism with their case-specific acceptance of contingency or resort to second-order counterfactuals.

Most troubling still—for determinist and nondeterminist alike—are the broader intellectual implications of the contingency of transformative events. They threaten some of our most important conceptual anchors. In the case of World War I, this includes a set of fundamental assumptions about the causes and likelihood of war, the consequences of industrialization and modernization, the advantages and vulnerabilities of democracy, the role of nationalism, the need and efficacy of deterrence, and the relative consequences of multi- versus bipolarity. World War I, its origins, conduct, and consequences, established a hierarchy of problems for theorists and a predilection to see certain kinds of theories and propositions as more appropriate and persuasive in exploring them.

If World War I or anything like it had been averted, I suggest in chapter 3, a successful Bolshevik coup in Russia could have been avoided—and World War II, the Holocaust, the Cold War, and perhaps even American hegemony. Amplifying changes would have moved European and world history away from the tracks they went down from 1914 to 1945 and might have produced a Europe closer to the one built on the ashes of World War II. The level of globalization reached in 1914 was not equaled again until after the end of the Cold War. With the sharp and sustained rupture in the mobility of ideas, trade, investments, and people across European and international borders, many long-standing historical rivalries might have become muted, if not resolved, as they were in the latter part of the century. In the absence of two disastrous wars and genocide, many intellectuals might still believe in progress. Colonial empires would have lasted longer, although their demise might not have been any less violent.

In this alternative world our frames of reference would have been very different. Realism would not have become the dominant paradigm, as it did after World War II in response to that conflict and a burgeoning Cold War between its principal victors. Without a Cold War and the divided nations it spawned, security would not have dominated the international relations literature, and the security subfield would not have focused on hegemonic war and its prevention. It might have been more concerned with economic development and the violence surrounding the breakup and partition of colonial empires. Liberalism and international law would almost certainly have continued to have maintained their ascendancy and would have generated different but sustained research agendas. As European intellectual life would have remained robust and German rivaled English as the language of science and social science, North American universities would not be as dominant as they are today. North American intellectual life would not have been enriched by the flood of refugees from Hitler's Germany and other European countries threatened by its expansion or indigenous fascist regimes. Not only would social science have developed differently in these circumstances, so would have literature, theater, and the arts. Americans would also be living in a different world, thinking different thoughts, doing different things, and being different people. For all these reasons, such a world is hard for us to imagine, and more demanding still if we try to insert ourselves into it.

Imagining alternative worlds is nevertheless a valuable, even essential enterprise, as *The Plot Against America* so effectively demonstrates. Identities are embedded in metanarratives. Counterfactuals can unmake the events on which those narratives rest. They accordingly have the potential to make us think about who we are and why we are who we are. Without counterfactuals we might not interrogate our identities and the conditions that enabled and sustain them. More mundane questions— of the kind social science seeks to answer—ultimately depend, as Weber understood, on the frameworks that lead us to these questions and their answers. To make effective analytical use of these frameworks we need to consider not only the conditions that gave rise to them, but the extent to which they have been "naturalized" by actors—and especially by researchers. We need to put ourselves in perspective, not only those we study. To understand our understandings, we must create alternative worlds. They give us an outside vantage point on ourselves and can help us recognize that the frameworks that we tend to accept as determined and natural are contingent, artificial, and local. Coming to terms with our own place in the world is a fundamental and essential step in becoming ethical and effective scholars.

In chapter 1 I sided with radical skeptics in rejecting the possibility of developing good predictive theories about social behavior. The principal reason for my pessimism is the open-ended, nonlinear nature of the social world. Critics of the behavioral revolution and its project of theory building also point to the seeming inability of social scientists to perform the cognitive tasks theory building and testing require. Thomas Kuhn levels a more fundamental objection against scientists: they are not nearly as open-minded as they think they are. The majority of scientists, he maintains, are committed to the conceptual, theoretical, and methodological truths of their epoch and reject, often out of hand, arguments and empirical findings of their critics.[57] Science still remains in large part a self-correcting process, as Kuhn himself notes, because dominant paradigms encounter anomalies, begin to breakdown when they resist explanation, and are ultimately replaced by new frameworks that provide convincing explanations and predictions. This process is an uphill struggle, but facilitated by the difficulty of denying the better correspondence between a new framework and the physical world, especially when it accounts for otherwise inexplicable anomalies and makes verifiable counterintuitive predictions. Social science does not work this way. None of its theories—and certainly not those in international relations—successfully predict major events in their respective domains, and endure despite repeated failures. In international relations, paradigms and theories tend to gain and lose adherents as a function of events in the political world; these prompt shifts in attention, as the end of the Cold War did, drawing scholars to paradigms they consider more appropriate to their new agenda. Maybe identity also plays a role. After making major investments of time and commitment to paradigms or theories, they help define who we are. We are correspondingly reluctant to give them up.

The surveys and experiments of chapters 5 and 6 lend some support to those who stress the cognitive limitations of historians and social scientists, and more support for the Kuhnian critique of the belief systems of scientists. The majority of our respondents remain committed to the overdetermination of major international developments and the related belief that big events have big (i.e., structural) causes. For the most part they resist contingency, or when they acknowledge it, tend to deny its potential to restructure the international environment. Many of the participants who resist contingency and its implications reveal a need for psychological closure or are committed to theory building. The two characteristics, as we have seen, are not unrelated. Other participants may simply find recognition of the consequences of contingency and the extreme unpredictability of the social world too threatening or intellectually disorienting. Whatever its causes, the rejection of contingency and the belief in structural causes serve to sustain not only the neopositivist project, but the deeper need to predict and control the future. As Max Weber noted, the demystification of the world and theory building are mutually supporting, if not mutually constitutive. The appropriate antidote may be the demystification of science. Counterfactuals are ideally suited to this test by virtue of their ability to encourage us to understand the similarities and differences between the physical and social worlds and the different kinds of limits they impose of understanding in the form of *epistēmē*.

Notes

ACKNOWLEDGMENTS

1. Richard Ned Lebow and Janice Gross Stein, "Back to the Past: Counter-factuals and the Cuban Missile Crisis," in Philip E. Tetlock and Aaron Belkin, eds. *Thought Experiments in World Politics: Logical, Methodological and Psychological Perspectives* (Princeton: Princeton University Press, 1996), pp. 119–48.

2. Richard Ned Lebow, "What's So Different about a Counterfactual?" *World Politics* 52 (July 2000), pp. 550–85, and "Contingency, Catalysts and International System Change," *Political Science Quarterly* 115 (Winter 2000–2001), pp. 591–616.

3. Philip E. Tetlock and Richard Ned Lebow, "Poking Counterfactual Holes in Covering Laws: Cognitive Styles and Political Learning," *American Political Science Review* 95 (December 2001), pp. 829–43.

4. Philip E. Tetlock, Richard Ned Lebow, and Geoffrey Parker, eds., *Unmaking the West: "What-If" Scenarios that Rewrite World History.* (Ann Arbor: University of Michigan Press, 2006).

5. George Breslauer and Richard Ned Lebow, "Leadership and the End of the Cold War: A Counterfactual Thought Experiment," in Richard K. Herrmann and Richard Ned Lebow, eds., *Ending the Cold War* (New York: Palgrave-Macmillan, 2003), pp. 161–88.

CHAPTER ONE

James Joyce, *Ulysses* (New York: Random House, 1990), p. 25.

1. *Genesis* 2–3, and *Ezekiel* 28:12–19, for a variant.

2. Richard Ned Lebow, *Gardens of Eden* (in progress), ch. 1, for a sociological analysis of this and other Golden Age myths.

3. Richard Ned Lebow and Mark Irving Lichbach, *Theory and Evidence in Comparative Politics and International Relations* (New York: Palgrave, 2007), for a dialog among researchers from different traditions and approaches, all of whom take evidence seriously and recognize the problems their own preferred approach has in its collection and evaluation.

4. Jack S. Levy, "Theory, Evidence, and Politics in the Evolution of International Relations Research Programs," in Lebow and Lichbach, *Theory and Evidence in Comparative Politics and International Relations*, pp. 177–98.

5. Gary King, Robert O. Keohane, and Sydney Verba, *Designing Social Inquiry* (Princeton: Princeton University Press, 1994), unreasonably contend that this is the only form of science. David Waldner, "Transforming Inferences into Explanations: Lessons from the Study of Mass Extinctions," in Lebow and Mark Irving Lichbach, *Theory and Evidence in Comparative Politics and International*

Relations, pp. 145–76, demonstrates how their primary example of "good science"—the hypothesis that a meteor impact was responsible for the extinction of the dinosaurs—was actually an instance of inductive reasoning based on the prior discovery of the Iridium layer.

6. King, Keohane, and Verba, *Designing Social Inquiry*, ignore this important condition and goal of science.

7. This is an ontological point, not an epistemological one. I am talking about how the world works, not our understanding of it.

8. See Alan Beyerchen, "Clausewitz, Nonlinearity and the Unpredictability of War," *International Security*, 17, no. 3 (Winter, 1992), pp. 59–90.

9. E. H. Carr, *What Is History?* (London: Macmillan, 1961), p. 127. According to A.J.P. Taylor, "a historian should never deal in speculation about what did not happen." *The Struggle for the Mastery in Europe, 1848–1918* (London: Oxford University Press, 1954). M. M. Postan writes: "The might-have beens of history are not a profitable subject of discussion," quoted in J. D. Gould, "Hypothetical History," *Economic History Review*, 2nd ser. 22 (August 1969), pp. 195–207. See also David Hackett Fischer, *Historians' Fallacies* (New York: Harper Colophon Books, 1970), pp. 15–21; Peter McClelland, *Casual Explanation and Model-Building in History, Economics, and the New Economic History* (Ithaca: Cornell University Press, 1975); E. P. Thompson, *The Poverty of Theory and Other Essays* (New York: Monthly Review Press, 1978), p. 300.

10. Robert Cowley, ed., *What If?* (New York: G. P. Putnam's Sons, 1998); Niall Ferguson, ed., *Virtual History: Alternatives and Counterfactuals* (New York: Basic Books, 1999); Philip E. Tetlock, Richard Ned Lebow, and Geoffrey A. Parker, eds., *Unmaking the West: "What-If?" Scenarios that Rewrite World History* (Ann Arbor: University of Michigan Press, 2006); Andrew Roberts, ed., *What Might Have Been: Leading Historians on Twelve "What Ifs" of History* (London: Weidenfeld and Nicolson, 2004); Gavriel Rosenfeld, *The World Hitler Never Made: Alternate History and the Memory of Nazism* (Cambridge: Cambridge University Press, 2005).

11. Max Horkheimer and Theodor W. Adorno, *Dialectic of Enlightenment*, trans. John Cumming (New York: Columbia University Press, 2001 [1944]); Joseph S. Nye Jr., *Bound to Lead: The Changing Nature of American Power* (New York: Basic Books, 1990).

12. For one of the first challenges to the conventional wisdom about the war's near inevitability, see Holger Afflerbach and David Stevenson, eds., *An Improbable War: The Outbreak of World War I and European Political Culture Before 1914* (New York: Berghahn Books, 2007).

13. On this last point, see the thoughtful essay by Ian Clark, "Democracy in International Society," forthcoming in *Millennium*.

14. Baruch Fischoff, "Hindsight Is Not Equal to Foresight: The Effect of Outcome Knowledge on Judgment under Uncertainty," *Journal of Experimental Psychology: Human Perception and Performance*, 1, no. 2 (1975), pp. 288–99; S. A. Hawkins and R. Hastie, "Hindsight: Biased Judgments of Past Events after the Outcomes Are Known," *Psychological Bulletin* 107, no. 3 (1990), pp. 311–27.

15. Richard E. Neustadt interview with Maxwell C. Taylor, Washington, D.C., 28 June 1983, in *Proceedings of the Hawk's Cay Conference, 5–8 March 1987*

(Cambridge: Harvard University Center for Science and International Affairs, Working Paper 89-1, 1989), mimeograph, p. 72.

16. Richard K. Herrmann and Richard Ned Lebow, "Policymakers and the Cold War's End: Micro and Macro Assessments of Contingency," *Cold War International History Project Bulletin*, no. 12/13 (Fall/Winter 2001), pp. 337–40.

17. Norman Angell, *The Great Illusion: A Study of the Relation of Military Power in Nations to Their Economic and Social Advantage* (London, Heinemann, 1910); Friedrich von Bernhardi, *Deutschland und der nächste Krieg* (Germany and the Next War), 2 vols. (Stuttgart: Cotta, 1912).

18. John Herz, *International Politics in the Atomic Age* (New York: Columbia University Press, 1959), p. 29.

19. Philip E. Tetlock, *Expert Political Judgment. How Good Is It? How Can We Know?* (Princeton: Princeton University Press, 2005), ch. 2, for the consistent failure of point predictions by experts and their general reluctance to acknowledge their failures.

20. Daniel Bell, *The End of Ideology: On the Exhaustion of Political Ideas in the 1950s* (Glencoe, Ill.: Free Press, 1960); Francis Fukuyama, *The End of History and the Last Man* (New York: Free Press, 1992).

21. Thomas Friedman, *The Lexus and the Olive Tree* (New York: Farrar, Strauss and Giroux, 1999).

22. Susan Stokes, "Region, Contingency, and Democratization," in Ian Shapiro and Sonu Bedi, *Political Contingency: Studying the Unexpected, the Accidental, and the Unforeseen* (New York: New York University Press, 2007), pp. 171–202, makes the case for the contingent nature of democratization.

23. Per Bak and K. Chen, "Self-Organized Criticality," *Scientific American* 264 (January 1991), pp. 46–53; James Gleick, *Chaos: Making a New Science* (New York: Viking, 1987), for further elaboration.

24. Tetlock, *Expert Political Judgment*, pp. 140–41, makes a similar although somewhat different point, arguing that the hindsight bias and belief-system defenses reinforce our self-images as rational beings.

25. David Hume, *An Inquiry Concerning Human Understanding*, ed. Tom L. Beauchamp (Oxford: Oxford University Pres, 1999), Part III, Book 2, sect. 9.

26. Martin Heidegger, *Being and Time*, trans. John MacQuarrie and Edward Robinson (London: SCM Press, 1962 [1927]), 18th Auflage.

27. J. Greenberg, T. Pyszczynski, and S. Solomon, "The Causes and Consequences of a Need for Self-Esteem: A Terror Management Theory," in F. Baumeister, ed., *Public Self and Private Self* (New York: Springer-Verlag, 1986), pp. 189–212; A. J. Rosenblatt, J. Greenberg, S. Solomon, T. Pyszcynski, and D. Lyon, "Evidence for Terror Management Theory I: The Effects of Mortality Salience on Reactions to those who Violate or Uphold Cultural Values"; J. Greenberg, T. Pyszczynski, S. Solomon, A. Rosenblatt, M. Veeder, S, Kirkland et al, "Evidence for Terror Management II: The Effects of Mortality Salience on Reactions to Those Who Threaten or Bolster the Cultural Worldview," *Journal of Personality and Social Psychology*, 58 (1990), pp. 308–18; J. Greenberg, L. Simon, T. Pyszczynski, S. Solomon, and D. Chatel, "Terror Management and Tolerance: Does Mortality Salience Always Intensify Negative Reactions to Others Who Threaten One's Worldview?" *Journal of Personality and Social Psychology*, 63 (1992),

pp. 212–20; J. Greenberg, T. Pyszczynski, S. Solomon, L. Simon, and M. Breus, "Role of Consciousness and Accessibility of Death-Related Thoughts in Mortality Salience Effects," *Journal of Personality and Social Psychology*, 67 (1994), pp. 627–37; J. Greenberg, S. Solomon, and T. Pyszczynski, "Terror Management Theory of Self-Esteem and Social Behaviour: Empirical Assessments and Conceptual Refinements," in M. P. Zanna, ed., *Advances in Experimental Social Psychology*, 29 (New York: Academic Press, 1997), pp. 61–139. On ontological security, see Anthony Giddens, *The Constitution of Society: Introduction of the Theory of Structuration* (Berkeley: University of California Press, 1984); Jenifer Mitzen, "Ontological Security in World Politics: State Identity and the Security Dilemma," *European Journal of International Relations* 12, no. 3 (2006), pp. 341–70.

28. Max Weber, "Science as a Vocation," in H. H. Gerth and C. Wright Mills, trans. and eds., *From Max Weber: Essays in Sociology* (London: Routledge and Kegan Paul, 1948), pp. 129–58.

29. Alexander L. George and Richard Smoke, *Deterrence in American Foreign Policy: Theory and Practice* (New York: Columbia University Press, 1974); Graham T. Allison, *Essence of Decision: Explaining the Cuban Missile Crisis* (Boston: Little, Brown, 1971), rely on conventional Cold War interpretations for their codings of cases. Paul K. Huth and Bruce Russett, "Deterrence Failure and Crisis Escalation," *International Studies Quarterly* 32, no. 1 (1988), pp. 29–45, and "Testing Deterrence Theory: Rigor Makes a Difference" *World Politics* 42, no. 4 (1990), pp. 466– 501, confirm the efficacy of deterrence with a data set, most of whose cases are not even deterrence encounters, and almost all of whose deterrence successes are deterrence failures. For critiques, see Richard Ned Lebow and Janice Gross Stein, "Deterrence: The Elusive Dependent Variable," *World Politics* 42 (April 1990), 336–69, and *When Does Deterrence Succeed and How Do We Know?* (Ottawa: Canadian Institute for International Peace and Security, 1990).

30. Gordon H. Chang, *Friends and Enemies: The United States, China, and the Soviet Union, 1948–1972* (Stanford: Stanford University Press, 1990); S. H. Zhang, *Deterrence and Strategic Culture: Chinese-American Confrontations, 1949–1958* (Ithaca: Cornell University Press, 1992); Ted Hopf, *Peripheral Visions: Deterrence Theory and American Foreign Policy in the Third World, 1965–1999* (Ann Arbor: University of Michigan Press, 1994); Richard Ned Lebow and Janice Gross Stein, *We All Lost the Cold War* (Princeton: Princeton University Press, 1994).

31. Max Weber, "Objectivity" in Social Science and Social Policy," in Edward A. Shils and Henry A. Finch, eds., *Max Weber, The Methodology of the Social Sciences* (Glencoe, Ill.: Free Press, 1949 [1904]), ch. 2.

32. Richard Thayer, "Anomalies: The January Effect," *The Journal of Economic Perspectives* 1, no. 1 (Summer 1987), pp. 197–201. A large fraction of the annual gains in this market used to occur in January, but no longer did so the moment the phenomenon was discovered and publicized.

33. Gabriel Almond, "Clouds, Clocks, and the Study of World Politics," *World Politics*. 29 (1977), pp. 496–522.

34. James D. Fearon and David D. Laitin, "Ethnicity, Insurgency, and Civil War," *American Political Science Review*, 97, no. 1 (2003), pp. 75–90.

35. Philip E. Tetlock, "Close-Call Counterfactuals and Belief System Defenses: I Was Not Almost Wrong but I Was Almost Right," *Journal of Personality and Social Psychology* 75 (1998), pp. 230–42, and *Expert Political Judgment*, chs. 2 and 5.

36. Hans J. Morgenthau, *Politics Among Nations: The Struggle for Power and Peace* (New York: Alfred Knopf, 1948); Kenneth N. Waltz,, *Theory of International Politics* (Reading, Mass.: Addison-Wesley, 1979); John Mearsheimer, *The Tragedy of Great Power Politics* (New York: Norton, 2001), are cases in point.

37. Robert Crowley, ed., *What If? The World's Foremost Military Historians Imagine What Might Have Been: Essays* (New York: Putnam, 1999), and *What If 2? The World's Foremost Military Historians Imagine What Might Have Been: Essays* (New York: Putnam, 2001); Philip E. Tetlock, Richard Ned Lebow and Geoffrey Parker, *Unmaking the West: "What-If" Experiments that Remake World History* (Ann Arbor: University of Michigan Press, 2006).

38. General Anatoliy Gribkov, "Operation 'Anadyr,'" *Der Spiegel*, no. 16, 1992, pp. 152–54; Lebow and Stein, *We All Lost the Cold War*, pp. 294–95.

39. Contingency has numerous meanings, and I try to use it throughout the book as meaning indeterminate and unpredictable. For a discussion of the concept, see Andreas Schedler, "Mapping contingency," in Ian Shapiro and Sonu Bedi, *Political Contingency: Studying the Unexpected, the Accidental, and the Unforeseen* (New York: New York University Press, 2007), pp. 54–78.

40. Richard Ned Lebow, *The Tragic Vision of Politics: Ethics, Interests and Orders* (Cambridge: Cambridge University Press, 2003).

41. Diedre McCloskey, "History, Differential Equations, and the Problem of Narration," *History and Theory* 30 (1999), pp. 21–36.

42. This point is made by Carl von Clausewitz and Hans J. Morgenthau, among others. For a discussion of their views on theory, see Lebow, *The Tragic Vision of Politics*. For the implications of such an understanding for social science, see Steven Bernstein, Richard Ned Lebow, Janice Gross Stein and Steven Weber, "Social Science as Case-Based Diagnostics," in Lebow and Lichbach, *Theory and Evidence in Comparative Politics and International*, pp. 229–60.

43. Friedrich Nietzsche, *Beyond Good and Evil*, in Walter Kaufmann, ed., *The Basic Writings of Nietzsche* (New York: Modern Library, 1966), pp. 179–436.

44. Weber, "The Meaning of Ethical Neutrality in the Social Sciences," and "'Objectivity' in Social Science and Social Policy," in Shils and Henry A. Finch, eds. and trans. *The Methodology of the Social Sciences* (Glencoe, Ill.: Free Press, 1949).

45. On this point, see Tracy B. Strong, *Thinking without a Banister: Essays on the Aesthetics in Political Thinkers of the Early Twentieth Century* (forthcoming), ch.3, "Max Weber, Magic, and the Politics of Social Scientific Objectivity."

46. King, Keohane, and Verba, *Designing Social Inquiry,* cited earlier, pp. 62–63.

47. Michael P. Colaresi, Karen Rasler, and William N. Thompson, eds. *Strategic Rivalries in World Politics: Position, Space and Conflict Escalation* (Cambridge: Cambridge University Press, 2007).

48. Lebow, *A Cultural Theory of International Relations*, ch. 8.

49. For example, Richard Ned Lebow and Janice Gross Stein, "Deterrence: The Elusive Dependent Variable," *World Politics* 42 (April 1990), pp. 336–69; James Fearon, "Selection Effects and Deterrence." *International Interactions* 28 (January–March 2000), pp. 5–29; David E. Spero, "The Insignificance of the Liberal Peace," *International Security* 19 (Fall 1994), pp. 50–86; William R. Thompson, "Democracy and Peace: Putting the Cart before the Horse?" *International Organization* 50 (Winter 1996), pp. 141–74.

50. An earlier version of the chapter appeared as a review essay, "What's So Different about a Counterfactual?" *World Politics* 52 (July 2000), pp. 550–85. The chapter drops the reviews of Niall Ferguson's two counterfactual books, revises and refines my suggested protocols for conducting counterfactual experiments and adds a new section that uses the rise of the West as a case in which to develop methods for distinguishing the relative importance of systematic and nonsystematic factors in key events and developments leading to this outcome.

51. Richard Ned Lebow, "Contingency, Catalysts and International System Change," *Political Science Quarterly* 115 (Winter 2000–2001), pp. 591–616.

52. George W. Breslauer and Richard Ned Lebow, "Leadership and the End of the Cold War: A Counterfactual Thought Experiment," in Richard K. Herrmann and Richard Ned Lebow, eds., *Ending the Cold War* (New York: Palgrave-Macmillan, 2006), pp. 161–88.

53. Philip A. Tetlock and Richard Ned Lebow, "Poking Counterfactual Holes in Covering Laws: Cognitive Styles and Political Learning," *American Political Science Review* 95 (December 2001), pp. 829–43.

54. Aristotle, *Poetics*, 1451a38–b11.

55. Francis Bacon, *Novum Organum*, trans and ed. Peter Urbach and John Gibson (Chicago: Open Court, 1994); Lorraine Daston, "Baconian Facts, Academic Civility, and the Prehistory of Objectivity, " *Annals of Scholarship* 8, nos. 3 and 4 (1991), pp. 338, 343; Peter Dear, *Discipline and Experience: The Mathematical Way in the Scientific Revolution* (Chicago: University of Chicago Press, 1995), p. 25.

56. On the latter view, see Mary Poovey, *A History of Modern Face: Problems of Knowledge in the Sciences of Wealth and Society* (Chicago: University of Chicago Press, 1998), p. 15 and ch. 3.

57. Everett Zimmerman, *The Boundaries of Fiction: History of the Eighteenth-Century British Novel* (Ithaca: Cornell University Press, 1996).

58. David Hume, *An Inquiry concerning Human Understanding*, ed. Charles W. Hendel (Indianapolis: Bobbs-Merrill, 1955), section iii, "Of the Association of Ideas," and "On the Study of History," in Eugene F. Miller, ed. *Essays: Moral, Political, and Literary* (Indianapolis, Ind.: Liberty Classics, 1885), pp. 563–68; Zimmerman, *The Boundaries of Fiction*, pp. 28, 130: Donald W. Livingston, *Hume's Philosophy of Common Life* (Chicago: University of Chicago Press, 1984), chs. 5 and 8.

59. Michael McKeon, *The Origins of the English Novel* (Baltimore: Johns Hopkins University Press, 1987), ch. 2; Clifford Haynes Siskin, *The Work of Writing: Literature and Social Change in Britain, 1700–1830* (Baltimore: Johns Hopkins University Press, 1997); Poovey, *A History of Modern Fact*, p. 198.

60. James Longenbach, *Modernist Poetics of History: Pound, Eliot, and the Sense of the Past* (Princeton: Princeton University Press, 1987), ch. 10.

61. Friedrich Nietzsche, *The Birth of Tragedy*, in *Basic Writings of Nietzsche*, trans. and ed., Walter Kaufmann (New York: Modern Library, 1962), sections 1 and 3.

62. Lionel Grossman "History and Literature: Reproduction or Signification," in Robert H. Canary and Henry Kozicki, eds., *Writing of History: Literary Form and Historical Understanding* (Madison: University of Wisconsin Press, 1978), pp. 3–39, on the changing relationship of literature to history.

63. Sinclair Lewis, *It Can't Happen Here* (Garden City: Doubleday Doran, 1935); Philip Roth, *The Plot Against America* (Boston: Houghton-Mifflin, 2004).

CHAPTER TWO

David Hume, *An Inquiry Concerning Human Understanding*, ed. Tom L. Beauchamp (Oxford University Press, 1999), in Section 3, "Of the Association of Ideas," p. 102.

1. Douglas R. Hofstadter, *Gödel, Escher, Bach: An Eternal Golden Brain* (New York: Vintage, 1979), and *Metamagical Themas: Questing for the Essence of Mind and Pattern* (New York: Basic Books, 1985), p. 232.

2. Alfred H. Bloom, *The Linguistic Shaping of Thought: A Study in the Impact of Language on Thinking in China and the West* (Hillsdale, N.J.: Erlbaum, 1981), maintains that the evidence for counterfactuals is weaker in languages that do not have "if-then" forms, such as Chinese. Subsequently studies contest this claim. See G. L. Liu, "Reasoning Counterfactually in Chinese: Are There Any Obstacles?" *Cognition* 21 (1985), pp. 239–70; Hazel Markus and Shinobu Kitayama, "Culture and the Self: Implications for Cognition, Emotion, and Motivation," *Psychological Review*, 98 (1991), pp. 224–53; D. Lardière, "On the Linguistic Shaping of Thought: Another Response to Alfred Bloom," *Language in Society* 21 (1992), pp. 231–52.

3. L. D. Stern, S. Marrs, M. G. Millar, and E. Cole, "Processing Time and the Recall of Inconsistent and Consistent Behaviors of Individuals and Groups," *Journal of Personality and Social Psychology* 47 (1984), pp. 253–62; Richard Hastie, "Causes and Effects of Causal Attributions," *Journal of Personality and Social Psychology*, 46 (1984), pp. 44–56; S. Kanazawa, "Outcome or Expectancy? Antecedent of Spontaneous Causal Attribution," *Personality and Social Psychology Bulletin*, 18 (1992), pp. 659–68; B. Wiener, "'Spontaneous' Causal Thinking," *Psychological Bulletin*, 97 (1985), pp. 74–84; Keith D. Markman, Igor Gavanski, S. J. Sherman, and Matthew N. McMullen, "The Impact of Perceived Control on the Imagination of Better and Worse Possible Worlds," *Personality and Social Psychology Bulletin*, 21 (1993), pp. 588–95; Matthew N. McMullen, Keith D. Markman, and Igor Gavanski, "Living in Neither the Best Nor Worst of All Possible Worlds: Antecedents and Consequences of Upward and Downward Counterfactual Thinking," in Neal J. Roese and James M. Olson, eds., *What Might Have Been: The Social Psychology of Counterfactual Thinking* (Mahwah, N.J.: Erlbaum, 1995), pp. 133–68; Neal J. Roese and James M. Olson, "Functions of Counterfactual Thinking," in Roese and Olson, *What Might Have Been*, pp. 169–98; Margaret Kasimatis and Gary L. Wells, "Individual Differences in

Counterfactual Thinking," in Roese and Olson, *What Might Have Been*, pp. 81–101; C. G. Davis, D. R. Lehman, C. B. Wortman, R. C. Silver, and S. C. Thompson, "The Undoing of Traumatic Life Events," *Personality and Social Psychology Bulletin*, 11 (1995), pp. 109–24; J. Landman, "Regret and Elation Following Action and Inaction: Affective Responses to Positive versus Negative Outcomes, *Personality and Social Psychology Bulletin*, 13 (1992), pp. 524–36; Daniel T. Gilbert, Carey K. Morewedge, Jane L. Risen, and Timothy D. Wilson, "Research Report Looking Forward to Looking Backward: The Misprediction of Regret," *Psychological Science*, 15, no. 3 (2004), pp. 346–50. Sean M. McCrea, "Counterfactual Thinking Following Negative Outcomes: Evidence for Group and Self-Protective Biases," *European Journal of Social Psychology*, 37 (2007), pp. 1256–71.

4. D. S. Dunn and T. D. Wilson, "When the Stakes Are High: A Limit to the Illusion of Control Effect," *Social Cognition*, 8 (1990), pp. 305–23; E. J. Langer, "The Illusion of Control," *Journal of Personality and Social Psychology*, 32 (1975), pp. 311–28; Margaret Kasimatis and Gary L. Wells, "Individual Differences in Counterfactual Thinking"; J. M. Burger and H. M. Cooper, "The Desirability of Control," *Motivation and Emotion*, 3 (1979), pp. 381–93; Neal J. Roese, "The Functional Basis of Counterfactual Thinking," *Journal of Personality and Social Psychology*, 66 (1994), pp. 805–18.

5. H. J. Einhorn and R. M. Hogarth, "Judging Probable Cause," *Psychological Bulletin* 99 (1986), pp. 3–19, on proxy experiments.

6. Daniel Kahneman and Amos Tversky, "The Simulation Heuristic," in Daniel Kahneman, Paul Slovic, and Amos Tversky, *Judgment under Uncertainty: Heuristics and Biases* (New York: Cambridge University Press, 1982), pp. 201–8; David Dunning and Scott F. Madey, "Comparison Processes in Counterfactual Thought," in Roese and Olson, *What Might Have Been*, pp. 103–31.

7. Examples from physics include R. Penrose, *Shadows of the Mind: A Search for the Missing Science of Consciousness* (Oxford: Oxford University Press, 1994); A. C. Elitzur and L. Vaidman, "Quantum-Mechanical Interaction-Free Measurement," *Foundations of Physics* 23, no. 7 (1993), pp. 987–97, which use information from non-events to test nuclear weapons; P. G. Kwiat, H. Weinfurter, H. Herzog, A. Zeilinger, and M. A. Kasevich, "Interaction Free Measurements," *Physics Review Letters* 74, no. 12 (12 June 1995), pp. 4763–66, which uses interaction-free measurements with a test particle to determine the presence of an object; Graeme Mitchison and Richard Josza, "Counterfactual Computation," Quantum-Ph/9907007, 2 July 1999, on counterfactual computation.

8. For example, Neal J. Roese and James M. Olson, eds. *What Might Have Been: The Social-Psychology of Counterfactual Thinking* (Mahwah, N.J.: Lawrence Erlbaum, 1995); Philip E. Tetlock and Aaron Belkin, eds., *Counterfactual Thought Experiments in World Politics: Logical, Methodological, and Psychological Perspectives* (Princeton: Princeton University Press, 1996); Raymond E. Wolfinger and Benjamin Highton, "Can More Efficient Purging Boost Turnout," paper presented at the 1994 annual meeting of the American Political Science Association; Ruy A. Teixeira, *The Disappearing American Voter* (Washington, D.C.: Brookings Institution, 1992); Steven J. Rosenstone and John Mark Hansen, *Mobilization, Participation, and Democracy in America* (New York: Macmillan, 1993); Gary J. Kornblith, "Rethinking the Coming of the Civil War: A Counter-

factual Exercise," *Journal of American History*, 90 (2003), pp. 76–105; Jeffrey M. Chwieroth, "Counterfactuals and the Study of the American Presidency," *Presidential Studies Quarterly* 32, no. 2 (June 2002), pp. 293–327; David R. Mayhew, "Events as Causes: The Case of American Politics," in Ian Shapiro and Sonu Bedi, *Political Contingency: Studying the Unexpected, the Accidental, and the Unforeseen* (New York: New York University Press, 2007), pp. 99–137.

9. Philip E. Tetlock and Aaron Belkin, "Counterfactual Thought Experiments in World Politics," in Tetlock and Belkin, *Counterfactual Thought Experiments in World Politics*, pp. 1–38.

10. Philip E. Tetlock and Geoffrey Parker, "Counterfactual Thought Experiments," in Philip E. Tetlock, Richard Ned Lebow, and Geoffrey Parker, *Unmaking the West: "What-If"? Scenarios that Remake World History* (Ann Arbor: University of Michigan Press, 2006), pp. 14–46.

11. Richard Ned Lebow and Janice Gross Stein, "Back to the Past: Counterfactuals and the Cuban Missile Crisis," in Tetlock and Belkin, *Counterfactual Thought Experiments in World Politics*, pp. 119–48, for our dissent.

12. Neal J. Roese and James M. Olson, "Counterfactual Thinking: A Critical Overview," in Roese and Olson, *What Might Have Been*, pp. 1–56.

13. Nelson Goodman, "The Problem of Counterfactual Conditionals," *Journal of Philosophy* 44 (1947), pp. 113–28.

14. Brian Skyrms, *Causal Necessity* (New Haven: Yale University Press, 1980), p. 95–102 on subjective conditionals.

15. S. J. Hoch, "Counterfactual Reasoning and Accuracy in Predicting Personal Events," *Journal of Experimental Psychology, Learning, Memory, and Cognition* 11 (1995), pp. 719–31; M. K. Johnson and S. J. Sherman, "Constructing and Reconstructing the Past and the Future in the Present," in E. T. Higgins and R. M. Sorrentino, eds., *Handbook of Motivation and Cognition: Foundations of Social Behavior* (New York: Guilford, 1990), vol. 2, pp. 482–526.

16. Private communication to the author.

17. *New York Times*, 27 November 1999, p. A1.

18. Yuen Foong Khong, "Confronting Hitler and Its Consequences," in Tetlock and Aaron Belkin, *Counterfactual Thought Experiments in World Politics*, pp. 95–118.

19. Lebow and Stein, "Back to the Past: Counterfactuals and the Cuban Missile Crisis."

20. Jay M. Winter, *The Great War and the British People* (London: Macmillan, 1986), 76–83.

21. Victoria Tin-bor Hui, *War and State Formation in Ancient China and Early Modern Europe* (Cambridge: Cambridge University Press, 2005). See also R. Bin Wong, *China Transformed: Historical Change and the Limits of the European Experience* (Ithaca: Cornell University Press, 1997).

22. Kenneth Pomeranz, *The Great Divergence: Europe, China and the Making of the World Economy* (Princeton: Princeton University Press, 200) and "Counterfactuals and Industrialization in Europe and China," in Tetlock, Lebow, and Parker, *Unmaking the West*, pp. 241–76.

23. Jon Elster, *Political Psychology* (New York: Cambridge University Press, 1993), p. 5; Sidney Tarrow, "Expanding Paired Comparison: A Modest Proposal,"

Comparative Politics Newsletter (Summer 1999), pp. 9–12; Doug McAdam, Sidney Tarrow, and Charles Tilly, *Dynamics of Contention* (Cambridge: Cambridge University Press, 2001).

24. Richard Ned Lebow and Janice Gross Stein, *We All Lost the Cold War* (Princeton: Princeton University Press, 1994).

25. Mark Elvin, *The Pattern of the Chinese Past: A Social and Economic Interpretation* (Stanford: Stanford University Press, 1973).

26. Kenneth A. Oye, "Explaining the End of the Cold War: Morphological and Behavioral Adaptations to the Nuclear Peace?" in Richard Ned Lebow and Thomas Risse-Kappen, *International Relations Theory and the End of the Cold War* (New York: Columbia University Press, 1995), pp. 57–84; Stephen G. Brooks and William C. Wohlforth, "Power, Globalization and the End of the Cold War: Reevaluating a Landmark Case for Ideas," *International Security* 25, no. 3 (2000/2001), pp. 5–53; James W. Davis and William C. Wohforth, "German Unification," in Richard K. Herrmann and Richard Ned Lebow, eds., *Ending the Cold War* (New York: Palgrave-Macmillan, 2006), pp. 131–60.

27. For example, Robert D. English, *Russia and the Idea of the West: Gorbachev, Intellectuals, and the End of the Cold War* (New York: Columbia University Press, 2000); Archie Brown, *The Gorbachev Factor* (Oxford: Oxford University Press, 1996); Jacques Lévesque, *The Enigma of 1989: The USSR and the Liberation of Eastern Europe* (Berkeley: University of California Press, 1997); Matthew Evangelista, *Unarmed Forces: The Transnational Movement to End the Cold War* (Ithaca: Cornell University Press, 1999.

28. E. H. Carr, *Socialism in One Country, 1924–1926*, 3 vols. (New York: Macmillan, 1958–1964), vol. 1, p. 151.

29. John Lukacs, "Counterfactual Is Wrong," *Historically Speaking*, 7, no. 2 (November–December 2005), and *Five Days in London May 1940* (New Haven: Yale University Press, 1999); Richard Ned Lebow, "John Lukacs, Meet Madame Jourdain," *Historically Speaking* 7, no. 4 (March/April 2006), pp. 50–51.

30. Lebow and Stein, *We All Lost the Cold War*, ch. 4; Raymond L. Garthoff, *Reflections on the Cuban Missile Crisis*, rev. ed. (Washington, D.C.: Brookings, 1989), for this evidence.

31. Robert Jervis, *Perception and Misperception in International Politics* (Princeton: Princeton University Press, 1976), pp. 17–42, 128–30, 187–91; Irving L. Janis and Leon Mann, *Decision Making: A Psychological Analysis of Conflict, Choice, and Commitment* (New York: Free Press, 1977), pp. 15, 55–57, 73.

32. G.E.M. Anscombe, "On Brute Facts," *Analysis*, 18 (1958), pp. 69–72.

33. John R. Searle, *The Construction of Social Reality* (New York: Free Press, 1995).

34. Donald Davidson and Jaakko Hintikka, eds., *Words and Objections: Essays on the work of W. V. Quine* (Dordrecht, D. Reidel, 1969).

35. Paul Diesing, *How Social Science Works* (Pittsburgh: Pittsburgh University Press, 1991), chap. 2; Steve Fuller, *Social Epistemology* (Bloomington: Indiana University Press, 1991); Roy Bhaskar, *The Possibility of Naturalism: A Philosophical Critique of Contemporary Human Sciences* (Brighton: Harvester Press, 1979); Friedrich V. Kratochwil, "Evidence, Inference, and Truth as Problems in

Theory Building in the Social Sciences," in Lebow and Lichbach, *Theory and Evidence in Comparative Politics and International Relations*, pp. 25–64.

36. Baruch Fischoff, "Hindsight Is Not Equal to Foresight: The Effect of Outcome Knowledge on Judgment under Uncertainty," *Journal of Experimental Psychology: Human Perception and Performance* 1, no.2 (1975), pp. 288–99; S. A. Hawkins and R. Hastie, "Hindsight: Biased Judgments of Past Events after the Outcomes Are Known," *Psychological Bulletin* 107, no. 3 (1990), pp. 311–27. The tendency was earlier referred to as "retrospective determinism" in comparative-historical studies by Reinhard Bendix, *Nation-Building and Citizenship* (New York: Wiley, 1964).

37. L. Ross, M. R. Lepper, F. Strack, and J. Steinmetz, "Social Explanation and Social Expectation: Effects of Real and Hypothetical Explanations on Subjective Likelihood," *Journal of Personality and Social Psychology*, 35 (1977), pp. 817–29.

38. Kenneth N. Waltz, *Theory of International Politics* (Reading, Mass.: Addison-Wesley, 1979); John Lewis Gaddis, *The Long Peace: Inquiries into the History of the Cold War Era* (New York: Oxford University Press, 1987); Robert Gilpin, *War and Change in World Politics* (New York: Cambridge University Press, 1981), pp. 232–33; Robert O. Keohane, *After Hegemony* (Princeton: Princeton University Press, 1984); Duncan Snidal, "The Limits of Hegemonic Stability Theory," *International Organization* 39 (Autumn 1985), pp. 579–614.

39. Leften Stavros Stavrianos et al, *A Global History of Man* (Boston: Allyn and Bacon, 1966).

40. Hui, *Rethinking War, State Formation, and System Formation*, p. 7.

41. Kwang-chih Chang, *Art, Myth and Ritual: The Path to Political Authority in Ancient China*, Cambridge: Cambridge University Press, 1983), pp. 128–29.

42. Roese and Olson, *What Might Have Been*, p. 11; Daniel Kahneman and C. A. Varey, "Propensities and Counterfactuals: The Loser that Almost Won," *Journal of Personality and Social Psychology* 59 (1990), pp. 1101–10; J. L. Mackie, *Cement of the Universe: A Study of Causation* (London: Oxford University Press, 1974): P. A. White, "Ideas about Causation in Philosophy and Psychology," *Psychological Bulletin* 108 (1990), pp. 3–18.

43. H. H. Kelley, "Attribution in Social Interaction," in E. E. Jones, D. E. Kanouse, H. H. Kelley, R. E. Nisbet, S. Valins, and B. Weiner, eds., *Attribution: Perceiving the Causes of Behavior* (Morristown, N.J.: General Learning Press,1972), pp. 1–26; Christopher G. Davis and Darrin R. Lehman, "Counterfactual Thinking and Coping with Traumatic Life Events," in Roese and Olson, *What Might Have Been*, pp. 353–74; Barbara A. Spellman and David R. Mandel, "When Possibility Informs Reality: Counterfactual Thinking as a Cue to Causality," *Current Developments in Psychological Science*, vol. 8 (1999), pp. 461–66; Barbara A. Spellman, Alexandra P. McKincannon, and Stephen J. Stose, "The Relations between Counterfactual and Causal Reasoning," in David R. Mandel, Denis J. Hilton, and Patrizia Catellani, *The Psychology of Counterfactual Thinking* (London: Routledge, 2005), pp. 28–43.

44. Robyn M. Dawes, "Counterfactual Inferences as Instances of Statistical Inferences," in Tetlock and Belkin, *Counterfactual Experiments in World Politics*,

pp. 301–8. Strictly speaking it does not follow that if x then y; therefore, if not-x, then not-y, because factors other than x may also cause y.

45. Donald Green and Alan S. Gerber, "Reclaiming the Experimental Tradition in Political Science." In Helen V. Milner and Ira Katznelson, eds., *Political Science: The State of the Discipline*, 3rd ed. (New York: Norton , 2002), pp. 805–32.

46. Harry Eckstein, "Case Study and Theory in Political Science," in Fred I. Greenstein and Nelson W. Polsby, eds. *Handbook of Political Science*, vol. 7: *Political Science: Scope and Theory* (Reading, Mass.: Addison-Wesley, 1975), pp. 94–137; Lijphart, "Comparative Politics and the Comparative Method"; Charles Ragin and Howard S. Becker, *What Is a Case? Exploring the Foundations of Social Inquiry* (Cambridge: Cambridge University Press, 1992); Alexander L. George and Andrew Bennett, *Case Studies and Theory Development* (Cambridge: M.I.T. Press, 2005); John Gerring, *Case Study Research: Principles and Practices* (Cambridge: Cambridge University Press, 2007).

47. See, for example, Alexander L. George and Richard Smoke, *Deterrence in American Foreign Policy: Theory and Practice* (New York: Columbia University Press, 1974); Alexander L. George and William E. Simmons, eds., *The Limits of Coercive Diplomacy* (Boulder, Colo.: Westview, 1994); Ted Hopf, *Peripheral Visions: Deterrence Theory and American Foreign Policy, 1965–1990* (Ann Arbor: University of Michigan Press, 1994); Robert Jervis and Jack Snyder, Eds., *Dominoes and Bandwagons: Strategic Beliefs and Great Power Competition in the Eurasian Rimland* (New York: Oxford University Press, 1991); Thomas Risse-Kappen, *Cooperation among Democracies: The European Influence on U.S. Foreign Policy* (Princeton: Princeton University Press, 1995).

48. Lars-Eric Cederman, "Rerunning History: Counterfactuals Simulation in World Politics," in Tetlock and Belkin, *Counterfactual Thought Experiments in World Politics*, pp. 247–67.

49. George W. Breslauer, "Counterfactuals Reasoning in Western Studies of Soviet Politics and Foreign Relations," in Tetlock and Belkin, *Counterfactual Thought Experiments in World Politics*, pp. 69–94, discusses this literature.

50. Tetlock, Lebow, and Parker, *Unmaking the West*.

51. John Mueller, *Retreat from Doomsday: The Obsolescence of Major War* (New York: Basic Books, 1989) and the debate on this subject between Mueller, "The Essential Irrelevance of Nuclear Weapons: Stability in the Postwar World," and Robert Jervis, "The Political Effects of Nuclear Weapons: A Comment," *International Security* 13 (Fall 1988), pp. 55–90.

52. Daniel Kahneman, Paul Slovic, and Amos Tversky, *Judgment under Uncertainty: Heuristics and Biases* (New York: Cambridge University Press,1982), pp. 201–8; Neal J. Roese, "The Functional Basis of Counterfactual Thinking," *Journal of Personality and Social Psychology*, 66 (1994), pp. 805–18; Near J. Roese and James M. Olson, "Counterfactual Thinking: A Critical Overview," in Roese and Olson, eds., *What Might Have Been*, pp. 1–56.

53. J. Landman, "Regret and Elation Following Action and Inaction: Affective Responses to Positive versus Negative Outcomes, *Personality and Social Psychology Bulletin*, 13 (1992), pp. 524–36; J. Baron, "The Effect of Normative Beliefs on Anticipated Emotions," *Journal of Personality and Social Psychology*, 63 (1992), pp. 320–30; David R. Mandel, "Counterfactuals, Emotions and Context," *Cogni-*

tion and Emotion, 17 (2003), pp. 139–59; Keith D. Markham and Matthew N. McMullen, "A Reflection and Evaluation Model of Comparative Thinking," *Personality and Social Psychology Review*, 7 (1993), pp. 244–67; Matthew N. McMullen, "Affective Contrast and Assimilation in Counterfactual Thinking," *Journal of Experimental Social Psychology*, 65 (1999), pp. 812–21; L. J. Sanna, "Defensive Pessimism, Optimism, and Simulating Alternatives: Some Ups and Downs of Prefactual and Counterfactual Thinking," *Journal of Personality and Social Psychology*, 71 (1996), pp. 1020–36; Keith D. Markham and Matthew N. McMullen, "Reflective and Evaluative Modes of Mental Simulation," in Mandel, Hilton, and Catellani, *The Psychology of Counterfactual Thinking*, pp. 77–93.

54. Richard Ned Lebow and Janice Gross Stein, *We All Lost the Cold War* (Princeton: Princeton University Press, 1994), for a strong statement of this argument.

55. Paul Johnson, "Glad Bush Is Still Around," *Forbes*, 5 May 2008. http://www.forbes.com/forbes/2008/0505/027.html.

56. See Yuen Foong Khong, *Analogies at War: Korea, Munich, Dien Bien Phu, and the Vietnam Decisions of 1965* (Princeton: Princeton University Press, 1992), for a strong statement of the former position with regard to historical analogies.

57. Alessandro Portelli, "Uchronic Dreams: Working-Class Memory and Possible Worlds," in *The Death of Luigi Trastulli and Other Stories: Form and Meaning in Oral History* (Albany: State University of New York Press, 1991), pp. 99-116.

58. L. Simon, J. Arndt, J. Greenberg, T. Pyszczynski, and S. Solomon, "Terror Management and Meaning: Evidence that the Opportunity to Defend the World-View in Response to Mortality Salience Increases the Meaningfulness of Life in the Mildly Depressed," *Journal of Personality* 66 (1998), pp. 359–82. Richard Ned Lebow, *A Cultural Theory of International Relations* (Cambridge: Cambridge University Press, 2008), for the relevance of the search for self-esteem and figurative immortality for politics and international relations.

59. Andrew D. Galinsky, Katie A. Liljenquist, Laura J. Kray, and Neal J. Roese, "Finding Meaning from Mutability," in David R. Mandel, Denis J. Hilton and Patrizia Catellani, *The Psychology of Counterfactual Thinking* (London: Routledge, 2005), pp. 111–25.

60. Tetlock and Belkin, "Counterfactual Thought Experiments in World Politics," for a discussion of these two kinds of counterfactuals.

61. John Elster, *Logic and Society: Contradictions and Possible Worlds* (New York: John Wiley, 1978); Geoffrey Hawthorn, *Plausible Worlds: Possibility and Understanding in History and the Social Sciences* (New York: Cambridge University Press, 1991), pp. 31–60.

62. This is a variant of the counterfactual (Bosnians as bottle-nosed dophins) used Tetlock and Belkin, *Counterfactual Thought Experiments in World Politics*, p. 14, fn. 23.

63. Ludwig Dehio, *The Precarious Balance: Four Centuries of the European Power Struggle* (New York: Knopf, 1995), argues that competition among many independent units produced "fertile friction" among Greek city-states and in modern Europe.

64. Newton reasoned that the energy reaching us from an individual star is E/r^2, where r is the distance of the star, and E is the average energy radiated by each star, and if the density (d) of stars in the universe is constant, the number of

stars would be d r^3. The total energy produced by these stars would grow in a linear fashion with r, and rise to infinity in an infinite universe—neither we nor the earth would exist. Hence, the density of stars must decrease or the universe must be finite.

65. Andrew Marvell, "To His Coy Mistress," Hug MacDonald, ed., *Andrew Marvell* (London: Routledge and Kegan Paul, 1952), pp. 21–22.

66. Francis Kaplan, ed., *Les Pensées de Pascal* (Paris: Les Éditions du Cerf, 1982), p. 209.

67. René de Doscinny and Albert de Uderzo, *Astérix et Cleopatre* (Neuilly-sur-Seine: Dargaud, 1965). Is it a coincidence that this publishing house is located at 12, rue Blaise-Pascal? The Turkish saying was brought to my attention by Prof. Orhan Tekelioglu of Bilkent University.

68. Niall Ferguson, ed. *Virtual History: Alternatives and Counterfactuals* (New York: Basic Books, 1999) and *The Pity of War: Explaining World War I* (New York: Basic Books, 1999).

69. Ferguson, ed. *Virtual History*, pp. 11–12.

70. Henry Ashby Turner, Jr., *Geissel des Jahrhunderts: Hitler and seine Hinterlassenschaft* (Berlin: Siedler, 1989); Geoffrey Parker, *The Grand Strategy of Philip II* (New Haven: Yale University Press, 1998), pp. 129–34; Geoffrey Parker, "The Repulse of the English Fireships," in Robert Cowley, ed., *What If?* (New York: G. P. Putnam's Sons, 1998), pp. 139–54.

71. Max Weber, "Objective Possibility and Adequate Causation in Historical Explanation," in *The Methodology of the Social Sciences* (Glencoe, Ill.: Free Press of Glencoe, 1949 [1905]), pp. 164–88.

72. P. Nash, "The Use of Counterfactuals in History: A Look at the Literature," *SHAFR Newsletter* (March 1991), pp. 2–12, offers a similarly restrictive definition.

73. Daniel Kahneman, "Varieties of Counterfactual Thinking," in Roese and Olson, *What Might Have Been*, pp. 375–96; P. A. White, "Ideas about Causation in Philosophy and Psychology," *Psychological Bulletin* 108 (1990), pp. 3–18. Nicholas Rescher, *Hypothetical Reasoning* (Amsterdam: North Holland, 1964), on conditions of counterfactual truthfulness.

74. Cederman, "Rerunning History," pp. 253, 255, for this criticism of Mueller.

75. Tetlock, "Distinguishing Frivolous from Serious Counterfactuals," unpublished paper.

76. Parker, *The Grand Strategy of Philip II*, pp. 281–96.

77. M. Maruyama, "The Second Cybernetics: Deviation-Amplifying Mutual Causal Processes," *American Scientist* 51, no. 2 (1963), pp. 164–79, contends that the very essence of the "butterfly effect" is that it cannot be discovered. He offers the example of a city built on the American plains because the first white settler awoke on an especially beautiful morning and took it as a sign to put down his stakes here rather than somewhere else. The coincidence of weather and intent was unpredictable, and would be invisible as a cause to researchers a century later attempting to discover why the city grew up where it did.

78. Fearon, "Causes and Counterfactuals in Social Science," in Tetlock and Belkin, *Counterfactual Experiments in World Politics*, p. 50.

79. Dawes, "Counterfactual Inferences as Instances of Statistical Inferences," in Tetlock and Belkin, *Counterfactual Thought Experiments in World Politics*, pp. 301–8.

80. Edgar Kiser and Margaret Levi, "Using Counterfactuals in Historical Analysis: Theories of Revolution," in Tetlock and Belkin, *Counterfactual Thought Experiments in World Politics*, pp. 187–210.

81. Elster, *Logic and Society*, pp. 184–85.

82. Weber, "Counterfactuals, Past and Future," pp. 278, 272.

83. Fearon, "Causes and Counterfactuals in Social Science," p. 54.

84. Richard Ned Lebow, "Contingency, Catalysts and International System Change."

85. On this question, see Steven Weber, "Counterfactuals, Past and Future," in Tetlock and Belkin, *Counterfactual Thought Experiments in World Politics*, pp. 268–90; David Waldner, "Transforming Inferences into Explanations: Lessons from the Study of Mass Extinctions," in Lebow and Lichbach, *Theory and Evidence in Comparative Politics and International Relations*, pp. 145–76.

86. Weber, "Counterfactuals, Past and Future."

87. Tetlock and Belkin, "Counterfactual Thought Experiments in World Politics," pp. 16–32; Philip Tetlock, "Distinguishing Frivolous from Serious Counterfactuals"; Lebow and Stein, "Back to the Past," pp. 146–47.

88. Geoffrey Hawthorn, *Possible Worlds: Possibility and Understanding in History and the Social Sciences* (Cambridge: Cambridge University Press, 1991), pp. 31–60.

89. Ibid, p. 54–60.

90. Robert Fogel, *Railroads and American Economic Growth: Essays in Econometric History* (Baltimore: Johns Hopkins University Press, 1964).

91. John Elster, *Logic and Society: Contradictions and Possible Worlds* (New York: Wiley, 1978), pp. 204–8; Tetlock and Belkin, "Counterfactual Thought Experiments," pp. 22–23.

92. Holger H. Herwig, "Hitler Wins in the East but Still Loses World War II," in Tetlock, Lebow, and Parker, *Unmaking the West*, pp. 323–62, for the many difficulties standing in the way of German victory in World War II.

93. Weber, "Objective Possibility and Adequate Causation in Historical Explanation."

94. Friedrich Engels suggested something similar. History was a "parallelogram of forces." If one person shook his arms to move one corner of the parallelogram, it affected parts of the figure far away and far removed from intentions of the actor. Richard J. Evans, *In Defense of History* (New York: Norton, 1999), p. 118.

95. Herwig, "Hitler Wins in the East but Still Loses World War II."

96. Lebow, and Parker, *Unmaking the West*.

97. Carl von Clausewitz, *On War*, trans. Michael Howard and Peter Parent (Princeton: Princeton University Press, 1976), pp. 119–21.

98. Lebow, *Cultural Theory of International Relations*, ch. 2 for a critical examination of level of analysis.

99. J. L. Mackie, "Causes and Conditions," in Myles Brand, ed., *The Nature of Causation* (Urbana: University of Illinois Press, 1976), pp. 308–44; Roy Chaska,

The Possibility of Naturalism: A Philosophical Critique of the Contemporary Human Science (Brighton: Harvester Press, 1979); Rom Haré and Peter Second, *The Explanation of Social Behavior* (Oxford: Basil Blackwell, 1973); Heikke Patomäki, "How to Tell Better Stories about World Politics," *European Journal of International Relations* 2 (March 1996), pp. 105–34.

100. Carlos N. Eire, "Religious Kitsch or Industrial Revolution," Kenneth Pomeranz, "Without Coal? Colonies? Calculus?" Joel Mokyr, "King Kong and Cold Fusion," in Tetlock, Lebow, and Parker, *Unmaking the West*, pp. 145–67, 241–76, 277–322.

101. Eire, "Religious Kitsch or Industiral Revolution," Jack A. Goldstone, "'Would the World Be 'Modern' If William III's Invasion of England in 1688 Had Failed?"; Carla Gardina Pestana, "A Response to Jack Goldstone's 'Europe's' Peculiar Path"; and Mokyr, "Counterfactual Analysis and the History of Technology," in Tetlock, Lebow, and Parker, *Unmaking the West*, pp. 145–67, 168–96, 197–204, 277–322.

102. Ross Hassig, *Aztec Warfare: Imperial Expansion and Political Control* (Norman: University of Oklahoma Press, 1988), pp. 236–51.

103. See chapter 5 for assessments of this question by historians.

104. Feng-husing Hsu, Thomas Anantharaman, Murray Campbell, and Andrew Nowatzyk, "A Grandmaster Chess Machine," *Scientific American* (October 1990) 263, pp. 44–50; "The Deep Blue Team Plots Its Next Move," www .research.ibm.com/deepblue/home/may11/story_1.html, a website that includes more articles, the games, and commentary on the play.

CHAPTER THREE

Moltke the Elder, quoted in Stig Förster, "Dreams and Nightmares: German Military Leadership and the Images of Future Warfare, 1871–1914," in Manfred F. Boemeke, Roger Chickering, and Stig Förster, eds., *Anticipating Total War: The German and American Experiences, 1971–1914* (Washington, D.C.: German Historical Institute, 1999), quote on p. 347.

Virginia von Hötzendorf, *Mein Leben mit Conrad von Hötzendorf*, 18 August 1914, p. 118, translation from Holger H. Herwig, *The First World War*: Germany and Austria Hungary, 1914–1918 (London: Arnold, 1998), p. 11.

1. F. H. Hinsley, "The Origins of the First World War," in Keith Wilson, ed., *Decisions for War, 1914* (New York: St. Martin's Press, 1995), p. 4.

2. In addition to Conrad, cited below, see the comments of Theobald von Bethmann-Hollweg and V. I. Lenin, quoted in James Joll, *The Origins of the First World War*, 2nd ed. (London: Longman, 1992), pp. 236–43, and David Lloyd George, *War Memoirs of David Lloyd George* (Boston: Little, Brown, 1933–37), vol. 1, p. 2.

3. Franz Conrad von Hötzendorf, *Aus meiner Dienstzeit*, 5 vols. (Vienna: Rikola, 1921–25), vol. 1, p. 8.

4. Princip told this to Dr. Martin Pappenheim, an Austrian psychiatrist, who conducted extensive interviews with him in Theresienstadt (Terezin) fortress in

1916. Cited in Z.A.B. Zeman, "The Balkans and the Coming of War," in R.J.W. Evans and Hartmut Pogge von Strandmann, eds., *The Coming of the First World War* (Oxford: Oxford University Press, 1988), p. 24.

5. Holger Afflerbach, "Topos of Improbable War Before 1914," in Holger Afflerbach and David Stevenson, eds., *An Improbable War: The Outbreak of World War I and European Political Culture before 1914* (New York: Berghahn Books, 2007), pp. 161–82.

6. Roger Chickering, "'War Enthusiasm?' Public Opinion and the Outbreak of War in 1914," in Afflerbach and Stevenson, *An Improbable War*, 200–212.

7. Sidney B. Fay, *The Origins of the World War*, 2 vols. (New York: Macmillan, 1928).

8. Fritz Fischer, *Germany's Aims in the First World War*, trans. Marian Jackson (New York: W. W. Norton, 1967) and *War of Illusions: German Policies from 1911 to 1914*, trans. Marian Jackson (New York: Norton, 1975).

9. R. H. Tawney, *The Agrarian Problem in the Sixteenth Century* (London: Longmans, Green, 1912), p. 177.

10. Charles Tilly, ed., *The Formation of National States in Western Europe* (Princeton: Princeton University Press, 1975), pp. 9, 14–15.

11. Alexander Demandt, *Der Fall Roms: die Auflosung des romischen Reiches im Urteil der Nachwelt* (Munich: Beck, 1984), p. 695, found 210 causes for the fall of Rome in the historical literature since 1600.

12. Paul W. Schroeder, "World War I as Galloping Gertie: A Reply to Joachim Remak," *Journal of Modern History* 44 (1972), pp. 319–45, reasons: "The fact that so many plausible explanations for the outbreak of war have been advanced over the years indicates on the one hand that it was massively overdetermined."

13. I am using the term *gestalt* here to imply a collection of psychological and symbolic entities that creates a unified configuration or pattern that is greater than the sum of its parts. Gestalt psychologists rejected elemental approaches that sought to understand perception by breaking it down into its constituent parts. They maintained that perception has properties that cannot be predicted from the study of its parts, just as the properties of a chemical cannot be predicted from knowledge of its individual molecules. The meaning, or properties, of perceptions is determined by the cognitive scheme imposed on them. Different cognitive schemas lead to different perceptions, as was the case in Germany, Austria, and Russia on the eve of the war. On gestalt psychology, see Kurt Koffka, *Principles of Gestalt Psychology* (New York: Harcourt, Brace and World, 1935); Wolfgang Köhler, *The Place of Value in a World of Facts* (New York: Liveright, 1938).

14. Fritz Stern, "Bethmann Hollweg and the War: The Limits of Responsibility," in Fritz Stern and Leonard Krieger, eds., *The Responsibility of Power: Historical Essays in Honor of Hajo Holborn* (Garden City, N.Y.: Doubleday, 1967), pp. 252–85; Konrad J. Jarausch, "The Illusion of Limited War: Chancellor Bethmann Hollweg's Calculated Risk, July 1914," *Central European History* 2 (March 1969), 48–76, and *The Enigmatic Chancellor: Bethmann Hollweg and the Hubris of Imperial Germany* (New Haven: Yale University Presses, 1973); Karl Dietrich Erdmann, "War Guilt 1914 Reconsidered: A Balance of New Research," in H. W. Koch, ed., *The Origins of the First World War*, 2nd ed. (Oxford: Oxford University Press, 1984), pp. 343–70; Wolfgang J. Mommsen, *Das Zeitalter des*

Imperialismus (Frankfurt, Fischer Bucherei, 1969) and "Domestic Factors in German Foreign Policy Before 1914," *Central European History* 6 (March 1972), pp. 3–43; Andreas Hilgruber, "Riezlers Theorie des kalkulieren Risikos und Bethmann Hollwegs politische Konzeption in der Julikrise 1914," *Historische Zeitschrift* 202 (1966), pp. 333–51; Egmont Zechlin, *Krieg und Kriegrisiko: Zur deutschen Politik im Ersten Weltkrieg* (Düsseldorf: Droste, 1979); David Kaiser, "Germany and the Origins of the First World War," *Journal of Modern History* 55 (1983), pp. 442–74; Hartmut Pogge von Strandmann, "Germany and the Coming of War," in Evans and Pogge von Strandmann, *The Coming of the First World War,* pp. 87–124; Herwig, *The First World War,* ch. 1; John C. G. Röhl, "Germany," in Keith Wilson, ed., *Decisions for War, 1914* (New York: St. Martin's Press, 1995), pp. 27–54; Richard Ned Lebow, *A Cultural Theory of International Relations* (Cambridge: Cambridge University Press, 2008), ch. 7. On Austria, see Samuel R. Williamson Jr., "Influence, Power, and the Policy Process: The Case of Franz Ferdinand," *The Historical Journal* 17 (1974), pp. 417–34, "The Origins of World War I," *Journal of Interdisciplinary History* 18 (1988), pp. 795–818, and *Austria-Hungary and the Origins of the First World War* (London: Macmillan, 1990); R. J. Evans, "The Habsburg Monarchy and the Coming of War," in Evans and Pogge von Strandmann, eds., *The Coming of the First World War,* pp. 33–56; Lebow, *Cultural Theory of International Relations,* ch. 7.

15. Kurt Riezler, *Tagebücher, Aufsatze, Dokumente. Eingeleidet und hrs. Von Karl Dietrich Erdmann* (Göttingen: Vandenhoeck and Ruprecht, 1972); Koch, ed., *The Origins of the First World War,* Introduction.

16. There is something of a consensus that Moltke expected a long and costly war. See Gerhard Ritter, *The Schlieffen Plan,* trans. Andrew and Eva Wilson (New York: Praeger, 1958); Jack L. Snyder, *The Ideology of the Offensive: Military Decision Making and the Disasters of 1914* (Ithaca: Cornell University Press, 1984), pp. 107–56; Annika Mombauer, *Helmuth von Moltke and the Origins of the First World War* (Cambridge: Cambridge University Press, 2001), pp. 72–105; Gunther E. Rothenberg, "Moltke, Schlieffen and the Doctrine of Envelopment," in Peter Paret, ed., *Makers of Modern Strategy: From Machiavelli to the Nuclear Age* (Princeton: Princeton University Press, 1985), pp. 296–325; Holger H. Herwig, "Germany and the 'Short War' Illusion: Toward a New Interpretation?" *Journal of Military History,* 66, no. 3 (July 2002), pp. 681–93. For Zuber's writings, see Terence Zuber, "The Schlieffen Plan Reconsidered," *War in History* 6, no. 3 (July 1999), pp. 262–305, "Debate: Terence Holmes Reinvents the Schlieffen Plan," *War in History* 8, no. 4 (November 2001), pp. 468–76, "Debate: Terence Holmes Reinvents the Schlieffen Plan—Again," *War in History* 10 no. 1 (January 2003), pp. 92–101, "Debate: The 'Schlieffen Plan' Was an Orphan," *War in History* 11, no. 2 (April 2004), pp. 220–25, *Inventing the Schlieffen Plan: German War Planning, 1871–1914* (Oxford: Oxford University Press, 2002); *German War Planning, 1891–1914: Sources and Interpretations* (Woodbridge, Sussex: Boydell, 2004). For Zuber's critics, see Terence M. Holmes, "Debate: The Reluctant March on Paris: A Reply to Terence Zuber," *War in History* 8, no. 2 (April 2001), pp. 208–32; "Debate: The Real Thing: A Reply to Terence Zuber's 'Terence Holmes Reinvents the Schlieffen Plan,'" *War in History,* 9 no. 1 (January 2002), pp. 111–20; Robert T. Foley, "Debate: The Origins of the Schlieffen Plan," *War in*

History 10, no. 2 (April 2003), pp. 222–32 and "Debate: The Real Schlieffen Plan," *War in History* 13, no.1 (January 2006), pp. 91–115; Annika Mombauer, *Helmuth von Moltke*, ch. 2, "Of War Plans and War Guilt: The Debate Surrounding the Schlieffen Plan," *Journal of Strategic Studies* 28, no. 5 (2005), pp. 857–85; Herwig, "Germany and the 'Short War' Illusion."

17. Keir A. Lieber, "The New History of World War I and What It Means for International Relations Theory," *International Security* 32, no. 2 (Fall 2007), pp. 155–91; Lebow, *A Cultural Theory of International Relations*, ch. 7.

18. Paul W. Schroeder, "World War I as Galloping Gertie: A Reply to Joachim Remak," *Journal of Modern History* 44 (September 1972), pp. 319–45, is the most forceful and well-respected statement of this argument.

19. Herwig, *First World War*, p. 11; F. R. Bridge, *The Habsburg Monarchy among the Great Powers, 1815–1918* (New York: Berg, 1990), pp. 335–36; Williamson, *Austria-Hungary and the Origins of the First World War*, pp. 190–212; Günther Kronenbitter, *Krieg im Frieden: die Führung der k.u.k. Armee und die Grossmachtpolitik Österreich-Ungarns 1906–1914* (Munich: Oldenbourg, 2003), p. 483; Graydon A. Tunstall Jr., "Austria-Hungary," in Richard F. Hamilton, and Holger H. Herwig, *The Origins of World War I* (Cambridge: Cambridge University Press, 2003), pp. 112–49; Lebow, *Cultural Theory of International Relations*, ch. 7.

20. D. C. Lieven, *Russia and the Origins of the First World War* (New York: St. Martin's, 1983); D. W. Spring, "Russia and the Coming of War," in Evans and Pogge von Strandmann, eds., *The Coming of the First World War*, 57–86.

21. L.C.F. Turner, *Origins of the First World War* (New York: Norton, 1970), "The Role of the General Staffs in July 1914," *Australian Journal of Politics and History* 11 (1965), pp. 305–23; "The Russian Mobilization in 1914," *Journal of Contemporary History* 3 (1968), pp. 65–88.

22. In chapter 10 above, Paul Schroeder argues forcefully that Franco-Russian efforts to "encircle" Austria-Hungary gave it little choice but to go to war.

23. Luigi Albertini, *The Origins of the War of 1914*, ed. and trans. Isabella M. Massey (London: Oxford University Press, 1953), vol. 2, p. 6, vol. 3, pp. 523–24; Zara S. Steiner, *Britain and the Origins of the First World War* (New York: St. Martin's Press, 1977), p. 227; David M. Calleo, *The German Problem Reconsidered: Germany and the World Order, 1870 to the Present* (Cambridge: Cambridge University Press, 1978), p. 34; Sean M. Lynn-Jones, "Détente and Deterrence: Anglo-German Relations, 1911–1914," *International Security* 11 (Fall 1986), pp. 121–50.

24. Karl Dietrich Erdmann, "War Guilt 1914 Reconsidered: A Balance of New Research," in Koch, *The Origins of the First World War*, pp. 343–70; Zechlin, *Krieg und Kriegsrisiko*; Jarausch, *The Enigmatic Chancellor*, pp. 167, 170.

25. Harry Elmer Barnes, *The Genesis of the World War: An Introduction to the Problem of War Guilt* (New York: Knopf, 1926); Kaiser, "Germany and the Origins of the First World War" in H. W. Koch, ed., *The Origins of the First World War* 2nd ed. (Oxford: Oxford University Press, 1984).

26. Karl Popper, *The Logic of Scientific Discovery* (New York: Harper, 1968).

27. On this distinction, see Isaiah Berlin, *The Hedgehog and the Fox* (New York: Simon and Schuster, 1966).

28. Imanuel Geiss, ed., *Julikrise und Kriegsausbruch des Ersten Weltkrieges* (Munich: 1965), ch 1.

29. On case studies, see Harry Eckstein, "Case Study and Theory in Political Science," in Fred Greenstein and Nelson Polsby, eds., *Handbook of Political Science* (Chicago: Addison Wesley, 1975), pp. 79–138; Alexander L. George, "Case Theories and Theory Development: The Method of Structured Focused Comparison," in Paul G. Lauren, ed., *Diplomacy: New Approaches in History* (New York: Free Press, 1979); Ian Lustick, "History, Historiography and Political Science," *American Political Science Review* 90 (September 1996), pp. 505–18.

30. Robert Jervis, *System Effects: Complexity in Political and Social Life* (Princeton: Princeton University Press, 1997).

31. Mombauer, *Helmuth von Moltke and the Origins of the First World War,* pp. 210–13; Hull, *The Entourage of Kaiser Wilhelm II*, p. 205; John G. Röhl, *Germany without Bismarck* (Berkeley: University of California Press, 1967), p. 161; Mombauer, *Helmuth von Moltke and the Origins of the First World War*, p. 24.

32. Barry Nalebuff, "Brinkmanship and Nuclear Deterrence: The Neutrality of Escalation," *Conflict Management and Peace Science* 9 (September 1985), pp. 19–30; Robert Powell, "Crisis Bargaining, Escalation, and MAD," *American Political Science Review* 81 (September 1987), pp. 717–27, and "Nuclear Brinkmanship with Two-Sided Incomplete Information," *American Political Science Review* 82 (March 1988), pp.155–78; Steven J. Brams, *Superpower Games* (New Haven: Yale University Press, 1985), pp. 48–85.

33. Richard Ned Lebow, "Beyond Parsimony: Rethinking Theories of Coercive Bargaining," *European Journal of International Relations* 4 (March 1998), pp. 31–66.

34. Ritter, *Sword and Scepter*, vol. 2, p. 234, quoting from minutes in the General Staff section of the Austrian War Archives; Virginia Conrad von Hötzendorf, *Mein Leben mit Conrad von* Hötzendorf (Leipzig, Grethlein, 1935), letter of 26 December 1908, pp. 30–31; Conrad's talk with Aehrenthal, 18 February 1909. Both cited in Herwig, *First World War*, p. 10; Tunstall, *Planning for War against Russian and Serbia*, pp. 167–88; Kronenbitter, *Krieg im Frieden*, pp. 455–86, on the role of revenge more generally for the Austro-Hungarian leadership.

35. Lebow, *Between Peace and War*, ch. 2.

36. Senator Gravel Edition, *The Pentagon Papers: The Defense Department History of United States Decisionmaking in Vietnam,* 4 vols. (Boston: Beacon Press, 1971), vol. 3, pp. 687–91; Townsend Hoopes, *The Limits of Intervention: An Inside Account of How the Johnson Policy of Escalation Was Reversed* (New York: David McKay, 1969), p. 30.

37. Remak, "1914—the Third Balkan War."

38. Bridge, *From Sadowa to Sarajevo*, pp. 334–5.

39. Remak, "1914—the Third Balkan War"; Bridge, *The Habsburg Monarchy,* pp. 335–37; Herwig, *The First World War*, pp. 8–18; Bridge, *From Sadowa to Sarajevo*, pp. 335–36; Sondhaus, *Franz Conrad von Hötzendorf*, pp. 94–95, 117; John Leslie, "The Antecedents of Austria-Hungary's War Aims: Policies and Policy-Makers in Vienna and Budapest before and during 1914," in Elisabeth Springer and Leopold Kammerhold, eds., *Archiv and Forschung: Das Haus-, Hof- und Staatsarchiv in seiner Beudeutung für die Geschichte Österreichs und*

Europas (Vienna: Verlag für Geschichte und Politik 1993), pp. 348–75; Kronen-bitter, *Krieg im Frieden*, passim.

40. Conrad's memorandum to Franz-Josef, 1 July 1914, *Osterreich-Ungarns Aussenpolitik von der bosnischen Krise 1908 bis zum Kriegsausbruch 1914*, vol. 8, no. 9978; Conrad von Hötzendorf, *Mein Leben mit Conrad von Hötzendorf*, 18 August 1914, p. 118; Ritter, *Sword and Scepter*, vol. 2, p. 235; Beller, *Francis Joseph*, pp. 213–30, for a more moderate account; Williamson, *Austria-Hungary and the Origins of the First World War*, pp. 192–93; Herwig, *First World War*, pp. 11–12.

41. Samuel R. Williamson Jr. to the author, 22 January 1999.

42. Albertini, *The Origins of the War of 1914*, vol. 2, pp. 129–30; Williamson, *Austria-Hungary and the Origins of the First World War*, p. 85.

43. Williamson, "Influence, Power, and the Policy Process," and *Austria-Hungary and the Origins of the First World War*, p. 51.

44. Georg Franz, *Erzherzog Franz Ferdinand und die Pläne zur Reform der Habsburger Monarchie* (Vienna: G.D.W. Callwey, 1943), p. 107, quotes a similar statement to his wife in 1913.

45. Williamson, "Influence, Power, and the Policy Process," and "The Origins of World War I."

46. Williamson, *Austria-Hungary and the Coming of the First World War*, p. 434; Stevenson, *The First World War and International Politics*, 14, believes war much less likely in general if Franz Ferdinand had remained alive and contin-ued to exercise restraint in Vienna.

47. Kronenbitter, *Krieg im Frieden*, pp. 462–65; Leslie, "Antecedents of Aus-tria-Hungary's War Aims"; Williamson, *Austria-Hungary*, pp. 192–94.

48. József Galántai, *Hungary in the First World War* (Budapest: Akadémiai Kladó, 1989), pp. 100–18; Vermes, *István Tisza*, pp. 230–31; Williamson, "Influ-ence, Power, and the Policy Process."

49. Mombauer, *Helmuth von Moltke and the Origins of the First World War*, pp. 210–13; Hull, *The Entourage of Kaiser Wilhelm II*, p. 205; John G. Röhl, *Germany without Bismarck* (Berkeley: University of California Press, 1967), p. 161; Mombauer, *Helmuth von Moltke and the Origins of the First World War*, p. 24; Lebow, *A Cultural Theory of International Relations*, ch. 7.

50. Konrad Jarausch, e-mail to the author, 4 January 1999.

51. Mombauer, *Helmuth von Moltke and the Origins of the First World War*, p. 286. Erich von Falkenhayn wrote in his diary on 29 June 1914 that the chan-cellor wanted Russia to mobilize first so that it would appear "responsible" for the war to German public opinion.

52. Moltke to Conrad, *Der grosse Politik der europäischen Kabinette*, ed., A., Mendelsohn-Bartholdy, I. Lepsius, and F. Thimme, 40 vols. (Berlin: Deutsche Ver-lagsgesellschaft für Politik und Geschichte, 1922–27), 10 February 1913, 38/1, No. 12,824; Conrad, *Aus Meiner Deinstzeit*, vol. 3, pp. 144ff. Showalter, "The Eastern Front and German Military Planning, 1871–1914; Herwig, *First World War*, pp. 51–52 on communications between the Austrian and German staffs.

53. Alfred von Tirpitz, *Politische Dokumente*, 2 vols. (Berlin: Cotta, 1924–26), vol. 1, p. 242; Cecil, *Wilhelm II*, pp. 194–95; Hull, *The Entourage of Kaiser Wilhelm II*, p. 265, and John C. G. Röhl, *Wilhelm II: The Kaiser's Personal Mon-archy, 1888–1900* (Cambridge: Cambridge University Press, 2004), pp. 541–45.

54. Lebow, *Between Peace and War*, pp. 133–47.

55. Ibid., pp. 122–29, on the hold of the Bosnian precedent on German leaders in 1914.

56. Irving L. Janis and Leon Mann, *Decision-Making: A Psychological Analysis of Conflict: Choice and Commitment* (New York: Free Press, 1977), pp. 59–60, 205; and Lebow, *Between Peace and War*, pp. 135–45.

57. Lebow, *Between Peace and War*, pp. 133–47.

58. Dedijer, *The Road to Sarajevo*, pp. 10–12, 408–9.

59. Ibid., pp. 13–15.

60. Herman Kantorowicz, *The Spirit of British Policy and the Myth of the Encirclement of Germany* (London, 1932), p. 360; and Imanuel Geiss, *German Foreign Policy, 1871–1914* (London: Routledge and Kegan Paul, 1976), p. 126.

61. Rogger, "Russia in 1914"; Mayer, "Domestic Causes of the First World War."

62. Zeman, "The Balkans and the Coming of War"; Dedijer, *The Road to Sarajevo*, ch. 7.

63. Ritter, *The Sword and the Scepter*, vol. 2, p. 196.

64. Dennis E. Showalter, "The Eastern Front and German Military Planning, 1871–1914—Some Observations," *East European Quarterly* 15 (1981), pp. 163–80.

65. Paul Kennedy, *The Rise of Anglo-German Antagonism, 1860–1914* (London: Allen and Unwin, 1980), pp. 425–65; Zara S. Steiner, *Britain and the Origins of the First World War* (London: Macmillan, 1977), pp. 211, 228–37; Keith M. Wilson, *The Policy of the Entente: Essays on the Determinants of British Foreign Policy, 1909–1914* (Cambridge: Cambridge University Press, 1985), pp. 135–47.

66. A. D. von Zoellner, "Schlieffens Vermachtnis," *Militarwissenschaftliche Rundschau*, supplementary issue, 1938, pp. 46–48, on the war games. Cited in Snyder, *Ideology of the Offensive*, p. 142, and 46–48 on the war games. Hew Strachan, *The First World War* (Oxford: Oxford University Press, 2001), pp. 213–15.

67. Stig Förster, "Der deutsche Generalstab und die Illusion des kurzen Krieges, 1871–1914: Metakritik eines Mythos," *Militärgeschichtliche Mitteilungen* 54/1 (1995), pp. 61–95.

68. On the militarism of the army's officers and leadership, see, Helmuth Haeussler, *General William Groener and the German Army* (Madison: State Historical Society of Wisconsin, 1962), p. 72; Jarausch, *The Enigmatic Chancellor*, pp. 181–86; Ritter, *The Sword and Scepter*, vol. 2, pp. 227–75; Martin Kitchen, *The German Officer Corps, 1890–1914* (Oxford: Oxford University Press, 1968, pp. 96–114.

69. Marginalia on telegram from Lichnowsky to Jagow, 23 July 1914. Quoted in Geiss, *July 1914*, p. 171.

70. Marginalia on telegram from Lichnowsky to Jagow, *24 July 1914*. Quoted in Geiss, July 1914, p. 184. Italics in original.

71. Quoted in Fischer, *War of Illusions*, p. 478.

72. Offer, "Going to War in 1914"; Lebow, *Cultural Theory of International Relations*, ch. 7.

73. Ritter, *The Schlieffen Plan*, p. 92.

74. Hajo Holborn, *The Political Collapse of Europe* (New York: Alfred A. Knopf, 1963), for an eloquent statement of this argument.

75. Niall Ferguson, *The Pity of War* (London: Allen Lane, 1998), contends that if Britain had not intervened, or intervened too late in 1914, Germany would have won the war and created a benign suzerainty over continental Europe. Michael Howard, "Out of the Trenches," *Times Literary Supplement*, 13 November 1998, pp. 23–24, rightly takes him to task for using contingency to establish a determined alternative world. Victory might just as easily have encouraged instead of restrained German militarism. The 1914 "September Program" might be cited in evidence, as it indicates that kinds of far-reaching territorial and economic demands German industrialists were willing to press on their willing government at the moment when hopes for victory were high.

76. I expect this would still have taken considerable time. See Daniel Chirot, *The Origins of Backwardness in Eastern Europe: Economics and Politics from the Middle Ages until the Early Twentieth Century* (Berkeley: University of California Press, 1989), for structural reasons retarding eastern-European economic growth independent of the consequence of two world wars.

77. For an early argument to this effect, see Gabriel Almond and Stephen J. Genco, "Clouds, Clocks, and the Study of Politics," *World Politics* 29 (July 1977), pp. 489–522.

78. Richard Ned Lebow and Janice Gross Stein, "Understanding the End of the Cold War as a Non-Linear Confluence," in Richard K. Herrmann and Richard Ned Lebow, eds., *Ending the Cold War* (New York: Palgrave, 2004), pp. 189–218.

79. As do Paul Senese and John A. Vasquez, *Steps to War: An Empirical Study* (Princeton: Princeton University Press, 2008).

80. Organski and Kugler, *The War Ledger*; Gilpin, *War and Change in World Politics*; Charles F. Doran and Wes Parsons, "War and the Cycle of Relative Power," *The American Political Science Review* 74 (December 1960), pp. 947–65.

81. Gilpin, *War and Change in World Politics*, pp. 191–92, 197.

82. William Wohlforth, "Realism and the End of the Cold War," International Security, 19, no. 3, (Winter 1994–1995), pp. 91–129; Richard N. Lebow, "The Long Peace, the End of the Cold War, and the Failure of Realism," *International Organization* 48 (1994), pp. 249–77.

83. Steven Weber, "Prediction and the Middle East Peace Process," *Security Studies* 6 (1997), 167–79; Janice Gross Stein, et al., "Five Scenarios of the Israeli-Palestinian Relationship in 2002: Works in Progress," *Security Studies* 7 (1998), pp. 195–212; Steven Bernstein, Richard Ned Lebow, Janice Gross Stein, and Steven Weber, "God Gave Physics the Easy Problems," *European Journal of International Relations*, 6 (March 200), pp. 3–76.

84. Lebow, *Between Peace and War*, ch. 2, on Justification of hostility crises.

85. Lebow, *A Cultural Theory of International Relations*, ch. 7, for a fuller discussion.

86. Kenneth N. Waltz, *Theory of International Politics* (Reading, Mass.: Addison-Wesley, 1979); Jervis, *System Effects*; Lars-Erik Cederman, *Emergent Properties in World Politics: How States and Nations Develop and Dissolve* (Princeton: Princeton University Press, 1997).

87. Lebow and Stein, "Understanding the End of the Cold War as a Non-Linear Confluence," for discussion.

88. Niklas Luhmann, *Die Gesellschaft der Gesellschaft*, 2 vols. (Frankfurt am Main: Suhrkamp, 1998), I, ch. 2.

89. Richard Thayer, "Anomalies: The January Effect," *The Journal of Economic Perspectives* 1, no. 1 (Summer 1987), pp. 197–201.

90. Lebow, *A Cultural Theory of International Relations*, for general theory of international relations based on this premise.

CHAPTER FOUR

1. Kenneth N. Waltz, "The Emerging Structure of International Politics," *International Security* 18 (Fall 1993), pp. 5–43; Kenneth Oye, "Explaining the End of the Cold War: Morphological and Behavioral Adaptations to the Nuclear Peace?" in Richard Ned Lebow and Thomas Risse-Kappen, *International Relations Theory and the End of the Cold War* (New York: Columbia University Press, 1995), pp. 57–84. For a critique of the realist argument, see Richard Ned Lebow and John Mueller, "Realism and the End of the Cold War," *International Security* 20 (Fall 1995), pp. 185–86. Representative liberal literature includes Michael W. Doyle, "Liberalism and the End of the Cold War," and Thomas Risse-Kappen, "Ideas Do Not Float Freely: Transnational Coalitions, Domestic Structures, and the End of the Cold War," in Lebow and Risse-Kappan, *International Relations Theory and the End of the Cold War*, pp. 85–108 and 187–222; Matthew Evangelista, *Unarmed Forces: The Transnational Movement to End the Cold War* (Ithaca: Cornell University Press, 1999). The literature on the end of the Cold War, including constructivist interpretations, is reviewed by Matthew Evangelista, "Internal and External Constraints on Grand Strategy: The Soviet Case," in Richard Rosecrance and Arthur Stein, eds., *The Domestic Bases of Grand Strategy* (Ithaca: Cornell University Press, 1993), pp. 154–78, and Richard Ned Lebow, "The Rise of and Fall of the Cold War," *Review of International Studies*, Special Issue, 25, no. 5 (December 1999).

2. On conjunctional causality, see Charles C. Ragin, *The Comparative Method: Moving Beyond Qualitative and Quantitative Strategies* (Berkeley: University of California Press, 1987), pp. 25–26.

3. William Wohlforth, "New Evidence on Moscow's Cold War: Ambiguity in Search of Theory," *Diplomatic History*, 21 (Spring 1997), pp. 229–42, reviews this literature and criticizes realists for explaining ex post facto what none of them predicted ex ante.

4. Steven Weber, "Prediction and the Middle East Peace Process," *Security Studies* 6 (Summer 1997), p. 196.

5. Baruch Fischoff, "Hindsight Is Not Equal to Foresight: The Effect of Outcome Knowledge on Judgment under Uncertainty," *Journal of Experimental Psychology: Human Perception and Performance* 1, no. 2 (1975), pp. 288–99; S. A. Hawkins and R. Hastie, "Hindsight: Biased Judgments of Past Events after the Outcomes Are Known," *Psychological Bulletin* 107, no. 3 (1990), pp. 311–27. The tendency was earlier referred to as "retrospective determinism" in

comparative-historical studies by Reinhard Bendix, *Nation-Building and Citizenship* (New York: Wiley, 1964).

6. Waltz, "The Emerging Structure of International Politics," *International Security* 18 (Fall 1993); Oye, "Explaining the End of the Cold War. In interviews with conservatives and reactionaries on the Gorbachev Politburo, conducted in Moscow in June 1999, respondents argued, for example, that a Politburo led by Yegor Ligachev during the second half of the 1980s would have acted very differently in domestic and foreign policy than did Gorbachev.

7. Norman N. Naimark, *The Russians in Germany: A History of the Soviet Zone of Occupation, 1945–1949* (Cambridge: Harvard University Press, 1995).

8. Lucius D. Clay, *Decision in Germany* (New York: Doubleday, 1950), pp. 365–66.

9. "Graduated Reciprocation in Tension-Reduction," a concept and strategy first suggested in Charles E. Osgood, "Suggestions for Winning the Real War with Communism," *Journal of Conflict Resolution*, no. 3 (1959), pp. 295–325. The strategy calls for making unilateral concessions and maintaining that posture, at least initially, even if the concessions are not reciprocated; in short, "don't take 'no' for an answer." This was the approach that Gorbachev embraced, though without necessarily being aware of Osgood or GRIT per se.

10. A man tried to shoot Gorbachev on November 7, 1990, but as he pulled the trigger, a police sergeant deflected his rifle. There was apparently an attempt to poison Gorbachev in September 1987, and the Gorbachevs were apparently shot at in September 1986. The KGB claimed in 1990 that it stopped attempts on Kremlin officials monthly. Similarly, someone shot at Brezhnev during a parade with four cosmonauts in January 1969. See Elizabeth Shogren, "Gorbachev's Would-Be Assassin," *Los Angeles Times*, 25 November 1990, p. A4; Philip Taubman, "Gorbachev Reappears at Kremlin," *New York Times*, 30 September 1987, p. A4; Antero Pietila, "Plot on Gorbachevs Rumored," *San Diego Union-Tribune*, 18 September 1986, p. A25; "KGB Tells of Foiling Kremlin Attacks," *Los Angeles Times*, 30 March 1990, p. A14; "Assassinations and Attempts," *New York Times*, 24 January 1969, p. A6; Werner Wiskari, "Brezhnev Is among World's Well-Wishers," *New York Times*, 1 April 1981, p. A21.

11. For an early sorting of Western speculation on this matter, and citations to the large Kremlinological literature on Gorbachev's rise to power, see George W. Breslauer, "From Brezhnev to Gorbachev: Ends and Means of Soviet Leadership Selection," in Raymond Taras, ed., *Leadership Change in Communist States* (London: Unwin Hyman 1989).

12. Archie Brown, *The Gorbachev Factor* (Oxford: Oxford University Press, 1996), pp. 82–88; Jerry F. Hough, *Democratization and Revolution in the USSR, 1985–1991* (Washington, D.C.: The Brookings Institution, 1997), ch. 3.

13. The notion of leadership as a process of "stretching constraints" is taken from Warren Ilchman and Norman University Presshoff, *The Political Economy of Change* (Berkeley: University of California Press, 1969).

14. On Khrushchev's foreign relations, see James G. Richter, *Khrushchev's Double Bind* (Baltimore: Johns Hopkins University Press, 1994). On Brezhnev's foreign policies, see Richard D. Anderson, *Public Politics in an Authoritarian Regime* (Ithaca: Cornell University Press, 1994); Harry Gelman, *The Brezhnev*

Politburo and the Decline of Détente (Ithaca: Cornell University Press, 1984). On U.S.-Soviet relations, John Lewis Gaddis, *Strategies of Containment* (London: Oxford University Press, 1982); Raymond L. Garthoff, *Détente and Confrontation: American-Soviet Relations from Nixon to Brezhnev* (Washington, D.C.: The Brookings Institution, 1985); Matthew Evangelista, *Unarmed Forces: The Transnational Movement to End the Cold War* (Ithaca: Cornell University Press, 1999). On the breakthrough in U.S.-Soviet relations in the 1980s, Raymond L. Garthoff, *The Great Transition* (Washington, D.C.: The Brookings Institution, 1997). On the ebb and flow of competitive and cooperative aspects of U.S. and Soviet foreign policies, Matthew Bencke, *The Politics of Space* (Boulder, Colo.: Westview, 1997).

15. George W. Breslauer and Philip Tetlock, eds., *Learning in U.S. and Soviet Foreign Policy* (Boulder, Colo.: Westview, 1991), passim; Richard Herrmann, "Conclusions: The End of the Cold War—What Have We Learned?" in Lebow and Risse-Kappen, International Relations Theory, pp. 259–84.

16. Louis Hartz, *The Liberal Tradition in America* (New York: Harcourt, Brace, 1955); Richard Herrmann, *Perceptions and Behavior in Soviet Foreign Policy* (Pittsburgh: University of Pittsburgh Press, 1985).

17. On the impact of the electoral and succession cycles on U.S.-Soviet relations, see I. M. Destler, Leslie H. Gelb, and Anthony Lake, *Our Own Worst Enemy* (New York: Simon and Schuster, 1984); Franz Schurmann, *The Logic of World Power* (New York: Pantheon Books, 1974); Gaddis, *Strategies of Containment*; George W. Breslauer, "Do Soviet Leaders 'Test' New Presidents?" *International Security* 8 (Winter 1983–84), pp. 83–101; Richter, *Khrushchev's Double Bind*.

18. On the distinction between innovative and visionary leadership, Howard Gardner, *Leading Minds: An Anatomy of Leadership* (New York: Basic Books, 1995), pp. 10–11.

19. For a detailed chronicle of Soviet policy in the early 1980s, Garthoff, *The Great Transition*, chs. 1–4. Conceptualization and categorization of types of policies pursued, however, is our own.

20. Some of these incidents are discussed in Garthoff, *The Great Transition*, pp. 149–51.

21. Although Brezhnev's policies toward the United States from 1980 to 1982 included elements of competition and conciliation, in general during this period Brezhnev temporized in order to wait and see what course the new Reagan administration would take. Brezhnev and other senior Soviet leaders hoped that Reagan would prove a second "Nixon," a conservative capable of salvaging detente. Garthoff, *The Great Transition*, pp. 54–74, esp. pp. 57, 60, and 67. See also Garthoff, *Détente and Confrontation*, pp. 1101–19.

22. Garthoff, *The Great Transition* pp. 131–36. Georgi Arbatov, *The System* (New York: Random House, 1992), pp. 276–77.

23. Jack Snyder, *Myths of Empire: Domestic Politics and International Ambition* (Ithaca: Cornell University Press, 1991), pp. 246–50.

24. *Moskovskaya pravda*, 22 February 1985; *Leningradskaya pravda*, 15 February 1985.

25. Hough, *Revolution and Democratization*; Anders Aslund, *Gorbachev's Struggle for Economic Reform*, 2nd ed. (Ithaca: Cornell University Press, 1991).

26. On Reagan's approach to the Soviet Union in his first term, George P. Schultz, *Turmoil and Triumph: My Years as Secretary of State* (New York: Charles Scribner's Sons, 1993), chs. 8, 12, 17–18, 25–26, and 30; Garthoff, *The Great Transition*, chs. 1–4; William C. Wohlforth, ed., *Witnesses to the End of the Cold War* (Baltimore: Johns Hopkins University, 1996).

27. We have decided not to pursue consideration of the counterfactual scenario that keeps a physically weakened Ronald Reagan in office and then has him win or lose the 1984 election, since we do not know how to estimate the likely behavior of a partially incapacitated Reagan.

28. Our image of George Bush is shaped by the following sources. George Bush and Brent Scowcroft, *A World Transformed* (New York: Knopf, 1998); James A. Baker III with Thomas M. DeFrank, *The Politics of Diplomacy: Revolution, War and Peace, 1989–1992* (New York: G. P. Putnam's Sons, 1995); Philip Zelikow and Condoleezza Rice, *Germany Unified and Europe Transformed: A Study in Statecraft* (Cambridge: Harvard University Press, 1995); Michael Beschloss and Strobe Talbott, *At the Highest Levels* (London: Little, Brown, 1993); and Stanley A. Renshon, ed., *The Political Psychology of the Gulf War: Leaders, Publics, and the Process of Conflict* (Pittsburgh: University of Pittsburgh Press, 1993).

29. Helen Dewar, "Senate Joins House in Backing Boycott of Moscow Olympics," *Washington Post*, 30 January 1980, p. A8. Peter Osnos, "Detente Is Dead," *Washington Post*, 30 December 1979, p. A1. Robert G. Kaiser, "Afghanistan: End of the Era of Détente," *Washington Post*, 17 January 1980, p. A1.

30. Schultz, *Turmoil and Triumph*, chs. 27, 29, 30, and 34; Garthoff, *The Great Transition*, chs. 5 and 6; Robert M. Gates, *From the Shadows* (New York: Simon and Schuster, 1996), chs. 18, 19, and 21.

31. Matthew A. Evangelista, "Cooperation Theory and Disarmament Negotiations in the 1950s," *World Politics*, 41 (July 1990), pp. 502–28.

32. Reference is to Bush's comment about President Manuel Noriega of Panama just before deciding to invade that country to seize Noriega and bring him to the United States for trial.

33. Lebow interview with Mikhail Gorbachev, Moscow, May 1989.

34. Those who, in retrospect, conclude that eastern Europeans would have overthrown communism with or without a Gorbachev in power in Moscow forget that Gorbachev's reforms, and his inhibitions about using force, combined to provide eastern European societies with a model to emulate and a realistic hope that defiance would not be met with repression; Gorbachev's model and policies also served to demoralize eastern European communist elites and to intimidate them in the face of societal defiance. Similarly, those who assume that the collapse of the Soviet Union would have followed on the heels of successful eastern European defiance vastly underestimate the intimidation level among Soviet citizens, and the collective action problems they faced, in the absence of Gorbachev's determined efforts to neuter the regime's capacity and will to use violence.

35. The term "offensive détente" is from Jack Snyder, *Myths of Empire*. Garthoff, *Détente and Confrontation*, for an encyclopedic demonstration that the detente of the 1970s was based on the mutual pursuit of unilateral advantage.

36. Witness, for example, two of Gorbachev's relatively early speeches. In his "Report to the Central Committee of the CPSU," Moscow, 27 January 1987,

Gorbachev declared that "we need democracy like air. If we fail to realize that, or if we realize it but make no real serious steps to broaden it, to advance it and to draw the country's working people extensively into the reorganization process, our policy will get choked." Also, in his 1986 party-Congress speech, he stated that "democracy is the wholesome and pure air without which a socialistic public organism cannot live a full-blooded life." Mikhail Gorbachev, "Speech to the Twenty-seventh Congress of the CPSU," Moscow, 25 February, 1986. See also Brown, *The Gorbachev Factor*, pp. 89–97; Robert G. Kaiser, *Why Gorbachev Happened* (New York: Simon and Schuster, 1991), 76–77; and Thomas H. Naylor, *The Gorbachev Strategy* (Lexington, Mass.: D.C. Heath, 1988) pp. 215–17.

37. See George W. Breslauer, "How Do You Sell a Concessionary Foreign Policy?" *Post-Soviet Affairs*, 10 (July–September 1994), pp. 277–90.

38. Michael R. Beschloss and Strobe Talbott, *At the Highest Levels* (Boston: Little, Brown, 1993), pp. 11, 29–30, 452–54. John Miller, *Mikhail Gorbachev and the End of Soviet Power* (New York: St. Martin, 1993), pp. 54–55. Christian Schmidt-Häuer, *Gorbachev* (Topsfield, MA: Salem House, 1986), pp. 115–22.

39. Brown, *The Gorbachev Factor*; Hough, *Revolution and Democratization*; Breslauer and Tetlock, *Learning in the United States and Soviet*, chs. by F. Griffiths, R. Legvold, and G. Breslauer.

40. Arbatov, *The System*, p. 294. Kaiser, *Why Gorbachev Happened*, pp. 62–73.

41. See Garthoff, *The Great Transition*, chs. 5–10.

42. The strongest statements for the view that Ronald Reagan deserves credit as the initiator of the overtures of conciliation that led to the end of the Cold War are found in Beth A. Fischer, *The Reagan Reversal: Foreign Policy and the End of the Cold War* (Columbia: University of Missouri Press, 1997); and Jack F. Matlock, Jr., *Autopsy on an Empire: The American Ambassador's Account of the Collapse of the Soviet Union* (New York: Random House, 1995).

43. H. M. Schroder, M. J. Driver, and S. Streufert, *Human Information Processing* (New York: Holt, Rinehart and Winston, 1967); and S. Streufer and S. C. Streufert, *Behavior in the Complex Environment* (New York: Wiley, 1978).

44. Nancy Reagan, *My Turn: The Memoirs of Nancy Reagan* (New York: Dell, 1989), pp. 370–71; Wohlforth, *Witnesses to the End of the Cold War*, pp. 164–65, 170, 180 (comments by Aleksandr Bessmertnykh); Schultz, *Turmoil and Triumph*, pp. 996 and 1138; Anatoly Dobrynin, *In Confidence* (New York: Random House, 1995), p. 504; Brown, *The Gorbachev Factor*, pp. 231–33.

45. Dan Oberdorfer, *The Turn: From the Cold War to a New Era: The United States and the Soviet Union, 1983–1990* (New York: Poseidon Press, 1991), p. 299; see also Beschloss and Talbott, *At the Highest Levels*, p. 132.

46. The argument is also made by Fred I. Greenstein, "Ronald Reagan, Mikhail Gorbachev, and the End of the Cold War: What Difference Did They Make?" in Wohlforth, *Witnesses to the End of the Cold War*, p. 216.

47. Brown, *The Gorbachev Factor*, pp. 230–31.

48. In Wohlforth, *Witnesses*, p. 107, and pp. 102–3 for the observation of Frank Carlucci, a cabinet member in the Reagan administration:

And the amazing thing is that the alchemy between these two disparate personalities seemed to work, that it somehow came together. There is no question that Ronald Reagan was very taken by Gorbachev; that he understood that Ronald Reagan was very taken by Gorbachev; that he understood this was a new figure in the Soviet Union; that this was a historical moment. And as our former Soviet friends have said, there's no question that Gorbachev recognized that this was a new, unique opportunity to establish a personal relationship and change the whole dynamic of the relationship.

49. George W. Breslauer, "Counterfactual Reasoning in Western Studies of Soviet Politics and Foreign Relations," in Tetlock and Belkin, *Counterfactual Thought Experiments*, pp. 69–94.

50. See chapter 3.

CHAPTER FIVE

1. Robert Fogel, *Railroads and American Economic Growth: Essays in Econometric History* (Baltimore: Johns Hopkins University Press, 1964); James Fearon, "Counterfactuals and Hypothesis Testing in Political Science," *World Politics* 43 (April 1991), pp. 474–84.

2. Donald (now Dierdre) N. McCloskey, "History Differential Equations and the Problem of Narration," *History and Theory* 36, no. 3 (1991), pp. 37–62.

3. Amos Tversky and Craig Fox, "Weighting Risk and Uncertainty," *Psychological Review* 102, no. 2 (1995), pp. 269–83.

4. Philip E. Tetlock, "Theory-Driven Reasoning about Possible Pasts and Probable Futures: Are We Prisoners of Our Preconceptions?" *American Journal of Political Science* 43 (April 1999), pp. 335–66.

5. Richard Ned Lebow, The *Tragic Vision of Politics: Ethics, Interests and Orders* (Cambridge: Cambridge University Press, 2003), chs. 3 and 4 on Thucydides' narrative.

6. Arie W. Kruglanski and Donna M, Webster, "Motivated Closing of the Mind: 'Seizing' and 'Freezing,'" *Psychological Review* 103, no. 2 (1996), pp. 263–68; Peter Suedfeld and Philip E. Tetlock, "Cognitive Styles," in Abraham Tesser and Norbert Schwartz, eds., *Blackwell International Handbook of Social Psychology: Intra-Individual Processes* (London: Blackwell, 2001), vol. 1, pp. 282–304.

7. Herbert A. Simon, *The Sciences of the Artificial* (Cambridge: MIT Press, 1996).

8. David K. Lewis, *Counterfactuals*, (Cambridge: Harvard University Press, 1973).

9. Robert Jervis, *Perception and Misperception in International Politics* (Princeton: Princeton University Press, 1976).

10. Scott Sagan and Kenneth Waltz, *The Spread of Nuclear Weapons: A Debate* (New York: Norton, 1995).

11. John A. Vasquez, "The Realist Paradigm and Degenerative versus Progressive Research Programs: An Appraisal of Neotraditional Research on Waltz's Balancing Proposition," *American Political Science Review* 91 (December 1997), pp. 899–912.

12. Mokyr, "King Kong and Cold Fusion."

13. Isaiah Berlin, "The Hedgehog and the Fox," in *The Proper Study of Mankind*, ed. Isaiah Berlin (New York: Farrar Straus and Giroux, 1997), pp. 436–98.

14. Philip E. Tetlock, "Close-Call Counterfactuals and Belief System Defenses: I Was Not Almost Wrong but I Was Almost Right," *Journal of Personality and Social Psychology* 75, no. 2 (1998), pp. 230–42.

15. Richard E. Neustadt and Ernest R. May, *Thinking in Time: The Uses of History for Decision-Makers* (New York: Free Press, 1986); Ian S. Lustick, "History Historiography and Political Science: Multiple Historical Records and the Problem of Selection Bias," *American Political Science Review* 90 (September 1996), pp. 605–18.

16. Vasquez, "The Realist Paradigm."

17. Amos Tversky and Daniel Kahneman, "Extensional versus Intuitive Reason: The Conjunction Fallacy as Probability Judgment," *Psychological Review* 90, no. 2 (1983), pp. 292–315; Derek Koehler, "Explanation Imagination and Confidence in Judgment," *Psychological Bulletin* 110, no. 3 (1991), 499–519.

18. Amos Tversky and Daniel Kahneman, "Extensional versus Intuitive Reason: The Conjunction Fallacy as Probability Judgment," *Psychological Review*, 90, no. 4 (1983), pp. 293–315.

19. Tversky and Fox, "Weighting Risk and Uncertainty."

20. Philip E. Tetlock and Geoffrey Parker, "Counterfactual Thought Experiments: Why We Can't Live without Them and How We Must Learn to Live with Them, " in Tetlock, Lebow and Parker, *Unmaking the West*, pp. 14–46.

21. Tversky and Fox, "Weighting Risk and Uncertainty."

22. Scott Hawkins and Reid Hastie, "Hindsight: Biased Judgment of Past Events after the Outcomes Are Known," *Psychological Bulletin* 107, no. 21 (1990), pp. 311–27.

23. William H. McNeill, *Pursuit of Power: Technology Armed Force and Society since A.D. 1000*, (Chicago: University of Chicago Press, 1982).

24. Stephen Jay Gould, *Dinosaur in a Haystack: Reflections in Natural History* (New York: Harmony Books, 1995).

25. Tetlock and Parker, "Counterfactual Thought Experiments."

26. E. H. Carr, *What Is History?* (London: Penguin Books, 1961).

27. The figure presents inevitability and impossibility curves for the rise of the West. The inevitability curve displays gradually rising likelihood judgments of some form of Western geopolitical dominance. The lower impossibility curve displays gradually declining likelihood judgments of all possible alternatives to Western dominance. The upper impossibility curve was derived by adding experts' likelihood judgments of six subsets of alternatives to Western domination. Adding values of the lower impossibility curve to corresponding inevitability-curve values yields sums only slightly above 1.0. Inserting values from the upper impossibility curve yields sums well above 1.0. The shaded area represents the cumulative effect of unpacking on the retrospective subjective probability of counterfactual alternatives to reality.

28. Tversky and Fox, "Weighting Risk and Uncertainty."

29. Hawkins and Hastie, "Hindsight: Biased Judgment of Past Events after the Outcomes Are Known."

30. Tetlock and Belkin, *Counterfactual Thought Experiments in World Politics*.

31. Koehler, "Explanation Imagination and Confidence in Judgment"; Tversky and Kahneman, "Extensional versus Intuitive Reason."

32. Koehler, "Explanation Imagination and Confidence in Judgment."

CHAPTER SIX

1. This point has subsequently been reiterated by Philip E. Tetlock, *Expert Political Judgment: How Good Is It? How can We Know?* (Princeton: Princeton University Press, 2005).

2. Fritz Heider and Marianne Simmel, "An Experimental Study of Apparent Behavior," *American Journal of Psychology*, 57 (1944), pp. 243–59; A. E. Michotte, *La perception de la causalité* (Louvain: University of Louvain Publications, 1946); Daniel Kahneman, "Varieties of Counterfactual Thinking," in Neal J. Roese and James M. Olson, eds., *What Might Have Been: The Social Psychology of Counterfactual Thinking* (Mahwah, N.J.: Erlbaum, 1995), pp. 375–96.

3. L. Ross, M. R. Lepper, F. Strack, and J. Steinmetz, "Social Explanation and Social Expectation: Effects of Real and Hypothetical Explanations on Subjective Likelihood," *Journal of Personality and Social Psychology*, 35 (1977), pp. 817–29.

4. Amos Tversky and Daniel Kahneman, "Extensional versus Intuitive Reason: The Conjunction Fallacy as Probability Judgment," *Psychological Review*, 90, no. 2 (1983), pp. 292–315.

5. Kahneman "Varieties of Counterfactual Thinking."

6. Tversky and Kahneman, "Extensional versus Intuitive Reason; Koehler, "Explanation, Imagination, and Confidence in Judgment," on the effects of vividness.

7. Neal J. Roese and James M. Olson, "Counterfactual Thinking: A Critical Overview," in Roese and Olson, *What Might Have Been*, pp. 1–56. Kasimatis and Wells, "Individual Differences in Counterfactual Thinking," find that counterfactuals typically posit worlds that are very close to real ones, containing one or, at most, a few features that differ. On mutating social behavior versus physical laws and controllable versus uncontrollable antecedents, see D. T. Miller, W. Turnbull, and C. McFarland, "Counterfactual Thinking and Social Perceptions: Thinking about What Might Have Been," in M. P. Zanna, ed., *Advances in Experimental Social Psychology* (New York: Academic Press, 1990), vol. 23, pp. 305–31; V. Girotto, P. Legrenzi, and A. Rizzo, "Event Controllability in Counterfactual Thinking," *Acta Psychologica*, 78 (1991), pp. 111–33; Eric P. Seelau, Sheila M. Seelau, Garry L. Wells, and Paul D. Windschild," Counterfactual Constraints," in Roese and Olson, *What Might Have Been*, pp. 67–79; Daniel Kahneman and Amos Tversky, "The Simulation Heuristic," in Daniel Kahneman, Paul Slovic, and Amos Tversky, *Judgment under Uncertainty: Heuristics and Biases* (New York: Cambridge University Press,1982), pp. 201–8, suggest that actions are more mutable than failures to act, as do Daniel Kahneman and D. T. Miller, "Norm Theory: Comparing Reality to Its Alternatives," *American Psychologist* 39 (1986), pp. 341–50; J. Landman, "Regret and Elation Following Action and Inaction: Affective Responses to Positive versus Negative Outcomes, *Personality and Social Psychology Bulletin*, 13 (1992), pp. 524–36; J. Baron, "The Effect of

Normative Beliefs on Anticipated Emotions," *Journal of Personality and Social Psychology*, 63 (1992), pp. 320–30. On availability, Amos Tversky and Daniel Kahneman, "Availability: A Heuristic for Judging Frequency and Probability," *Cognitive Psychology*, 5 (1973), pp. 207–32. On proximity and exceptional versus normal features, see H.L.A. Hart and A. M. Honoré, *Causation in Law*, 2nd. ed. (Oxford: Oxford University Press, 1985); Daniel Kahneman and D. T. Miller, "Norm Theory: Comparing Reality to the Alternatives," *Psychological Review*, 93 (1986), pp. 136–53; D. J. Hilton and B. R. Slugoski, "Knowledge-Based Causal Attributions: The Abnormal Conditions Focus Model," *Psychological Review*, 93 (1986), pp. 75–88; Igor Gavanski and G. L.Wells, "Counterfactual Processing of Normal and Exceptional Events," *Journal of Experimental Social Psychology*, 25 (1989), pp. 314–25; M. L. Buck and D. T. Miller, "Reactions to Incongruous Negative Life Events," *Social Justice Research*, 7 (1994), pp. 29–46; C. D. Lundberg and G. E. Frost, "Counterfactuals in Financial Decision Making," *Acta Psychologica*, 79 (1992), pp. 227–44; G. L. Wells, B. R. Taylor, and J. W. Turtle, "The Undoing of Scenarios," *Journal of Personality and Social Psychology*, 53 (1987), pp. 421–30; Daniel Kahneman, "Varieties of Counterfactual Thinking," in Roese and Olson, *What Might Have Been*, pp. 375–96.

8. P. Brickman, K. Ryan, and C. B. Wortman, "Causal Chains: Attribution of Responsibility as a Function of Immediate and Prior Causes," *Journal of Personality and Social Psychology*, 32 (1975), pp. 1060–67; Wells, Taylor, and Turtle, "Undoing of Scenarios"; D. T. Miller and S. Gunasegaram, "Temporal Order and the Perceived Mutability of Events: Implications for Blame Assignment," *Journal of Personality and Social Psychology*, 59 (1990), pp. 1111–18. An important exception to these principles concerns people coping with trauma, who will generate counterfactuals to undo events even in situations that lack readily mutable features. See Christopher G. Davis, Darrin R. Lehman, Camille B. Wortman, Roxanne Cohen Silver, and Suzanne C. Thompson, "The Undoing of Traumatic Life Events," *Personality and Social Psychology Bulletin*, 21, no. 2 (1995), pp. 109–24.

9. Holger Afflerbach and David Stevenson, eds., *An Improbable War? The Outbreak of World War I and European Political Culture Before 1914* (New York: Berghahn, 2007), represents the first serious effort by historians to challenge the inevitability thesis.

10. W.K.C. Guthrie, *The Sophists* (Cambridge: Cambridge University Press, 1971); Kerferd, *The Sophistic Movement* (Cambridge: Cambridge University Press, 1981).

11. Richard Ned Lebow, *Tragic Vision of Politics: Ethics, Interests and Orders* (Cambridge: Cambridge University Press, 2004), ch. 4.

12. Tversky and Kahneman, "Judgment under Uncertainty," p. 226, and "Extensional versus Intuitive Reason; Koehler, "Explanation, Imagination, and Confidence in Judgment."

13. Richard Ned Lebow, "Unmaking the Holocaust," ongoing and unpublished study.

14. Leon Festinger, *A Theory of Cognitive Dissonance* (Evanston, Ill.: Row, Peterson, 1957).

15. Christophere G. Davis, Darrin R. Lehman, Camille B. Wortman, Roxanne Cohen Silver, and Suzanne C. Thompson, "The Undoing of Traumatic Life Events," *Personality and Social Psychology Bulletin*, 21, no. 2 (1995), pp. 109–24; Orit E. Tykocinski, "I Never Had a Chance: Using Hindsight Tactics to Mitigate Disappointments," *Personality and Social Psychology Bulletin*, 27, no. 3 (2001), pp. 376–82; Orit E. Tykocinski, Dana Pick, and Dana Kedmi, "Retroactive Pessimism: A Different Kind of Hindsight Bias," *European Journal of Social Psychology*, 32 (2002), pp. 577–88.

16. Richard E. Nisbet and Lee Ross, *Human Inference: Strategies and Shortcomings of Social Judgments* (Englewood Cliffs, N.J.: Prentice-Hall, 1980). Richard E. Nisbet and Eugene Borgida, "Attribution and the Psychology of Prediction," *Journal of Personality and Social Psychology*, 32, no. 5 (1975), pp. 932–43.

17. Eugene Borgida and Richard E. Nisbett, "Character Proof and the Fireside Induction," *Law and Human Behavior*, 3 (1977), pp. 258–71; Shelly Chaiken and Alice H. Eagley, "Communication Modality as a Determinant of Message Persuasiveness and Message Comprehensibility," *Journal of Personality and Social* Psychology, 36, no. 4 (1979), pp. 605–14; R. Hamill, T. D. Wilson, and Richard E. Nisbet, "Insensitivity to Cample Bias: Generalization from Atypical Cases," *Journal of Personality and Social Psychology*, 39 (1980), pp. 578–89; Andrew A. Mitchell and Jerry C. Olson, "Are Product Attribute Beliefs the Only Mediator of Advertising Effects on Brand Attitude?" *Journal of Marketing Research*, 18 (March 1975), pp. 932–43; P. R. Dickson, "The Impact of Enriching Case and Statistical Information on Consumer Judgments," *Journal of Consumer Research*, 8 (1982), pp. 398–406; R. Hamill, T. D. Wilson, and Richard E. Nisbet, "Insensitivity to Sample Bias: Generalization from Atypical Cases," *Journal of Personality and Social Pscyhology*, 39 (1980), pp. 578–89; Jolita Kisielius and Brian Sternthal, "Detecting and Explaining Vividness Effects in Attitudinal Judgments," *Journal of Marketing Research*, 21 (February 1984), pp. 54–64.

18. Shelly Taylor and S. Thompson, "Snaking the Elusive 'Vividness' Effect," *Psychological Review*, 89 (1982), pp. 155–81.

19. Jolita Kisielius and Brian Sternthal, "Detecting and Explaining Vividness Effects in Attitudinal Judgments." *European Journal of Social Psychology*, 32 (2002), pp. 577–88.

20. Ibid., Nisbet and Ross, *Human Inference*.

21. Ann L. McGill and Punan Anand, "The Effect of Vivid Attributes on the Evaluation of Alternatives: The Role of Differential Attention and Cognitive Elaboration," *Journal of Consumer Research*, 16 (September 1989), pp. 188–96.

22. Thomas Kuhn, *The Structure of Scientific Revolutions* (Chicago: University of Chicago Press, 1970), p. 42.

CHAPTER EIGHT

Philip Roth, *The Plot Against America* (Boston: Houghton Mifflin, 2004), p. 114.

1. Sinclair Lewis, *It Can't Happen Here* (Garden City: Doubleday Doran, 1935); Philip Roth, *The Plot Against America* (Boston: Houghton-Mifflin, 2004).

2. *The Iliad of Homer*, trans. Richard Lattimore (Chicago: University of Chicago Press, 1951), Book Two, lines 135–210; pp. 80–81.

3. Wikipedia: http://en.wikipedia.org/wiki/Counterfactual_history; Amazon.com, 25 May 2007; Google, 25 May 2007.

4. Examples of this genre include Ward Moore, *Bring the Jubilee* (New York: Ballantine Books, 1953); Philip K. Dick, *The Man in the High Castle* (New York: Vintage, 1962); Robert Harris, *Fatherland* (London: Hutchinson, 1992). On the American Revolution, see Robert Sobel, *For Want of a Nail: If Burgoyne Had Won at Saratoga* (London: Greenhill Books, 1997).

5. Michael Chabon, *The Yiddish Policeman's Union* (Ontario: Harper-Collins, 2007).

6. D. James Kennedy's *What If Jesus Had Never Been Born* (Nashville: Thomas Nelson, 1997).

7. Erskine Childers, *Riddle of the Sands: A Record of Secret Service* (Boston: Charles E. Lauriat Company, 1927 [1902]); H. G. Wells, *The War in the Air* (New York: Macmillan, 1922).

8. Edward Bellamy, *Looking Backward, 2000–1887* (Boston: Houghton, Mifflin, 1889); Theodore Herzl, *Old-New Land* [*Altneuland*], trans. Lotta Levinson (New York: Bloch, 1960 [1902]); Roth, *The Counterlife*, p. 151.

9. The articles appeared in the *Jewish Daily Bulletin* in April–May 1933. Richard R. Lingemann, *Sinclair Lewis: Rebel from Main Street* (New York: Random House, 2002), 394.

10. Dorothy Parker, *I Saw Hitler!* (New York: Farrar and Rinehart, 1932), p. 35.

11. Lingemann, *Sinclair Lewis*, pp. 399–400.

12. Ibid, p. 400.

13. Huey P. Long, *Every Man a King: An Autobiography of Huey P. Long* (New Orleans: National Book Co., 1933).

14. Lingemann, *Sinclair Lewis*, p. 400.

15. "Utopia, or Uncle Tom's Cabin," Review of *It Can't Happen Here*, *The Nation*, 30 October 1935, p. 516; William Plomer, "Fiction," *Spectator*, 8 November 1935, p. 790.

16. R. L. Duffus, "Free or Fascist," *Survey Graphic* 29, no. 12 (December 1935), pp. 620–22.

17. Peter Quennell, "New Novels," *The New Statesmen and Nation*, 10, no. 245, 2 November 1935, pp. 644–45.

18. R. P. Blackmur, "Utopia, or Uncle Tom's Cabin," *The Nation*, 141, no. 3669, 30 October 1935, p. 516.

19. Mr. Lewis Says It Can."

20. "Peter Quennell, "New Novels,"

21. *Common Sense*, 9, no. 12 (December 1935), pp. 24–25. Geoffrey Stone, "An Ironical Tract," *The Commonweal*, 23, no. 4, 22 November 1935, pp. 107–8.

22. Stolberg, "Sinclair Lewis Faces Fascism in the U.S."

23. Edith H. Walton, "The Book Parade," *Forum*, 94, no. 6 (December 1935), p. vi; Geoffrey Stone, "An Ironical Tract," *The Commonweal*, 23, no. 4, 22 November 1935, pp.107–8; Herschel Brickell, "Book Reviews," *North American*

Review, 240, no. 3 (December 1935), pp. 543–44; Stolberg, "Sinclair Lewis Faces Fascism in the U.S."

24. "Mr. Lewis Says It Can"; "An Ironical Tract."

25. Vincent, "Social Fiction Notes."

26. Stone, "An Ironical Tract."

27. J. Donald Adams, "American under the Iron Heel, *New York Times Book Review*, 20 October 1935, p. 1; Duffus, "Free or Fascist."

28. Erich Eyck, *A History of the Weimar Republic*, trans. Harlan Hanson and Robert Waite, 2 vols. (Cambridge: Harvard University Press, 1962–63), vol. 2, pp. 350–488; Andreas Dorpalen, *Hindenburg and the Weimar Republic* (Princeton: Princeton University Press, 1964), pp. 301–446; Wolfgang Mommsen, *The Rise and Fall of Weimar Democracy*, trans. Elborg Forster and Larry Jones (Chapel Hill: University of North Carolina Press, 1996), pp. 357–456, 494–95, 535–37.

29. On Tulsa, see http://www.tulsareparations.org/FinalReport.htm, *The Final Report of the Oklahoma Commission to Study the Tulsa Race Riot of 1921*, compiled by Danny Goble.

30. Alexis de Tocqueville, *Democracy in America*, trans. and ed. Harvey C. Mansfield and Debra Winthrop (Chicago: University of Chicago Press, 2000), vol. II.1.2, pp. 409–10; I, 2.2, p. 169; II.1.2, pp. 409–10.

31. "Mr. Lewis Says It Can"; Vincent, "Social Fiction Notes."

32. Duffus, "Free or Fascist." H. G. Wells, *Things to Come* (New York: Macmillan, 1935) is the book of based on his 1933 novel, *The Shape of Things to Come*.

33. Duffus, "Free or Fascist"; Stone, "An Ironical Tract"; Melvin J. Vincent, "Social Fiction Notes," *Sociology and Social Research*, 20 (1956), p. 297.

34. Justus D. Doenecke, *Storm on the Horizon: The Challenge to American Intervention, 1939–1941* (Lanham, Md.: Rowman and Littlefield, 2000); Max Wallace, *The American Axis: Henry Ford, Charles Lindbergh and the Rise of the Third Reich* (New York: St. Martin's 2003).

35. Roth, *The Plot Against America*, p. 305. There is also a reference to Lewis's novel in *American Pastoral* (Boston: Houghton, Mifflin, 1997), where the hero's father says about the Nixon administration: "You know the book *It Can't Happen Here*? There's a wonderful book, I forget the author, but the idea couldn't be more up-to-the-moment. These people have taken us to the edge of something terrible."

36. Philip Roth, "The Story behind *The Plot Against America*," *New York Times*, Book Review Section, 19 September 2004, pp. 10–12.

37. Ibid.

38. "The Plot Again," Jeffrey Brown talks to Philip Roth, *Online New Hour*, 27 October 2004, http://pbs.org/newshour/bb/entertainment/july-dec04/philip-roth_10-27.html

39. Ibid.

40. Phil A. Roth, "Goodbye, Columbus," in *Goodbye, Columbus and Five Short Stories* (New York: Modern Library, 1966 [1959]), p. 58.

41. Philip A. Roth, "Eli the Fanatic," in *Goodbye, Columbus and Five Short Stories*, pp. 247–98; Timothy Parrish, "Introduction: Roth at Mid-Career," in

Timothy Parrish, ed., *The Cambridge Companion to Philip Roth* (Cambridge: Cambridge University Press, 2007), pp. 1–8; Victoria Aarons, "American-Jewish Identity in Roth's Short Fiction," in Parrish, *The Cambridge Companion to Philip Roth*, pp. 9–21; Michael Steinberg, "Roth and the Holocaust," in Parrish, *The Cambridge Companion to Philip Roth*, pp. 52–67.

42. Philip A. Roth, *Operation Shylock* (New York: Simon and Schuster, 1993), p. 334.

43. Parrish, "Introduction: Roth at Mid-Career," and "Roth and Ethnic Identity"; Aarons, "American-Jewish Identity in Roth's Short Fiction."

44. Roth, "Eli the Fanatic," and "I Always Wanted You to Admire My Fasting, or, Looking at Kafka," *Reading Myself and Others* (New York: Farrar, Strauss and Giroux, 1975), pp. 247–70; *The Ghost Writer* (New York: Farrar, Strauss and Giroux, 1979). Ellen Feldman, *The Boy Who Loved Anne Frank: A Novel* (New York: Norton, 2005), is another novel in which Anne Frank figures prominently. It is about Peter, a young boy, who is sent to the death camps with the Franks, survives, and comes to New York after the war where he gives up his Jewish identity.

45. Steinberg, "Roth and the Holocaust."

46. Roth, "The Story behind *The Plot Against America*."

47. Roth, *A The Plot Against America*, pp. 220, 359.

48. Ibid., p. 326.

49. On Roth's penchant for autobiography, see Hanna Wirth-Nether, "Roth's Autobiographical Writings," Michael Steinberg, "Roth and the Holocaust," in Parrish, *The Cambridge Companion to Philip Roth*, pp. 158–72.

50. Roth, *A The Plot Against America*, p. 301.

51. Ibid., p. 7.

52. Aristotle, *Poetics*, 1149b27–28

53. Charles Segal, *Tragedy and Civilization: An Interpretation of Sophocles* (Cambridge: Harvard University Press, 1981), p. 48.

54. See the essays in Peter Suedfeld, ed., *Light from the Ashes: Social Science Careers of Young Holocaust Refugees and Survivors* (Ann Arbor: University of Michigan Press, 2001).

55. W. G. Sebald, *Austerlitz* (Munch: Hanser, 2001); Günther Grass, *Im Krebsgang: eine Novelle* (Göttingen: Steidl, 2002).

56. Roth, "The Story behind *The Plot Against America*."

57. Roth, *The Plot Against America*, p. 362.

58. Roth, "The Story behind *The Plot Against America*."

59. Ibid.

60. Lee Henderson, "Alternate Roths," *Globe and Mail* (Toronto), 2 October 2004, p. D11, notes the parallel between Lindbergh and Bush; Tom Callahan, "The Plot Against America," http:/www/bookreporter.com/reviews2/1400079497. asp, describes Lindbergh's measures against Jews as reminiscent of the Patriot Act; Jonathan Yardley, "The Plot Against America," *Washington Post*, 3 October 2004, p. BW2, argues that the novel gives every appearance of being an attack on Bush and his administration; James Woolcott, "The Counter-Life," *The Nation*, 22 November 2004, pp. 23–28, maintains that Roth has no need to make explicit

any parallels because they stand out too sharply; Geoffrey Galt Hapham, "Inadmissible Evidence: Terror, Torture, and the World Today," *Chronicle of Higher Education*, 52, issue 8, 15 October 2004, pp. B12–13, makes the connection between Roth's novel and post 9/11. America; Michael Wood, "Just Folks," *London Review of Books*, 4 November 2004, pp. 3–5, contends that contemporary politics is not the focus of the novel but it certainly puts the events of 9/11 and the global war against terror into perspective; Michael Schaub, "The Plot Against America," *Bookslut*, October 2004, argues that it is easy to read Roth's disdain for Bush in his depiction of Lindbergh and his administration; Gabriel Brownstein, "Flight or Fight," *Village Voice*, 27 September 2004, contends that "The references to George W. Bush's America are impossible to miss."

61. Michael Gorra, "A Kitchen Table in Newark," *The Times*, 8 October 2004.

62. David Gates, "It Can't Happen Here," *Newsweek* 144, issue 12, 20 September 2004, p. 56.

63. Michiko Kakutani, "A Pro-Nazi President, a Family Feeling the Effects," *New York Times*, 21 September 2004.

64. J. M. Coetzee, "What Philip Knew," *New York Review of Books*, 18 November 2004.

65. Roth, *The Plot Against America*, pp. 196, 256, 197.

66. Roth, *A The Plot Against America*, p. 256.

67. Aristotle, *Poetics*, 11.1452a32 and 24.1460a27–31.

68. This point is made by Coetzee, "What Philip Knew."

69. Roy Foster, "No Place for a Jew," *Financial Times Weekend Magazine*, Book Reviews, p. 30.

70. Paul Berman, "*The Plot Against America*: What If It Happened Here?" *New York Times*, Book Review Section, 3 October 2004.

71. Max Watman, "Worse Yet, Real Life," *New Criterion*, November 2004, pp. 54–60. See also, Schaub, "The Plot Against America."

72. Timothy Parrish, "The Plot Against America," *Philip Roth Studies*, 1, no. 1 (Spring 2005), pp. 93–101, 111.

73. Clive James, "Fatherland," *Atlantic Monthly*, November 2004, pp. 143–49.

74. Ross Douthat, "It Didn't Happen Here," *Policy Review* (February–March 2005), no. 125, pp. 75–78.

75. Adam Mars-Jones, "*The Plot Against America*," *Observer*, 17 October 2004.

76. Hana Wirth-Nesher, "Roth's Autobiographical Writings"; Michael Steinberg, "Roth and the Holocaust," in Parrish, *The Cambridge Companion to Philip Roth*, pp. 158–72.

77. Michael Winock, *Nationalisme, antisemitisme, fascisme en France* (Paris: Seuil, 1990); Herman Lebovics, *True France: The Wars over Cultural Identity, 1930–1945* (Ithaca: Cornell University Press, 1992).

78. Andreas Dorpalen, *Hindenburg and the Weimar Republic* (Princeton: Princeton University Press, 1964), pp. 302–3, 316–17, 472; Erich Eyck, *A History of the Weimar Republic*, trans. Harlan Hanson and Robert Waite, 2 vols. (Cambridge: Harvard University Press, 1962–63), vol. 2, pp. 203–52; Martin Broszat, *Hitler and the Collapse of Weimar Germany*, trans. V. R. Berghahn (New York:

Berg, 1987), pp. 94–115; Ian Kershaw, *The "Hitler Myth": Image and Reality in the Third Reich* (Oxford: Oxford University Press, 1987); Denis Mack Smith, *Mussolini* (New York: Knopf, 1982), pp. 56–61; Adrian Lyttelton, *The Seizure of Power: Fascism in Italy 1919–1929* (Princeton: Princeton University Press, 1988), pp. 77–93.

79. Max Weber, "Objective Possibility and Adequate Causation in Historical Explanation," in *The Methodology of the Social Sciences* (Glencoe, Ill.: Free Press, 1949 [1905]), pp. 164–88.

80. Ken Tucker interviews Philip Roth, "Philip Roth Makes History," *Entertainment Weekly*, 1 October 2004, p. 42.

81. Roth, "The Story behind *The Plot Against America*."

82. Ibid.

83. Roth, *The Plot Against America*, p. 326.

84. Holger Herwig, "Hitler Wins in the East but Germany Still Loses World War II," in Philip E. Tetlock, Richard Ned Lebow, and Geoffrey Parker, *Unmaking the West: "What-If" Scenarios that Rewrite World History*, pp. 323–62.

85. Susan Berman, Introduction to Alessandro Manzoni, *On the Historical Novel*, trans., and ed. Sandra Berman (Lincoln: University of Nebraska Press, 1984).

86. Roth, *The Plot Against America*, pp. 180, 113–14, 154.

87. Wirth-Nesher, "Roth's Autobiographical Writings."

88. G.E.M. Ansombe, "On Brute Facts," *Analysis,* 18 (1958), pp. 69–72. John R. Searle, *The Construction of Social Reality* (New York: Free Press, 1995).

89. Hayden V. White, *The Content of the Form: Narrative Discourse and Historical Representation* (Baltimore: Johns Hopkins University Press, 1987).

90. Richard Ned Lebow, *The Tragic Vision of Politics: Ethics, Orders and Interests* (Cambridge: Cambridge University Press, 2004), ch. 4.

CONCLUSIONS

Sigmund Freud, "Delusions and Dreams in Jensen's *Gradiva*," in *The Standard Edition of the Complete Psychological Works of Sigmund Freud* (London: Hogarth Press, 1907), vol. IX, p. 8.

1. David Hume, *An Inquiry Concerning Human Understanding*, ed. Tom L. Beauchamp (Oxford: Oxford University Pres, 1999), sec. XII, "On the Probability of Causes." See also David Wooton, "From Fortune to Feedback: Contingency and the Birth of Modern Political Science," in Ian Shapiro and Sonu Bedi, *Political Contingency: Studying the Unexpected, the Accidental, and the Unforeseen* (New York: New York University Press, 2007), pp. 21–53.

2. Montesquieu, Charles de Secondat, *Considérations sur les causes de la grandeur des Romains et de leur décadence*, trans. David Lowenthal (New York: Free Press, 1965), ch. 18.

3. Richard Ned Lebow, "Beyond Parsimony: Rethinking Theories of Coercive Bargaining," *European Journal of International Relations* 4, no. 1 (1998), pp. 31–66.

4. Richard Ned Lebow, *A Cultural Theory of International Relations* (Cambridge: Cambridge University Press, 2008).

5. Richard Ned Lebow, *Between Peace and War: The Nature of International Crisis* (Baltimore: Johns Hopkins University Press, 1981).

6. For an exchange on this question, see William Thompson, "A Street Car Named Sarajevo: Catalysts, Multiple Causality Chains, and Rivalry Structures," *International Studies Quarterly* 47, no. 3 (September 2003), pp. 453–74; Richard Ned Lebow, "A Data Set Named Desire: A Reply to William P. Thompson," *International Studies Quarterly,* 47 (June 2003), pp. 475–58.

7. Hein E. Goemans, *War and Punishment: The Causes of War Termination and the First World War* (Princeton: Princeton University Press, 2000), for the strongest argument about why a negotiated peace was unlikely.

8. John Lukacs, *Five Days in London, May 1940* (New Haven: Yale University Press, 1999), on how close the British came to responding positively to Hitler's peace overtures. Holger Herwig, "Hitler Wins in the East but Germany Still Loses World War II," in Philip E. Tetlock, Richard Ned Lebow, and Geoffrey Parker, *Unmaking the West: "What-If" Scenarios that Rewrite World History*, pp. 323–62, on why Germany would still have lost the war even if they had won in the east.

9. Interviews with Indian and South Korean officials, Washington, D.C., Columbus, Ohio, Beijing, China, January 1999, March 2001, September 2007.

10. Gabriel A. Almond and Stephen J. Genco, "Clouds, Clocks and the Study of Politics," *World Politics*, 29, no. 4. (1977), pp. 489–522, for an early but still powerful argument to this effect.

11. Barbara Geddes, "How the Cases You Choose Affect the Answers You Get: Selection Bias in Comparative Politics," *Political Analysis* 2 (1990), pp. 131–50; Ian Lustick, "Multiple Historical Records and the Problem of Selection Bias," *American Political Science Review* 90: (1996), pp. 505–18; Robert Jervis, *System Effects: Complexity in Political and Social Life* (Princeton: Princeton University Press, 1997).

12. Milja Kurki, *Causation in International Relations: Reclaiming Causal Analysis* (Cambridge: Cambridge University Press, 2008).

13. Rom Harré and Peter Secord, *The Explanation of Social Behaviour* (Oxford: Blackwell, 1973); Roy Bhaskar, *The Possibility of Naturalism. A Philosophical Critique of the Contemporary Human Science* (Brighton: Harvester Press, 1979); Andrew Collier, *Critical Realism: An Introduction to Roy Bhaskar's Philosophy* (London: Verso, 1994); Heikki Patomäki, "How to Tell Better Stories about World Politics," *European Journal of International Relations* 2 (1996), pp. 105–34; Jervis, *System Effects*.

14. Remarkably, this is not a bias that has been identified or tested by cognitive psychology.

15. Richard Ned Lebow, *Between Peace and War: The Nature of International Crisis* (Baltimore: Johns Hopkins University Press, 1981), chs. 7 and 9 for these conditions and relevant cases.

16. Richard Ned Lebow, *A Cultural Theory of International Relations* (Cambridge: Cambridge University Press, 2008), ch. 7.

17. Matthew L. Wald and Kenneth Chang, "Minneapolis Bridge Had Passed Inspection," *New York Times*, 22 May 2008.

18. Ibid., ch. 7, for details.

19. Holger H. Herwig, *The First World War: Germany and Austria-Hungary 1914–1918* (London: Arnold, 1997), pp. 312–17.

20. Ibid.

21. George W. Breslauer and Richard Ned Lebow, "Leadership and the End of the Cold War: A Counterfactual Thought Experiment," in Richard K. Herrmann and Richard Ned Lebow, eds., *Ending the Cold War* (New York: Palgrave-Macmillan, 1006), pp. 161–88; Lebow and Stein, "Understanding the End of the Cold War as a Non-Linear Confluence."

22. Michael R. Beschloss and Strobe Talbot, *At the Highest Levels: The Inside Story of the End of the Cold War* (Boston: Little, Brown, 1993), pp. 13–17, 19–21, 45–46.

23. The term is from G. L. Wells, B. R. Taylor, and J. W. Turtle, "The Undoing of Scenarios," *Journal of Personality and Social Psychology*, 53 (1987), pp. 421–30.

24. H.L.A. Hart and A. M. Honoré, *Causation in Law*, 2nd ed. (Oxford: Oxford University Press, 1985), on unfolding chains.

25. Bernstein, Lebow, Stein and Weber, "Social Science as Case-Based Diagnostics."

26. Quoted in Hanna Wirth-Nether, "Roth's Autobiographical Writings," Michael Steinberg, "Roth and the Holocaust," in Parrish, *The Cambridge Companion to Philip Roth*, pp. 158–72.

27. Arnold Davidson, "Carlo Ginzburg and the Renewal of Historiography," in James Chandler, Arnold I. Davidson, and Harry Harootunian, eds. *Questions of Evidence: Proof, Practice and Persuasion across the Disciplines* (Chicago: University of Chicago Press, 1994), pp. 304–20.

28. Chaim Perelman and L. Olbrechts-Tyteca, *The New Rhetoric: A Treatise on Argumentation*, tr. John Wilkinson and Purcell Weaver (Notre Dame: University of Notre Dame Press, 1968).

29. John Zinman, *Reliable Knowledge: An Exploration for the Grounds of Belief in Science* (Cambridge: Cambridge University Press, 1978).

30. Tullio Maranhão, "Recollections of Fieldwork Conversations, or Authorial Difficulties in Anthropological Writing," in Jane H. Hill and Judith Irvine, eds. *Responsibility and Evidence in Oral Discourse* (Cambridge: Cambridge University Press, 1993), pp. 260–88. I am indebted to Dorothy Noyes for the arguments in this paragraph.

31. See chapter 1 for a discussion.

32. Paul Ricoeur, *Time and Narrative*, trans. and ed. Kathleen McLaughlin and David Pellauer, 3 vols. (Chicago: University of Chicago Press, 1984–88), vol. I, pp. 352–54.

33. Barbara Herrnstein Smith, *On the Margins of Discourse: The Relations of Literature to Language* (Chicago: University of Chicago Press, 1978), pp. x–xi, 10–11.

34. I am indebted to Dorothy Noyes for this example.

35. G.E.M. Ansombe, "On Brute Facts," *Analysis,* 18 (1958), pp. 69–73; John R. Searle, *The Construction of Social Reality* (New York: Free Press, 1995).

36. Hayden V. White, *The Content of the Form: Narrative Discourse and Historical Representation* (Baltimore: Johns Hopkins University Press, 1987). Arthur C. Danto, *Narration and Knowledge* (New York: Columbia University Press, 1985), ch. 8, on the process of emplotment from the perspective of analytical philosophy.

37. John Locke, *An Essay concerning Human Understanding*, ed. A. S. Pringle-Pattison (Oxford: Oxford University Press, 1924), Book II; Hume, *An Inquiry Concerning Human Understanding*, part II, 2–3.

38. Susan E. Fiske and Shelley Taylor, *Social Cognition* (New York: McGraw-Hill, 1991), for a good overview.

39. John R. Searle, *Expression and Meaning: Studies in the Theory of Speech Acts* (Cambridge: Cambridge University Press, 1979), p. 65.

40. Steven Saylor, *The Judgment of Caesar* (New York: St. Martin's, 2004); Colleen McCullough, *Caesar: A Novel* (New York: Harper Collins, 1997); George Thomas Clark, *Hitler Here: A Biographical Novel* (London: Three Points Press, 2004); Ron Hanse, *Hitler's Niece* (New York: Harper Collins, 1999); Don DeLillo, *Libra* (New York: Viking, 1998); Robert S. Levinson, *The John Lennon Affair* (New York: Forge Books, 2001). Maurice Samuels, *The Spectacular Past: The Historical Novel in Nineteenth Century France* (Ithaca: Cornell University Press, 2004), on the cult of Napoleonic fiction, the commercial incentives for publishers, and the influence of the romantic novel on the portrayal of the emperor.

41. Philip E. Tetlock, *Expert Political Judgment: How Good Is It? How Can We Know?* (Princeton: Princeton University Press, 2005).

42. Richard Ned Lebow, "British Historians and Irish History," *Eire-Ireland* 8 (December 1973), 3–38.

43. Thierry Meyssan, *The Big Lie* (London: Carnot, 2002).

44. Richard Ned Lebow and Janice Gross Stein, "Reagan and the Russians," *Atlantic Monthly* 273 (February 1994), pp. 35–37; Richard K. Herrmann, "Learning from the Cold War," in Richard K. Herrmann and Richard Ned Lebow, eds., *Ending the Cold War* (New York: Palgrave-Macmillan, 2004), pp. 219–38.

45. *JFK* (1991), directed by Oliver Stone. DeLillo, *Libra*.

46. Becky Ebenkamp, "Only the Grassy Knoll Knows—Gallup Poll Examines Public Opinion Regarding the John F. Kennedy Assassination," *Brandweek*, 9 April 2001, http://findarticles.com/p/articles/mi_m0BDW/is_15_42/ai_73409412; Gary Langer, "Legacy of Suspicion Decades after, Few Accept the Official Explanation of the Kennedy Assassination, "ABC News, 16 November 2003, http://abcnews.go.com/sections/wnt/US/JFK_poll_031116.html.

47. Gerd Krumeich, "Die Dolchstoss-Legende," in Etienne Francois and Hagen Schulze, eds., *Deutsche Erinnerungsorte* (Munich: Beck, 2000), pp. 585–99; Bernd Seiler, "'Dolchstoss' und 'Dolchstosslegende,'" *Zeitschrift für Deutsche Sprache* 22 (1966), pp. 1–20.

48. Bertrand Russell, "On Denoting," in Farhang Zabeeh, E. D. Klemke, and Arthur Jacobsen, eds., *Readings in Semantics* (Urbana: University of Illinois Press, 1974 [1905]), pp. 143–58.

49. Gottlob Frege, "Über Begriff und Gegenstand," *Vierteljahrsschrift für Wissenschaftliche Philosophie* 16 (1892), pp. 192–205, reprinted in Peter Geach and

Max Black, eds., *Translations from the Philosophical Writings of Gottlob Frege*, 3rd ed. (Oxford: Blackwell, 1980), pp. 42–55.

50. On possible worlds, see B. Mates, "Leibniz on Possible Worlds," in B. van Rootsellar and J. F. Straal, *Logic, Methodology, and Philosophy of Science* (Amsterdam: North-Holland, 1968), vol. 3, pp. 507–29; Raymond Bradley and Norman Swartz, *Possible Worlds* (Oxford: Blackwell, 1979); Jaakko Hintikka, "Exploring Possible Worlds, " in Allén Sture, ed., *Possible Worlds in Humanities, Arts, and Sciences: Proceedings of the Nobel Symposium 65* (Berlin: de Gruyter, 1989), pp. 52–73; M. J. Cresswell, *Semantical Essays: Possible Worlds and Their Rivals* (Dordrecht: Kluwer, 1988); David Lewis, *On the Plurality of Worlds* (Oxford: Blackwell, 1966); Robert Stalnaker, "Possible Worlds," *Nous* 10 (1976), pp. 65–75, and *Inquiry* (Cambridge: M.I.T. Press, 1984); Ruth Ronen, *Possible Worlds in Literary Theory* (Cambridge: Cambridge University Press, 1994).

51. Gary King, Robert Keohane, and Sidney Verba, *Designing Social Inquiry* (Princeton: Princeton University Press, 1994). For critiques, Terry M. Moe, "On the Scientific Status of Rational Models," *American Journal of Political Science* 23, no. 1 (1979), pp. 215–43; Richard Ned Lebow and Mark I. Lichbach, eds., *Theory and Evidence in Comparative Politics and International Relations* (New York: Palgrave-Macmillan, 2007).

52. Donald (Dierdre) McCloskey, *The Rhetoric of Economics* (Madison: University of Wisconsin Press, 1985).

53. Aristotle, *Poetics*, 1448b4–24. Erich Auerbach, *Mimesis: The Representation of Reality in Western Literature* (Garden City, N.Y.: Doubleday, 1957 [1946]), attempts to restate the authority of mimesis following the modernist attack on the concept.

54. Lubomír Doležel, *Heterocosmica: Fiction and Possible Worlds* (Baltimore: Johns Hopkins University Press, 1998), pp. x, 33–37.

55. James Frey, *A Thousand Little Pieces* (New York: Anchor, 2005).

56. Rigoberta Menchu, *An Autobiography* (New York: Verso, 1998).

57. Thomas Kuhn, *The Structure of Scientific Revolutions* (Chicago: University of Chicago Press, 1970), p. 42.

Index

Able Archer (exercise), 128
Adam, 3, 279
Aehrenthal, Alois Lexa von, 78
affirmative action, 43
Afflerbach, Holger, 70
Afghanistan, 107–8, 116–17, 123, 271–73
Alba, Duke of (Fernando Álvarez de
    Toledo), 47–49
Alsace-Lorraine, 78, 87
Altneuland (Herzl), 224
American Historical Society, 171
American Pastoral (Roth), 247
American Political Science Association,
    142, 171
American Political Science Review, 23
Ames, Aldrich, 30
Anand, Punan, 192
Andropov, Yuri, 109, 113–14, 116–18, 264
Anscombe, G.E.M., 35, 258
Anthony, Mark, 47–48, 54
anti-Semitism, 210–11, 225, 231–37,
    241–50, 281
Apis (Dragutin Dimitriević), 88
Arbeitskreis Militaergeschichte Histo-
    risches Institut, 171
Aristotle, 25, 243, 247–48, 256–57
arms control, 10, 103, 108, 115–17, 120,
    124–25, 130, 271–73
arms races, 16
Astérix, 46
Athens, 20, 216, 243, 245
Augustus, 279
Auschwitz, 69
Austerlitz (Sebald), 244
Austria, 55
Austria-Hungary, 7, 23, 49–50, 60, 69–93,
    94, 97, 100, 170, 172–82, 208–16,
    261–63, 270–71
availability valence hypothesis, 192
Aztec Empire, 63

Bacon, Francis, 25
balance of power, 36, 141–42
Balkan League, 80–82
Barnes, Harry Elmer, 74

Bay of Pigs invasion, 31
Belgium, 89, 143, 180, 270
belief systems, 6, 12, 167, 269–70
Belkin, Aaron, 45, 54
Bell, Daniel, 11
Berchtold, Leopold, 80, 82–83
Berlin crises, 13, 16, 31, 35, 51, 107, 267
Berlin Wall, 103, 125
Berlin, Isaiah, 143, 162
Bernhardi, Friedrich von, 70
Bessmertnykh, Aleksandr, 130
Bethmann Hollweg, Theobald, 73, 80,
    84–85, 91, 261, 270
Between Peace and War (Lebow), 261
biases, 17, 147–48, 155, 163
bible, 26
binary complementarity, 149–54
Bismarck, Otto von, 78, 179–81
Black Death, 54, 144
Black Legion, 225
Bonaparte, Napoleon, 65, 141–42, 253
Bosnia-Herzogovina, 78, 83, 88
Bosnian Annexation crisis, 77
bounded rationality, 140
Bourbons, 62
Breslauer, George, 23, 34, 262–63, 272
Brest-Litovsk, Treaty of, 70
Brezhnev, Leonid, 108, 113–14, 116–17,
    126
Britain, 7, 10, 15–16, 31, 43, 55, 72, 74,
    78, 143–44, 180, 263
Brooklyn College, 11
Bryan, William Jennings, 225
Bukharin, Nikolai, 132
Bulgaria, 81
Bundy, McGeorge, 81
Bush, George H. W., 23, 103–9, 116–24,
    129–31, 247–48, 262, 272–73
Bush, George W., 43, 99
butterfly effect, 274

Calvin, John, 259
Canada, 226, 232–33, 240, 254–55
Carr, E. H., 6, 34, 159
Carter, Jimmy, 116–17

Castro, Fidel, 51
catalysts, 261, 268–76
causation, 6, 166–95; Humean, 4, 17, 265–66
Cederman, Lars-Eric, 42
Central Intelligence Agency (CIA), 30
Chang, Kwang-chih, 40
Charlemagne, 279
Chernenko, Konstantin, 15, 34, 105, 109, 113–14, 118–19, 121, 264
Chernobyl, 108, 127
Chernyayev, Anatoliy, 127
chess, 65–66
Chickering, Roger, 70
China, 7, 13, 19, 32–33, 40, 54, 141, 144, 159–60
Christianity, 26, 46
Churchill, Winston, 10, 34, 252
Civil War (U.S.), 223
Clausewitz, Carl von, 61–62
Cleopatra, 46–48, 54
closure, 24, 143–56, 160, 164, 259–60
Coetzee, J. M., 247
cognitive styles, 139–41, 143–50, 164–65
Cold War, 6, 8–11, 13–16, 22–23, 28, 33–35, 38–40, 42–43, 69, 93, 96–97, 103–83, 260, 263–65, 271–74, 280, 283–84
colonialism, 284
Columbine, 46
communism, 69
comparative analysis, 41–42
confluence. *See* nonlinearity
Congress of Vienna, 213, 218, 220
Constantine, 59
constructivism, 4
contingency, 6, 23–25, 58–64, 70–72, 259–60, 266–76. *See also* counter-factuals, nonsystematic factors
Cortés, Hernán, 63
Cosi fan Tutte (Mozart), 207, 256, 270
Counterfactual Thought Experiments in World Politics (Tetlock and Belkin), 29
counterfactuals: close call, 24–35, 137–65, 166–82,193; enabling, 181, 213–14; folk, 30, 46–47; long-short counter-factuals, 24–25, 168, 179, 182–86, 192–93; make your own, 175–186, 192–93; miracle, 30, 44–46, 179; plausible, 30, 44–49, 105–13; second order, 51–52, 275–76; smuggled in, 34; surgical, 50; tests, 47–58; upward, 43

Counterlife (Roth), 239–40, 243
Countess Sophie Chotek, 44, 86–87, 167, 193
covering laws, 137–43
Craig, Gordon, 91
Crohn's Disease, 62
Cuban missile crisis, 9, 13–16, 31–32, 34–35, 37, 50–51, 137–38, 140, 149–58, 267
Cultural Theory of International Relations, 261
Czechoslovakia, 55

Darfur, 45
Daughters of the American Revolution, 229
Dawes, Robyn, 52
de Gaulle, Charles, 103
De Klerk, F. W., 103
Deep Blue, 65–66
Delian League, 59
DeLillo, Don, 280
Democratic Peace, 4, 20
demystification (*Entzauberung*), 19
Denmark, 181
Designing Social Inquiry (King, Keohane and Verba), 19–20, 36, 281
détente, 16
deterrence, 13–14, 31, 43, 141, 158
Diary of Anne Frank, 243, 250
Disraeli, Benjamin, 217
divided nations, 264–65
Dogger Bank affair, 78
Dolchstoss (stab in the back), 70
Doležel, Lubomír, 282
Don Giovanni (Mozart), 207
Dr. Seuss (Theodore Seuss Geisel), 45

Eden, Garden of, 3, 19
Egypt, 38
Eichmann, Adolf, 244
Einstein, Albert, 212, 254
election of 2000 (U.S.), 177–78
"Eli the Fanatic" (Roth), 237
Eliot, T. S., 26
Elvin, Mark, 32–33
Ending the Cold War (Herrmann and Lebow), 271
England, 52, 57. *See also* Britain
English language, 15, 284
Entente Cordiale, 72, 78
epistemology, 19
erklären, 4

Elster, Jon, 52
Euclid, 46
Europe, 7–8, 13, 17, 33, 62, 92–93, 114, 130, 210–11, 271
Every Man a King (Long), 225
evidence, 33
extensionality principle, 148
external validity, 21

fact vs. fiction, 25, 35, 256–60, 276–83
factual vs. counterfactual, 21, 29, 32, 34
Farnese, Alexander (Duke of Parma), 48
Fashoda crisis, 72, 78, 267
Fatherland (Dick), 223
Fearon, James, 13–14, 52–53
Federal Bureau of Investigation (FBI), 188, 233, 241, 253
Ferguson, Niall, 47–49, 54
fiction, 25–27. *See also* fact vs. fiction
Fielding, Henry, 26
Finnegan's Wake (Joyce), 258
Fischer, Fritz, 70, 74
Fischoff, Baruch, 38
Florida, 44–45
Fogel, Robert, 55
Ford, Henry, 225, 233, 240
Fox, Craig, 138, 148, 154
France, 7, 10, 15–16, 19, 31, 55, 73–74, 79, 84–85, 87, 89–90, 103, 141, 143–44, 159, 217, 219, 250
Franco-Prussian War, 181
Franco-Russe, 72, 84, 87, 180
Frank, Anne, 237, 250
Frankfurt Parliament, 185
Frankfurter, Felix, 232
Franz Ferdinand, 9, 15, 22, 44, 49, 56, 60–61, 73, 80, 82–83, 86–89, 167, 170–3, 176, 178, 193, 211, 262–63, 268, 270
Franz Josef (Austria), 80, 82–85, 89, 211, 261, 270
Frederick III (Prussia), 180
Frege, Gottlob, 281
French Revolution, 8, 12, 71
Freud, Sigmund, 259
Friedman, Thomas, 11
Fukuyama, Francis, 11
fundamentalism, 46
Future to Come (Wells), 230

Geiss, Imanuel, 74
Genghis Khan, 141, 144, 159–60

Genscher, Hans-Dietrich, 125
German-American Bund, 226, 236
German language, 15, 284
Germany, 172–82, 208, 210–11, 213, 219, 262–64, 268–71; Federal Republic, 39, 123, 125; imperial, 7–8, 10, 19, 23, 43, 49–50, 56, 69–93, 94–95, 100, 143–45; Nazi, 16, 55, 57, 70, 145, 251–56, 281; 272, 284; Weimar, 70
gestalt shifts, 80
The Ghost Writer (Roth), 250
Ginzburg, Carlo, 277
glasnost, 125
globalization, 283–84
Godunov, Boris, 279
Goering, Hermann, 231
Gonzalez, Elián, 44–45, 177–78
Goodbye Columbus (Roth), 237
Gorbachev, Mikhail, 15, 23, 33–35, 103, 108–11, 113, 115, 118–31, 264, 271–73
Gore, Albert, 45, 177–78
Gould, Stephen Jay, 30, 158, 218
Greece, 84
Gresham's Law, 281
Grey, Edward, 74
Grishin, Victor, 34, 100, 108–110, 131
GRIT, 108
Gromyko, Andrei, 110

Haarlem, 48
Habsburg dynasty, 62, 83
Harding, Warren, 226
Hassig, Ross, 63
Hawthorn, Geoffrey, 54
Hegel, 257
Hegel, G.W.F., 100
hegemony, 20, 45, 141, 158–62
Heidegger, Martin, 12
Helsinki Accords (1975), 130
Herder, Johann Gottfried, 209
Herodotus, 258
Herrmann, Richard, 9
Herwig, Holger, 57, 73
Herz, John, 10
heuristics, 169
Himmler, Heinrich, 252
Hinckley, John Jr., 48, 61, 109, 116
Hindenburg, Paul von, 15, 250, 281
hindsight bias, 8, 38–39, 274
Hinsley, F. H., 69
historians, 6, 39–41, 260

history, 25, 258
Hitler, Adolf, 8, 10, 15, 28, 31, 43, 47, 50, 55, 61, 92, 94, 141–42, 208, 210, 226, 228, 250–52, 255, 262, 281
HIV, 62
Holland, 48
Hollywood, 8, 46
Holocaust Museum, 238, 244
Holocaust, 7, 27, 43, 49–50, 183–84, 186, 205, 243–44, 277, 280, 283
homosexuality, 227
Hötzendorf, Conrad von, 70, 78, 80, 82–89
Howard, Sidney, 225
Hoyos Mission, 83, 85
Human Stain (Roth), 237
Hume, David (see also, causation, Hume), 12, 26, 259, 277–78, 280
Hungary, 83, 92

I Saw Hitler (Parker), 225
identity, 283–86
Iliad (Homer), 222
India, 54, 268
Indochina War, 11, 35, 81, 107–8
Inferno (Dante), 224
influenza pandemic, 180
Iraq: invasion of, 43–45
Irving, David, 280
isolationism, 230, 252
Israel, 39, 223
It Can't Happen Here, 27, 222, 225–30, 234–35, 246, 249, 256, 277. *See also* Lewis, Sinclair
Italy, 7, 56, 84, 91

"Jabberwocky" (Carroll), 278
Jagow, Gottlieb von, 80
January effect, 13
Japan, 8, 39, 57, 61, 94
Jervis, Robert, 140
Jesus, 61, 279
Jews, 43, 47, 210–11, 225, 231–50, 276, 281
Johnson, Lyndon B., 81, 96
Joll, James, 74
Joyce, James, 3, 26
July crisis. *See* World War I, origins

Kafka, Franz, 238, 248, 250
Kahneman, Daniel, 25, 147, 167, 169, 176
Kakutani, Michiko, 246
KAL 007, 114

Kasparov, Gary, 65–66
Kempelen, Wolfgang von, 65
Kennedy, John F., 15, 31–32, 34–35, 51, 106, 140, 150–51
Kennedy, Paul, 93
Khrushchev, Nikita S., 9, 31–32, 34–35, 50–51, 106
Kiselius, Jolita, 192
Kiser, Edgard, 52
Kissinger, Henry, 272
Kohl, Helmut, 125
Im Krebsgang (Grass), 244
Kripke, Saul, 281
Ku Klux Klan (KKK), 226, 245
Kuhn, Thomas, 195, 285
Kurki, Milja, 265

La Clemenza di Tito (Mozart), 207
LaGuardia, Fiorello, 232, 234, 253
Laitin, David, 13–14
Landon, Alf, 225
Laos, 16
Last Judgment (Bosch), 224
law: international, 284
leadership, 103–33
Lebow, Richard Ned, 214, 218–19
Leibniz, Gottfried, 281
Lend Lease (1941), 252, 254
Lenin, V. I., 42
Levi, Margaret, 52
Lewis, Sinclair, 6, 27, 222, 234–35, 246, 249, 256
liberalism, 284
Licinius, Valerius Licinius, 59
Ligachev, Yegor, 34, 108, 110, 131, 273
Lindberg, Anne Morrow, 232–33
Lindberg, Charles, 27, 222, 231–33, 239, 241, 247, 252–55
Lindbergh kidnapping, 252
literature, 17–18, 25–26
Locke, John, 278
Long, Huey, 225
Looking Backward (Bellamy), 224
Louis XIV (France), 19
Luhmann, Niklas, 97
Lukacs, John, 34

MacArthur, Douglas, 228
Macaulay, Thomas, 280
Malamud, Bernard, 237
Mandela, Nelson, 103

Manhattan Project, 254
Maranhão, Tullio, 277
Marne, Battle of (1914), 143
Marriage of Figaro (Mozart), 207
Martin, Colin, 51–52, 57
Marvel, Andrew, 46
Marx, Karl, 10
Marx, Karl, 217–18, 257
McCloskey, Diedre,18, 281
McGill, Ann, 192
McNamara, Robert, 51, 151
Medvedev, Vadim, 127
Mein Kampf (Hitler), 226
Menchu, Rigoberta, 281
Meso-America, 63
methods, 3, 19
Mexico, 143
Michelson-Morley experiment, 212
Middle East War, 1973, 14
Military History Society, 171
Mill, John Stuart, 101
Milvian Bridge, 59
mimimal rewrite counterfactuals. *See*
    counterfactuals: close call
Minneapolis, 268
modernization, 210
Moltke, Helmuth von (the elder), 69
Moltke, Helmuth von (the younger), 73,
    78–80, 83–84, 89–91, 262–64, 268,
    270–71
Mondale, Walter, 109, 118, 120–124, 130–32
Mongols, 47, 61, 140, 159–60
Montenegro, 84
Montesquieu, Charles de Secondat, 259
Moors, 159
Moroccan crises, 72
Moses, 47, 279
motives, 32
Mozart, Wolfgang Amadeus, 27, 49–50,
    52, 56, 183–85, 205–20
Mueller, John, 42–43, 46, 50
Munich Agreement (1938), 15
Mussolini, Benito, 8, 226, 247, 252
Mussorgsky, Modest, 279

Naimark, Norman, 106
Napoleon et la conquête du Monde
    (Geoffrey-Chateau), 222
narratives, 282–83
nationalism, 22
neo-positivism. *See* positivism

New Deal, 225–26, 230, 236, 250–51
New York City, 30
New York Times, 232
Newton, Isaac, 46
Nietzsche, Friedrich, 18–19, 27
"Night of the Long Knives" (1934), 228
9/11, 45, 47,188, 246, 264, 280
1984 (Orwell), 234, 251
Nisbet, Robert E., 192
Nixon, Richard, 51, 126, 248
nonlinearity, 11, 17, 22–23, 93–99, 175,
    194, 259–76
nonsystematic factors, 15, 21, 33. *See also*
    contingency
North Atlantic Treaty Organization
    (NATO), 14, 102, 256, 272
nuclear war, 16, 256
nuclear weapons, 43, 57, 129, 140–42, 144

O'Connell, Daniel, 208
Oakley, Annie, 180
Oedipus, 205–6, 211
ontology, 23
Operation Shylock (Roth), 237, 239, 243
Oswald, Lee Harvey, 280
Ottoman Empire, 7, 54, 87

Parker, Dorothy, 224–25, 234
Parker, Geoffrey, 29, 42, 51–52, 57
partitioned countries, 264–65
Pašić, Nikola, 91
path dependence, 175
Patton, George, 228
Pausanias, 59
Pearl Harbor, 253, 255
Peloponnesian War, 216
perestroika, 125
Pericles, 61
peripeteia (reversal), 247–48
Persia, 59
Persian Gulf War, 264
Philip II (Spain), 19, 51, 141–42
Philip III (Sparin), 51
Planck, Max, 212
The Plot Against America (Roth), 6, 27–28,
    46–47, 222, 230–58, 277, 284. *See* Roth,
    Philip
poetry, 26, 256
Poincaré, Henri, 212
Poitiers, battle of, 217
Poland, 89, 126

Politburo, 109, 123
Political Science Quarterly, 23
political science, 6
Pomerantz, Kenneth, 32
Portelli, Allesandro, 44
positivism, 4, 18–19, 27
postclassicism, 49–50
Potiorek, Oskar, 83, 86
Pound, Ezra, 26
prediction, 11, 14, 195
Princip, 60–61, 70, 87
probability, 49–50
psycho-logic, 149, 183, 205, 219–21
psychology, 4–6. *See also* cognitive styles, gestalt shifts
punctuated equilibria, 5
Pushkin, Alexander, 279

Quine, Willard van Orman, 37

racism, 228. *See also* anti-Semitism
Reagan, Ronald, 23, 48–49, 61, 103, 108–9, 113–26, 128–31, 264, 272
realism, 16, 34, 284
regularities, 4, 13, 17, 20. *See also* causation: Humean
Remak, Joachim, 82
Reno, Janet, 44, 177
Repeal Movement (Ireland), 208
revolution of the 1960s, 11
Reykjavik summit (1986), 129
Rhineland, 15
Ribbentrop, Joachim, 231, 247
Richardson, Samuel, 26
Ricoeur, Paul, 277
Riddle of the Sands (Childers), 224
Riezler, Kurt, 73
Ritter, Gerhard, 91
Roland, 279
Roman Empire, 8, 47–48, 59, 71
Romanov, Grigoriy, 34, 108–110, 115
Romanov dynasty, 83
Romanticism, 184–85, 207–8, 212–13
Romanticism, 49–50
Roosevelt, Franklin, 10, 27, 222, 230, 232–33, 236–37, 246, 251–55
Ross, Lee, 192
Ross, Lepper, Strack and Steinmetz (1977), 38, 169
Roth, Philip, 6, 27–28, 46, 222, 234, 236–39, 250–51, 257, 276–78, 284

Rousseau, Jean-Jacques, 185, 240
Russell, Bertrand, 281
Russia, 7, 23, 56, 60, 71, 78–81, 83, 85, 87–91, 93–94, 97, 172, 179, 261, 263, 270–71. *See also* Soviet Union
Russian revolution, 16, 34, 92, 159, 181
Russo-Japanese War, 77, 88
Rust, Matthias, 34, 127

el-Sadat, Anwar, 103–4
Saddam, 264
Salamis, 59, 61
Sarajevo, 8, 60, 71, 137, 170, 172, 261–263, 268. *See also* World War I: origins
Schindler's List, 238, 245
Schlesinger, Arthur M., Jr., 234
Schlieffen Plan, 73, 143, 270
Schlieffen, Alfred von, 89
Schroeder, Paul, 74
Schultz, George, 103
Searle, John, 279
self-esteem, 44
September Program (1914), 70
Serbia, 9, 23, 71–73, 77–81, 82, 84, 88, 184, 262, 271
Shaknazarov, Georgiy, 127
Shevardnadze, Eduard, 103, 127
Silver Shirts, 226
Simon, Herbert, 140
SIOP (Single Integrated Operational Plan), 128
Smith, Adam, 100
Social Darwinism, 22, 209
Social Democrats (Germany), 84, 261
social facts, 36–38
social imperialism, 181
socialism, 7, 16
Society of Diplomatic and Military Historians, 142
Sociology, 16
soft power, 8
sophism, 175
Southeast Asia, 7
Soviet Union, 9–10, 13, 15–17, 33–35, 55, 103–83, 144–45, 150–51, 256, 280
Spain, 7, 19, 46, 57
Spanish Armada, 48, 51
Sparta, 59, 216
Spinoza, Baruch, 259
Stalin, Josef V., 34, 42, 103, 106, 132, 144–45, 280

statistical inference, 219–21
Steele, Richard, 26
Stein, Janice Gross, 32
Sternthal, Brian, 192
Stone, Oliver, 280
Strategic Defense Initiative (Star Wars), 115, 117, 280
subadditivity, 157
Sunarić, Josip, 89
supreme court (U.S.), 226–27, 230
Szilard, Leo, 254

Taiwan Straits crises, 13
Tawney, R. H., 70
Taylor, Maxwell, 10
Taylor, Shelley, 192
temperature, 36
terror management theory, 12
testing and evaluation, 40–42
Tetlock, Philip E., 8, 23–24, 29, 37, 42, 45, 54, 214, 218–19
theory building, 5, 14–20, 266–76
Things to Come (Wells), 229
Third World, 114–15, 117, 121, 123, 130, 273
Thompson, Suzanne, 192
A Thousand Little Pieces, (Frey), 281
Thucydides, 258
Tikhonov, Nikolai, 110
Tilly, Charles, 71
Time-Life, 280
timing, 264–66
Tin-bor, Victoria Hui, 32
Tirpitz, Alfren von, 84
Tisza, István, 83
Tocqueville, Alexis de, 229
tragedy, 243, 247–48
The Tragic Vision of Politics (Lebow), 17
Translylvania, 81
Tree of Knowledge, 3
Tripoli, 81
Trotsky, Leon, 280
Truman, Harry, 256
Tversky, Amos, 25, 138, 147–48, 154, 167, 169, 176
typologies, 36

Uchronia (website), 223
Union of Social Justice, 226
United Kingdom. See Britain

United States, 7–9, 15–16, 19, 39, 43, 48, 90, 94, 96, 103–83, 143, 150–51, 272
Unmaking the West (Tetlock, Lebow, and Parker), 58–59, 63, 66, 144
Ustinov, Dimitri, 110

Versailles, Treaty of, 8, 70
Verstehen, 4
Vidal-Naquet, Pierre, 277
Vienna Summit, 35
Vietnam War. See Indochina War
vividness, 192

War in the Air (Wells), 224
Warsaw Pact, 103, 105, 126, 272
Washington, George, 61
Watergate, 247–48
Waterloo, battle of, 253
Weber, Max, 5, 12–13, 19, 48, 55, 195, 251, 286
Weber, Steven, 53–54
Werther (Mozart), 207
Western civilization, 58–64, 141, 144–45, 158–62
What if Jesus Had Never Been (Kennedy), 223
Wheeler, Burton, 232
White, Hayden, 258, 277
Wilhelm I (Germany), 78, 80, 82, 85, 91, 179, 261, 270–71
Wilkie, Wendell, 225, 251
William of Orange, 61
Williamson, Samuel R., Jr., 86
Winchell, Walter, 232
Winter, Jay, 31–32
Woodstock (music festival), 11
World History Association, 142
World War I, 5–6, 9–11, 15–16, 18, 22–23, 43, 50, 53, 55–56, 59–60, 69–102, 143–45, 167–8, 170–82, 183–86, 193–94, 219–20, 260–63, 266, 283
World War II, 7–8, 10, 13, 16, 22, 34, 42, 55, 57, 145, 223, 231–34, 244–50, 256, 260–64, 266–68, 270–71, 274, 280, 283,
World War III, 140

Y2K computer bug, 30
Yakovlev, Aleksandr, 127

Ziman, John, 277
Zuber, Terence, 73